A *DEUS EX MACHINA* REVISITED

THE ATLANTIC WORLD

Europe, Africa and the Americas, 1500-1830

EDITORS

Wim Klooster (Clark University)
Benjamin Schmidt (University of Washington)

VOLUME VIII

A *DEUS EX MACHINA* REVISITED

Atlantic Colonial Trade and European Economic Development

EDITED BY

P.C. EMMER, O. PÉTRÉ-GRENOUILLEAU AND J.V. ROITMAN

BRILL
LEIDEN · BOSTON
2006

Cover illustration: View on the harbour of the French Atlantic Port of La Rochelle (after Claude-Joseph Vernet, 1762).

This book is printed on acid-free paper.

Library of Congress Cataloging-in-Publication Data

A C.I.P. record for this book is available from the Library of Congress.

ISSN 1570–0542
ISBN 90 04 15102 8
978 90 04 15102 4

PRINTED IN THE NETHERLANDS

CONTENTS

PART II

REGIONAL AND NATIONAL APPROACHES

NOTES ON CONTRIBUTORS

Dan H. Andersen, Ph.D. was born in 1956. He is a part-time lecturer at the Saxo Institute, Department of History, University of Copenhagen. He has published on Danish eighteenth century price history, shipping, trade, naval history, and Denmark's relationship with the Ottoman Empire and the Barbary States.

Manuel Bustos-Rodriguez is a Professor of Modern History at the University of Cádiz. He has published extensively on the History of the city of Cádiz and its relationship with the outside world. He has also worked on the interrelationship of the various regions of Spain with one another and their trade with the colonies.

François Crouzet is Professor Emeritus of the Department of History at the University of Paris-Sorbonne, is the author of *The Victorian Economy: The First Industrialists*; *Britain, France, and International Commerce: From Louis XIV to Victoria*. He has published extensively on the origins and early stages of modern industrialisation in Britain and in France as well as numerous other studies of the European economy.

Guillaume Daudin finished his Ph.D. in Economics at Université Paris Panthéon-Sorbonne (Paris-I) and the London School of Economics in 2001. After a year as a post doctorate at Stanford University, he is now an economist at the Globalisation department of the Observatoire français des conjonctures économiques (OFCE), which is part of Science Po. He works on historical and contemporaneous globalisation and growth.

Pieter C. Emmer is Professor in the History of the European Expansion at the University of Leiden. He was a visiting fellow at Churchill College, Cambridge, UK, the *Wissenschaftskolleg* Berlin and at the *Netherlands Institute for Advanced Study* (2002–2003), The Netherlands. He served as visiting professor at the University of Texas at Austin and at the University of Hamburg, Germany (1996–97). He is the author of *The Dutch in the Atlantic Economy, 1580–1880* (Aldershot, 1998) and of *De Nederlandse slavenhandel, 1500–1850* (Amsterdam, 2000)

[The Dutch Slave Trade, 1500–1850, translations in English and French]. In 2004 he was nominated as a member of the European Academy (London).

Bouda Etemad is Professor of History at the Universities of Geneva and Lausanne. He is the author of *La possession du monde. Poids et mesures de la colonisation* (Complexe, Bruxelles 2000) and *De l'utilité des empires. Colonisation et prospérité de l'Europe* (Armand Colin, Paris 2005).

Gérard Le Bouëdec is Professor of Modern History at the University of South Brittany and is the director of SOLITO. He has published more than fifty articles. He is the author or co-author of 15 works dealing with coastal traffic, the activities and innovations of companies based on the seaboard, and on the merchants, soldiers and fishing industry in French ports from the sixteenth through the nineteenth centuries.

Michel Morineau, now retired, began his career by studying the effect of the arrival of precious metals from the Americas on Europe. He then began studying colonial trade and agriculture. He is the author or co-author of many books, as well as the author of several hundred articles. He is one of the best-known and most well-respected Historians of the European Economic History in the 16th, 17th, and 18th centuries

Leos Müller, Ph.D. (1998) is Associate Professor of History at Uppsala University, Sweden. His recent publications include *The Merchant Houses of Stockholm, c. 1640–1800. A Comparative Study of Early-Modern Entrepreneurial Behaviour (1998)*, and *Consuls, Corsairs, and Commerce. The Swedish Consular Service and Long-distance Shipping, 1720–1815* (2004). He is also co-editor of *Statehood Before and Beyond Ethnicity. Minor States and Eastern Europe, 1600–2000* (2005).

Patrick O'Brien, FBA, former Director of the Institute of Historical Research, University of London and President of the British Economic History Society is currently Centennial Professor of Economic History at the London School of Economics where he convenes the Global Economic History Network and a masters programme in global economic history. His last book was P. K. O'Brien, ed., *Urban Achievement in Early Modern Europe: Golden Ages in Antwerp, Amsterdam and London* (2001).

Olivier Pétré-Grenouilleau, Ph.D. (1994), University of Rennes, is a Professor in Modern and Contemporary History at the University of Lorient (France) and a fellow of the Institut Universitaire de France. He has published ten of books since 1995 mainly devoted to the history of Nantes, of the French maritime economy, of the colonial expansion of Europe and of the slave trades. His most recent work is the critically acclaimed, *Les traites négrières; Essai d'Histoire Globale*, (2004) which has received the Prix de l'Académie Française, and the Prix du Sénat.

Horst Pietschmann is currently retired. He was the chair of Latin American History at the University of Hamburg from 1985—2005. He is a specialist in Early Modern Iberian History, and in Colonial Latin American History, as well as in European expansion. He has published eight books and over 200 articles.

Pierrick Pourchasse is a senior lecturer and research fellow in the Department of History at the University of West Brittany in Brest. His research deals with economic relations between France and Northern Europe in the eighteenth century. He is the author of *Le commerce du Nord. Les échanges entre la France et l'Europe septentrionale au XVIIIe siècle*, (Rennes: PUR, 2006).

Jessica V. Roitman is a Ph.D. candidate in the History of European Expansion at the University of Leiden. Her work focuses on Sephardic trade networks in the Portuguese and Dutch Atlantic. She has forthcoming publications in *Migration, Integration, Minorities, a European Encyclopaedia* to be published by Cambridge University Press and in the *Portuguese Studies Review*.

Patrick Verley has spent the greater part of his career in France where he has taught Economic History and Economic Statistics at the University of Paris—I Sorbonne and, later at the University of Paris—viii, between 1969–1990. He has published extensively on global Economic History as well as on Western Industrialisation. He has been President of the Association of Economic and Social Sciences,

Vice-President of the French Association of Economic Historians, a member of the Scientific Committee for data exchange in the Social Sciences, a member of the National Council of Universities, a member of the Board of Directors of the l'Ecole Normale Supérieure Lettres (Lyon), and a member of the editorial committee of the journal *Histoire et Mesure*. He is currently Professor of Economic History at the University of Geneva.

INTRODUCTION
COLONIAL TRADE AND THE EUROPEAN ECONOMY

Pieter C. Emmer, Olivier Pétré-Grenouilleau,
and Jessica V. Roitman

The effects of the expansion of Europe have fascinated historians and economists, as well as the public at large, for centuries. One of the most intriguing and controversial effects of Europe's expansion has been the trade that resulted from this movement out of Europe and into other regions of the world. The role of foreign trade in Europe's economic growth—and especially in its industrialisation—has long been hotly contested. As early as 1776, Adam Smith discussed the role of foreign trade as a catalyst of economic growth, while Karl Marx treated the Industrial Revolution and economic development in *Capital*.[1] Interest in the effects of foreign trade on Europe's economic growth has never entirely faded away, and historians such as Paul Mantoux, who published *The Industrial Revolution in the Eighteenth Century*, which was translated to English in 1928, were certainly influential.[2]

However, it was historians seeking the factors influencing development, or the lack thereof, of various regions of the world up to the present day who fueled a resurgence of interest in the topic around the mid-20th century. By then it had become apparent that decolonisation by itself was not a sufficient condition for economic growth and that there were other inhibiting factors at work. There existed in the mid-20th century—and still exists, for that matter—a tenacious stereotype that the West became rich by exploiting those countries that are now part of the so-called Third World. The prevailing popular and, to some extent, scholarly, opinion has been that,

[1] A. Smith, *An Inquiry into the Nature and Causes of the Wealth of Nations*, R. H. Campbell, A. S. Skinner and W. B. Todd, eds. (Indianapolis: Liberty Classics, 1981); Karl Marx and Frederick Engels, *Collected Works* (New York and London: International Publishers, 1975).

[2] P. Mantoux, *The Industrial Revolution in the Eighteenth Century* (Chicago: University of Chicago Press, 1983).

in exchange for a few trinkets, European traders were able to rob Africans, Asians, and Amerindians of their wealth—wealth that led to the dominant economic position Europe now enjoys. The assumption has been that the impact of European expansion in the New World, Africa, and Asia was so dramatic and, at times, so devastating that it must have been beneficial to the economy of Europe. Therefore, historians began to look for possible links between the possession of colonies and the growth in overseas trade in the 18th century and the development of the European economy and its concomitant or subsequent industrialisation. For example, M. H. Dobbs and K. Polanyi both treat this subject in their influential works.[3] In the early to mid-1960s, this line of thought was especially prevalent. K. E. Berrill, P. Dean, and H. J. Habakkuk, to name a few, were proponents of this view.[4] The most famous historian commenting on the links between overseas trade, colonies, and industrialisation, though, was E. J. Hobsbawm, who published *Industry and Empire* in 1968. In this well-known work he writes that, "The new kind of relationship between the 'advanced' areas and the rest of the world, unlike the old, tended constantly to intensify and widen the flows of commerce. The powerful, growing and accelerating current of overseas trade . . . swept the infant industries of Europe with it . . . [and] sometimes actually created them."[5]

Hobsbawm's assumption still lives on, in spite of the fact that during the past decades modern historical research has called into question this notion of economic growth fueled by intercontinental trade. A wealth of studies indicated that, during the period of modern imperialism, the conquest of colonies in Africa was a losing proposition. This was the case for most European colonies in Asia as well.

[3] M. H. Dobbs, *Studies in the Development of Capitalism* (London: Routledge & Kegan Paul, 1946), and *Some Aspects of Economic Development: Three Lectures* (Delhi: Delhi School of Economics, 1951); K. Polanyi, *Origins of Our Time: The Great Transformation* (London: Gollancz, 1945).

[4] K. E. Berrill, "International trade and the rate of economic growth," *Economic History Review*, 12 (1959–60), 351–54; P. Dean and H. J. Habakkuk, "The Take-off in Britain," in *The Economics of Take-Off into Self-Sustained Growth*, ed. W. Rostow, (London: Macmillan, 1963), 77–80; P. Deane, *The First Industrial Revolution* (Cambridge, UK: Cambridge University Press, 1965); H. J. Habbakuk, *American and British Technology in the 19th Century: the Search for Labour-Saving Inventions* (Cambridge, UK: Cambridge University Press, 1962).

[5] E. J. Hobsbawm, *Industry and Empire: An Economic History of Britain since 1750* (Weidenfeld and Nicolson: London, 1968), p. 36.

Some of the most respected scholars in the field have denied that there was any vitally important role for exports. Thomas and McCloskey concluded that "the strongest effect between commerce abroad and industry at home was from industrialisation to commerce, not the reverse. Trade was the child of industry."[6] Trade theorists such as Charles Kindleberger and Ronald Findlay share this opinion.[7] One of the leading scholars of trade in the 18th century, Ralph Davis, writes,

> I share the view that overseas trade did not have an important direct role either in bringing about the Industrial Revolution or in supporting the first stages of its progress. The initiative came from the supply side, from technical change . . . Though a combination of changes made up the Industrial Revolution, the principal driving forces came from the nature of the inventions in the textile industry . . . and the efficacy of these inventions, which lifted the market for these inventions, at home and abroad, to an entirely new level . . . Overseas trade made little contribution to the advent of the Industrial Revolution itself and was not essential in the early stages of its development. Its importance reappeared in the further expansion of the mature industrial economy.[8]

Patrick O'Brien began to attack the inflated estimates of the contribution of the colonial world to the economy of Early Modern Europe. In a seminal article he summarised his findings in a by now famous—phrase: "*The contribution of the periphery was peripheral.*"[9]

The discussion on the effects of intercontinental trade has centred on Great Britain, where the growth of non-European trade, particularly the trade in slaves and sugar across the Atlantic, was more pronounced than in any other country during the 18th century. During the second half of the 18th century, Great Britain was the

---

[6] R. P. Thomas and D. N. McCloskey, "Overseas Trade and Empire, 1700–1860," in R. C. Floud and D. N. McCloskey, eds., *The Economic History of Britain Since 1700*, Vol. I (Cambridge, UK: Cambridge University Press, 1981).

[7] C. P. Kindleberger, *Economic Growth in France and Britain, 1851–1950* (Cambridge, Mass.: Harvard University Press, 1964), pp. 264–66, and R. Findlay, "Trade and Growth in the Industrial Revolution," in C. P. Kindleberger and Guido di Tella, eds., *Economics in the Long View: Essays in Honour of W. W. Rostow*, Vol. I (New York: New York University Press, 1982).

[8] R. Davis, *The Industrial Revolution and British Overseas Trade* (Leicester: Leicester University Press, 1979), pp. 62–63.

[9] Patrick O'Brien, "European Economic Development: The Contribution of the Periphery," *Economic History Review*, 2nd Series, Vol. 35, 1982, pp. 1–18.

first nation in the world to industrialise. Nevertheless, according to O'Brien, England's trade with the periphery, and the profits from it, were still too small a percentage of its total economy to explain its expansion through the 18th century. Paul Bairoch has argued that the "core" countries, including Great Britain, had an abundance of the minerals necessary for industrialisation such as iron ore and coal. Therefore, they were almost totally self-sufficient in raw materials and, in fact, exported energy to the present-day Third World nations, making the exploitation of colonies for these resources a moot point.[10]

Along these same lines of thought Britain's early industrialisation has led some historians to the hypothesis that the profits from slavery and the slave trade were instrumental in bringing about the first Industrial Revolution. The classic attempt to link colonial expansion and the slave trade with the Industrial Revolution was provided by the West Indian historian and former Prime Minister of Trinidad and Tobago, Eric Williams. In a Ph.D. dissertation later published as *Capitalism and Slavery* in 1944, Williams put forward the thesis that the Atlantic slave trade and plantation slavery in the New World provided re-investable profits and cheap raw cotton on a scale essential for the British Industrial Revolution.[11] Williams inspired a whole generation of historians studying the relationship between imperialism, economic growth, and industrialisation, including E. J. Hobsbawm, who wrote, "the industrialisation of Lancashire prolonged and developed slavery in America."[12]

As Stanley Engerman put it, in Williams' version, history becomes a morality play in which one evil—the Industrial Revolution—arises from another, perhaps greater, evil—slavery and imperialism.[13] Perhaps because of the enduring attraction of such a neat moral paradigm

---

[10] P. Bairoch, *Economics and World History: Myths and Paradoxes* (London: Harvester, 1993), p. 172; see also P. Bairoch, "The main trends in economic disparities since the Industrial Revolution," in Paul Bairoch and Maurice Lévy-Leboyer, eds., *Disparities in Economic Development Since the Industrial Revolution* (New York: St. Martin's Press, 1981); and "International Industrialisation Levels from 1750 to 1980," *Journal of European Economic History* 11, 2 (Spring 1982): 269–333.

[11] Eric Williams, *Capitalism and Slavery* (Chapel Hill: University of North Carolina Press, 1944).

[12] Hobsbawm, p. 7.

[13] S. L. Engerman, "The Slave Trade and British Capital Formation in the Eighteenth Century: A Comment on the Williams Thesis," *Business History Review*, 1972, 46: 430–43, p. 430.

for historians, it took more than three decades to deconstruct the inaccuracies of the "Williams Thesis." Two studies were of particular importance in undermining the hypothesis that the Industrial Revolution was based on the exploitation of Africa and its slaves: Roger Anstey's *The Atlantic Slave Trade and British Abolition* and Seymour Drescher's *British Slavery in the Era of Revolution*.[14] Yet foreign trade as an essential impetus to the growth of the British economy is a tenacious concept.

Despite the strong refutation that Anstey and Drescher seem to have given to Williams' thesis, several volumes of collected essays, as well as a special issue of *The Journal of Interdisciplinary History* in 1989, have appeared since their works were published showing that, for some historians, the "Williams Thesis," albeit in a more nuanced and better-researched form, is still alive and kicking.[15] In fact, the debate continues to this day, fuelled, in part, by a recent publication by Joseph Inikori that stresses the important role of Africa in the making of the British Industrial Revolution.[16]

Yet recent work has not been very successful in substantiating Williams' claim that the profits from this trade "provided one of the main streams of that accumulation of capital in England which financed the Industrial Revolution."[17] Engerman demonstrates that the quantitative effects of the slave trade on the British Industrial Revolution were negligible. D. Richardson points out that the slave trade depended on the demand for sugar which itself was a function of economic changes in the sugar-consuming economies in Western

[14] Roger Anstey, *The Atlantic Slave Trade and British Abolition, 1760–1810* (London: McMillan, 1975); Seymour Drescher, *Econocide, British Slavery in the Era of Revolution* (Pittsburgh: University of Pittsburgh Press, 1977).

[15] *Journal of Interdisciplinary History* 17 (1987); B. L. Solow and S. L. Engerman, eds., *British Capitalism and Caribbean Slavery* (Cambridge, UK: Cambridge University Press, 1987); J. Tracy, ed., *The Rise of Merchant Empires: Long Distance Trade in the Early Modern World, 1350–1750* (Cambridge, UK: Cambridge University Press, 1990), and *The Political Economy of Merchant Empires. State and World Trade, 1350–1750* (Cambridge, UK: Cambridge University Press, 1991); J. J. McCusker and K. Morgan, eds., *The Early Modern Atlantic Economy* (Cambridge, UK: Cambridge University Press, 2000); P. O'Brien and L. Prados de la Escosura, eds., "The Costs and Benefits of European Imperialism from the Conquest of Ceuta, 1415, to the Treaty of Lusaka, 1974," *Revista de Historia Económica* (vol. XVI), 1998–1 (proceedings of the Twelfth International Economic History Congress held in Madrid in 1998).

[16] Joseph E. Inikori, *Africans and the Industrial Revolution in England* (Cambridge, UK: Cambridge University Press), 2002.

[17] Williams, p. 52.

Europe.[18] And, as R. Findlay notes, in the absence of West Indian Slavery, Britain would have had to drink bitter tea, but it still would have had an Industrial Revolution, if perhaps at a marginally slower pace.[19]

Therefore, the findings of recent historical research on the history of European expansion abroad, and of industrialisation at home, have shown time and again that: 1) the profitability of colonial operations was not particularly out of the ordinary, albeit usually slightly higher than profits made at home; 2) during the first phase of the Industrial Revolution, the captains of industry had only a tenuous connection with colonial trade; 3) during the first stages of industrialisation, investments in industries were small and easily obtainable at home; and 4) endogenous factors of development (such as the volume of domestic commerce and the size of a national market) have played a key role in making industry a permanent sector of the European economy.

Additionally, the internal economy of Europe was already ahead of that of other continents, even before the beginnings of transoceanic trade, otherwise the countries of Western Europe could not have expanded overseas in the first place. The early maritime expansion of Great Britain is treated by D. Eltis in *The Rise of African Slavery in the Americas*. In this work, he stresses the fact that the British expansion overseas was preceded by social changes at home. Eltis goes on to ask why "despite the clear chronology, scholars have generally searched harder for the effects of overseas expansion on European economic performance than vice versa."[20] Long before Eltis' work, however, F. Braudel wrote that in order to achieve expansion overseas, "you need a power, slowly matured," adding that, in addition to the accumulation of capital, the nature of European social hierarchies was an even more important precondition for expansion.[21]

[18] D. Richardson, "The Slave Trade, Sugar, and British Economic Growth, 1748–1776," *Journal of Interdisciplinary History*, 17, 1987: pp. 739–69.

[19] R. Findlay, *The "Triangular Trade" and the Atlantic Economy of the Eighteenth Century: A Simple General Equilibrium Model* (Princeton: Princeton University Press, 1990), p. 40. For more on this debate, see: Olivier Pétré-Grenouilleau, *Les traites négrières. Essai d'histoire* globale (Paris: Gallimard, 2004).

[20] David Eltis, *The Rise of African Slavery in the Americas* (Cambridge, UK: Cambridge University Press, 2000), p. 30.

[21] Fernand Braudel, *La dynamique du capitalisme* (Paris: Flammarion, 1988).

Moreover, it is interesting to consider the gap that exists between the beginnings of industrialisation in Europe on one hand, and the start of colonial commerce on the other. The first countries to profit from colonial trade were Spain and Portugal, yet these two countries were among the last in Europe to industrialise. Similarly, the volume of French colonial trade far exceeded that of the United Kingdom, but France did not start to industrialise until 1850. This was at least a half-century later than Britain, and certainly much later than during the heyday of its colonial trade at the end of the 18th century. Both Switzerland and Belgium, two non-imperial nations, were successful and relatively early industrialisers, whereas Holland and Portugal, both of which possessed large and rich colonies, lagged behind. In fact, in the case of the Netherlands, the process of industrialisation did not start until the end of the 19th century and, thus, was completely divorced from the important Dutch role in the Atlantic trade during the first half of the 17th century.

Furthermore, if we look beyond the narrow question of industrialisation and, instead, look at the wider issue of Europe's standard of living, the chronological gap between colonial trade and industrialisation becomes even wider. According to P. Bairoch, Europe did not move ahead of other continents—North America excepted—until the 1950s, by which time Europe's colonial epoch had long ended. In short, trade with the empire may have been important, although this is debatable, before the Industrial Revolution, but it lost any primacy it might have had in the years after 1780 when it would have been needed most.[22]

Thus, colonial countries like Britain, France, the Netherlands, Portugal, and Spain have been characterised by a slower rate of economic growth and industrialisation than largely noncolonial nations such as Belgium, Germany, Sweden, Switzerland, and the United States. The "rule" is, to a certain extent, also valid for the 20th century. Thus Belgium, by becoming a colonial power in the early 20th century, also began to suffer from slow growth. The loss of the Netherlands' colonial Empire after World War II was followed by increased economic development. Colonialism, as Bairoch and others argue was, therefore, not a necessity for industrial growth in

[22] Bairoch, 1993.

Europe; in fact, it may have, instead, been a stumbling block to economic growth and development there. If one compares the rate of growth during the 19th century it appears that noncolonial countries had a more rapid economic development than colonial ones.[23]

Since, as has been seen above, historiography has moved beyond mono-causal and linear explanations for industrialisation, it now seems an outdated idea that colonial commerce and slavery, and the slave trade in particular, might have been at the root of Europe's development. Therefore, some historians are looking at non-economic factors in their attempts to defend the importance of the colonial world for the development of Europe. One of these scholars, R. Blackburn, continues to stress the importance of the profits of slavery and the slave trade, but, at the same time, redirects the debate toward cultural rather than economic factors, as can be seen from the subtitle *From the Baroque to the Modern* of his last book *The Making of New World Slavery*. According to Blackburn, colonial trade not only brought profits to Europe, but it also stimulated a more "qualitative" change.[24] Similarly, C. Shammas insists that we should adopt a different perspective from that of the nation state and, instead, look at the volume of trade within one colonial empire instead of at the volume of trade between nation states. Trade between nation states usually dwarfed trade within one colonial empire. She argues that this intracolonial trade was not important during the colonial period. Instead, it was the colonial links that mattered.[25] Though this suggestion is original, it hardly explains why twenty million inhabitants in the same empire were more important to trade, production, and consumption than the sixty million living in other empires. However, Shammas's theory does have some validity, because the colonial consumers and producers were more important to some cities and regions of the European nation states than to others. The colonial impact differs greatly from nation-state to nation-state, as will be seen in the contributions to this volume.

---

[23] Ibid., p. 77.

[24] Robin Blackburn, *The Making of New World Slavery. From the Baroque to the Modern, 1492–1800* (London: Verso, 1997).

[25] Carole Shammas, "The Revolutionary Impact of European Demand for Tropical Goods," in John J. McCusker and Kenneth Morgan, eds., *The Early Modern Atlantic Economy* (Cambridge: Cambridge University Press, 2000), 163–85.

In addition to discussing the trade between Europe and the colonies, recent studies indicate that inter-colonial trade should not be neglected. In *The Early Modern Atlantic Economy*, K. Morgan prefers to analyse "the growth of aggregate demand in relation to Britain's early industrialisation produced by a combination of domestic and external factors, rather than resorting to the traditional distinction between home and foreign demand."[26] And, in the same volume, David Hancock proposes replacing the model of the "hub and spoke" by what he calls a "spider-web trade."[27] The "hub and spoke" can be illustrated by the traditional trades in sugar and tobacco, organised and dominated by traders in the European port cities. The "spider-web" trade emerged later, when the Atlantic economy had become integrated, thereby reducing the importance of the European port cities in favour of the colonial ports. The existence of this spider-web trade can best be exemplified by the trade in Madeira wine, which was related to a "decentralised" system, organised directly between the areas of production and consumption, far away from the centres of European commerce.

Because of the growing awareness that the link between colonial trade and the development of Europe was much more complex than hitherto believed, we felt the need to bring the various specialists in this area of study together. Their brief was to assess the new directions in the historiography of this subject matter in relation to their specific fields of expertise. Ideally, these assessments should lead to new answers to old questions, to new questions, and, hopefully, to new research. With this intention an international conference was organised at the University of Lorient, France, in September 2001.

A second purpose of the conference was to widen the debate on the impact of colonial trade to all the countries and not to Britain alone, as has so often been the case in the last decades. In addition to Britain, France, Spain, Portugal, the Netherlands, Denmark, and Sweden were analysed during the conference. The contributions to *Deus ex Machina* also focus on a longer time-period than the 18th century alone, again a deviation from the usual analysis. The

[26] John J. McCusker and Kenneth Morgan, eds., *The Early Modern Atlantic Economy* (Cambridge: Cambridge University Press, 2000).

[27] David Hancock, "A Revolution in the Trade: Wine Distribution and the Development of the Infrastructure of the Atlantic Market Economy, 1703–1807," in *The Early Modern Atlantic Economy*, 105–53.

contributions to this volume not only deal with the period between 1500 and 1800, but also with the 19th and 20th centuries. Several contributions specifically discuss the transition period between 1750 and 1850, bridging the classical divide between the "old" and "new" colonialism. Furthermore, this collection of essays presents new information regarding the non-European trade of countries other than Britain, and most contributors pay special attention to the impact of the slave trade and of slavery on the economy of the mother country that they analyse.

The collection offers six contributions discussing the general aspects of the economic impact of Europe's expansion followed by eight contributions dealing with individual countries. In the first part of this book, Patrick O'Brien sets the tone by reiterating his previous claim that foreign trade did not help to bring about the Industrial Revolution. The volume and the profits of that trade were simply too small in relation to the general economy. Even if we look for qualitative arguments, a connection is difficult to establish. Only in Great Britain, and only during the second half of the 18th century, did the trade to non-European parts of the world increase more rapidly than trade in general. Even then, it constituted less than half of all British trade. In addition, none of the goods imported from outside Europe were vital to the European societies at the time. Sugar provided only a small share of the calories consumed, and cotton became important to British industry only after industrialisation. In sum, internal, not external, factors helped Great Britain and the other European countries to achieve the growth necessary to finance and establish their Industrial Revolutions. In reviewing the majority of the modern theories about the "European miracle," O'Brien makes two observations regarding the period between 1500 and 1750. First, he states that the Great Divergence between Europe and the rest the world occurred much later than has hitherto been assumed. Second, O'Brien points to the extreme diversity of the factors that might have played a role in bringing the so-called miracle about, such as imports and exports, improvements in farming, social and political structures, cultivable land, and coal resources, to name a few. Before 1750, it was impossible to determine which factor would be of importance in the subsequent growth spurt. The old paradigms were linked to a small and clearly identifiable range of "pre-conditions" on which the industrial takeoff was supposed to have been based. O'Brien now advances a much more refined idea of a set of progressively emerging plateaus from where the transition to an industrial market economy became feasible.

This conclusion is fully endorsed by Michel Morineau, the *doyen* of historians of Early Modern trade. He states that the concept of what was a "trump" in economic development fluctuated over time and depended very much on the personal opinion of the observer. In addition, Morineau recalls that the debate regarding the economic importance of the slave trade and of slavery itself has led to the conclusion that these branches of the economy had only an indirect influence on insurance, banking and manufacturing—what he calls "limited sectorial developments in space and in time." Rather than singling out certain causes and the opinions of the "grand masters," Morineau suggests that we return to the observations of the contemporaries regarding economic assets. According to O'Brien and Morineau colonial trade was only one advantage among many during the course of Europe's economic development.

Colonial trade might have been an asset, but in quantitative terms it was of very limited importance according to Bouda Etemad in the opening contribution to the section "From quantitative to dynamic approaches" in this volume. By providing the statistical evidence regarding the volume of trade for the five colonial empires between 1750 and 1950, Etemad shows that Great Britain was the only colonial power to enjoy uninterrupted trade and migration with the colonial world in the period between the 1750s and 1850s. His tables also highlight the fact that, overall, for European nations the trade with one another was far more important than their colonial trade, with the exception of a few decades in the case of Britain, Spain, and Portugal. During the course of the 18th century, international trade had become more colonial, but this trend was reversed during the 19th and 20th centuries. And, after decolonisation, only 3% of the trade of the former colonial powers was directed toward their former tropical colonies. Even that percentage was inflated because of re-exportations on both sides.

Patrick Verley points out that, during the late 18th and early 19th centuries, colonial trade was a vital link in the complex world of trade and payments. However, he adds that this observation is the result of an economic distortion. He asserts that intercontinental trade was marginal both in volume and value, that it consisted mainly of luxury goods, and that growth in this trade was easy to achieve because incomes in Europe rose and the demand for intercontinental luxury goods was highly elastic. Verley writes that, when we look at trade in general, there is no doubt that most trade occurred between the countries of Europe and between Europe and the United States. Colonial trade usually functioned as a replacement for markets lost elsewhere. The impact of colonial trade on the economy should have increased after Europe moved from being a demand economy to a supply economy during the second half of the 19th century. In historical reality, however, the reverse is true.

In concluding the first part of the volume, Gérard Le Bouëdec discusses a forgotten sector of development—that of European coastal shipping. He recalls that coastal shipping played a determinant role in the rise of commercial networks in Europe long before European ships began sailing to other continents. This coastal trade enabled the various regions in Europe to develop their competitive advantages and to integrate their economies. In order for colonial trade to grow, it was necessary to use the established circuits of the traditional coastal traffic. He goes on to assert that this coastal trade always remained far more important for Europe than all the non-European trade combined. It was not until the transport revolution of the 19th century that coastal shipping gradually lost its importance. Toward the end of the 19th century, France, according to Le Bouëdec, neglected its international coastal traffic and began to specialise in colonial shipping, because French coastal shipping was unable to compete, while colonial shipping enjoyed government protection.

The second part of the volume consists of contributions on Portugal, Spain, and the Netherlands, the first European countries to be involved in transoceanic exploration and trade. The history of the Iberian countries shows a remarkable cleavage between the fabled importance of empire and the economic reality. Around 1500 both Portugal and Spain were the two most advanced countries in Europe. They were the first countries to expand beyond the borders of Europe; they had, as it were, first choice of the overseas territories and, as a result, they seemed to have assembled a particularly promising collection of colonial assets. Spain conquered the most developed parts of the New World—those areas possessing plenty of local labour and natural treasures such as precious metals. Portugal was able to monopolise the trade with Asia and also developed Brazil into the world's major sugar producer. Yet, after three centuries of colonial exploitation, the economies of both Portugal and Spain no longer ranked among the foremost in Europe. Instead, the Iberian Peninsula had become an economic, social, and political backwater, and it remained so until recently.

Manuel Bustos-Rodriquez explains why Spain's promise was not fulfilled. He points to the limited impact of the trade with the New World on the Spanish economy and to the fact that the range of export products from Spain was confined to textiles and alcoholic beverages, and even some of these were re-exports. This explains why, during the first decade of the 19th century, the impact of the Continental Blockade on the Spanish domestic economy was limited. The author makes note of the fact that Catalonia experienced some modernising effects from its trade with America, but emphasises Catalonia's unique position in comparison with the rest of Spain. During the Middle Ages, Catalonia had been the most advanced area of Spain, and this legacy allowed it to profit more from colonial trade than any other region in Spain. Over time, colonial trade became no more than a *niche* for Spanish merchants who could not compete in the European markets.

In a similar fashion, H. Pietschmann and N. Wiecker point to the limited effects of intercontinental trade on the economic development of Portugal. The authors start out by saying that, in the Iberian Peninsula, "transatlantic connections in the 18th century were primarily of an economic nature," but their contribution highlights the importance of political and cultural rather than economic factors. The gold imports from the Americas are a case in point. These compensated for Portugal's deficit in her balance of trade with England. That deficit was the result of an unbalanced economic treaty concluded on the basis of domestic and international political considerations. In the end only a small amount of gold remained in Portugal. The authors conclude their contribution by discussing the link between the fiscal crisis and the changes in the political relationship between Brazil and Portugal during the second half of the 18th century. In addition, Pietschmann and Wiecker suggest that the nature of the political subordination of the colonies to the mother country should be reconsidered. We know too little about the relationship between politics and the economy. This relationship was of the utmost importance in the trade connections between Portugal and the rest of Europe. We are similarly ill-informed about the networks, strategies, and culture of the Portuguese and Brazilian merchants, nor do we know enough about the impact of the large out-migration from Portugal, including such successful groups as the Sephardi Jews.

Another interesting case is presented by the Dutch Republic (1600–1806) and the Kingdom of the Netherlands (1806–present). In many ways, the mercantile activities of the Dutch developed side by side with those of Britain. The outcome, however, was quite different, as is argued by Pieter Emmer. The impact of the trade with Asia on the Dutch economy was considerable, but, over time, that impact declined even though the Dutch kept investing in the trade with Asia and each year continued to send thousands of young men there as sailors and soldiers. In the Atlantic, the Dutch suffered bad luck. Their conquest of part of Brazil (1630–54) was short-lived and cost them dearly when the Portuguese retook it. In the following century, the Dutch invested far too much money in their Caribbean plantation colonies, resulting in a crash of the stock exchange and heavy losses for the investors. In spite of these negative developments, the importance of the colonies to the Dutch economy increased because, after 1750, Dutch shipping and trading firms were driven out of the competitive markets in Europe, which increased their dependence on the protected colonial markets.

What about France, the second largest colonial power during the modern as well as the contemporary periods? Guillaume Daudin makes a statistical comparison between the non-European trade of Britain and France and concludes that France only received 7% of her economic growth from intercontinental trade. Had there been no intercontinental trade at all, France's national income would have been lowered by a mere 1.5 to 2%. There is no reason to assume that French merchant firms involved in colonial trade would invest more than an average amount in manufacturing and, if they did, their investments would have been limited to the industries in the port cities where they were located. Intercontinental and colonial trade did little more than increase the number of traders and postpone the moment in which investment in trade would suffer from diminishing returns. In sum, Daudin suggests that colonial trade was important as an investment opportunity for wealthy traders in the French ports, but that, on the whole, the colonies cost France more than they yielded.

This argument is carried even further by Olivier Pétré-Grenouilleau who argues that France, in fact, might have incurred heavy economic losses because of its overseas expansion. That conclusion is, in part, based on research into the costs and benefits of the French overseas empire during the 19th and 20th centuries. The author is inclined to draw similar conclusions for the preceding period. Before their entry into the transoceanic trade, French trading and shipping firms were already well developed. They used the colonial markets in order to escape the more competitive markets. In the long run, avoiding competition turned out to be detrimental to French shipping and trade. Pétré-Grenouilleau also theorizes that industrialisation triggered by overseas trade remained limited to a few port cities, and that these port cities were not well connected to the rest of the French economy.

François Crouzet underpins O'Brien's contribution by providing both the data and the analysis regarding British foreign trade during the crucial years between 1750 and 1850. Crouzet shows that Britain "Americanised" her trade during the second half of the 18th century, but that Europe remained her most important market, especially for industrialised goods. There is, indeed, a remarkable growth in Britain's trade with some parts of the colonial world, but the share of colonial trade remained modest at best. After 1850, British production and trading firms sought refuge in the colonial markets in order to escape competition elsewhere. In times of war, Great Britain used its colonial markets to replace those on the Continent.

The last section of the book is devoted to the Baltic. Pierrick Pourchasse demonstrates that French, Spanish, and Portuguese shipping in this region was not competitive in the Baltic trade—the so-called mother of all European trades. In the case of France, shipping costs were too high. Employing too many sailors made French shipping too expensive. The French merchants also neglected building up a trading network in the North. In contrast, Dutch and British merchant ships employed a far smaller crew and could rely on well-organised commercial networks, which explains why the lucrative trade to the Baltic remained firmly in their hands.

The colonial impact on the economies of Denmark and Sweden was far less important than elsewhere in Western Europe as pointed out by Dan Andersen and Leos Müller. Both contributors argue that, in the beginning, the intercontinental trade and overseas expansion of Denmark and Sweden were linked to international politics. Economic considerations came second. Over time, the intercontinental trade networks of both countries comprised an Atlantic as well as an Asian section, but the volume of trade was marginal compared to the Nordic trade in general, though this was more the case for Sweden than for Denmark. There was no way in which the profits of the slave trade, and of slave-produced products, could have contributed to the modernisation of the Nordic economies.

The three articles devoted to the Baltic region demonstrate that interregional trade was far more important to Europe's economic development than were the global trade networks. In addition, these last three articles show that colonial products increased the volume of intra-European trade, and that the Baltic was able to profit from more trade in spite of the fact that the region was paying for the imports with primary goods such as minerals and wood. What looked like an unequal exchange turned out to be advantageous for the Baltic, as trade linked the region firmly with the rest of Europe. The region's involvement with the non-European world was marginal and limited to periods of war when Denmark and Sweden could profit from their neutral positions.

Writing from various geographical perspectives, all the contributors to this volume arrive at a number of common conclusions. First, they point to the fact that—with the possible exception of Britain—trade to and from the non-Western world was marginal and served as a *chasse gardée* for uncompetitive firms, as well as for firms that might have been competitive, but became less so because of their involvement in colonial trade and the ensuing mercantilist policies. And, even when individuals, private firms or shareholder companies made a profit from trading with the non-European world, the overall result was still negative due to both the large public expenditure and the casualties incurred in defending and administering the various colonies, trading forts and sea routes. In quantitative terms, maritime trade in Europe might have been small by present-day standards, but it was many times larger than the trade to Africa, Asia and the New World at the time.

Second, all authors agree that the spin-off effects of non-European trade were limited in economic as well as in geographical scope. This means that the links between colonial trade and European economic development could be better studied at a local and a regional level. In addition, as pointed out by Morineau, the strategies of merchants, merchant firms, and politicians require further scrutiny, as do the ways in which trade, particularly overseas trade, and the colonies were represented at the time. Cultural and political factors have had more impact on changes in the economy than has been assumed.

Third, most contributions confirm the fact that the "British model" of expansion and colonial trade seems to have been the exception, not the rule. Between 1500 and 1650, the trade in luxury goods, the exploitation of silver mines, and some limited production of cash crops sufficed to make the colonies worthwhile. Between 1650 and 1800, the production of cash crops dominated. Portugal was unable to keep up with the other colonial powers. In fact, it was only due to the compartmentalisation of the sugar market that, after 1650, Brazil continued to produce sugar and coffee, and even experienced a second boom in production after 1750. Spain was unable to keep her place in the market, and the Cuban sugar boom during the 19th century was mainly based on non-Spanish investments, shipping, and consumption. The Dutch tried to change from trade to a combination of trade and production, but never fully succeeded. France was able to work wonders in the production of cash cops, as demonstrated by the growth of the coffee and sugar output of Saint Domingue, but lacked efficient transport and marketing systems. Only Britain succeeded in both diversifying its investments abroad and devising an efficient tax system that allowed for the construction and operation of the most effective navy at the time. Yet, even in the British case, there are signs that the exploitation of its colonial empire benefited a few at the expense of many.[28]

Before leaving the reader to make up his or her own mind, we would like to thank the University of South Brittany at Lorient, and the *Institut Universitaire de France* for their unstinting support in enabling Olivier Pétré-Grenouilleau to organise the international conference at which the contributions to this volume were first presented, and for having these contributions translated. Anne Simpson of the Netherlands Institute of Advanced Study at Wassenaar, where Pieter Emmer spent the academic year 2002–3, has also provided editorial support. Judith A. Christie has translated the papers three, five, six, seven, and 12 from French to English.

[28] L. E. Davis and R. A. Huttenback, *Mammon and the Pursuit of Empire. The Political Economy of British Imperialism, 1884–1912* (Cambridge: Cambridge University Press, 1986).

Part I

Global Approaches

Colonial Trade: A Trump Among Others

CHAPTER ONE

A CRITICAL REVIEW OF A TRADITION OF META-NARRATIVES FROM ADAM SMITH TO KARL POMERANZ

Patrick O'Brien

Marx and Weber

Along with histories of hegemony and power, histories of material life and economic growth are the most popular of meta-narratives currently published in the field of global history. Indeed no surprise will be occasioned by the appearance in times marked by the debate about "globalisation" of histories seeking to encompass a "world economy." These histories of a so-called "world economy" deal with chronologies going back millennia, and are written to expound upon the disparate levels of material progress achieved by tribes, societies, communities, and national economies on all continents. Such concern with the disparate levels of the material progress of various peoples has, since Herodotus, been the litmus test of the mission of global economic history, which is to keep "humanity in view." After all, most people, in most places for most of history have been preoccupied with obtaining food, shelter, clothing, and other manufactured artifacts required to sustain either a basic, or a comfortable standard of living.

The modern tradition of historical inquiry into the wealth and poverty of nations owes its paradigms for investigation to the towering intellects of two cosmopolitan, but perhaps equally "Eurocentric" Germans: Karl Marx and Max Weber. Both scholars maintained a serious interest (admittedly as a counterpoise to Europe) in the evolution of the Indian, Chinese, American, and Russian economies, although Weber's investigations into Oriental religions, philosophies, cities, and states look far more serious than anything written by Marx or Engels.

The vocabularies and concepts borrowed by generations of historians from the corpus of writings left by Marx and Weber can no longer be presented as coherent theory. Nevertheless, it is still useful—when trying to understand material progress and relative decline across continents over long spans of time—to distinguish Marxian from Weberian approaches. The former has classically been concerned with investigating the potential for material progress embodied in distinctive "modes of production" observed in different parts of the world, while the Weberian "research programme" can be divided into two major strands of inquiry: first, a comparison of hegemonic systems of belief, operating to promote or constrain personal and group behavior in material life; and second, an empirical analysis of the political, legal, and institutional frameworks within which economic activity has operated historically around the world.

In classical Marxian thought, the only mode of production capable of generating sustained material progress—"capitalism"—is based upon wage labour and the accumulation of capital. Marx found that the first transition from precapitalist to capitalist modes of production occurred in Western Europe. Thereafter global historians (working within a Marxian tradition) have addressed his question of when and why the transition occurred in Western Europe prior to considering the obverse question: what sorts of "precapitalist" modes of production prevailed throughout Africa, Asia, and the Amerindian Americas that delayed or arrested comparable transitions to capitalism upon these continents?

Recently a "deviant" (or supplementary) Marxian paradigm has been elaborated in detail by the World Systems School of Historical Sociology—namely that the transition to capitalism (or commercial society), which led, eventually, to the establishment of successful industrial market economies, occurred first in Western Europe because Europeans reaped timely and decisive gains from intercontinental trade and the colonisation of the Americas for some three or more centuries before the onset of the French and Industrial Revolutions. Europe's economic benefits from centuries of participation in *intercontinental* commerce and imperialism are broadly conceived to encompass positive externalities as well as a range of favourable political, institutional, and cultural feedback and spin-offs connected to ever increasing flows of commodities shipped into European ports from all over the world, and especially from across the Atlantic.

Unsurprisingly, the World System School's emphasis upon the extension of markets for European exports in Asia, Africa, and the Americas—and, above all, its insistence on the persuasive significance of imports (embodying productive knowledge) from other continents—has been contested. Classical Marxist scholars defend canonical texts concerned with progressive and nonprogressive modes of production and, thereby, implicitly join forces with neoclassical economic historians who continue to regard the particularities of Europe's own history as the motor of its earlier transition to capitalism or commercial society. Parenthetically, and for this particular debate, neither of these representations—nor that other unresolvable discussion about continuous versus discontinuous transformations from one kind of traditional economic system to another, and ultimately more progressive, system—seem to matter. What is now at issue is to specify and measure the significance of endogenous vs. exogenous forces promoting economic growth in one part of the world economy (Europe) and restraining a similar momentum on the continents of Asia, Africa, and Southern America.

Unfortunately, Marxian scholarship concerned with Asiatic modes of production, and with the presence or absence of peculiar forms of "feudalism" found outside Europe, now looks more theoretical than historical. Perhaps because the tradition ossified and was ostracised during the Cold War, classical Marxism seems less influential than its Weberian counterpart in establishing the parameters, structure, and vocabulary of a discourse concerned with restraints which, for several centuries, operated to prevent Asiatic economies from following the "European trajectory" that was leading toward divergent standards of living between the "West and the Rest" that became conspicuous over the course of the 19th and 20th centuries. Furthermore, the ad hoc comments made by Marx on Asian societies are now regarded as little more than typical Eurocentric speculations of his time, which, alas, led generations of his followers down a blind alley in search of supposedly ubiquitous and unchanging Asiatic modes of production.

Max Weber's erudition is more impressive. His approach, questions, and topics for investigation have effectively set the parameters for the construction of global histories of material progress written in recent decades. He dealt with long spans of time, read widely about classical and oriental civilisations and used comparative methods in order to comprehend why capitalism arose in the West and not in the East. Reading over chronologies covering millennia, he recognised that the economies of India and China displayed impressive scientific and technical precocity. Weber appreciated that

Arabs and Asians had established sophisticated systems and efficient institutions for the conduct of internal and overseas trade long before European ships and merchants began to sail regularly into and around the Indian Ocean and China seas during the 16th and 17th centuries.

Weber remained less impressed than Adam Smith and Karl Marx with the economic significance for European development of the discovery of the Americas. He was not inclined to inflate the gains from transatlantic trade and colonisation above endogenous forces operating over centuries of history to promote economic growth within Europe. Along with Marx, Weber retained an appreciation of how and why the accumulation of capital and the evolution of slave labour, through feudal to free markets, mattered as "proximate" determinants of material progress in Western Europe.

For scholars concerned with including an analysis of intra- and inter-continental trade in meta-narratives about the "long run" history of material progress, Weber elaborated upon themes that have exercised a powerful impact on modern stories told about the economic success of the West and the relative failures of the East over the past millennium. Along with Montesquieu and other thinkers of the Enlightenment, Weber (and Weberians) believed that the discernible differences between Europe and Asia in the manner in which the institutional, ideological, and legal frameworks within which economic activities (including trade) functioned had already existed for several centuries. These differences between Europe and Asia were marked by divergences in religious beliefs, cultural conditioning, family life, and political systems. It was these contrasting frameworks which, according to the Enlightenment thinkers and the Weberians, promoted divergent paths of economic growth and eventually produced a clear divide within the world economy into affluent and poor nations.

The New Global History of "Surprising Resemblances"

In recent decades, a modern generation of economic historians has carried forward the Weberian tradition of attempts to reconfigure the now highly visible economic achievements of Western societies in a global context. Weber left them with an approach, a vocabulary, and several suggestive hypotheses that have been modified and rejected by two generations of postwar and postcolonial research. There are now libraries of books and articles dealing with "Eastern" agricultures, industries, towns, commercial networks, communications, trade, science, technologies, cultures, business organisation, taxation, state systems, government policies, and economic cosmologies, covering the last millennium and written in large part by historians from universities not long emancipated from imperial rule. This impressive, but still far from comprehensive, volume of historical research has, moreover, been communicated to the West by specialists in area studies from North American, European, Australian, and Japanese universities. Not long after the Second World War and during the era of decolonisation, economic historians were offered an opportunity—provided by the accumulation of a large and sophisticated body of knowledge (long available in Europe and North America), but emerging on Asia, the Middle East, Africa, and Latin America—to reposition their hitherto disconnected histories of wealth and poverty against one another in order to construct global histories of material progress that might have satisfied the aspirations of Montesquieu, Voltaire, Smith, and their "enlightened" followers, as well as pleasing Max Weber.

Clearly, and as a prelude to analysis and explanation, it is necessary to date that divergence in living standards between the Western and Eastern ends of the Eurasian landmass because the assumption that unmistakable gaps in real incomes per capita and labour productivities (measured for the decade preceding the Great War) must have prevailed for centuries prior to that time and cannot be supported with hard economic data. Indeed, historical research on Asia has produced some partial, regionally specific, and still inconclusive evidence to suggest that standards of living in Western Europe and the maritime provinces of China and South India may not have differed perceptibly much before the late 18th century.

This contestable suggestion about differing living standards has led global historians, represented as "Eurocentric" by their opponents, to fall back upon unqualified Weberian (and Marxist) assertions that the economies of North Western Europe were surely on potentially more promising trajectories for early transitions to efficient industrial market economies for several centuries before even the most developed regions of Asia. Europe's cultures, political systems, property rights, legal frameworks, regimes for the discovery and diffusion of reliable knowledge, commercial and financial organisations, trading networks, markets for commodities, labour, and capital are represented by these global historians as more capable of producing systems of production than were Asia's. These historians point out that the preconditions for factories, industry, and mechanised transportation by land and sea; for the generation of inanimate forms of energy; for the relocation and reorganisation of agriculture, manufacturing, and commerce into concentrated locations and functional firms were much more firmly entrenched in Europe than in Asia.

More than three decades ago, Marshal Hodgson (one of the godfathers of modern global history) opined that "all attempts to invoke pre-modern seminal traits in the Occident to account for the divergence in living standards can be shown to fail under close historical analysis." Two generations of postcolonial research on India, China, and South East Asia (synthesised in the recent writings of Fernand Braudel, Kirty Chaudhuri, Jack Goody, Gunder Frank, Ken Pomeranz, Kaoru Sugihara, and David Washbrook) has seemed to have proven his point. From his own impressive and detailed comparisons of levels and types of economic development achieved by European and Asian economies during the Early Modern period, Braudel inferred that "the populated regions of the world faced with demands of numbers seem to us to be quite close to each other." But there is, he observed, "a historiographical inequality between Europe and the rest of the world. Europe invented historians and made good use of them. Her own history is well lit and can be called as evidence or used as claim. The history of non-Europe is still being written. And until the balance of knowledge and interpretation has been restored, the historian will be reluctant to cut the Gordian knot of world history." One distinguished historian of Europe, David Landes, displays no such reluctance, and his celebrated book, *The Wealth and Poverty of Nations* elaborates over some 600 pages the "historical record" of Weberian preconditions which he claims demonstrates why "for the last thousand years Europe (the West) has been the prime mover of development and modernity."

Modern historical research, has, however, "degraded" (or severely qualified) repetitions of Marxist and Weberian assertions that the political, institutional, and cultural frameworks within which economic activities in Asia were embedded for centuries, before the Industrial Revolution, differed from Europe in ways that clearly and *significantly impeded* the evolution and integration of commodity and factor markets, the development of financial intermediation, the spread of private property rights, the operations of mercantile networks, proto-industrialisation, and, above all, commercialisation within agriculture. What recent syntheses of the libraries of historical research on the economies of Asia (as well as Europe) observe and document are not only a range of both advanced and less developed regions across Western Europe, but also a "World of Surprising Resemblances" across Eurasia. Surveys of monographic literature have effectively rendered a whole corpus of Marxian and Weberian interpretations redundant. It can no longer be taken for granted that, for centuries before the Industrial Revolution, European economies experienced virtually exceptional transitions to capitalism; evolved differentiated legal, behavioral, institutional, and political frameworks for the formation, integration, and operation of markets, and thereby allowed for progress (albeit at a slow rate and with limited help from new technologies) down a path prescribed for in models of Smithian growth. Historians of Asia have also located and analysed cultures that encouraged industrious and ambitious households to transform their extra earnings into displays of possessions and luxuries. Their work reveals that, contrary to the expectations of Werner Sombart (and his modern European followers), common attributes of material life appeared in too many cities, towns, and villages across the Eurasian landmass for anyone to single out the "rise of material culture" as something peculiar to the acquisitive households of Western Europe.

Before the era of liberal capitalism (1856–1914), states everywhere placed impediments in the path of Smithian growth; but the endlessly repeated endemic (but always implausible) notion that dynastic and territorial rivalries among European states consistently provided more favourable (less unfavourable) conditions for the spread and integration of markets during the Early Modern era of mercantilism and warfare has also been undermined. More simplistic versions of that hypothesis conflate virtuous circles and cycles of development flowing from "competition" with the destructive violence and rivalries of Early Modern European power politics. Furthermore, historical scholarship positing notions (which have been floating around since Montesquieu) that the emperors and bureaucracies of despotic Eastern empires ruled over the economies (and, ergo, their fiscal bases) in irrational ways that can be represented as more predatory, arbitrary, and consistently and peculiarly maligned toward Smithian growth now look increasingly obsolete.

In the recently reconstructed economic histories of a "world of surprising resemblances," canonical accounts of Smithian growth—of European economies growing up gradually but inexorably on distinctive trajectories within their restricted and relatively underdeveloped promontory of Eurasia—look untenable simply because too many of Hodgson's seminal traits of the Occident turn out to be not only ubiquitous, but also already extant features of the Orient as well. Perhaps such Weberian (and/or Marxian) perceptions will be revived and underpinned by future research and debate. That scholarship (or even search among extant histories) might *delineate* and perhaps measure discernible differences in the scale, scope, and intensity of Smithian growth across time and space. Meanwhile, as recent reconfigurations of Asian economic history became acceptable (to all but an anachronistic generation of historians) and debate moves on from the realm of acrimony toward conversation, we may well witness a revival of more nuanced and carefully specified long run historical explanations for divergences in productivity and living standards between East and West—divergences that historians have long agreed became unmistakable during the 19th century and starkly apparent during the 20th century.

A "Eurocentric" Comeback

To suggest that an unexpected and unpredictable conjuncture between East and West quite suddenly appeared in the late 18th century remains fragile as a hypothesis about long-run global economic development. That is so because revisionists offer three contested explanations for both the "late" and the "great" divergence, and to each proposition there are counter arguments. The first is that, in different ways, for different reasons, and along different chronologies, imperial governmental structures in the Orient became increasingly inefficient and incapable of providing their subject populations and territories with the good order, protection against external aggression and other public goods required to maintain satisfactory levels of private economic activity, market integration, and innovation. In short, political, geopolitical, and administrative defects and decline within the Safavid, Ottoman, Mughal, and Ming-Qing empires, preceded, and thereby made space for, the rise of the West. Investigations into the nature, extent, and significance of this decline (clearly affecting Oriental empires in the 18th century) continue, and may well lead to the kind of insights now coming from comparative histories of Early Modern European States—studies concerned with contrasting the evolution of political arrangements and policies and whether they were conducive or obstructive toward economic growth and innovation within Western Europe. This debate about forms of government and the behavior of states will only be taken forward by historians who know something about the foundation and evolution of political and other subordinate institutions, their diverse forms and the precise ways they interconnected with the economic activities of households, farms, and firms, not only in Early Modern Europe, but in Asia as well. As the literature now stands, repetition of recycled Enlightenment equations between Republican Liberty, and Parliamentary forms of government on the one hand, and transitions to industrial market economies on the other, seem less and less satisfactory.

Second, and at the heart of the revisionist explanation for the divergence between East Asia and Western Europe, is a quintessentially classical growth story which traduced an impressive array of historical scholarship around concepts, connections, and mechanisms derived, ultimately, from the writings of Smith, Malthus, and Ricardo. For example, Pomeranz represents cultivable land as a relatively fixed factor of production and suggests that additions to the stocks of useful and reliable knowledge allowed only for incremental and limited technological progress. Upswings in population growth led (only *in extremis* and in some regions) to Malthusian crises, but, more commonly both in Western Europe and in the Ming-Qing Empire, to constricting shortages of land intensive crops and agrarian raw materials, including: basic foodstuffs, timber utilised for manufacturing and construction, wood converted into fuel and energy for both industrial and domestic purposes, and fibers derived from plants and animals for purposes of transformation into textiles.

Over some two or more centuries, before 1750, when population growth rates in Europe and China advanced at comparable rates, the Chinese economy coped with the "pressure of numbers" by intensifying labour in order to relieve shortages of food and agrarian raw materials. For Pomeranz and other scholars who reject Eurocentric explanations for the great divergence cast in terms of Smithian growth, the problem is to explain how and why European economies did not proceed down the same path as China but instead avoided diminishing returns on labour engaged in agriculture and proto-industries, and gradually diffused mechanised techniques of production across manufacturing and transportation. Pomeranz restates this key question cogently: "Why," he inquired, "did England's economy not continue to develop like the economy of the Yangtze Delta?" In other words, revisionism, as Marc Bloch advised long ago, rests on carefully specified *reciprocal* comparisons.

The answers offered are carefully supported with a reflexive reading of modern scholarship, and refer to contrasts between the endogenous and exogenous potential for the avoidance of diminishing returns on land available in China and to Europe. After millennia of successful land management, Chinese agriculture stood closer to its production possibility boundary than European agriculture. Possibilities for coping with population pressures through extensions to margins of cultivation and cropping, tenurial reform, investments in the infrastructure for intra-regional trade and specialisation, the reallocation of pasture to arable land, the control of water, food stabilisation policies, etc., had already been carried further in China than Europe.

Europe not only enjoyed some discernible (alas, immeasurable) opportunities for taking up "slack" within the agrarian system, but the potential gains from trade and specialisation in foodstuffs and raw materials within Northern and Southern, Eastern and Western parts of our continent remained greater than the long-exploited patterns of interregional trade within the Chinese Empire. Indeed, and when demographic pressures intensified over the 18th century, the potential for trade diminished because, unfortunately, rates of population increase became faster among China's poorer, less urbanised regions of primary production. The empire's Northern and inland regions adjusted by reallocating surplus agricultural labour into proto-industry consuming higher proportions of both the food and agrarian raw materials produced within their boundaries, and importing fewer manufactured goods. Thus China's precocious Smithian growth, high levels of trade and dependency upon a mix of labour intensive crops (particularly rice), rendered the imperial economy more "ecologically vulnerable" than Europe to population pressures when they intensified over the century before the Industrial Revolution.

Nevertheless, revisionists insist (and have traduced a not entirely sufficient or convincing body of evidence to support the view), that Britain and other European economies were also on a similar trajectory of diminishing returns and rising costs for the production of food, fuel, and fibers, but that the West postponed the onset of more severe ecological problems and shortages during the early phases of industrialisation in the 18th century and circumvented them throughout the 19th century by exploiting two "windfalls" of massive significance, namely: endowments of cheap and accessible energy in the form of coal, and the fecund soils and abundant natural resources of the Americas.

In bringing to the foreground the contribution of the Americas, revisionists have, in effect, returned the attention of historians to exogenous (overseas) sources of Western Europe's economic advance—the same sources underlined by Adam Smith and Karl Marx, and reified in recent decades into a "*primus mobile*" by Wallerstein, Chase, Dunn, Blaut, Frank, and others in the World Systems School of Historical Sociology.

However, they must also recognise that Wrigley and an earlier generation of British economic historians had already explored the profound significance and widespread ramifications of endowments of cheap fossil fuels in allowing Britain to escape (before the rest of Europe) from potential "Malthusian traps." Although precise calculations are difficult to make, and several competing figures (including the revised estimates from Pomeranz) have come to the fore, the tradition of energy accountancy goes back to the 19th century. And it is not difficult to accept its major conclusions—namely that the substitution of coal and steam power to provide for the heat and energy previously supplied to Britain (and other economies) by horses, wood, and manpower, for various benchmark decades after the Napoleonic Wars, would (counterfactually) have absorbed ever increasing and implausibly large shares of Europe's virtually fixed supplies of agricultural land. Furthermore, all forms of heat- and energy-intensive industry and transportation (metallurgy, glass, pottery, beer, sugar and salt, refining soap, starch, railways, and ships) benefited from the substitution of coal for other more costly and less efficient organic forms of energy. Feedback and spin-offs from the mining, transportation, and utilisation of coal, including the construction of canals, precision engineering, and, above all, the impetus provided by coal for the development, improvement, and diffusion of engines for the provision of energy from steam, remain impossible to calculate. They became central for the aptly named "Age of Steam." Yet that age (1846–1914) remained imminent rather than dominant during the first stages of the Industrial Revolution, which occurred decades before that particular golden age of liberal capitalism.

Furthermore (and to revert to Bloch's reciprocal mode of comparative history), the question of why China failed to exploit its known and very considerable deposits of coal—and thus become more like England, Belgium, and Westphalia—is, perhaps, not pursued in the depth that such a salient contrast demands. Chinese coal may well have been more combustible and less well located than European deposits, but it stayed below ground as an abundant and, presumably, potentially more efficient source of energy, especially when compared with the manpower, wind, and water that the Chinese, Japanese, and other Asian economies continued to utilise throughout the 19th century. References to geology and geography do not seem to be sufficient for explaining why China remained virtually an outsider throughout the Age of Steam.

Finally (to return to Adam Smith and overseas expansion), Europeans (not Chinese, Arabs, or Indians) discovered, conquered, infected, plundered, colonised, and eventually established mutually beneficial commercial relationships with the Americas. That protracted enterprise should not be designated as "peripheral" (as I suggested, before climbing onto a learning curve some 18 years ago) nor reified (as it continues to be in the writings of Immanuel Wallerstein, James Blaut, and the World Systems School of Historical Sociology) as the "motor" driving the continents' benign transformation toward successful industrial market economies over the course of the 19th century.

Material benefits did not come into being for a long time after 1492, and accrued disproportionately to two latecomers and free riders: the Netherlands and England. No doubt quantitative exercises in national accountancy designed to measure the macro-economic significance of transatlantic commerce for either the development of Europe as a whole, or even for particular countries such as the Netherlands or Britain specifically, are fraught with conceptual and statistical difficulties. No economic historian could deny that the establishment of colonies regulated along mercantilist lines together with slave plantations in the New World, turned the terms and conditions for transatlantic trade in favour of Europe. This is especially true when compared to commerce with Asia, and certainly is the case when contrasted with a counterfactual scenario, whereby the settlement and the buildup of viable and independent economies in the Americas depended upon unregulated but unprotected private investment and the immigration of free labour from Europe rather than the enslavement of Africans. Furthermore, recent research has clarified the importance of the complex and multifaceted role played by Chinese, Indian, and South East Asian demand for New World silver in maintaining the profitability and momentum of European investment in the Americas for some two centuries before the Industrial Revolution. That investment also promoted an entirely gradual movement toward the integration and growth of an embryonic global economy, within which the separated maritime towns and regions of Europe, Africa, Asia, and the Americas interacted—usually with positive effects for both European and Asian development.

Nevertheless, a national accounts framework continues to be the only viable perspective available to historians who wish to specify and quantify the overall significance of variables, such as intercontinental exports and imports for national (and European wide) rates of capital formation and structural change and innovation from 1492 to 1815. If (as Bairoch's imperfect and badly referenced data suggest), European exports to other continents and imports from the Americas, Asia, and Africa are but small percentages of the total value of European output, then inferences that either the Americas (or the non-European world as a whole) continued, as late as the end of the 18th century, to play a comparably minor role in the advance of the West European economy could only be challenged in two ways. First (and this logic seems illuminating), in Early Modern Europe, economic growth took place at specific margins, and if a large share of the annual *incremental* increase to total European (or even to particular national products) growth can be connected directly or indirectly to intercontinental commerce, then an overpublicised and glamorous subsector of several maritime economies might, indeed, be plausibly represented as highly significant for the continent's economic advance. Quantitative tests could then relate the gains from intercontinental trade to net capital formation and to aggregated volumes of potentially tradable outputs in order to manufacture ratios that are more relevant for locating, dating, and comprehending the sources of economic growth from, say, 1500 to 1800. Historians who take their perceptions from Adam Smith will prefer to shift the focus of concentration to Britain, which became more involved than any other European economy with intercontinental commerce and colonisation.

Another, less parsimonious, route can be followed in order to make the case for the role of intercontinental trade. This route comes closer to the details of micro-dynamism favoured by historians like Fernand Braudel, Immanuel Wallerstein, and Ken Pomeranz, and constructs narratives built around the array of imports that Europeans transshipped from the New World and Asia back into famous maritime ports (Lisbon, Seville, Cadiz, Antwerp, Amsterdam, Bordeaux, and London). Imports represented tangible manifestations of the bounty that Europe obtained from investments in commerce and colonisation in the Americas and, by way of extension and linkages, to gains from trade with Asia as well. American and Asian imports included bullion, foodstuffs, manufactured goods, industrial inputs, and raw materials. Imports, obtained in very large part through coercion at favourable terms of trade, increased in volume with the incorporation of maritime Atlantic economies into global commerce—slowly at first, but more rapidly as the infrastructure and organisations required for long distance trade were built up over the 16th and 17th centuries. Histories of spin-offs and externalities have been woven around most of the major imports from other continents carried into European ports. Their connections to the maintenance and extension of benefits from long-established patterns of intra-European trade, to the foundation of new processing industries, to geopolitical rivalry and state formation, to the growth in the wealth and powers of merchant oligarchies, to the rise of maritime cities, to changes in science, technology and the arts; indeed to almost all aspects of European economic, political, and urban life have been elaborated in numerous histories of sugar, tea, coffee, cocoa, maize, rice, tobacco, tropical fruit, tomatoes, beans, chili peppers, potatoes, timber hardwoods, dyes, wax, fish, oils, cotton fibers, quinine, sarsaparilla, pecal, laxatives; porcelain, silk and cottons, textiles, and above all, silver and gold. That bibliography is long. The volumes imported fluctuated, but overall, they increased. Points of entry and distribution for Asian and American imports changed through time from city to city and from country to country. The problem is how to connect imports from other continents to narratives (or models) of Early Modern European development, in which national economies are carried forward to plateaux of possibilities from where transitions to industrial market economies became probable.

Fernand Braudel, Giovanni Arrighi, and Charles Kindleberger find the mechanisms with which to explore in a geopolitical matrix of dynamic circuits between maritime cities, big merchants, and nation states. Pomeranz devotes his research and analysis to two possible macroeconomic connections. One operates through a recently elaborated thesis about Europe's premodern "industrious" revolution, which emanated from decisions by myriad households to work harder and allocate more of the labour time and other resources under their control to production for markets. Behind such decisions made by households are shifts in tastes or propensities to consume, stimulated by the availability of "exotic" and "addictive" foodstuffs such as sugar, tea, coffee, cocoa, tobacco, tropical fruits, tomatoes, and spices, as well as pharmaceuticals and luxurious, but affordable, Asian manufactures such as silks, cottons, jewels, and porcelain imported from the Americas as well as the East. In brief, the rise of material culture in Europe has been linked, in carefully specified ways, to intercontinental trade, while colonisation has been linked to changes in consumption and investment as well as to the patterns of work by European households.

Nothing comparable occurred in Asia because the consumption of tropical groceries, porcelain, silk and cotton textiles, and other indigenous products had already diffused down the social scale. In the Orient, imperial states had no fiscal or other interest in the promotion of commerce and colonisation that might, in the fullness of time, pay for itself in the form of imported and taxable luxuries. At the same time, Chinese and Indian demands for foodstuffs and manufactures produced in Europe remained limited in volume and scope. This demand remained limited even though New World silver was exchanged by European merchants for Asian foodstuffs, manufactures, and raw materials. This exchange presumably promoted monetary transactions and internal trade in China and India in the same way that American bullion did within Europe; yet the outcome of this exchange was very different.

Revisionists make the most of a not unconvincing case for symbiotic linkages between the luxurious, exotic, addictive, and desirable characteristics embodied in imports from Asia and the Americas to: the industrious revolution, the maintenance of European commitments to intercontinental trade, the enslavement of Africans, and flows of investment into colonisation and plantations in the New World. They cite literature that locates the impetus for development from urban processing industries (sugar refining, coffee roasting, tea and tobacco blending, etc.) in maritime cities, which were heavily engaged in transoceanic commerce. They are familiar with histories that explain how the manufacture of cotton textiles in Britain developed in the 18th century within a matrix of trade with India, the import of cotton fibers from plantations in the Americas, state involvement with the East India Company, and the promotion of a functional process of import substitution by English Parliaments between 1660 and 1721.

Nevertheless, it is necessary to examine closely this new and heuristic narrative foregrounding the role of the Americas in bringing about divergent economic developments between Western Europe and East Asia. First, the share of the calorific intake supplied by sugar, tea, and other tropical groceries could only have been small. Growing proportions of British merchant ships were indeed built in the North American colonies (and in Asia) even before the French blockades cut off supplies of Baltic timer and other naval stores (pitch, tar, and hemp) during the Napoleonic Wars. Nevertheless, the established patterns of East-West and intra-European trade in timber reverted to normal after that war, and iron rather than American forests seriously alleviated European shortages of wood for construction and shipbuilding in the 19th century.

A statistically more compelling case for the substitution of cotton fibers grown on slave plantations in the Americas for supplies of flax, hemp, silk, and wool grown in Europe can be made. Once again, the *scale* of imports in relation to total consumption of indigenous fibers becomes important later rather than earlier in the 19th century. The suggestion that supplies of cotton wool from the Americas had long been virtually indispensable for the development of mechanised cotton textile production in Europe is not convincing because an equally plausible counterfactual scenario can be formulated to suggest that the accumulating and steadily improving capacity to produce mechanised cotton yarn and cloth, first in Britain and then elsewhere on the continent, would have stimulated other primary producers in Asia (even in China) and the Middle East to respond to European demand for cotton fibers.

Economic history consigned axioms of indispensability to the realms of improbability more than three decades ago. Yes, there is certainly a more nuanced, but less dramatic, argument to be made for the importance of supplies of slave-produced cotton fibers—namely that cheap raw materials promoted the growth of one major manufacturing industry in Europe, and that the engineering problems involved in the mechanisation of spinning and weaving cloth were more easily solved with fibers having the tensile properties of cotton, than silk, wool, flax, and hemp. Indeed, the problems of mechanising all major processes in the production of cloth made from the entire range of natural fibers were solved. By then, supplies of cheap flax from Russia and wool from Australia, Argentina, and other primary producers became readily available to supply Europe's textile industries with all the fibers they could process mechanically.

Divergence and Convergence

The problem of "the Great Divergence" between Western Europe and East Asia is stimulating to address. We can agree that the early shift from organic to inorganic forms of energy provided Europe (particularly Britain) with an early start. Nevertheless, and for several reasons, the other leg of the revisionist explanation (which follows the line taken by Adam Smith, Karl Marx, and the World Systems School)—that the discovery, conquest, and exploitation of the Americas also generated comparably large windfall gains and allowed Western Europe to circumvent the problems of diminishing returns afflicting the Qing empire—carries far less conviction.

First, classical theories of diminishing returns effecting land seem less applicable to India and South East Asia than China, and the convergence of Japan with Europe, despite a poor endowment of natural resources, contradicts histories based on classical growth models. Second, recasting and reconfiguring of the data now available to measure the significance of intercontinental commerce shows that standard exercises in national income accountancy are unlikely to provide persuasively large ratios of commerce. The now fashionable post-modern retort that large outcomes could flow from small changes to exogenous variables simply destroys any claims that economic history might have to precision. We might rhetorically inquire if small outcomes could flow from large changes to endogenous variables?

Third, it is not at all clear that the arable land, pastures, forests, and seas of Western Europe, together (and through trade) with its periphery to the East, could not have sustained the rates of population growth, industrialisation, and urbanisation experienced, say, down to the mid-19th century without massive imports of primary produce from the Americas. To hark back to the central point of

Mark Elvin's classic book, was it not the case that China had exhausted more of the potential gains from intraregional trade, intensification of labour inputs, and agrarian improvements well before the growth of its population accelerated in the 19th century? Elvin's thesis can moreover, be reformulated in the language of classical economics. Compared to Western Europe, how far was China (and other regions of Asia) away from their (technologically constrained) production possibility boundaries before 1750? Classical economists (Smith and Malthus) both perceived that China had proceeded further and continued to move faster down the path of diminishing returns.

Leaving coal aside, intercontinental trade data suggests that Europe possessed the foodstuffs and agricultural raw materials required to persist with Smithian growth, and the subsequent urbanisation and industrialisation of the workforce without recourse to massive imports of primary produce from the Americas until well into the 19th century. Meanwhile, the testing and application of a body of reliable knowledge required to carry the mechanisation and transformation of industry and transport, the deployment of steam power, urbanisation, and reorganisation of finance and commerce had proceeded a long way and, perhaps, beyond a point of no return or to what historians of China refer to as involution.

With this observation, which is concerned with the unavoidable and important demarcation of the relevant chronologies in place, I wish to underline a distinction that has perhaps not been made clearly enough throughout the modern debate between the Industrial Revolution and the Great Divergence. The Industrial Revolution owed something—but probably not a lot—to the incorporation of the Americas into global commerce. That remains clear if we look again at the volume and array of imports entering European ports before 1846. On the whole (and with the conspicuous exceptions of maize, potatoes, and cotton fibers) imports merely supplemented supplies of the continents' own basic foodstuffs and raw materials. Imports were dominated by tropical groceries and manufactured luxuries. At most they embodied attributes that scholars find appealing to place at the centre of their narratives about the origins of the North-South divide.

It is clear that the Great Divergence and the Industrial Revolution form part of an interconnected narrative. It is also clear that the degree of divergence in labour productivities and real incomes between Europe and China—a divergence that had so clearly appeared by

1914—is inconceivable without the massive supplies of basic foodstuffs and raw materials imported from the Americas and other primary producers. But since those supplies became available over the course of the second half of the century, the questions of what started versus what sustained the Industrial Revolution should not be conflated.

In most of its essentials, the Industrial Revolution—which demarcates the beginnings of this divergence—had appeared several decades earlier. During its early stages, tenuous (but not highly significant) connections can be constructed between intercontinental commerce on the one hand and the substitution of coal-based forms of heat and power for traditional forms of energy derived from wood, wind, water, animals, and human muscles on the other. Some elements of early and gradual mechanisation of industrial processes (particularly for textiles) can be linked to transoceanic trade, but again, the connections still seem more peripheral than central. There are missing chapters in explanations for divergence that should be concerned with "regimes" for the production and diffusion of useful and reliable knowledge in Europe and China. Technology really mattered for the Industrial Revolution, and if the English and follower economies on the mainland might well (but for coal and then close involvement with the Americas) gone the way of the Yangtze Delta, then why has even that commercialised and advanced region of the Manchu Empire taken such a long time to regain the economic rank and status it held in the world economy in the mid-18th century?

CHAPTER TWO

TRUMPS, NO TRUMPS, A HANDFUL OF TRUMPS: A NEW DEALING OF CARDS

M. Morineau

The role and importance of the global expansion of Europe is a classic subject in historiography. The purpose of this paper is to establish and measure the role and importance of this expansion while also taking into account the influence colonies had on the expanding European nations themselves. The colonies were, after all, considered to be economic extensions of their "home" countries. Much study has focused on the phase of European expansion from around the mid-18th century until well into the 19th century, and the economic relationships that were formed during this time. More recently, however, interest has shifted to both a much longer period of time, and to the evolution of the economic relationships up to the present day.[1]

The Trump

Politically, colonies have ceased to exist. However, there still exists a more veiled or subtle control known as "neocolonialism." Clearly, all aspects of colonisation did not vanish when agreements on independence were reached and signed between the colonised and the colonisers. The hypocritical and clandestine persistence of colonisation is of some importance to the way we perceive today's situation, as well as to how we perceive the past. We have to look at the past and see what has been brought about by today's rich nations and what has been suffered by today's poor ones.

[1] See Patrick O'Brien and Leandro Prado de la Escosura, eds., "The costs and benefits of European imperialism from the conquest of Ceuta, 1415, to the Treaty of Lusaka, 1974," *Revista de Historia Económica*, xvi, 1, Winter.

At the beginning of the 20th century, commentators and historians viewed the legacy of colonialism in a totally different light. This was a time during which the imperial power of European nations was at its peak. There was no hesitation or reservation about the absolute triumph of the West, and no possible objection to its legitimacy nor to its origin. It was viewed as the proof, the reward, and the consequence of an innate superiority, and, therefore, the manifestation of an inherent inferiority of the native populations—populations that could, in turn, be categorised as lazy savages. This justified, in the eyes of many Europeans, the use of force against the supposedly savage native populations. This use of force was, quite simply, viewed as necessary. Some Westerners even believed that this use of force was a benediction for the enslaved populations, and a way for them to integrate into their masters' civilisation.

It is hard to imagine such a radical reversal of the representation of the present and past as there has been between the early 20th century and the early 21st. In the present day, many commentators and historians view as inevitable the conflict between a Western world that has been enriched as a whole, despite all the defects of its economic and social organisation, on the backs of its former colonies, and the rest of the world, which is forever doomed to misery. In order to provide some answers to these contemporary problems, it is essential to clarify the influence of colonial trade on the development of Europe, or, conversely, on the weakening of the Third World.[2]

Background: exploration and colonisation to the early 19th century

It is necessary to look at the beginnings of colonisation in order to understand its ramifications fully. In fact, we should include in our study of colonisation the Venetian and Genoese excursions in the Mediterranean as early as the 13th century, as well as Portuguese prospecting along the African coasts and in the middle of the Atlantic Ocean decades before Christopher Columbus discovered America.

---

[2] It should be noted that Denmark and Sweden never possessed more than small territories. See Leos Müller's essay in this volume. Germany and Italy had none before the end of the 19th century.

The different modes of economic and social exploitation which were implemented in Crete, Chio, São Tome, and in the Azores were testing grounds, or even models, for entry into the New World.[3]

On the European stage the acquisition of unknown lands by the Kings of Castile and Aragon, as well as the King of Portugal's direct access to the pepper and spice producing regions, were perceived as providing undeniable increases in power. These regions also supplied new wealth that gave them *ipso facto*—superiority on the international stage. These regions can be, and, in fact, were, seen as a winning trump, an ace card in a continuing game between nations and princes. Ships returned with more and more goods, and the abundance of gold and silver never seemed to end, all of which reenforced the prestige for the fortunate princes and the loss in wealth and prestige for the others. The losing princes did not have these trump cards in their hands.

Over time, however, this favourable opinion about the wealth colonies brought to the colonising nations has begun to change. Jean Bodin was one of the first and most important historians to question the prevailing wisdom of the benefit of colonies for the colonisers. He brought up the fact that the American wealth that was imported to Spain did not remain in Spain. The needs of the population led to the exportation of this wealth in exchange for essential goods such as wheat, but also for commodities such as clothes—or even in order to pay for an immigrant workforce. That meant that the trump card was no longer in the same hands. Spain no longer had the winning card—the neighbouring nations, especially France, were the winners, according the Bodin. Or, one could also say that the assumed trump card had lost its power. Instead, colonial goods were a diversion in comparison to the "real" products coming from the soil and the workers of Europe.

In fact, Spain could have and should have kept the colonial treasures for herself so as to create a modern, capitalist economy. Under such circumstances, Spain would have automatically been promoted to the rank of "first industrial nation" of the Western world. Portugal made similar errors by ignoring the basic paradigms of colonisation.[4]

---

[3] The transfer of the sugar cane industry from the Mediterranean regions to America is a spectacular example. This transference was facilitated by the Genoese who participated in the journeys of discovery made by the Portuguese and Spanish.

[4] The Spanish turned to foreign producers of clothes and linen simply because

Spain faced more problems when the Low Countries revolted against Philip II. The so-called sea beggars engaged in a sort of guerrilla warfare, while the Hollanders and the Zealanders organised fleets in 1598 to take the East Indies, a territory that had been reserved for the Portuguese. Portugal, therefore, lost the monopoly over pepper and spices, which had been one of its main assets. And, some twenty years later, another attempt was made to deprive the Portuguese of yet another of their assets—Brazil's sugar. Furthermore, the Dutch began encroaching in the Caribbean and setting up plantations.

Initially, this non-Iberian colonisation appeared to be neither a total nor a lasting triumph. Even the Dutch, from the United Provinces to the East Indies, had some difficulties in supplanting their Lusitanian rivals and controlling the seas and the trade they had entered into. They often had to defer to the dictates of the regional powers such as China and Japan. Furthermore, they suffered a serious setback in Formosa. The occupation of Brazil ended in a nonrenewal of the privileges of the West India Company. Then the English colonies were developed in a completely different manner than were most of the Iberian and/or Dutch colonies. Colonies on the American continent were self-sufficient and did not send much to England. On the other hand the merchandise from the Caribbean—tobacco, indigo, and sugar—was sent to England, but the quantities produced during the 17th century were so small they could only be considered as being of minor importance. *A fortiori* the same conclusion is also valid for the French possessions, including those in the Caribbean.

It should also be noted that there were different types of colonies. In the beginning of European exploration, there were primarily small landing areas, which were used only as points of embarkation for further exploration and/or for the simple exchange of goods. In the mid to latter part of the 17th century, in contrast, there began to appear some established settlements with a sizeable presence of European immigrants and their descendants, as well as with established farming, which produced the basic necessities for subsistence. Between these two extremes of colonisation, there were the trading posts that were subject to the authorisation of the native princes,

---

it was financially advantageous, in the same way that European industrialists now relocate their factories in Asia. Gold and silver were used firstly for the political aims of the king, but a part of it must have been distributed to the country as a whole. The same holds true for Portugal in the 18th century.

and were dependent on these princes' tolerance. From such trading posts, the Europeans negotiated for the exchange of goods with the local producers and traders. At a more intensive level, there were the plantation colonies where the Europeans were fully sovereign over the land. These settlements were divided into properties that belonged to the European colonisers and on which the workforce was invariably of African and/or Indigenous origin. These plantations produced goods almost entirely for export, and depended completely on their European homeland for the transport of the goods, as well as for their own re-supply. Similar systems of organisation, with minor differences, also existed in Portuguese Brazil and in the Spanish Americas.[5]

These differences in the sorts of colonies set up by the Europeans are of some importance when we attempt to consider the general influence of colonies on the development of Europe as a whole, as well as on individual nations specifically. But this is not the only issue to consider. The economic management of the colonies and the nature of their relations with their metropoles are elements we have to consider when making an assessment. Colonial trade is contingent upon the creation of colonies, a bilateral exchange between the colonies and the home country and the home country and colonies, the financing of this exchange, and, eventually, re-export. The French West Indies constitute a textbook case of all such issues inherent in the study of colonial trade.

The 18th-century "person on the street" considered these colonies to be of great importance to France's prosperity and splendour. This opinion is still held by numerous historians, one of whom even went so far as to declare a "Glorious Sixty," which the country had experienced between 1716 and 1775. If we look at the statistics up to 1789 we can see that the volumes and value of sugar, coffee, and other goods coming from the West Indies were multiplied nearly fifteen times. Their re-exportation throughout Europe at the end of the absolute monarchy, reached the value of 150 million *livres tournois*, which represented 40% of France's total exports. Clearly then, the West Indies and Saint-Domingue must be viewed as an important asset for the nation.

---

[5] The theoretical possession of immense territories in America by the Spanish and the Portuguese did not necessarily mean effective occupation.

But let us look more closely at this asset. The wealth derived from the area depended on the work of an extravagant number of slaves (in 1789 there were over 400,000 in Saint-Domingue). Their number had increased greatly during the previous 20 years and, because of a high mortality rate, they had to be replaced frequently. In exchange for these new slaves, as well as for the supplies they received from the home country, the planters traded their products. The islands' economy was occasionally shaken by various problems—crops were affected by adverse environmental changes, and trade was affected by war.

The home country, or, more precisely, the ship owners and merchants at the ports dealing in the colonial trade, enjoyed a monopoly on traffic with the colonies and, therefore, the benefits from the freight that came with it. They were also in charge of the redistribution of colonial goods abroad, although their ships did not export cargoes from France to Amsterdam, Hamburg, or any other foreign port. Rather, it was Dutch or German merchants instead of French ones who worked on these routes. If we are to believe the French figures on the balance of trade, the outcomes of these exchanges were always positive, and traders collected gigantic benefits that allowed them to maintain the country's economy at a high level. These figures are exaggerated, however, and do not take into account the mysteries of financing. Countries that took part in that trade managed to reduce their outlays and, as a consequence, to reduce French profits to reasonable levels, and even sometimes to very mediocre levels indeed.[6]

The consumption of sugar and coffee in France remained at a low level compared with the rates in other countries. Moreover, exports to the colonies only reached the value of 100 million *livres tournois* at the end of the 18th century. In addition, the contribution of the various sectors of the metropolitan economy in providing goods to the colonies was unequal. The Caribbean islands consumed 75% to 80% of all exported flour, 20% of all exported wines, and 10% of all exported brandy. These volumes are not small, but they

[6] French ports worked in a very cosmopolitan way. Moreover, military spending by the monarchy sent a lot of money abroad—money that was then used by foreigners for trade. M. Morineau, "La vraie nature des choses et leur enchaînement entre la France, les Antilles et l'Europe (17ᵉ–19ᵉ siècle)" in *Revue Française d'Histoire d'Outre-Mer*, 1997, vol. 84, no. 314, 3–24.

dwindle when compared with the production intended for the internal market. And not all supplies for the colonies were produced in France. For instance, the colonies were dependent on cheese from Switzerland and Holland and salted meat from Ireland. Also, the trade in slaves depended on imported textiles from Asia which were popular on the African coast. Lastly, a third of all linen cloth produced in France went to the West Indies, compensating for the decline in exports to Spain.[7]

As far as we can judge, colonial trade was not small when compared with the overall production of France. But we must not inflate its importance either. Continuing prosperity relied on the slave trade, as well as on the maintenance of peace and authority in the colonies. The economy of Saint-Domingue did not survive the insurrection. It collapsed and brought down with it the wealthy ports in the home country—ports that never recovered. Therefore, it is clear that there was a limited, sector-based, development in some places and for a limited amount of time that development was attributable to colonial trade. The effect of colonial trade on later economic development in France, however, was very limited, if not nonexistent.[8]

Colonial trade proved no more profitable for the United Provinces. Their main South American colony—Suriname—was shaken by a slave revolt, which required long and expensive repression, resulting in considerable debt. The mortgage arranged to pay for the suppression of the insurrection was as disastrous for the sponsors as it was for the borrowers. The situation in 1789 in the French West Indies was no better, and, probably, worse than that in Suriname, even if it was worse for different reasons.

What was the situation in the East? The Dutch East India Company (VOC) continued to prosper from its monopoly, even though its sugar and coffee cargoes were controlled in ports like Amsterdam, Rotterdam, or Middleburg by competitors trading in the Atlantic, including via France. The privileges, including the freedom of trade, that the VOC enjoyed had a pernicious influence on some industries in the country that depended on the VOC's imports of cloth, as

[7] The localisation of the producing areas in the Islands was very precise and very limited. The main outlets for woolen cloth and silk were Italy and Germany. Brittany particularly suffered from the restrictions upon its trade with Spain.

[8] Bordeaux and Nantes did not recover from the loss of Saint-Domingue until the second half of the 19th century.

well as on its exports. The VOC also suffered some misfortunes on the oceans, got involved in expensive wars, and made some errors in policy that worked in favour of the English East India Company, as well as being evicted from prosperous markets such as Bengal. The VOC was crippled by its debts, and it had to rely on the indulgence of the Bank of Amsterdam in order to obtain new *equipagies*. The losses it suffered during the 1784 Treaty of Paris were worsened during the French Revolution and the subsequent emergence of the French Empire. Basically, the VOC had lost everything by the end of the 18th century. Although the United Provinces did not become impoverished, its wealth came from economic activities other than colonial trade.[9]

The 19th century was, of course, the century of the European Nations' great colonial expansion. But when we look back in time, in order to consider our material and understand it better, we have to analyse the period from the beginnings of exploration and colonisation until the beginning of the 19th century, as we have done above. In fact, English historians often distinguish an "Old" and a "New" Empire. The "Old" one was partly, but severely, dismantled by the emancipation of the Thirteen American Colonies, which eventually formed the United States. After the loss of the American colonies, the English hold on Bengal, as well as on the whole of India, became the core of the "New" Empire—an empire that grew ever bigger through annexations all over the globe.

The loss of colonial assets was more dramatic for France. Saint-Domingue's insurrection and eventual secession deprived France of its most important colony, which had been vital for the supply of various tropical goods—goods that were, at least according to some commentators, essential to its foreign trade. By 1815 the French colonial Empire was comprised of bits and pieces. The new leaders' ambition was to regain a global presence equal to that of the English Empire. Hence, France engaged in a nearly constant spate of colonial conquests ranging from the regency of Algiers to the protectorate over Morocco, and including expeditions in Africa, Indochina, and in the Indian and Pacific Oceans. Spain and Portugal were more

---

[9] The resumption of colonial trade with Indonesia occurred after 1815, and the "modern" industrialisation of the low countries did not take place until the end of the 19th century.

affected by the gradual and definitive decline of their respective empires. Nearly the whole of Latin America escaped their authority, either through insurrection, peaceful separation, or through loss of their colonies to other foreign powers. The fact of it being a gradual loss does not compensate for the eventual great loss, in both territorial and financial terms, that the Iberian powers suffered.

We shall now examine the case of England which, in the early 19th century, had wonderful cards in its hand. This is when the famous "Industrial Revolution" took place—a revolution that was both the embryo of, and the engine for, the later transformations that eventually created the wealth of the Western World.

The English and the origins of the Industrial Revolution: Fact versus Fiction

Nearly every historian agrees that England was the first industrial nation, and we must, therefore, look toward England to find the origins of industrialisation, if there are any. Indeed, multiple causes for the Industrial Revolution have been debated. Alas, no mutually accepted cause has been agreed upon. We can find many examples of this disagreement in the literature. For example, some of the various causes for England's early industrialisation that have been posited are: religion and mentality; natural resources; political structure; increase in demand; a growing tendency toward proletarianisation; an agricultural "revolution;" a drift from the land and consequent urbanisation; international trade; colonisation; primitive accumulation of money and the creation of a bourgeoisie; pre-industrialisation; technical innovation; mechanisation; and liberalism. It is important that we extract from this miscellany the part that can be imputed to colonial trade.[10]

Generally speaking, the English seem to have colonised in the same manner as the French and the Dutch. The economy of their plantation colonies was based on the production and sale of tropical goods. They used a labour force of slaves whom they bought in Africa. The colonies were linked to England by an exclusive contract.

---

[10] Paul Bairoch, *Victoires et déboires. Histoire économique et sociale du monde du XVIe siècle à nos jours*. Vol. 1 (Paris: Gallimard, 1997). Immanuel Wallerstein, *The Modern World System: The Second Era of Great Expansion of the Capital World Economy 1730–1840s* (San Diego, New York: Academic Press, 1989).

The main difference was that Britain was the centre of the consumption of goods such as sugar and tea. Tobacco was the only commodity to be re-exported on a large scale. Although it is not easy to make a thorough comparison between the different East India companies, the Dutch VOC proved to be the most lucrative. The interests of West Indies planters on the American continent were well defended in London, and, therefore, they prospered. There is no evidence that they invested their money in new industries, nor did those who had been in Asia. We can find no evidence of a decisive contribution from the colonies to new industries.

Many years ago, Eric Williams presented a controversial thesis. According to him, in the late 18th century, some groups in England were in favour of the abolition of the slave trade for economic reasons. Williams theorised that, had the slave trade continued to grow, slavery would have led to a decrease in financial returns. He also stated that, thanks to the colonial regime, capital in England had already reached a sufficient level to continue with industrialisation without outside financing. Williams believed that the use of slaves had been profitable for a time, especially for the initial accumulation of capital, but had become much less so later on.[11] Williams, however, does not offer any concrete proof in favour of a prior accumulation of capital nor of a payout to shareholders, which was the case in the other nations such as France and the United Provinces. The thesis is initially framed in a Marxist way of thinking and, furthermore, it is rooted in the belief that large assets were required to trigger the Industrial Revolution. This idea has been questioned. François Crouzet, for example, noted that the first phases of industrialisation were based on quite modest funds and that, moreover, the expansion of industrialisation was not entirely and solely due to these funds—whether modest or not.

There are many other theories about the beginnings of industrialisation in Britain, as well. The "demographic revolution" for example, has been offered as an explanation. However, this so-called revolution was, in fact, just a return to conditions that had temporarily disappeared, and which were of more importance in Ireland than in England anyway. Another theory is the so-called agricultural revolution, which has more or less automatically been imputed to a

[11] Eric Williams, *Capitalism and Slavery* (London: Andre Deutsch, 1944, reprinted in 1966).

transformation of agrarian structures, but which was, in fact, so inefficient that the average level of bread consumption by the English continually decreased between 1750 and 1850. Urbanisation is another theory offered up as the reason behind Britain's early industrialisation. However, urbanisation took place at the same time in the Low Countries, regions of Italy, and the South of France, none of which industrialised as early as Britain. Mechanisation, accompanied industrialisation, but did not generate it. What about Britain's natural resources? Cotton, which was the most important commodity during the Industrial Revolution, was not collected on the Thames' banks, and iron and coal only became important as the Industrial Revolution progressed. Therefore, none of these factors can, by itself, satisfactorily explain Britain's early industrialisation.

Let us now look at agriculture. In the middle of the 18th century, the number of people in England involved in agriculture was lower than that of the population working in other sectors. Some historians have suggested that the lower percentage of the population involved in agriculture promoted the individual productivity so characteristic of the English countryside. But this is not true if we look at other countries. This low percentage of the population engaged in agriculture actually seems to suggest the existence of other jobs of every sort other than that of farming. An important part of the population worked in the craft industry, which was more rural than urban, and most of these craftspeople worked with wool and in other textiles. This shift toward crafts began in 1337, when Edward III decided that his country should not remain a simple purveyor of raw materials to other countries but should instead produce its own textiles.

The shift in the population's economic activities in order to achieve Edward's aims did not take place overnight. Additionally, analogous situations existed throughout the world, and they did not have long-term repercussions on the economic system—particularly when the domestic market, as was the case in China, could absorb most of the domestic production. The situation was different in England, however, because the English woollen industry was quickly able to export, and the quality of its cloth ensured a durable and substantial turnover. In general the British were able to use trade to their national advantages by protection, by set prices, and by diplomatic and judicial measures—measures like the obligation to balance sales and purchases and the successive Navigation Acts. Other nations also enacted protectionist policies, but they never took the same form, nor were they ever as dominant as in England. In fact, the English practiced a tough form of mercantilism, making them capable of opposing competition with the local craft-workers. For example, in 1686 imports of Indian cloth were forbidden or marginalised in order to "save" the woollen industry. Moreover, the British had quite a knack for finding and exploiting foreign markets.[12]

This does not mean that any of these conditions were the sole cause of the Industrial Revolution. Increased output would have perhaps happened under any circumstances. Innovation in cotton spinning acted as a catalyst for industrialisation, as it increased the production capacity and diminished production costs, all of which facilitated the sale of products—provided, of course, that there were sufficient buyers. At this point we must challenge the romantic image of the Industrial Revolution as a violent and instantaneous economic upheaval. While it is true that this transformation exceeded the initial technical boost as it developed itself, none of this could have come about without a favourable environment. Liberalism provided such an environment. Liberalism can be seen as an improved form of mercantilism, as it does increase the power to sell.

Each of these factors was useful, and probably necessary, for Britain's industrialisation. But Britain also had to make good use of them in order to become so successful.

The Reality: Colonial Trade and Industrialisation in England and France

Dependency on foreign markets was not only characteristic of the English economy; it was the case for every nation or industry involved in international trade. A prime example of this was the United Provinces, and the Leiden drapery industry in particular. In France this dependency on foreign markets affected the silk industry in Lyon which was linked to Central Europe; the woollen industry in Languedoc, which was linked to the Levant; and the manufacture of linen in Brittany, which was linked to the Spanish Americas

[12] The Great Fire of London in 1664 led to an increase in the importation of wood from Norway as well as for the compensating exports. The English concentrated their trade efforts successively on the Levant, and then on Brazil via Portugal, and then on the Levant again when imports from Lisbon began to decrease.

through Cadiz. When demand for these products dropped, it created a slump, and, in the more dramatic cases, a decline from which these industries could never recover. England's dependency on foreign markets was even greater than that of other nations because of the widespread craft industries and because of the size of its production.

The English colonies, just like the French ones, could, of course, absorb a proportion of the exports from England or France. But we have to look at the percentages with greater precision. The West Indies and North America reached 15.5% of total exports in the fiscal year 1750–51, a figure that could be raised by one percentage point if we were to add the goods sent to Africa. If we are to evaluate the colonies' contribution to their colonising nations' economies, we should also look at the imports to the homeland corresponding to the exports to the colonies—this proportion is about 30%. But these figures cannot be attributed only to the plantations and the slaves they used. These figures also include goods from New England and the adjacent areas, as well as the gum from Africa, but their volume and value were limited. Therefore, we can estimate that the slave workforce represented nearly a third of the colonies' financial contribution to the homeland.[13]

Therefore, it is indisputable that slavery was important and had a powerful impact on a nation that was still a "traditional" economy. This would not have been the case if we were to consider the creation of capital and, furthermore, its investment in the pioneering industries of the "Industrial Revolution." Slavery also played an important role in the colonial production of gold. If the production of gold, with the help of slave labour, were included, the figures mentioned in the previous paragraph would have to be increased by two-fifths or even by half, depending on the period.[14]

Twenty years later, during the fiscal year 1772–73, the increase in the production of the colonies in Northern America and the West Indies was outstanding. The imports to England nearly doubled, and

---

[13] To establish these proportions, I used: B. R. Mitchell and Phillys Deane, *Abstract of British Historical Statistics* (Cambridge: Cambridge University Press, 1971, reprinted).

[14] See M. Morineau, *Incroyables Gazettes et Fabuleux Métaux* (Paris: MSH, 1985), "Les frappes monétaires en France au XVIIIe siècle" in John Day, ed., *Etudes d'histoire monétaire* (Lille: Presses universitaires, 1985), and "Quodlibet. Or brésilien, macro-économie et croissance économique en France et en Angleterre au XVIIIe siècle," *Revue d'Histoire Moderne et Contemporaine*, 48/3, 2001, 245–306.

the re-exports to continental Europe were significant. The trade engaged in by France's colonies were, more or less, the same as that of the English colonies, with the notable exception being that England re-exported tobacco instead of sugar and coffee. The demand for slaves in the French colonies might not have been equal to the English demand, but it was analogous. British industries' shipments to these colonies increased by more than a half in value and more than twice in percentages—to 37.2%. The imports from the East India Company doubled in value. However, their overall effect on the English economy as a whole is ambiguous. Most of the cotton imported at the time was brought in by the East India Company. Cotton spinning in Manchester, and the subsequent production of cotton fabrics, had already begun in this fiscal year, but the general productive trend remained geared toward "traditional" industries, which shows that tradition did not inhibit change and development.[15]

English colonial trade received its first blow with the American insurrection a few years later, although the existing network of trade was rapidly restored. Therefore, British industry was able to continue finding outlets for its products, and even increase its market penetration thanks to competitive pricing. A constant and sufficient supply of cotton was necessary to drive this industrial production. The reorientation of the economy of the Southern part of the United States, the West Indies, and of Brazil toward cotton provided this vital product. At the same time, this increased orientation toward cotton in the United States, the West Indies, and Brazil stimulated the English cloth export industry. Consideration of the slaves' participation and their contribution to the emergence of this industrial landscape must not be overlooked. Their contribution was of great importance, even if it is difficult to evaluate quantitatively. In 1808 European exports to the New World, including the Spanish and Portuguese colonies, exceeded those to Europe by nearly a half. They also exceeded New World imports.

The transformation of the English economy in the middle of the 18th century, improperly called the "Industrial Revolution," did not

[15] Imports of cloths from India provoked a crisis in England in 1686, and the use of imported Indian cloth was subsequently curbed by the implementation of prohibitionist measures. This example shows how colonial trade could have a bad influence on the economy of the importing country. It is very possible that the imports brought in by the VOC had the same effects in the United Provinces.

happen in one day, nor in a few years. Therefore, the persistence of historians in looking for a certain "cause" of the Industrial Revolution, and, more precisely, in looking for the exact part played by colonial trade in this economic shift, makes no sense, since there were no direct, definable causes, and it is certainly almost impossible to extract what part of later industrialisation was imputable to colonial trade. But in 1815, soon after the wars with France, the process of industrialisation in England was already well under way, and, essentially, irreversible. We must not forget about the cultural factors that led to industrialisation, starting with those intrinsic to the first industrialising nation—the United Kingdom. These factors include: inventiveness, the art of looking for resources on its own soil in order to exploit what is available; ability to react quickly to market changes; and ability to exploit already existing advantages for further gain.

Needless to say, similar transformations were taking place in other nations that, at least at the beginning, had a similar set of circumstances as did Britain, but who did not industrialise. For instance, the Low Countries were in possession of a sizeable colonial empire, just as Britain was, yet their industrial take-off did not occur until the end of the 19th century. However, eventually, all the countries in Western Europe saw their economies grow rapidly, and, subsequently, the world became divided into two economic zones: the dynamic West and "the rest."

The disparity between the two zones raises some fundamental questions. Historians agree, at least a majority of them do, on the equality, or near equality, between these two zones at the beginning of the Early Modern era. By the beginning of the 21st century, however, the gap has widened tremendously and, in many cases, reached extraordinary dimensions. But what was the driving force behind this divergence? One answer is that colonial trade and the use of slave labour necessary for this trade created Western prosperity. However, we have seen above that this hypothesis is untrue.

The Rise of the West: Some Tentative Conclusions

The situation in every country in each of the zones was different. The West benefited from the vast open spaces of its colonies. This advantage created an emigrating-immigrating flow that allowed Europe to survive a demographic explosion. The agricultural development of these vast areas of land, and the control over their natural resources, was the result of European migration. Europe's lead in economic development did not stop with the invention of the spinning wheel in the cotton industry. Technical and scientific inventions followed one after the other in an uninterrupted flow. They were the fruits of a state of mind, of an education turned toward progress, of an atmosphere of success and of the "culture of benefit," which was exacerbated by international competition. This had the effect of generating growth in the West, which resulted in ever more power and wealth. This also had the effect of increasing the zone's strength in penetrating other economies.

We have to make several distinctions when considering the second, non-Western zone. There were some open spaces to exploit such as in Africa or Indonesia. But they were unequally distributed. For instance, there was little free space available in India, and, according to exactly which area is under consideration, available space could be further diminished by natural constraints such as forests or deserts. None of the countries in the second zone had a similar population density. Asia was already swarming with people and was relatively poor. America and Africa had scattered populations, as did the Canadian Great North or Australia. And the resources of each country were different, whether we are considering vegetal growth such as palm trees and rubber trees or minerals and fertilizers like phosphates, guano, gold, copper, and uranium.

No wonder that, after a couple of centuries, the situation was as different as it could be for the two zones. Some former colonies did become part of the first zone. The United States won independence from Britain and remained in the rich countries' group. New Zealand, Australia, and South Africa also joined this successful group. The different nations of Latin America underwent fluctuations, sometimes enjoying prosperity, sometimes falling into depression, and then, finally, reaching an uncertain position—either in debt or on the verge of bankruptcy. Many other countries in Asia or Africa experienced some precarious or truncated changes, but they never fully developed and sometimes even fell back to their original level at the beginnings of European colonisation. Then there are those nations that remain at the margins and completely underdeveloped—countries that simply deteriorate every day. The paradox is that the differences between the former colonial nations continue to increase even after decolonisation.

It would be wrong not to mention the role the West played in its own development. The West constituted a zone which finally found within itself, and between the different countries that comprise this zone, the main markets for the exchange of its goods, and which managed to reduce its dependence on outside countries, except for petrol and some rare metals. The progress of the West also had effects on the non-Western zone. One effect was, for instance, the abolition of the transoceanic slave trade, and the repression of the slave trade in Africa. In addition, the colonisation of the non-Western world provided the colonies with administrative and medical structures, as well as roads, railways, and other public works, in addition to the creation of effective agricultural methods, mining, and industrial enterprises.

Nevertheless, the conquest of lands by the Europeans meant the expropriation of the lands held by the previous inhabitants—Amerindians in the New World, Inuit in the Great North, Maori in New Zealand, Algerians in Northern Africa, Kikuyu in Kenya, and Shonas in Zimbabwe, to name but a few. Moreover, slavery continued in the United States until 1864 and in Brazil until 1888, meaning that black people were harvesting the cotton that was necessary to the development of that industry in the West. Elsewhere, populations were often subjected to hard labour which, in most cases, was badly paid, and the fruits of which were confiscated by the dominating power. For example, the Dutch employed a system of forced cropping in the East Indies. The wealth produced was misappropriated, which created frustration. The local elite were often accused of intervention and dishonest compromises—Indian chiefs, Javanese regents, and, at the same time, the black kings who supplied slaves for the traffickers. Multinational companies are the last avatar of this more or less regulated dissection of the globe.

Contact with European colonisers also dislocated the indigenous industry. Native craftsmen could not compete against Western technology. For example, African ore casters could not compete with imported iron, the Bengalis could not compete with imports from the textile industry of Blackburn and Bolton or with the fabrics of Manchester. The inducement to develop crops with commercial value had some pernicious effects on the cultivation of food for subsistence.

The food requirements of the urban populations, which have been rapidly increasing since 1950, are now supplied by imports from the United States and Europe, at low prices, which makes non-Western produce uncompetitive and, therefore, generates impoverishment of the countryside and reinforces the drift from the land—all of which are legacies of the emphasis on colonial cash crops. It shows that even good intentions can have perverse effects.

This situation does not mean that these nations cannot overcome their inferior position. The past has shown that the value of the goods and the raw materials exported by a producer of primary goods can match the costs of the manufactured goods it imported. This happened in Africa during the first half of the 19th century because England was eager for the gum and palm oil needed by its industries. In the case of raw silk, imports from Japan were so important to France and Italy that the cultivation of mulberry trees and the breeding of bombyxes were abandoned. For a long time, the European colonies in the Southern hemisphere only supplied raw materials—wool from Australia and South Africa and meat from New Zealand and Argentina. Until 1914 the United States exported both manufactured goods and raw materials.

No country was ever able to maintain a monopoly over any one particular form of production. During the previous centuries, sugar cane and the coffee tree were transplanted from the Eastern Mediterranean to America. Even many spices, which were closely controlled by the Dutch in the Molucca Islands, escaped their control by the end of the 18th century and were transplanted to the Indian Ocean, ending up in Zanzibar. Therefore, pre-eminence in certain commodities can be uncertain, and exports can decline for different reasons—sometimes because of a difference in quality, as was the case with the superiority of Egyptian cotton over Indian cotton—and sometimes because the price was lower. These fluctuations can still be felt, as is shown by the different crisis in cocoa, coffee, and petrol. However, the West, as the main importer of these products, has always managed to get through these crises.

From Quantitative to Dynamic Approaches?

CHAPTER THREE

COLONIAL AND EUROPEAN DOMESTIC TRADE: A STATISTICAL PERSPECTIVE OVER TIME

Bouda Etemad

The present study is a short exercise in compiling and organising dispersed and disparate data. The main purpose of this study is to reconstruct the geographical structure of the exports and imports of Spain, Portugal, Great Britain, France, and the Netherlands at seven crucial dates, namely: circa 1720, 1750, and 1780 for the 18th century; circa 1830, 1880, and 1913 for the 19th century; and 1938 in the 20th century, which was a milestone year that marked the pinnacle of the modern European empires.

These countries have been chosen because, collectively, their colonies accounted for anywhere between 85% and 100% of the total surface area and population of all European colonies since the 16th century (see Table 1). The choice of dates was determined by the quality of the sources available. Commercial data are more extensive for the 18th and 19th centuries than for the 16th and 17th centuries.

The results of this exercise are summarised and presented in tables that constitute the backbone of this study. While these results fill a void in the existing research and provide useful information in and of themselves, there is limited analysis attached to the quantitative data that are presented in this paper. This limited analysis is due to the fact that we have confined ourselves to studying only the colonial trade of the European powers. The role colonial trade played in the economic development of the European powers might have been to foster and support, in a sustainable or in a superficial manner, a process of growth for particular economic sectors and/or geographical regions. Or, on the other hand, colonial trade may have severely hampered the economic development of the European colonial powers. The roles colonial trade may have played, then, depended on a dynamic combination of factors. The limitations of my approach, which is based on a single indicator—the geographical structure of exports and imports—are, therefore, quite real. Keeping these limitations in mind, what can we learn from these statistics?

Table 1. Surface area and population of colonies held by colonial powers in 1760, 1830, 1880, 1913, 1938 (expressed as a percentage, totals expressed in millions of km^2 and millions of inhabitants).

	1760	1830	1880	1913	1938
Surface area					
France	0.3	0.2	3.0	18.2	21.3
United Kingdom	13.0	90.1	92.8	60.8	59.3
of which dominions	12.9	46.5	73.1	35.6	33.3
The Netherlands	0.8	3.1	1.7	3.9	3.7
Portugal	35.1	1.0	0.8	1.5	3.7
Spain	50.8	5.7	1.7	0.6	0.6
Belgium	–	–	–	4.4	4.2
Italy	–	–	–	3.8	6.0
Germany	–	–	–	5.5	–
Total Europe	100.00	100.00	100.00	98.8	98.9
United States	–	–	–	0.6	0.6
Japan	–	–	–	0.6	0.6
Total (millions of km^2)	24.2	8.2	24.5	53.2	56.7
Population					
France	2.2	0.3	2.3	8.7	9.7
United Kingdom	10.3	91.9	86.8	71.2	68.6
of which dominions	6.3	0.6	2.9	3.6	4.1
The Netherlands	12.0	5.4	7.7	9.0	9.4
Portugal	6.0	0.3	0.6	1.0	1.5
Spain	69.5	2.1	2.7	0.2	0.1
Belgium	–	–	–	2.0	2.0
Italy	–	–	–	0.3	1.8
Germany	–	–	–	2.2	–
Total Europe	100.0	100.0	100.0	94.7	93.1
United States	–	–	–	1.8	2.6
Japan	–	–	–	3.5	4.3
Total (millions of inhabitants)	27.1	205.6	312.3	554.1	724.2

See appendix for sources and notes.

Colonial trade

Tables 2 and 3 illustrate what importance European colonial powers placed both on distant and nearby markets. Tables 1, 4, and 5 show how that importance varied, depending on both the geographical size and the population figures of the various colonial empires. Some empires would profoundly change not only geographically, but also in the composition of their populations over the two centuries that are the focus of this study.

One of those changes occurred between 1760 and 1830 and was marked by a shift in colonial interests from the Americas to Asia. This shift also precipitated radical changes in the hierarchy of European colonial powers. Spain's virtual disappearance from the colonial scene following the loss of the greater part of her empire in the Americas effectively left the seat of the leading colonial power vacant. That seat would be filled by Great Britain, which assumed the leading role all the more easily because of the Industrial Revolution. The Industrial Revolution thrust Britain into the role of the leading world economic power, and gave it a vital edge over its European rivals. So much of an edge that, between 1830 and 1880, Great Britain controlled up to 90% of all colonial lands and populations.

This brings us to another criterion of differentiation between the European colonial powers—their level of development. This level of development was often, though not always, parallel with the size of the empires. One comparison would be the trade relations between Great Britain, the leading industrialised nation of the world, and its colony of India. India was a territory that, until the middle of the 18th century, was considered one of the main economic centres of the world, and was fifteen times larger and ten times more populous than the British Isles. Therefore, the trade relations between these two "giants" were obviously more important and more diverse than those between Portugal, one of the poorest and least industrialised nations of 19th century Europe, and its African colonies with their rudimentary economic structures.

One of the peculiarities of the British case, which Tables 2 and 3 clearly illustrate, is that it managed to maintain a large share (25 to 30%) of total colonial trade throughout the two centuries under consideration. Unlike the vast majority of other cases, there was no break in colonial trade between the 18th and 19th centuries. This continuity of trade can doubtless be explained by the fact that the independence of the United States (1776–1783) was a loss quickly compensated for by the conquest of India. Britain's considerable share of total colonial trade can also be explained by the development and establishment of other settlement colonies such as Canada, Australia, New Zealand, and South Africa, all of which would prove to be good, reliable trading partners.

Another factor of differentiation in the case of the British colonies was the high numbers of white settlers early on. Toward the middle of the 18th century, Europeans already made up half of the total population of the British colonies. In the other non-British colonies, that proportion was significantly lower: 16–18% for Spanish colonies; 24% for Portuguese colonies; 11% for French colonies; and 1% for Dutch colonies. A hundred and fifty years later, this divergence would persist. Around 1913, 15 million Europeans would inhabit the four British dominions, whereas there were a mere two million white residents in the 160 or so tropical colonies of the other European colonial powers.[1]

Spain, Portugal, and France were not as fortunate as Britain in their colonial endeavours. The end of the *ancien régime* empires marked a turning point in the geographical structure of their overseas trade. The loss of the Spanish possessions in the Americas, of Portuguese Brazil, and of French Haiti would account for the drastic decline in the colonial share of exports and imports for these three metropolitan powers (see Tables 2 and 3).

It should be noted that the method of calculating the share of colonial trade by excluding re-exports mitigates the role of overseas possessions as supply sources for the European economies. However, this exclusion does mean that an increase in the colonies' contribution as outlets for the production activities of the metropolitan powers can be seen.

The higher the re-exported share of colonial imports, the more this "double effect" was felt. The rate of re-export was close to 65% for France in 1787, roughly 60% for Great Britain in 1780, approximately 50% for the Netherlands in the 1770s and over 75% for Portugal in 1796. In the case of Portugal, 99% of re-exports, which were composed almost exclusively of Brazilian products, were sold on European markets.

---

[1] B. Etemad, *La possession du monde. Poids et mesures de la colonisation (XVIIIe–XXe siècles)*, (Brussels: Editions Complexe, 2000). pp. 196, 263–65.

In the case of France, deducting the re-exports of colonial products from the equation—products that merely transited the country, often without being manufactured—means that, at the end of the 18th century, it lost more outlets than supply sources in the Americas. In 1787 the colonial markets absorbed 22.1% of French exports (including re-exports) and 40% of total exports of domestically produced products. On the other hand, the contribution of the colonies to the importation of products consumed within France itself was 20.2%, which was lower than its share of total imports, which was 37.4%. (See Table 2)

Table 2. Estimated share of colonies and Europe in the foreign trade (excluding re-exports) of Spain, Portugal, Great Britain, France, and the Netherlands circa 1720, 1750, and 1780 (expressed as a percentage of the total value of each country's exports and imports).

	Exports			Imports		
	c. 1720	c. 1750	c. 1780	c. 1720	c. 1750	c. 1780
Colonial share						
Spain	...	...	48.8	...	...	26.1
Portugal	...	...	41.7	...	...	22.9
Great Britain	13.9	15.6	38.3	25.0	30.1	32.1
Settlement colonies	6.7	10.6	16.5	8.6	11.2	1.5
Tropical colonies	7.2	4.9	21.8	16.4	18.9	30.6
France a)	4.3	14.9	22.1	13.5	33.9	37.4
France			40.0			20.2
The Netherlands	11.0	...	12.9	16.7	...	20.3
European share						
Spain	...	...	49.2	...	...	70.2
Portugal	...	...	53.3	...	...	70.1
Great Britain	81.8	77.0	55.7	53.1	55.3	61.4
France a)	94.2	74.1	71.1	80.6	53.2	52.3
France			47.7			62.6
The Netherlands	81.0	...	80.0	78.0	...	75.0

a) Including re-exports
See appendix for sources and notes.

It was only between the 1780s and the 1830s that France would suffer the same fate as its Iberian counterparts, whose colonial trade shrunk drastically at the end of the *ancien régime*. The colonies retained by Spain (Cuba, Puerto Rico, the Philippines, as well as a number of enclaves in North Africa) and Portugal (Angola, Mozambique, Guinea, Cape Verde, São Tomé, and Principe, Macão)—as well as a few enclaves in India and the Indian Archipelago—in the 19th century provided selling and supply markets which were far less profitable than the vast and prosperous former Iberian possessions of the Americas.

To compensate for their losses in the late 18th and early 19th centuries, France managed to construct a new colonial domain centred in North Africa, Indochina, and sub-Saharan Africa. These colonies would occupy a significant place in French foreign trade (see Table 3). The establishment of what was virtually a settlement colony in Algeria helped consolidate the importance this colony played in French foreign trade. In fact, Algeria became, after a century of colonisation, France's leading trade partner.

Given the atypical manner in which the colonial share of Dutch foreign trade evolved, I have decided to treat this case last. The Dutch situation is peculiar due, in part, to the fact that, unlike the other colonial powers, the Netherlands never really managed to carve out for itself a colonial domain in the true sense of the word in the Americas. Dutch Guiana (present day Suriname) and the Netherlands Antilles are the American vestiges of a colonial empire that was dominated, from beginning to end, by the Indian Archipelago. The fate of Dutch colonial trade would be decided upon, from the very outset, in Asia, not the Americas.

An example of this "Asian bias" would be Dutch trade with their Indonesian possessions. From 1830 to 1880, the disproportionate exploitation of the island of Java would foster trade with the Netherlands at time when, everywhere else, the colonial share of metropolitan trade was lessening or dwindling (see Table 3). The intensive trade ties between the Netherlands and the Dutch East Indies, are generally underestimated because of statistical bias (see appendix), which is clearly illustrated in Table 7.

Table 3. Estimated share of colonies and Europe in the foreign trade (excluding re-exports) of Spain, Portugal, Great Britain, France, and the Netherlands in 1829–31, 1879–81, 1911–13, and 1936–38 (expressed as a percentage of the total value of each country's exports and imports; three-year annual averages).

	Exports				Imports			
	1829–31	1879–81	1911–13	1936–38	1829–31	1879–81	1911–13	1936–38
Colonial share								
Spain	18.3	11.5	0.8	2.5	16.4	6.5	0.4	1.8
Portugal	2.0	3.2	14.1	11.6	1.5	2.0	3.2	10.5
Great Britain	22.9	33.0	36.0	43.6	25.2	22.2	20.4	35.6
Settlement colonies	7.3	14.8	18.0	25.1	7.1	10.7	11.8	22.4
Tropical colonies	15.6	18.2	18.0	18.5	18.1	11.5	8.6	13.2
France	11.8	6.2	14.0	29.0	13.8	4.8	10.7	26.4
The Netherlands	20.5	19.5	21.0	9.1	34.0	25.0	17.5	9.3
Average a)	18.9	21.5	26.2	34.2	23.3	16.5	16.2	29.6
b)	15.2	13.8	16.3	19.3	19.0	10.1	9.7	15.5
European share								
Spain	73.3	77.0	70.0	70.5	76.6	71.5	63.5	55.3
Portugal	. . .	70.8	62.3	62.9	. . .	74.2	76.6	64.0
Great Britain	38.1	35.0	33.7	34.9	37.5	38.6	44.2	34.6
France	57.6	71.5	67.3	53.5	61.1	61.2	51.0	37.4
The Netherlands	73.5	74.5	63.5	71.7	58.5	60.5	63.5	59.7
Average	. . .	52.9	48.5	45.4	. . .	48.3	49.3	42.9

a) Including British white settlement colonies
b) Excluding British white settlement colonies

See appendix for sources and notes.

Trade with Europe

Colonial trade rarely ever surpassed inter-European trade for any of the empire-building nations in Europe. For Spain and Portugal, colonial outlets were on a par with European outlets at the end of the 18th century. This quasi parity would recur between 1879 and 1881 in the case of Great Britain, which was the country whose colonies would also absorb a higher share of metropolitan exports than did other European nations in the years between 1911 and 1913. This relative "superiority" of the British colonies would continue during the period between the two World Wars and, during this time, would temporarily extend to imports as well (see Table 3).

Generally, the intra-European share of the total foreign trade of the five colonial powers under consideration in this study would lose ground in the 18th century. Then, except for the case of Great Britain, the intra-European market would gain some small amount of ground against the colonial markets during much of the 19th century. These gains would be erased in the 1880s when, once again, colonial markets came out ahead.

The intra-European share of the colonial powers' foreign trade depended on various factors. Obviously, as was the case with the colonial share, the intra-European portion fluctuated depending on the expansion and contraction of the empires themselves. Another factor was the evolution of the economic structures in the metropolitan countries. The rapid pace of industrialisation among the colonial powers of Europe throughout the 19th century, which expanded greatly from the 1860s onward, would account for changes in the commodity structure of the metropolitan exports.

A number of tropical colonies proved to be successful outlets for first-generation industrial goods such as textiles and iron and steel products. The standard of living of their populations and the structures of their economies, however, did not make them good clients for second-generation manufactured products such as chemicals, machinery, and automobiles. Hence, the trend to "Europeanise" trade by increasing the intra-European share.

Conclusion

The data collected for this study shows that there was a process of "colonisation" of European trade in the 18th century, and that the trend was reversed in the 19th century with the advent of the "Europeanisation" of trade, when the colonial powers (with the exception of Great Britain) turned increasingly toward partners who were close both in terms of geography and in their levels of economic and industrial development. This shift toward greater intra-European trade would be interrupted during the period between the two World Wars, as the colonial powers of Europe would fall back on their empires as their trading partners. However, the shift toward "Europeanisation" was inexorable, and the process would be renewed and intensified after the Second World War.

The political independence of the colonies, gained half a century ago, would place a great strain on relations between the European nations and their former possessions. On the eve of the Second World War, roughly 15% of the foreign trade of the European colonial powers was conducted with their own overseas possessions (excluding British white settlement colonies). In the case of Great Britain and France, the two dominating colonial powers, the proportion would be ever greater. At the end of the 20th century, the former colonies accounted for a mere 3% of the external trade of the five nations considered in this study.[2]

Therefore, the former colonies in the Americas, Asia, Africa, and Oceania ceased to be the primary trading partners for their former colonial masters. Europe would turn its attention away from the endless horizon of its overseas empires and toward the industrialised Western world. Today, more than ever, the industrialised countries trade and invest with and among each other. In fact, roughly 80% of their exports and over 90% of their direct foreign investment remain inside the borders of the West.

[2] For further details on the 20th century, see B. Etemad, "L'Europe et le monde colonial. De l'apogée des empires à l'après-décolonisation" in *Revue économique*, volume 51, number 2, March 2000, pp. 257–68.

Table 4. Surface area and population of colonies per region in 1760, 1830, 1880, 1913, and 1938 (expressed as a percentage, totals expressed in millions of km^2 and millions of inhabitants).

	1760	1830	1880	1913	1938
Surface area					
Africa	0.3	5.9	7.1	48.8	51.4
North Africa	–	0.0	1.3	9.9	7.9
Sub-Saharan Africa	0.3	5.9	5.8	38.9	43.5
Americas	98.0	15.9	39.3	19.4	18.2
Asia	1.6	45.2	20.8	15.7	15.3
Middle East	–	–	–	–	0.6
Oceania	–	32.9	32.8	16.1	15.1
Total (millions of km^2)	24.2	8.2	24.5	53.2	56.7
Population					
Africa	0.4	0.4	2.7	20.4	19.9
North Africa	–	0.0	1.3	4.6	2.6
Sub-Saharan Africa	0.4	0.4	1.4	15.8	17.3
Americas	78.3	1.6	2.7	2.1	2.3
Asia	21.0	97.7	93.5	76.0	76.2
Middle East	–	–	–	–	0.8
Oceania	–	0.0	1.0	1.4	1.5
Total (millions of inhabitants)	27.1	205.6	312.3	554.1	724.2

Note: Great Britain's "European" colonies of Gibraltar, Malta, and Cyprus, excluding Northern Ireland, are included in the totals, although they do not appear above since their relative importance is insignificant. From 1760 to 1938, their surface area was less than half of the unit used. Their population did not exceed 0.1 to 0.3% of the total.

See appendix for sources and notes.

Table 5. Ratio between colonial and metropolitan populations in 1760, 1830, 1880, 1913, and 1938 (expressed as a percentage).

	1760	1830	1880	1913	1938
France	2.3	1.8	18.9	120.6	168.1
United Kingdom					
with dominions	25.1	794.5	783.2	865.6	1,045.9
without dominions	9.9	789.2	757.5	821.5	982.6
The Netherlands	166.3	425.8	602.9	804.0	785.9
Portugal	70.7	22.9	38.4	94.0	141.5
Spain	208.9	31.5	49.4	4.6	4.1
Belgium	–	–	–	144.7	170.2
Italy	–	–	–	5.4	29.5
Germany	–	–	–	18.6	–
Total Europe					
with dominions	54.6	272.0	320.0	230.2	368.0
without dominions	51.1	270.3	310.9	221.0	351.6
United States	–	–	–	10.3	14.3
Japan	–	–	–	37.9	43.1
Grand total	54.6	272.0	320.0	147.1	188.0

See appendix for sources and notes.

Table 6. Surface area and population of colonial powers in 1760, 1830, 1880, 1913, and 1938 (expressed in thousands of km² and millions of inhabitants).

		Surface area	Population				
			1760	1830	1880	1913	1938
Spain		505	9.0	13.5	16.8	20.4	25.6
Portugal		92	2.3	3.0	4.7	6.0	7.5
United Kingdom	a)	244	11.1	23.8	34.6	45.6	47.5
France		552	25.2	32.7	37.5	39.8	42.0
The Netherlands	b)	41	2.0	2.6	4.0	6.2	8.7
Germany		357	–	–	–	67.0	–
Belgium		31	–	–	–	7.6	8.4
Italy		301	–	–	–	35.2	43.6
Total		2.123	49.6	75.6	97.6	227.8	183.3
Japan		378	–	–	–	51.7	71.9
United States	c)	9,373	–	–	–	97.2	130.0
Grand total		11,872	49.6	75.6	97.6	376.7	385.2

a) Great Britain (England, Wales, Scotland) and Northern Ireland
b) Including internal waters
c) Excluding Hawaii and Puerto Rico
See appendix for sources and notes.

Table 7. Estimated exports to and imports from colonies of Spain, Portugal, Great Britain, France, and the Netherlands for 1829–31, 1879–81, 1911–13, 1936–38 (per capita, in current US dollars, 1936–38 in old dollars, three-year annual averages).

	1829–31	1879–81	1911–13	1936–38
Per capita exports				
Spain	0.3	0.8	0.1	0.0
Portugal	0.1	0.2	0.9	0.5
Great Britain	0.7	10.0	18.8	12.8
Settlement colonies	0.6	4.5	9.4	7.4
Tropical colonies	1.2	5.5	9.4	5.4
France	0.3	1.1	4.4	3.8
The Netherlands	3.8	7.3	14.5	3.4
Average a)	0.9	4.4	9.6	6.1
b)	0.7	2.8	6.0	3.4
Per capita imports				
Spain	0.3	0.5	0.0	0.1
Portugal	0.1	0.2	0.4	0.8
Great Britain	3.0	12.2	13.6	18.9
Settlement colonies	0.8	5.9	7.8	11.9
Tropical colonies	2.1	6.3	5.8	7.0
France	0.4	1.2	4.3	5.7
The Netherlands	8.2	12.8	14.7	4.7
Average a)	1.4	5.4	7.5	9.1
b)	1.2	3.3	4.6	4.7

a) Including British white settlement colonies
b) Excluding British white settlement colonies
See appendix for sources and notes.

APPENDIX

NOTES AND SOURCES FOR TABLES

Key to symbols:
. . . not available
0,0 smaller than half of the unit used
- strictly zero or negligible

Dominions: 13 colonies of North America, Canada, Australia, New Zealand, and South Africa.

As percentages are rounded off, totals and sub-totals are not always equal to the exact sum total of their components

Sources—Tables 1, 4, 5, 6
B. Etemad, *La possession du monde. Poids et mesures de la colonisation (XVIIIe–XXe siècles)*. (Bruxelles, Editions Complexe: passim, 2000).

Sources—Table 2
Spain, 1792: L. Prados de la Escosura, "Comercio exterior y cambio económico en España (1792–1849)" in J. Fontana ed., *La economia española al final del Antiguo Régimen*, Volume III, *Comercio y Colonias* (Madrid: Alianza Editorial/Banco de España, 1982), pp. 189–90.

Portugal, 1796: A. Balbi, *Essai statistique sur le Royaume du Portugal et d'Algarve*, Volume I (Paris: Rey et Gravier, 1822), pp. 430–45.

Great Britain, 1719–21 and 1749–51 (England and Wales), 1779–81: B. R. Mitchell with the collaboration of P. Deane, *Abstract of British Historical Statistics* (Cambridge: Cambridge University Press, 1962), pp. 279–312. In the 18th century and in 1830, the Ottoman Empire was included in Europe.

France, 1716, 1755, and 1787: P. Butel, *L'économie française au XVIII^è^ siècle* (Paris: SEDES, 1993), pp. 85–88.

The Netherlands, 1720 and the 1770s: J. de Vries & A. Van der Woude, *The First Economy, Success, Failure and Perseverance of the Dutch Economy, 1500–1815* (Cambridge: Cambridge University Press, 1997), pp. 496–99.

Sources—Table 3
Spain, circa 1830: L. Prados de la Escosura, "Comercio exterior y cambio económico en España (1792–1849)" in J. Fontana ed., *La economía española al final del Antiguo Régimen*, Volume III, *Comercio y Colonias* (Madrid: Alianza Editorial/Banco de España, 1982), pp. 211, 221, 245, and 249. 1879–1881: *Statistical Abstract for the Principal and Other Countries in Each Year from 1872 to*

1881/82, tenth edition, London, 1883, pp. 126–27. 1911–13: *Estatistica general del comercio exterior de España*, Direccín general de aduanas, 1912 and 1914 editions, Part I, Madrid 1913 and 1915, pp. XII–XIV. 1935 (figures for 1936–38 not available): *Anuario estadtistico de España. Año XX. 1943*, Direccín general de estadtistica, Madrid, 1943, pp. 694–95.

Portugal, circa 1830: share of colonies in total exports estimated from P. Lains, "An Account of the Portuguese African Empire, 1885–1975," in *Revista de historia economica*, año XVI, No 1, Invernio 1998, p. 240; and *Estatisticas de comercio externo*, 1968, volume I, Lisboa, p. XXVIII. 1879–81: *Statistical Abstract for the Principal and other Countries in each year from 1872 to 1881/2*, tenth number, London, 1883, pp. 125. 1911–13: *Estatistica comercial. Comercio e navegação. Ano de 1913*, Direcçao geral de estatistica, Lisboa, pp. XVIII–XIX. 1936–38: *Comercio externo. Ano de 1938*, Instituto nacional de estatistica, Lisboa, 1939, p. XXI.

Great Britain, circa 1830: R. Davis, *The Industrial Revolution and British Overseas Trade* (Leicester: Leicester University Press, 1979), pp. 86, 89, 91; supplemented by B. R. Mitchell, with the collaboration of P. Deane, *Abstract of British Historical Statistics* (Cambridge: Cambridge University Press, 1962), pp. 313–14. 1879–81, 1911–13 and 1936–38: *Statistical Abstract for the* United Kingdom, Board of Trade, London, various issues. In the 19th century, there were declared values, whereas in the 18th century, there were official values.

France, 1829–31: *Tableau décennal du commerce de la France avec ses colonies et les puissances étrangères 1827 à 1836*, Administration des douanes, Paris, April 1838, pp. XLIV–XLV and XLVIII–XLIX. 1879–81, 1911–13 and 1936–38: *Tableau général du commerce extérieur* (title varies slightly), Direction générale des douanes, Paris, various issues.

The Netherlands, circa 1830: *Résumé statistique pour le Royaume des Pays-Bas 1850–83*, The Hague, 1884, p. 28. 1879–81: *Jaarcijfers over 1883 en vorige jaren, omrent Bevolking, Landbouw, Handel, Belastingen, Onderwijs enz., Statistiek in Nederland*, No 3, The Hague, 1884, p. 28. 1911–13 and 1936–38: *Statistiek van den in-, uit- en doorvoer*, Departement van financien, The Hague, various issues.

Trade statistics for the Netherlands, reputedly largely unreliable for the 19th century, have been adjusted. For the value of exports and imports see A. Lewis, "The Rate of Growth of World Trade, 1830–1973" in S. Grassman and E. Lundberg eds., *The World Economic Order. Past and Prospects*, (London: Macmillan 1981, pp. 35 and 41–48.) For the geographical structure of trade, see J. T. Lindblad and J. L. Van Zanden, "De Buitenlandse Handel van Nederland, 1872–1913" in *Economischen Sociaal-Historisch Jaarboek*, volume 52, 1989, pp. 231–69; and P. Van der Eng, "Exploring Exploitation: The Netherlands and Colonial Indonesia 1870–1940" in *Revista de historia económica*, año XVI, No 1, Invernio 1998, pp. 294–96. Without these adjustments, the portion represented by the colonies would have been much lower.

Sources—Table 7
Figures obtained according to the data in Tables 3 and 6 combined with the following estimates of the total exports and imports of the five colonial powers cited in this study (in current US dollars, 1936–38 in old dollars, three-year annual averages):

	1829–31	1879–81	1911–13	1936–38
Exports				
Spain	20.5	119.0	199.6	47.7
Portugal	7.8	24.6	37.4	29.7
Great Britain	180.5	1,052.1	2,379.2	1,393.2
France	90.9	659.9	1,265.0	551.0
The Netherlands	48.0	149.0	429.0	323.4
Total	347.7	2,004.6	4,310.2	2,345.0
Imports				
Spain	22.0	126.6	216.0	71.1
Portugal	10.5	35.5	83.9	58.8
Great Britain	278.8	1,899.9	3,032.8	2,525.9
France	86.6	932.0	1,589.7	912.1
The Netherlands	63.0	204.0	522.0	441.3
Total	460.9	3,198.0	5,444.4	4,009.2

The figures appearing above were calculated using the data provided in the references for Table 3, and were converted into US dollars based on the exchange rates mentioned below.

Exchange rates used

One US dollar is equivalent to:

4.933 Spanish pesetas from 1848 to 1864; 5.18 pesetas from 1864 to 1914; and 12.32 pesetas in 1935.

1.105 Portuguese milreis from 1829 to1831; 0.925 milreis from 1854 to 1913; 37.43 escudos in 1936; 37.79 escudos in 1937; and 38.24 escudos in 1938.

0.2055 pounds sterling from 1816 to 1914; 0.3397 pounds in 1936; 0.3425 pounds in 1937; and 0.3465 pounds in 1938.

5.183 French francs from 1803 to 1914; 27.62 francs in 1936; 41.84 francs in 1937 and 58.82 francs in 1938.

2.488 Dutch guilders from 1817 to 1914; 2.621 guilders in 1936; 3.252 guilders in 1937 and 3.079 guilders in 1938.

The US dollar was devalued by 40.94% on January 30, 1934. For 1936–38, "old dollars" were used. To convert "old dollars" into "new dollars", multiply the figure by a coefficient of 1.693.

CHAPTER FOUR

FROM ONE INTERNATIONAL TRADE TO ANOTHER: CHANGES IN EUROPEAN TRADE DURING THE NINETEENTH CENTURY

Patrick Verley

Since the 18th century, the economic growth of European countries seems to be related to their access to international trade, and, thereby, to their level of integration in the international economy. It seems their periods of greatest growth corresponded to a development in their international economic relations. However, we must be cautious about drawing conclusions from this apparent corollary. We must not assume that a chronological coincidence is evidence of a relationship. Colonial trade was the most dynamic segment of European trade in the 18th century. Therefore, it was logical that European economic history, which was long dominated by the question of the "origins of the Industrial Revolution" anyway, would then lead us to question the link between European development and colonial trade. This question of the relationship between industrialisation and colonial trade was of particular interest to historians, due to the light it might shed on the development of relationships between countries—some of which would proceed along a trajectory of growth, others of which would become, or remain, underdeveloped. However, looking for links between colonial trade and industrialisation, or for connections between colonies and the origins (or lack thereof), or development, has led historians to ignore the fact that the industrialisation of Europe was placed on a secure footing by re-directing the flow of trade between developed countries. In fact, the colonies played a minor role in industrialisation, and many of these colonies were actually decolonised between 1770 and 1830—the time at which industrialisation was beginning.

Analysis of the colonies and their supposed links to development and industrialisation is made particularly difficult due to the problems inherent in establishing criteria for comparing the stage of economic development in each country. We shall look at them from a different perspective, according to whether we define them by their colonial link, their low level of development, their function as a supplier of primary goods in the international division of labour, or by their passive integration within the international economy. An example of the difficulty of establishing an objective criterion is shown by the case of the United States. During the 19th century, the United States was an ex-colony, as well as a supplier of primary products, just like Brazil and Argentina. If, as defining criterion, we take the level of development as the most appropriate criterion for comparison of countries in the 19th century, we would have to classify the 13 colonies of North America with the European developed countries rather than with the tropical colonies.

The difficulty in choosing the criteria for making comparisons affects the conclusions that can be drawn from the statistical evidence available. It is possible to speak of "Europeanisation" of international trade during the 19th century. Indeed, Europe was responsible for 65% of exports and 70% of imports worldwide in the 1870s. However, this observation has only a limited significance because the European countries themselves did not constitute a homogeneous "centre" in relation to a homogeneous "periphery." Not all European countries functioned as an economic unit. Indeed, the most developed European countries had a symbiotic relationship with the economy of the United States, which became ever more important. For example, in the second half of the 19th century, this American-European trading block was very important because it was responsible for 75% of all imports and exports.

Since, as we have seen above, it is difficult to draw valid conclusions from a statistical approach due to lack of homogenous units of analysis, it is better to look at the qualitative development of international economic relations. We can then see the structural changes between the international system of the 18th century—often conflictual because of commercial rivalries engendered by colonial relations—and that of the 19th century, during which a system encouraging lasting, peaceful relations between the great political and economic powers emerged. The international economy of the 18th century was conflict-ridden because there was virtually no international commercial system in place. Such a system provides for the organisation of relations between partners with a dominant economy and a sufficiently advanced division of labour, so that each country's contribution to the whole would appear more complementary than competitive. In the 19th century, we can see an international economic system because there was a dominant economy—that of Great Britain. And, Great Britain was recognised as being the dominant player by the other participating countries. This meant there was a system of trade with a hierarchy and with complementary roles. In the 19th century, this system of trade, and the payment flow through it, had at least two successive configurations—one in the middle of the century, and the other at the beginning of the 1890s. The period between 1870 and 1890 was the least recognisable as an international system.

The characteristics of the 18th century and the genesis of a system based on an international division of labour

Colonial economies within the international division of labour

In the 18th century, the international division of labour was brutal and rudimentary. This division of labour set the colonial economies, which provided tropical goods, against the economies of the more advanced European countries, which sold basic foodstuffs and manufactured goods made in proto-industrial structures. These European nations used basically the same techniques and, therefore, had largely the same levels of productivity. Since international trade, in general, increased more rapidly during this century than did European production specifically—and coupled with the fact that the main feature of international trade at the time was its increasing "Americanisation"—it is tempting to attribute a driving role to the apparently most dynamic element: insatiable American demand as the main stimulant to European growth in a mutually beneficial symbiosis.

The importance of colonial trade for internal European growth cannot be denied. Paul Bairoch proves this in his well-known article.[1] Whereas the European markets were relatively inflexible because growth in the standard of living could only sustain a very limited

[1] P. Bairoch, "Commerce international et genèse de la révolution industrielle anglaise," *Annales, Economie, Société, Civilisation*, vol. 28, no. 2, 1973, pp. 541–71.

increase in sales of manufactured goods due to short-term entrepreneurial decisions, colonial outlets represented a degree of freedom, giving added impetus—the effect of which was even greater as it was concentrated in certain industries, certain regions or even certain factories. But the colonial consumers did influence changes in the share of the market held by each producer. Historians have tended to posit colonial production as the prime element in the growth of trade between the colonies and Europe. For example, historians have thought that the growth in sugar production enabled colonial markets to develop as outlets for European industries which then benefited from this production of sugar.

However, this reasoning seems rather implausible because there is little evidence of a large increase in plantation productivity before 1780. The driving force of the system of mutual growth was, therefore, in the long-term, the rise in living standards and consequent consumption in Europe. This rise was weak, but its effect was increased by the demand for colonial luxury goods, as well as colonial products with high price flexibility. The price of goods fell due to the reduction in the cost of transport. This reduction in transport costs was due, in turn, to technical progress and economies of scale at both a production and commercialisation level resulting from this increase in consumption.

Finally, it would be wrong to see this trade as a flow between unconnected economic entities, because the colonies and the home countries were hardly different economies. For instance, there were not always distinct monetary units in use between the two, and the merchants working in both the colonies and the home countries were mostly the same. There is little sense in attempting to establish the balance of payments between European countries and their colonies. These colonies had the status of productive appendices. Therefore, the transfer of profits to the home country could not be likened to the movement of capital between distinct economies—a necessity for establishing a balance of payments.

The type of international division of labour which predominated was that of opposing countries with access to colonial economies, some of which then re-exported tropical products. The importance of re-export for general trade was one of the important features of the international economy in the 18th century. It must certainly have increased in relation to previous centuries, but this assertion is difficult to quantify. Re-exports certainly decreased later. For example, Great

Britain, centre of the global raw materials market in 1914, and industrialised by 1850, was in a much weaker position for re-export than it had been a century earlier.

Bipolarisation of the international economy in the 18th century

Great Britain and France found themselves in relatively similar and, therefore, competitive positions as both suppliers and consumers of colonial products. It is hardly surprising, then, that the balance of payments of the two countries was the same as with all their other partners combined at the end of the 1780s. In this bipolar system, it was not possible to have real complementarity between the two countries, nor much connection between their mutual creditors and debtors. This was particularly true since the division of labour was also very limited between the European economies, excluding re-exports, of course.[2] Although for products such as silk goods there was a division of labour according to quality between the producers of Lyons, Italy, the Netherlands, and England, competition was more direct between the large-scale clothing manufacturers, and even more so for textile manufacturers.[3] Of the few open markets outside Europe where general protectionism did not hamper trade, competition was fierce. This inspired states to create industrialisation policies supporting producers, which had the added effect of creating work and avoiding social unrest.

Due to both colonial and industrial rivalry, a not insignificant part of the running costs of international trade was based on military expenditure. Once the United Provinces were no longer competitive colonially or industrially, the conflict focused on the confrontation between two blocks—the Spanish-French block and the Luso-British block. Each of the two commercial poles had structured systems of partial payment. There was, therefore, an opening up of multilateral systems of payment or, to be more precise, the circulation of precious metals between producer countries and countries building up their capital. As an example, Samuel Berrick Saul points to Great Britain during the middle of the 18th century. Great Britain was

[2] Patrick Verley, *L'échelle du monde* (Paris: Gallimard, 1997), pp. 466–69.

[3] C. Poni, "Mode et innovation: les stratégies des marchands de soie de Lyon au XVIIIe siècle," *Revue d'Histoire Moderne et Contemporaine*, 45–3, July–September, 1998.

able to compensate for the constant trade deficit with the Far East and the Baltic by obtaining precious metal from the Iberian colonies.[4] Comparable circuits also existed in the French economy. Bipolarisation resulting from the relationship of the home country with colonial economies was an obstacle to the development of an international economic system.

Product innovations and the international division of labour

During the 19th century, colonisation was no longer of particular importance for the international economy and, from then on, a complex division of labour was set up between exporters of manufactured goods. This division of labour within the manufacturing sector was founded upon the diversification of products at two levels. The first level consisted of the successive stages in the manufacturing process. Therefore, the industrialisation process gave rise to an increasing number of intermediary products. There was also a diversification of products by quality. This evolution was particularly relevant for consumer goods such as fabrics, but it also included raw materials and semi-manufactured goods such as threads, metals and different varieties of coal. This was a conscious decision on the part of the producers so that they might better adapt to and encourage consumer demand while also promoting the obsolescence of products and, therefore, ensuring captive markets. From the 1820s onward, so-called novelty products came on the market, and the variety of products offered to the client increased greatly. Commercial strategies such as product innovation and the segmentation of markets rapidly spread to all consumer goods, including the intermediary products. The variety of fabrics produced required a great variety of threads, and the increase in the use of semi-finished products like metallurgical goods, or even coal, resulted in an increase and specialisation in quality. Moreover, prices could vary widely. This division by quality enabled the producer to market their products to their best advantage. Due to the increasing diversification in the range of manufactured goods, the division of labour between the countries increased. This division of labour is also evident in the

[4] Samuel Berrick Saul, *Studies in British Overseas Trade 1870–1914* (Liverpool: University Press, 1960), p. 7.

international trade in half-finished industrial products. The rate of product diversification is reflected in the many new product names used by customs officials.[5]

The international commercial system in the mid-19th century

A commercial system is characterised by a series of customs regulations, and by exchanges that are both complementary and hierarchical. In the first half of the 19th century, there was widespread and intense protectionism by international trading partners. This eased off gradually from 1840, but remained the rule during the middle decade of the century. A high level of protectionism can only have a dissuasive effect on the growth of trade. Whereas the 1820s and the beginning of the 1830s were years of experimentation when exporters were looking for new outlets and endeavoured to adapt their products to the clients targeted, there was a very rapid growth in trade from 1840—much more rapid, in fact, than that of production. So many new markets were opening up that many European countries became very dependent upon imports and exports. Did protectionism limit the development of the international economy? The trade boom seems to suggest otherwise.

Protectionism, national specialisation, and the international division of labour

As far as government protection is concerned, everything depends on the type of products and, therefore, the economic sectors the governments have chosen to protect. Apart from customs duties, which are comparable to taxes on consumption and were mainly instituted in order to generate government income, or import duties such as the "sliding scale" aimed at regulating the market for cereals, the customs' duties served, above all, to protect the leading industries such as iron and textiles, because the technological level differed greatly from country to country. It was, therefore, an "educational" protectionism, as analysed by Carey and List, protecting the sectors

[5] Between 1850 and 1860, the "Tableaux du commerce de la France" already included a considerable number of items—around 800. There were as many imports as exports included. The table only roughly indicated the differences in quality between similar products.

where productivity increased most rapidly, and not a defensive protectionism, protecting the sectors in decline.

The effect on the British economy was to reinforce specialisation of exports. Protectionism by other industrialising countries, and especially the ban on the importation of textiles, prompted Manchester industrialists to develop markets outside Europe—for example in India, where there was a large population with low purchasing power. For that reason, textiles suitable for the Indian market needed to be low in price and made of a coarse fabric. From 1830 onward, British exports to India and China exceeded those to the United States. The export dynamics of textiles were based on what had previously been favoured in the domestic market. During the 1820s and 1830s, exports surpassed domestic consumption. The profits from these exports, however, were not used to benefit the workers, and this lack of "re-investment," in turn, further limited domestic consumption. Thus, many profits were stashed in savings of various sorts, leading to slower economic growth. Also, the limited opportunities for investment in Britain stimulated the exportation of capital abroad.

British exports to other countries in Europe and to the United States consisted of two types of goods, which the protectionist barriers allowed through because the national economies could not provide them, yet still needed them. The first were goods that companies in other countries either did not know how to manufacture or else did not yet produce in sufficient quantities. This was the case of many half-finished products like cast iron, rails, certain machines, and fine threads required by industries further up the production line. The German and Italian states and Russia were examples of such states into which these half-finished goods from Britain were exported. The second sorts of goods for export were the surprisingly important primary products. France, for example, bought silk, cotton, wool, coffee, and coal from Great Britain. The fact that this dominant economy also exported primary products is explained by Britain's comparative advantage in setting up efficient marketing networks outside Europe, as well as by its superiority in the manufacturing industries. The result was that the market for raw materials became located in Great Britain. The structure of British trade was, therefore, based on highly mechanised heavy industry, technological superiority, and an interface between Europe, Asia, and Latin America, as well as control of the market for raw materials. Because Britain was so dominant, other partners in international trade had to find alternative or complementary specialisations. This was due to the fact that direct competition with British production was virtually impossible in a global market, especially a market in which protectionist regulations only permitted the importation of certain products.

The various national economies can, therefore, be classed in three categories according to their trade structure and level of internal development: advanced industrialised countries, underdeveloped countries, and "in-between" countries. In the first group of countries, of which Great Britain is part, foreign trade corresponds to this degree of progress. Mid-century, there were four countries—Great Britain, France, Switzerland, and Belgium—all of which were mainly exporters of manufactured goods and importers of primary products. The second category, underdeveloped countries, had not yet begun the industrialisation process and imported manufactured products and sold primary products. They were Asia, Latin America, the Ottoman Empire, the Southern Italian states, and Greece. The "in-between" countries will be discussed below. At any rate, the development of trade between developed and undeveloped countries could not be balanced, and exports from industrialised countries could only find buyers in other economically advanced countries with sufficient purchasing power to sustain the growth in imports. The rapid growth in international trade was, therefore, only possible under two conditions.

The first condition was that the industrially advanced countries were, by necessity, the main outlets for their own trade. It was not difficult to see a division of labour between the industrialised countries, as there were very few of them. Among the four industrialised countries in the middle of the 19th century, two stood out: Great Britain and France. Trade between these countries was generally complementary. Maurice Lévy-Leboyer has studied the French specialisation in quality products, such as silk goods, for export. The main outlet for these French exports was the middle and upper classes in the United States. The United States was replaced in the 1860s by Great Britain, a market that was all the more dynamic since the middle and upper classes were quite rapidly becoming wealthier. This specialisation of French exports encouraged a dualism in the French economy, which Lévy-Leboyer has emphasised.

During the 19th century other exporters of manufactured goods had to find a specialisation in the gaps left by British production and trade. These countries had a tendency toward a bipolarisation of their industry—meaning one sector worked for the home market and the other for the export market. However, this bipolarisation was the opposite of what was to happen a century later when the domestic sector was modern and mechanised, and the export sector was outdated. Indeed, the situation of the "followers" of Great Britain in the mid-19th century cannot be compared to that of the "new industrial countries" of the second half of the 20th century. The differentials in productivity, even in the mechanised industries, were greater than the differentials in wages. For example, the French cotton industry had lower wage costs at the end of the 1850s, and could produce cotton for the same price, or, sometimes, even more cheaply, than could the British.[6]

The second condition for solving the problem of export outlets for manufactured goods was the existence of a third category of countries, mentioned above, which were rapidly industrialising, but in which the commercial infrastructure still resembled that of an underdeveloped country. For example, these countries would export primary goods and import manufactured goods, but also import the raw materials necessary for their developing industries. This was the case of the German States (Zollverein primarily) and the United States, as well as the Austrian Empire and the Scandinavian countries. The Russian Empire and the Northern Italian States were probably about to join this group of countries—those in which the relationship between finished and semi-finished goods gives an indication of their development. The imports of these countries were comprised not only of consumer goods that they did not themselves produce in sufficient quantities, but also of semi-finished products like thread or cast iron and equipment such as machines or rails. This third group of in-between countries financed their industrialisation based on their domestic market, combined with the export of primary products.

The in-between countries could only progress as the structure of their trade aligned with the structure of their productive system. They had to catch up with the advanced industrialised countries and, therefore, find specialisations complementing those of the industrially advanced nations. Otherwise, it was necessary to enter into competition and conflict with the advanced nations, particularly if they had the same export structure. The more participants there

[6] There are various accounts in *Conseil supérieur de l'agriculture, du commerce et de l'industrie, Enquête, Traité de commerce avec l'Angleterre*, Imprimerie impériale, 1860.

were in the international division of industrial labour, the more difficult this division was to maintain, and whatever the level of development within the trade sector was, the greater the risk of conflict between the nations. Trade within the German Empire evolved in this way during the 1870s. It happened very slowly in the United States which, until 1914, principally remained a primary exporter of cotton and wheat. This was because the difference in productivity between American and European agriculture was much greater than that between industrial productivity, prompting the United States to export agricultural products.

The global system of compensation and the role of Paris as a second financial centre in the mid-19th century

The different trade flows did not balance bilaterally but, instead, gave rise to a system of compensation based on a multilateral system of payments with a financial centre. In order to play the role of financial centre in the 19th century, a city had to have a banking infrastructure capable of carrying out operations on an international scale, with companies whose signature was recognised in the international trading community, as well as possessing a national currency whose convertibility into precious metal inspired total confidence. However, it was also necessary that the structure of the balance of trade encouraged the development of compensatory activities. In fact, this last condition was the most important one because it explains the development of trading and banking infrastructures directed toward international operations. These infrastructures took a long time to become established, but once they were, they worked like a magnet that slowed down the development of competing markets. This is why, among the three main partners of international exchange—Great Britain, France, and the United States—until 1913 the New York market played only a very limited role as a financial centre compared to London or Paris.[7]

A diagram of compensations can be drawn by calculating the bilateral balance of sales of merchandise between the three main commercial powers and the other countries grouped here, for reasons of

[7] Until 1870, it is difficult to consider "German" commerce as a homogeneous entity, although after the institution of the Zollverein there was a certain unification of the economic area.

legibility, according to type of trade and as to whether the current balance of payments was positive or negative.[8] The London market was the centre of compensation for payment deficits for US trade—a country with plentiful credit in the London banks. The Anglo-American negotiating houses, represented on both sides of the Atlantic, had deposits in London. This credit enabled the trading companies to compensate for the trading deficits of the US with Brazil and, particularly, with China. Apart from its roles as credit holder and in long-term investment, London was also a centre for payments and short-term loans because most of the worldwide export and import flows were financed through these systems of payment.

Calculations of the balance in flows of trade and precious metals show that, on the European continent, it was the Paris market that played a major role.[9] Sales of wine, alcohol, silk and other manufactured goods to the United States and Great Britain—the two main French export markets—guaranteed credits with French traders in both these countries which had been left on deposit with Parisian bankers. The United States and Great Britain had credit in continental Europe, particularly with the German states. The German balance of trade was in deficit with Great Britain due to the large imports of tropical goods such as coffee, which were then re-exported by British merchants. The German and Mediterranean countries were very much in deficit with the United States because they bought cotton and raw materials for industrialisation without being able to sell to the United States the goods they sold to other European countries—primary products like wood, wheat, leather and cattle. These primary products were much cheaper in the United States, but transport costs to the United States would have made them prohibitive under any circumstances. The Germans or the Italians could have exported similar goods to those of the French to the United States,

[8] Strictly speaking, it would be appropriate to calculate the current sales of the balance of payments and not the trading balance, including monetary transfers by permanent or seasonal migrants and the remuneration of capital lent abroad. For a more complete analysis, see P. Verley, "Spécialisations industrielles, structures sociales, activités financières et intégration économique internationale au XIXe siècle: le cas de la Grande-Bretagne et de la France," *Revue d'Histoire du XIXe siècle*, special edition, May 2002.

[9] Verley, op. cit., p. 605. For French trade, we rely on the data in the "Tableaux décennaux du commerce de la France avec ses colonies et les puissances étrangères." See also, Maurice Lévy-Leboyer, *Les banques européennes et l'industrialisation internationale dans la première moitié du XIXe siècle* (Paris: PUF, 1964).

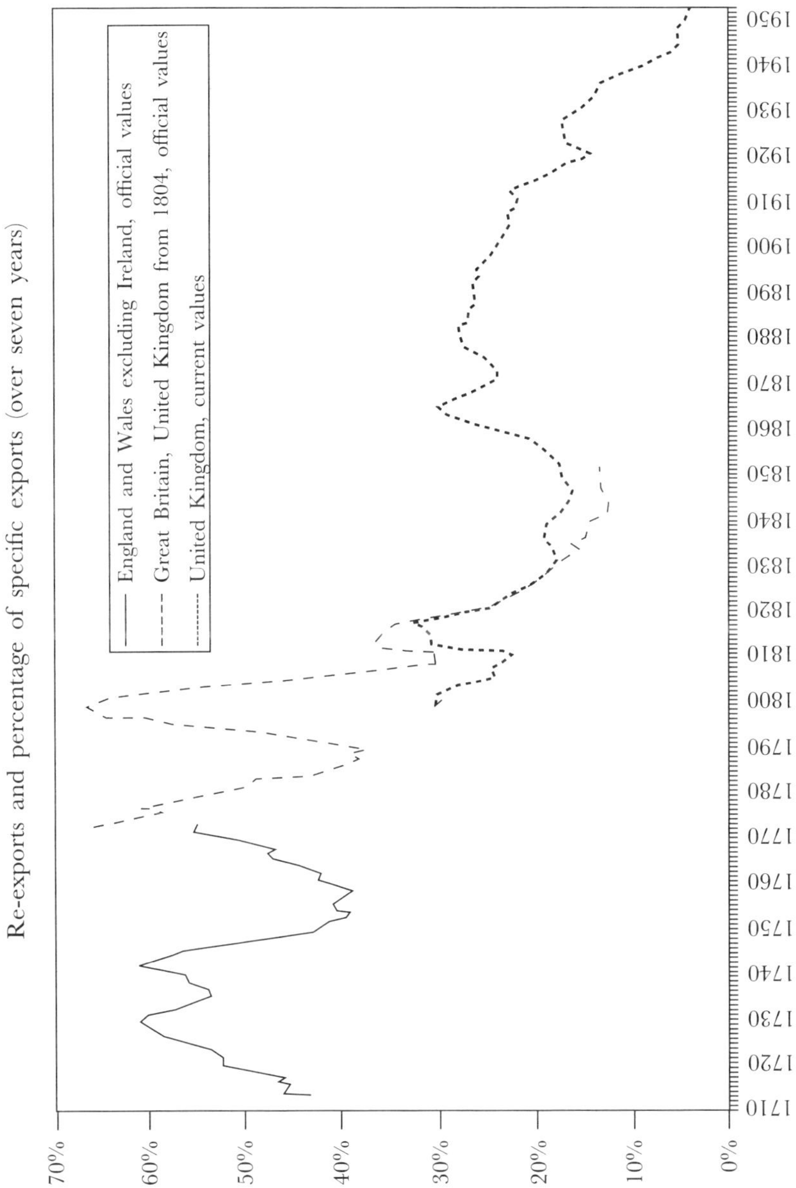
Re-exports and percentage of specific exports (over seven years)
England and Wales excluding Ireland, official values
Great Britain, United Kingdom from 1804, official values
United Kingdom, current values
70%
60%
50%
40%
30%
20%
10%
0%
1710
1720
1730
1740
1750
1760
1770
1780
1790
1800
1810
1820
1830
1840
1850
1860
1870
1880
1890
1900
1910
1920
1930
1940
1950

Diagram 1.

because the skilled workers were using the same techniques as the French. However, the manufacturers of German, Italian, or Swiss silk goods did not manage to penetrate the American market sufficiently. The Germans and the Italians did not manage to balance their trade because they had not yet set up commercial networks across the Atlantic. Their networks were directed to the East, specifically to the markets of Russia and the Middle-East.

However, the Germans, Italians, and Belgians could pay off their debts by approaching the Parisian bankers who managed their assets. Indeed, Zollverein, the Italian States, Belgium, and the Netherlands exported more to France than they imported, because the French bought primary products but were unable to develop large-scale sales of wine or "semi-luxury" goods. This failure to develop a significant market in wine or other semi-luxury goods is most likely due to the fact that the standard of living in these neighbouring countries was less than that in America or Britain. It could also be because their industries often manufactured similar goods. The movement of precious metals further increased the French trade deficit with these countries.[10]

As a consequence, the German, Italian, and Belgian bankers had credit in Paris. In fact, in the 1820s, many bankers from the Rhine valley settled in Paris. Their deficit was easily compensated for by economising as much as possible on the transport of precious metals, though this was complicated by the existence of two world standards. Looking at these flows in more detail, it seems that there may have

[10] An estimate of the current bilateral balance of payments of France (millions of francs). Annual averages 1827–66.

Balances of . . .	General trade (A)	Precious metals (B)	A + B	Tourism	Total
Great Britain	160,7	−112	49	70	119
United States	56,5	−17	39	8	47
Latin America	52,1	−8	44	44	
Italian States	−2,1	3	1	1	
Northern countries	−22,4	0	−22	−22	
Russia	−35,5	2	−34	−34	
Asia	−51,7	17	−35	−35	
Germanic States	−18,1	−22	−40	−40	
Of which Zollverein	*−26,6*	*−23*	*−49*	*−49*	
Belgium/Netherlands	−65,2	−11	−76	−76	

been other financial networks and other centres, but the reality of the flow of payments must be confirmed by research in the archives of banks and trading houses. A really reliable reconstitution of all the flows requires detailed research, taking into account customs statistics for all European countries, particularly the Italian States. Working from only French, British, German, and American sources, we can obtain some idea of these flows, however.

Belgium, the Netherlands, and the Italian States occupied a similar position to the Zollverein. These countries had surpluses with France through their sales of raw materials and agricultural commodities. For example, Belgium sold France coal, scotched flax, and livestock, while the Netherlands exported cheeses, zinc, wool fleece, and tin ore to France, and the Italian States traded in silks, olive oil, and livestock. In this way these different countries compensated for their deficits with Great Britain. Russia and the Scandinavian countries had considerable surpluses with France and Great Britain through their sales of raw materials—cereals, textile fibres, tallow, and wood.[11] The simplest trade circle was based on Great Britain and Zollverein. A secondary circle involved the Parisian bankers and the Northern countries—France, Great Britain, and Zollverein. In both cases, German bankers such as Bleichröder and Mendelssohn of Berlin and the Bethmann brothers of Frankfurt played a major role.

The role of the Paris market in international payments was reinforced by its position in the flow of precious metals, since the bimetallism of the franc allowed it to be traded in countries using the silver standard—the German states and the Asian countries—and those using the gold standard—mainly Great Britain and Portugal. However, payments in Asia remained the overall problem of the international system in the mid-19th century. Although the cultivation of tea in India gave exporters credit in London, and the Opium Wars had forcibly opened markets, trade still remained unbalanced with the Far East.[12] This asymmetrical position of Asian trade was

[11] It should be noted that, until the reform bill of 1857, French statistics did not show the origin or the final destination of the merchandise, but, rather, the immediate origin and destination. Thus, the trade with the Hanseatic towns could also include Russia or Austria. This inhibits a detailed understanding of continental trade.

[12] M. Greenberg, *British Trade and the Opening of China, 1800–1842* (Cambridge: Cambridge University Press, 1951).

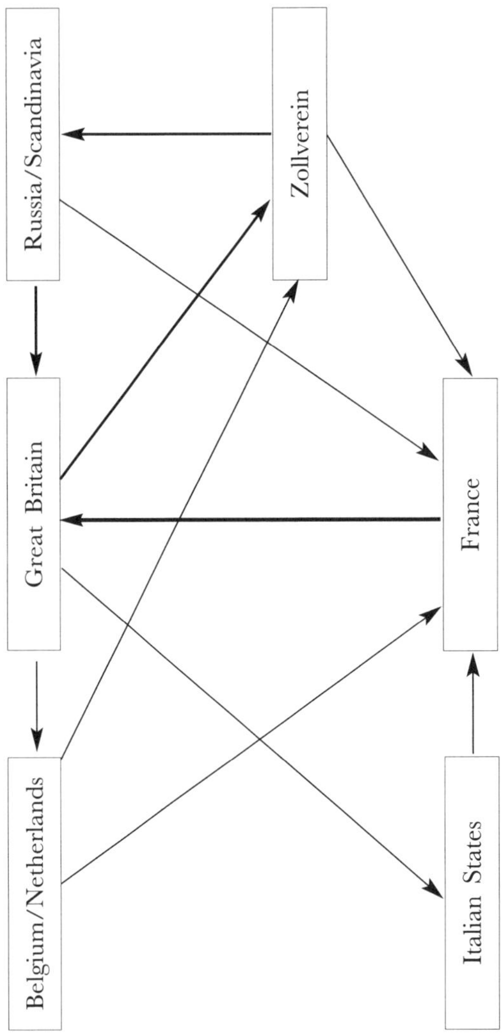
Russia/Scandinavia
Zollverein
Great Britain
France
Belgium/Netherlands
Italian States

Diagram 2

the only factor which prevented a perfect multilateralism in the mid-19th century. Therefore, the Asian countries were not a "fringe" element in the system of international flows; on the contrary, they "completed" the system by the end of the century.

The breakdown of the compensations system during the middle of the 19th-century

This relatively harmonious system broke down from the 1860s onward because two trade balances that corresponded to major trade flows were radically altered. Due to the American Civil War, American trade suddenly fell, both exports—particularly cotton—and imports. French exports to the United States collapsed because the demand for high-quality goods—those much more susceptible to political and economic changes than everyday commodities—fell drastically.[13] This drop in the sales of silk goods and wines was counterbalanced by the collapse of cotton imports, since part of the cotton was bought in Great Britain. The current French balance of payments with the United States remained positive, but the total was greatly reduced.[14] Basically, the Parisian bankers no longer had the same credit available on the New York market.

At the same time, French exporters had advanced on the Italian markets by selling more top-of-the-range goods in a country where the accumulation of wealth had been slow.[15] The French had also been selling industrial equipment as the Italian process of industrialisation got under steam.[16] Railway construction in France, dominated by financial groups, had encouraged a reproduction of the

[13] Buyers working for New York wholesalers came once a year to Paris and Lyons who then re-sold for the entire country through auctions held in New York had been common before the War. This practice does not seem to have been started up again after the War was over. For a description of this practice, see Jeanne Gaillard, *Paris, la ville 1852–1870* (Paris: Champion, 1977).

[14] On the evolution of the French balance of trade with the United States and the Italian states, see P. Verley, op. cit.

[15] D. Soleymani, op. cit. vol. I, p. 251, explains the boom of textile exports from 1850 by the increase in revenue and by the reduction of transport costs due to the railways.

[16] The work already mentioned by Soleymani shows the inflation of French exports "of metal items" to the German states from 1855. On the other hand, the shift in national production to imports seem to have been made earlier for "machines and mechanisms" D. Soleymani, Vol. II, pp. 92–95.

same model in neighbouring countries. From the 1850s onward, some Parisian financial groups participated in the construction of a rail network, and these direct investments abroad encouraged exports—exports that explain the growth toward a positive French balance of payments at the same time. Paris' function as a commercial and financial centre was about to change. Paris became less and less a centre of payment and compensation for international trade. Instead, bankers began to turn toward direct investment abroad, especially in Italy, Spain, and Austria.

The emergence of the Anglo-Saxon trading system at the end of the 19th-century

From one sort of protectionism to another

By the last quarter of the 19th century, the global system of compensation was concentrated in only one centre—London. This was because the role of the Paris market in international payments, especially for short-term movements of capital, was diminishing. This trend away from Paris was accentuated by the inconvertibility of the franc between 1870 and 1878, and by the crisis in French exports—in particular that of luxury and semi-luxury goods.[17] The slowdown in growth experienced by the industrial countries during the 1880s affected revenues derived from property and from shares in, or ownership of, companies. Therefore, it was the revenues gained by the wealthy classes, rather than the actual wages, that tended to increase. From then on, the unstable income gained from selling quality consumer goods had a detrimental effect on French exports. The breakup of the system of international trade from the middle of the century, along with changes in the level of industrial development and in the location of production areas explain the more conflictual nature of international economic relations from this period onwards.

The consequence of these changes was increased intervention by governments and a concomitant rise in protectionism. Moreover, this protectionism was of a very different type than that of the first half

[17] P. Verley, "Dynamique des marchés et croissance industrielle," in *Histoire de la France industrielle*, M. Lévy-Leboyer, ed. (Paris: Larousse, 1996).

of the 19th century. The protectionism of the 1820s–1850s was "Listian," aiming to protect "new" industries such as the nascent cotton or metallurgical industries. Between 1890 and 1900, government intervention endeavoured to protect, in addition to agriculture, declining industries. This protection had a definite negative effect on economic growth, since it slowed down the reallocation of the labour force and of capital by sector.[18] Ultimately, it was the consumer who paid the price. However, these government interventions also had a positive social effect since they limited the social cost which a sudden re-structuring of productivity would have implied.

The French decline and the Anglo-Saxon circle of trade and compensations

From the 1890s, a new system was created by restructuring international commercial and financial exchange. After 1890, in relative terms, France did not win back the position it once had occupied, whereas Germany became the second leading global exporter of manufactured products and, gradually, approached the level of Britain. Although there is no detailed study to evaluate the development of French trade from 1880 onward, the result of Alfred Maizels' work confirms the hypotheses that, intuitively, seem plausible.[19] This hypothesis is that the growth in the absolute value of French trade at the end of the 19th century, as opposed to that of Germany and the United States, was a passive response to the resumption of economic growth in general rather than a sign of dynamism. Diversification in terms of markets was weak. There was hardly any movement away from markets of weak potential growth toward more promising markets. Diversification in terms of products was not very satisfactory either. This is because the value in exports from the leading industries, like the car industry, must not be overestimated in relation to that of the old export sectors with weak growth in productivity, such as the silk industry, for which world demand was becoming less and less flexible.

[18] Jean-Pierre Dormois and Michael Dintenfass, *The British Industrial Decline* (London: Routledge, 1999).

[19] Alfred Maizels, *Industrial Growth and World Trade* (Cambridge: Cambridge University Press, 1971), pp. 476–84.

The share of manufactured goods in global exports

	1899	1913
United Kingdom	33.2	30.2
Germany	22.4	26.6
United States	11.7	13.0
France	14.4	12.1
Belgium-Luxembourg	5.5	5.0
Italy	3.6	3.3
Switzerland	4.0	3.1

Source: Alfred Maizels, *Industrial Growth and World Trade* (Cambridge: Cambridge University Press, 1971), p. 189.

In the 1890s a new international circuit of compensating payments was set up based on the complementary balance of payments of the United Kingdom and the new suppliers of agricultural products—the United States and India. It was an Anglo-Saxon system, giving the central role in the global economic relations to the United Kingdom, which S. B. Saul has described.[20] His findings will not be reproduced here. British trade remained the most important in the world but it was regressing in relative terms in the majority of markets apart from India, Australia, New Zealand, and Canada, where it increased in percentage. India became the main market, absorbing 23% of British manufactured goods exported in 1899 and purchasing 26% in 1913. India, Australasia and Canada together guaranteed an outlet for nearly 50% of the British manufactured goods exported in 1913.

Although Germany was to approach the level of the United Kingdom in export value in 1910, the British remained, by far, the most important global importers. Britain remained the most important commercial and financial partner for the majority of countries, which always placed it at the centre of global multi-lateralism.

[20] Saul, op. cit., chapters 2 and 3.

The multilateralism of the exchanges in 1910
(The differences between current transactions added to the number in millions of livres)

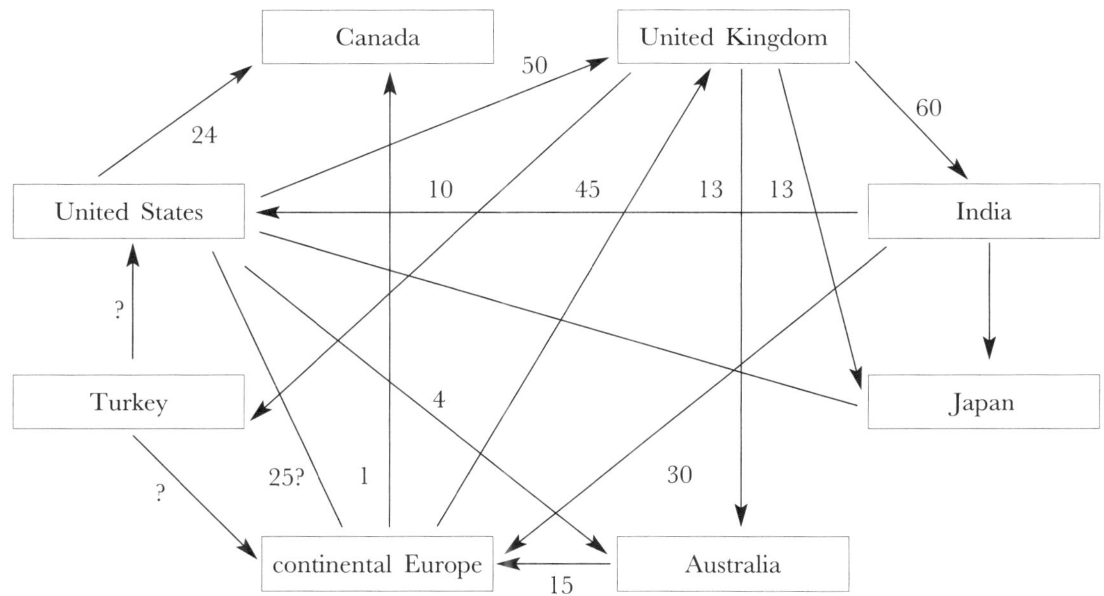

Note: The arrow is pointing at the debtor country.
Source: Saul

Diagram 3. S.B. Saul's diagram[21]

[21] Ibid., pp. 56–58.

The British balance in 1910 was in deficit. The countries surveyed in Saul's diagram showed £145 million debit and £118 million credit which makes a negative balance of £27 million. The compensation of world payments was, therefore, made between these credits and debts. The United Kingdom's principle debts were to the United States, continental Europe and the new suppliers of agricultural goods—Canada and, at the end of the 19th century, Australia and Argentina. Twenty years previously, continental Europe had been the main creditor. Its surplus diminished after 1900 due to the large exports of British coal. After 1900 the role of the United States changed with a reduction in the British deficit because Great Britain purchased less of its foodstuffs from the United States and more from Argentina and Canada. In Argentina and Canada, however, imports of US-manufactured goods tended to replace British goods, thereby upsetting the British balance of payments.

In 1910 the United Kingdom compensated for £120 million of debt—83% of the £145 million outstanding—by trade with the United States, continental Europe, and Canada. This was possible because the United Kingdom had a large trade surplus with India, Australia, Japan, and China. Canadian debt was transferred to the United States since Canada had a positive balance with Great Britain and a negative balance with the United States. The United States was always the second pivot in the system of compensations since it was a large creditor of the United Kingdom. However, the United States had a deficit with India and Japan that allowed for direct compensation. India was the third pivot in the system. It was the sale of British manufactured goods to India that ensured the functioning of the international economy. However, a more important part of the debt was compensated for in continental Europe. If we believe Saul's diagram, continental Europe used the £30–40 million in credit it had with Great Britain to pay its debts to Australia, India, and Turkey, all of which were in debt to the United Kingdom.

Saul's diagram did not break down the unit of "continental Europe," which clearly included countries with very different commercial structures. Saul believed that, in 1910, continental Europe had, overall, a positive balance of trade with Great Britain and the United States. His work brings to the fore some important subtleties, such as a source of dollars in Europe being Italy, Austro-Hungary and, to a lesser degree, France, due to their emigrant nationals remitting money.[22] However, the countries playing a role in the global system of compensating payments were only those having a positive balance of trade with the United Kingdom. Detailed research is necessary to highlight the bilateral balances of payments with all the individual European countries. Nevertheless, looking at the balance of trade in goods could help in the formulation of some assumptions.

In 1909	British imports from	British exports to	Balance
Russia	36898	18326	−18572
Sweden	9245	7114	−2131
Norway	6574	3835	−2739
Denmark	19427	5705	−13722
Germany	40115	47169	7054
Netherlands	37372	16304	−21068
Belgium	29218	19285	−9933
France	50691	31515	−19176
Portugal	2913	2777	−136
Spain	13363	5352	−8011
Italy	3634	13275	9641
Austro-Hungary	1208	4333	3125
Greece	1613	1514	−99
Bulgaria	151	902	751
Romania	3395	1750	−1645
Total	255817	179156	−76661

Millions of marks, calculations according to B. Harms's data, op. cit., p. 172.

Although Saul insists on the commercial progress of Germany in the European markets, it seems that Germany remained in deficit in 1909 and did not participate in the Anglo-Saxon system of compensation centred in Great Britain. On the other hand, the hierarchy of trading creditors with the United Kingdom always emphasised the role of Russia and the Northern countries—from the Netherlands to Scandinavia—and France, which was no longer central to the compensatory flows with the United States and Great Britain. Although the continental European countries could use their credit with the

[22] Ibid., pp. 51–52.

United Kingdom to pay their debts in their balance of payments with the United States, they could not rectify the fact that Britain was in debt to the United States. France participated in the system of compensating payments because of the many French imports from India between 1900 and 1913. In this period, India became the third largest creditor country to France, after the United States and Russia, and most of the deficits in the French balance of payments with British India were compensated for by French credit in its trade with Great Britain. A question mark remains regarding the French balance of payments with Russia, which showed a considerable trade deficit and were reduced to the level of the current balance of payments by interest on capital. Saul raises the point that these financial revenues were sufficient to change the current balance of payments from negative to positive (or vice versa). However, this requires further research.

Continental trade credits with the United Kingdom in 1909 (millions of marks)

Russia and Scandinavia (including Denmark)	37164	38%
Netherlands and Belgium	31001	32%
France	19176	20%
Portugal and Spain	8147	8%
Greece, Romania	1744	2%
Total credits with the United Kingdom	97232	100%

Thus, we see that by the early part of the 20th century, France played a minor role in the flow of short-term payments, and was only a secondary centre of compensation, but that it had become a long-term financial centre in the division of labour with London. If we push the idea further, Paris placed state loans, and London financed the development of the international production of raw materials and bulk agricultural commodities. On a monetary level, the complementary nature of France and Great Britain's role was also confirmed by the Bank of England's function as general regulator and the Bank of France's function as a depository for gold and silver reserves.

Conclusion

Between the mid-19th century and 1900–13, the international system of trade flows exhibited certain features such as the relative stability of trade between the industrial countries and/or the developed countries and, therefore, between the industrial and/or developed countries. Between the second half of 1870 and 1913, the total exports and imports in Europe (including Russia) and North America changed from 76.4% to 75.2% of the world as a whole—too small a difference to be significant.[23] This geographical grouping does not fit the definition of industrial and nonindustrial countries nor does it fit the distinction between developed and nondeveloped countries. It does not even work as a distinction between exporters of manufactured goods and exporters of primary products, although it comes close. This indicates that the colonial world only had a marginal impact on the international economy.

This global analysis of international trade puts into perspective Great Britain and France's specific development. These two countries increased their exports to their colonies just as they were losing markets in the United States due to competition with Germany. However, the increased dependency of British industry on colonial markets was partially compensated for by the development of exports to Australia, New Zealand, and Canada—countries with a high standard of living. As far as French exports to the colonies are concerned, the importance of Algeria must not be exaggerated. Weak sales of French manufactured goods to its main client, Great Britain, whose share of the total sales fell from 37% to 27% between 1900 and 1912, was only compensated for by the 3% increase in exports to Algeria—from 11% to 14%. In fact, the increase in French exports to the United States was larger, going from 9.3% to 13.7%.

The evolution of the international system in the last third of the 19th century and at the beginning of the 20th century was, therefore, mainly a redistribution of roles between the industrial powers, due to the dynamism of the German and American economies—both of which were gaining market share to the detriment of English

[23] Calculated according to P. Lamartine Yates, *Forty Years of Foreign Trade* (London: Allen & Unwin, 1959), pp. 32–33.

and French trade. However, the consequence of the weaker competition and diversification (to use the classic analysis of Maizels) of British and French exports was a more marginal role for France as centre for international banking. By reorienting to other partners, English trade remained the most important in the world. What had been the characteristics of international economic relations became, in reality, the characteristics of international trade.

The reorientation of Great Britain to the markets of underdeveloped countries gave countries such as India and Australasia a place in the international economy of the 19th century that statistics alone cannot reflect. In the middle of the 19th century, India and the Far East found themselves on the fringes of the trade system and of the international system of payments because they were at the outer limits of the trade circle and were major creditors with the all the other countries—and, therefore, were only integrated in a small way into the multilateral flows. The reversal in the balance of payments between Great Britain and India at the time, as well as the development of Australasian market, were major events because they integrated these countries into the international system of payments. Without giving in to the temptation of contra-factual history, one can, nevertheless, imagine that a drop in British sales on the Indian market would have resulted in a complete upset in the international economy, endangering a large number of bilateral payments. It does not mean, however, that India became a financial centre. It is at this level that the colonised countries played an essential role in the international economy. Between the two wars, the role of India and Australasia proved very important in the system of international payments.

CHAPTER FIVE

INTRA-EUROPEAN COASTAL SHIPPING FROM 1400 TO 1900: A LONG-FORGOTTEN SECTOR OF DEVELOPMENT

Gérard Le Bouëdec

The historical research undertaken by French and other European historians about trade in Northern Europe is impressive. Until the 1970s, the study of the intra-European trade constituted a major theme in French historical research. Mediaevalists, as well as historians specialising in the 16th century, have published a wealth of studies regarding this trade during the first period of coastal shipping. This period was the time during which the short-haul routes between the Southwest of France, the Netherlands and England,[1] along with those routes connecting the Atlantic ports with the Iberian Peninsula, predominated. [2] The integration of the Northern countries and the Baltic into the European trade networks is central to the work of P. Jeannin,[3] M. Morineau[4] and M.-L. Pelus-Kaplan.[5] However,

[1] M. Mollat, *Le commerce maritime normand à la fin du Moyen-Age* (Paris: Plon, 1952); H. Touchard, *Le commerce maritime Breton à la fin du Moyen-Age* (Paris: Les Belles Lettres, 1967); E. Trocme and M. Delafosse, *Le commerce rochelais de la fin du XVe au début du XVIIe siècle* (Paris: Centre de Recherches Historique, 1952); J. Craeybeckx, *Un grand commerce d'importation. Les vins de Fransaux anciens Pays-Bas (XIIIe–XVe s.)* (Paris: S.E.V.P.E.N., 1958); J. Bernard, *Navires et gens de mer à Bordeaux (1450–1550)* (Paris: École des Hautes Études en Sciences Sociales, 1968); P. Dollinger, *La Hanse (XIIIe–XVIIe s.)* (Paris: Aubier, 1964).

[2] J. Tanguy, *Le commerce du Port de Nantes au milieu du XVIe siècle* (Paris: S.E.V.P.E.N., 1963); J. Delumeau, *L'alun de Rome, XVe–XIXe siècle* (Paris: S.E.V.P.E.N., 1963); H. Lapeyre, *Une famille de marchands les Ruiz : contribution à l'étude du commerce entre la France et L'Espagne au temps de Philippe II* (Paris: Colin, 1955).

[3] P. Jeannin, Philippe Braunstein and Jochen Hoock, *Marchands du Nord : espaces et trafics à l'époque moderne* (Paris: Presses de l'École Normale Supérieure, 1966).

[4] M. Morineau, "Le commerce de la Baltique dans ses rapports avec le commerce hors de la Baltiques (du milieu du XVIe à la fin du XVIIIe)" in W. J. Wieringa, et al., eds., *The interaction of Amsterdam and Antwerp with the Baltic Region (1400–1800): proceedings of the 3rd international conference, Utrecht, Aug/Sept, 1982* (Leiden: Nijhoff, 1983), pp. 31–42 and "Au bord de la mer en Normandie avant et après J. B. Colbert" in *Les Ports Normands: Un Modèle* (Rouen: University of Rouen Press, 1999), pp. 27–38.

[5] M. L. Pelus-Kaplan, "L'enseignement des registres originaux du péage du Sund"

their research hardly goes beyond the end of the 17th century. As far as the research regarding this trade in the 18th century is concerned, the study of Europe's coastal trade seems to be only a poor relation when compared with all the research dealing with the colonial trade, with a few exceptions.[6] Intra-European trade might have been neglected, but even less research has been done on the coastal trade. My own work[7] and that of G. Buti[8] has tried to remedy that situation. As far as the study of the coastal trade during the 20th century is concerned, the lack of research is even more striking. Apart from the publications by the Chamber of Commerce in Marseille, we must rely on older studies that were not specifically aimed at coastal trade.

A major place in the historiography is given to the long-distance intra-European trade from the Baltic to the Mediterranean in the 17th and 18th centuries, when the demand for naval stores and the re-exportation of colonial goods increased, adding to the existing trade in wine and salt. This trade is central to the integration of the Northern economies into a global economy, as is shown in the works of I. Wallerstein,[9] J. Israel,[10] J. V. T. Knoppers[11] and, more

---

in *Les hommes et la mer dan l'Europe du nord-ouest de l'Antiquité à nos jours*, special edition of *Revue du Nord*, no. 1, 1986, pp. 323–41; "Les Européen et la Baltique (1690–1790)," *Bulletin of the SHMC*, 1997, pp. 99–129, and *Wolter Von Holstein, marchand Lubeckois dans la seconde moitié du SVI*^e^ *siècle* (Cologne: Böhlau, 1981).

[6] J. M. Biziere, *Croissance et Protectionnisme: L'exemple du Danemark au XVIII*^e^ *siècle* (Paris: Publisud, 1994); P. Vos, *Bordeaux et les villes Hanséates*, unpublished thesis, (Bordeaux, 1995); A. Kraatz, *La Compagnie française de Russie. Histoire du commerce franco-russe au XVII*^e^ *et XVIII*^e^ *siècles*, (Paris: François Bourin, 1993); P. Pourchasse, *Les relations commerciales entre les pays de la baltique et de Scandinavie et la Bretagne au XVIII*, unpublished thesis, (University of South Brittany, 1997).

[7] G. Le Bouëdec, "Le cabotage sur la façade atlantique au XVIIIe siècle," in *La circulation des marchandises dans la France d'Ancien Régime: Journée d'études tenue à Bercy le 12 décembre 1997 (Histoire économique et financière de la France)* (Paris: Comité pour l'histoire économique et financière de la France, 1998), pp. 53–83; "La Compagnie des Indes et le cabotage atlantique au XVIIIe siècle," *Bulletin de la SHMC*, 1997, pp. 140–67; "L'Etat et le cabotage en France et en Europe aux XVIIe et XVIIIe siècles," in Le Bouëdec and F. Chappe, eds., *Pouvoirs et Littoraux aux XV*^e^ *et XX*^e^ *siècles* (Rennes: PUR, 2000).

[8] G. Buti, "Le 'chemin de la mer' ou le petit cabotage en Provence (XVIIe–XVIIIe s.)," Proceedings from the 44th Conference of the Historical Society of Provence, Digne, Oct. 1999, unpublished, pp. 297–320.

[9] I. Wallerstein, *The Modern World System*, Vol. 2: *Mercantilism and the consolidation of the European world-economy, 1600–1750* (New York: Academic Press, 1980).

[10] J. Israël, *Dutch Primacy in World Trade (1585–1740)* (Oxford: Clarendon Press, 1989).

[11] J. V. T. Knoppers, *Dutch trade with Russia from the time of Peter I to Alexander I: a quantitative study in eighteenth century shipping* (Montreal: I.C.E.S., 1976).

recently, of J. Maarbjerg,[12] J. P. Lemmink and J. Van Koningsbrugge,[13] D. Kirby[14] and M. North.[15] This important trade also features in the work of O. F. Johnsen,[16] P. Bamford,[17] E. Cieslak,[18] H. Kellenbenz,[19] S. E. Aström,[20] H. C. Johansen[21] and E. K. Newman.[22] These studies illustrate the choices and strategies of the different European countries. The United Provinces and England were the only countries that maintained a maritime presence both in the colonial and in the European trade routes. During the 17th century, however, French shipping appears to have abandoned the maritime trade routes in the North of Europe. French shipping was mainly directed toward the colonies in Asia and the West Indies. At the same time, the fleets from the Baltic and Scandinavia, as well as those from the Hansa ports, increased their presence in the long-haul European routes.

Coastal Trade and Coastal Shipping

During the 14th and 15th centuries, trade routes were established along the Northern European route, from Novgorod to Reval, Lübeck, Bruges, and London. The main products of this trade moving from

[12] J. Maarbjerg, *Scandinavia in the European world-economy 1570–1625: some local evidence of economic integration* (New York: Peter Lang, 1995).

[13] J. P., Lemmink, and J. Van Koningsbrugge, eds., *Baltic Affaires: relations between the Netherlands and North-Eastern Europe 1500–1800* (Nijmegen: Instituut voor Noorden Oosteuropese Studies, 1990).

[14] D. Kirby, *Northern Europe in the Early Modern Period: the Baltic World (1492–1772)* (London: Longman, 1990).

[15] M. North, *From the North Sea to the Baltic: Essays in Commercial Monetary and Agrarian History (1500–1800)* (Aldershot: Variorum, 1996).

[16] O. F. Johnsen, "Le commerce entre la France méridionale et les pays du nord sous l'Ancien Régime," *Revue d'Histoire moderne*, 1927, pp. 81–98.

[17] P. W. Bamford, "French shipping in Northern European trade 1600–1789," *The Journal of Modern History*, Vol. XXVI, Sept. 1954, pp. 207–219.

[18] E. Cieslak, "Seaborne trade between France and Poland in the XVIIIth century," *The Journal of European Economic History*, vol. 6, no. 1, 1997, pp. 49–61.

[19] H. Kellenbenz, "Les escales hanséatiques," *Recueil de la Société J. Bodin*, vol. XXXII, pp. 366–379.

[20] S. E. Aström, "English timber imports from Northern Europe, in the eighteenth century," *Scandinavian Economic History Review*, XVIII-1, 1970, pp. 12–32.

[21] H. C. Johansen, *Shipping and Trade between the Baltic area and Western Europe, 1784–95* (Odense: Odense University Press, 1983).

[22] E. K. Newman, "Hamburg in the European Economy, 1660–1750," *Journal of European Economic History*, 14, 1985, pp. 57–83.

East to West were furs and wax, while Flemish and English cloth moved in the opposite direction.

However, it is important to remember, as noted by Philippe Dollinger, that "the establishment of regular lines of trade seems to have been determined more by the need to purchase than to sell, more by the necessity to obtain an article requested by a client than by the need to sell goods." The German traders went to Novgorod to obtain furs, to Malmö and Bergen to buy fish to Flanders, for woollen cloth, and to Bourgneuf for salt.[23] This did not result in an equal trade balance, and the deficit had to be evened out by the transfer of money. This is how the coastal trade in Europe started. The increasing demand for salt in Europe could not be satisfied by the production of the Lüneburg salt mines, and during the second half of the 16th century this need for salt stimulated the Hansa fleets to use the *Baienfahrt* routes along the coast of Southwest Europe. However, during the 16th century the demand was reversed. Trade and shipping between the North, the West, and the South of Europe increased in volume because of the growing demand for cereals which, until the end of the 17th century, were mainly produced in Prussia and Poland.[24] In addition, the direct maritime trade route between Italy and Flanders dating from the 13th century should not be ignored. However, it is undeniable that the intensification of intra-European trade was due both to the demand for salt and wine by the Northern countries and the demand for cereal and ready-made construction materials by the countries on the Atlantic and Mediterranean seaboards.

From the vineyards and the salt marshes between the Loire and the Gironde, the shipping routes for wine and salt were supplemented by the routes along which dried herring and woollen cloth were exported from English and Flemish ports. The trade between Southern Brittany and the Southwest of France consisted of cereals, wood for cooperage, sailcloth, wine, and salt. The cross-channel trade between Léon and Devon was comprised of fabrics and fine linen that were exchanged for woollen cloth. The surplus from the agri-

[23] Dollinger, op. cit., pp. 264–265.
[24] P. Jeannin, "Marchands du nord," op. cit., "Introduction," pp. xiv–xvi.

cultural hinterlands stimulated trade in goods such as wine from Libourne, which was exchanged for salt from Aunis-Saintonge.[25]

The globalisation of trade and the development of large navies increased the volume of the intra-European trade. P. Jeannin emphasised "the interdependence between the development of transoceanic shipping and the mobilisation of Northern resources."[26] In fact, the European ports specialising in the trade with the New World and Asia also developed large ship building facilities that demanded a large supply of naval materials. The demand for such materials first appeared in the Iberian countries during the 16th century, and increased dramatically during the 17th and 18th centuries in those European countries that witnessed a substantial increase in the trade with their colonies and in the size of their navies.

Despite the careful management of national resources, the administration of "*eaux et forêts*" (waterways and forests) in France had to turn to the Baltic in order to obtain sufficient wood, pitch, hemp, iron, copper (for lining the hulls), and tar for the French shipyards. The massive sale of these materials provided the Baltic and Scandinavia with the purchasing power necessary in order to import high-value merchandise such as goods from the colonies. In the trade from the North to the South of Europe, cereals became less important than did the materials for shipbuilding, while in the opposite direction, wine and salt were superseded by sugar, coffee, tobacco, and indigo, which were re-exported from ports specialising in the trade with the West Indies and Asia.[27] However, this new dynamic development, which Jeannin called a spiralling process, should not undermine the impetus given to the intra-European trade by the departure and arrival of the Spanish fleets in Cadiz—a port that, at least on paper, claimed to have a monopoly on the trade to and from Spanish America. From the 16th century onwards, these fleets stimulated the importation of linen from Brittany and Normandy, cloth from England, woollens from Holland, and silks from Genoa into Spain, all via the sea. The return freight was measured in *piastres*.[28] The incoming and

[25] G. Le Bouëdec, "Le cabotage sur la façade atlantique," op. cit., p. 59.

[26] P. Jeannin, *Marchands du nord*, op. cit., p. 269.

[27] P. Butel, *Les Négociants Bordelais, L'Europe et Les îles au XVIIIe Siècle* (Paris: Aubier, 1974).

[28] A. Lespagnol, *Messieurs de Saint-Malo: Une élite négociante au temps de Louis XIV*, (Paris: PUR, 1997).

outgoing colonial trade did lead to a significant increase in the coastal trade, and helped to reinforce the existing shipping. The increase in the amount of provisions for the crews employed in intercontinental shipping, as well as in the amount of trade goods, combined to lead to a substantial growth in the existing coastal and regional trade. Coastal trade was thus continuously renewed, growing because of the introduction of new products and new demands as well.

A similar development took place during the 19th century. The composition of the cargoes shipped in Europe reflected the changes in the European economy. This is why the beginning of the industrial period resulted in a qualitative and quantitative change in port traffic. Trade statistics rocketed with the new generation of heavy goods such as coal, oil, and ores, as well as with the increase in the amount of finished products such as steel, chemicals, cotton, and food.[29]

Coastal shipping completed the maritime part of internal transport to the interior of various regions at every level. The success of, and the preference for, coastal shipping were based on its competitive costs. Transport via sea or river routes was not only the least expensive, but also, until the construction of a railway network, the only alternative solution for the transport of raw materials and bulky merchandise.

The term "port" is sometimes used incorrectly to describe the numerous harbours that came into existence along the coasts. Such a heterogeneous port landscape was organised as a complete and hierarchical network. Three functions determined the growth of a port: 1) its function as a market; 2) its function as a place of transit; and, 3) its function as a centre for shipbuilding. The importance of ports was measured according to their impact on their hinterlands, in addition to the radius of their links across the sea. The hinterland was primarily an area for obtaining and distributing merchandise. The largest ports had vast hinterlands, and their inland connections were always based on rivers. European ports were the main warehouses for such river networks. For example, Saint Petersburg benefited from the Volga river network; Danzig controlled the 4,000 navigable kilometres of the Vistula; the Dutch ports of Amsterdam

[29] O. Pétré-Grenouilleau, *Les Négoces Maritimes* (Paris: Belin, 1997).

and Rotterdam depended on the traffic on the Rhine; Hamburg was the port that gave access to the German hinterland with 763 kilometres of the Elbe and Oder network; while Le Havre, Rouen, Nantes, and Bordeaux were also connected with a vast fluvial hinterland.

The ships used on the rivers had a small draught allowing goods to be transported even on the small tributaries of such a river network. No wonder, then, that different European countries constructed canals in order to link their rivers into a vast system of waterways.[30]

International politics played a decisive role in the use of ports. That Hamburg was vital to its German hinterland was the result of the fact that many coastal ports along the German section of the North Sea and the Baltic belonged to other countries. In fact, most of the Baltic coast belonged to non-German powers: Livonia belonged to Sweden, Estonia to Poland, and Kurzeme to Russia. Only the Oder provided access to the German interior from the Baltic. However, from 1698 to 1714, Stettin, Wismar, and Stralsund, at the mouths of the Oder, were Swedish.

The hierarchical organisation of a group of ports in an estuary with a primary centre and several secondary ones occurred in the great estuaries of the Vistula, Thames, Seine, Loire, Garonne, and Guadalquivir.[31] Such a pyramid of ports existed in France, on the North coast of Brittany and on the West of the Cotentin peninsula around Saint Malo, on the South Breton coast around Nantes and Lorient, between the Somme and the Vire around Rouen-Le Havre,[32] in Provence from Arles to Antibes around Marseilles, in Denmark around Copenhagen, and in Sweden around Stockholm.[33] The institution of the *Stapelrecht* allowed certain ports in the North of Europe to exclude other ports from international trade by prohibiting the "*ungewöhnliche Häfen*" and "*Nichthansen*"; i.e., the right for coastal shipping to use them as a port of call.[34]

---

[30] Colbert initiated the construction of canals between the different river basins of the Loire and the Seine, and between the Seine and the rivers and tributaries in the North of France—the "two seas canal." In 1688 the Frederic-Guillaume Canal joined the Elbe to the Oder.

[31] O. Pétré-Grenouilleau, op. cit., p. 60.

[32] P. Dardel, *Navires et marchandises dans les ports de Rouen et du Havre au XVIIIe siècle* (Paris: S.E.V.P.E.N., 1963), p. 606.

[33] G. Buti, "Le chemin de la mer," op. cit.

[34] H. Kellenbenz, "Les escales hanséatiques," op. cit. and E. Cieslak, "Les grandes

There existed a division of shipping between the primary and secondary ports in an area, but it would be a mistake to think that the large ports specialising in colonial trade were not interested in coastal shipping. However, the coastal trade of the large ports was limited to long-distance shipping, which is exemplified by the preferential trading contacts established by the ship-owning merchants of Le Havre and Rouen with the large Southern ports of Bilbao, Cadiz, and Lisbon. The intra-European coastal shipping in the Baltic was a *Hochseefahrt* controlled by a few large ports.

In the North of Europe, the long-haul coastal trade was carried out through ports that also equipped ships for colonial destinations. Within the various port complexes, the secondary ports usually specialised in equipping ships for the coastal trade. Having neither the necessary loading nor unloading facilities, they commanded a fleet that prospered due to the dynamics of the commanding ports. In the Bordeaux port complex, the coastal fleets had as home ports: Saint Estèphe, Blaye, Plassac, Roque de Thau, Bourg, Caverne, and the Isle d'Yeu.[35] In the Baltic, the numerous ports past the Sound—which were not recognised as international ports of call and whose horizons were restricted to the Baltic inshore waters were coastal shipping ports responsible for collecting and redistributing merchandise to and from the main ports that participated in shipping on the high seas.

This hierarchy of ports regulated the organisation of the trade. Within each port area, there was a coastal trade between the main port and its secondary ones. However, the fact that the fleets of many such secondary ports (like that of Rostock) rarely crossed the Sound was not only due to the application of the "port-of-call" legislation; there were additional factors at play. Each system of coastal shipping was, in practice, enclosed by three major boundaries: the Sound, the most Western point of Brittany, and Gibraltar. These points delineated the four main areas of coastal shipping: the Baltic; the North Sea and the Channel; the Bay of Biscay; and the Mediterranean. Each region had its own coastal shipping traditions that determined the nature of the freight and the characteristics of its ships. As the method of passing on nautical knowledge by word of

escales de la Baltique (XVe–XVIIIe siècles)," in *Les Grandes Escales*, vol. II, (Les Temps Modernes) (Brussels: Librairie Encyclopedique, 1972), pp. 299–334.

[35] G. Le Bouëdec, "Les companies des Indes et le cabotage," op. cit.

mouth did little to encourage innovation, coastal shipping generally was limited to by zones. Crossing these boundaries demanded a leap forward in technology, finance, and trading policies that only certain communities of ship owners and sailors were ready to consider. In each of these zones coastal shipping could be divided into three large sectors: local coastal shipping; coastal shipping within a specific zone; and long-distance, national, and international coastal shipping.

Although a single-haul voyage (or an unplanned voyage, picking up cargo here and there) was often considered to be the most typical type of coastal trading, the reality sometimes proved to be more complex. Trading links came into existence between the principal ports that offered year-round trade. These links were often like circles involving the large ports of the Atlantic seaboard. During certain seasons such trading links also existed in coastal shipping within areas that had complementary trade, such as Southern Brittany and Southwestern France. In the autumn, cereals and sardines were traded for wine and salt from ports between the Garonne and the Loire. However, on European routes, ships sometimes sailed empty. The imbalance of trade and tonnages caused ships to sail in ballast. During the 18th century, many Dutch *flutes* returned in ballast, because the cargoes of wine and colonial goods were not of the same volume as the cargoes of raw materials on the voyage out. The density of the coastal shipping also revealed its commercial organisation. It testified to the existence of networks of agents, brokers, and freight exchanges such as in Ellsinore and Amsterdam. The master who bartered salt, cereal, or wine on his own account was disappearing.

There was no typical vessel that sailed along the coasts. The diversity in coastal trading and in regional and local traditions explains the great diversity of coastal fleets. In fact, any ship could be used in the coastal trade. Ships flying the flag of a Scandinavian country and sailing between the Baltic and the ports of Western and Southern Europe, were usually *flutes*, a ship of 150 to 300 tons, but up to as much as 400 or 500 tons. Most coastal trade in the Baltic was done by small *galéasses* (combined sailing and rowing boats), and that explains why 53% of the Rostock fleet were vessels of less than 50 tons.[36]

---

[36] N. Spella, *Renaissance et crise du négoce maritime à Rostock (1800–1820)* (MM: UBS), 2000.

During the 18th century, typical coasters sailing along the Atlantic seaboard were small-decked craft of 50 tons or more, and these gave way to new rigs that had appeared earlier in the Channel such as *bricks* (brigs), brigantines, and *senaux* (large brigs). Between 1750 and 1850 the *chasse-marée* (shallow draught vessel) was introduced into Southern Brittany. The *gabares* (barges), not to be confused with the *allèges* (lighters) of the estuaries, were large coasters of 80 to 200 tons, specialising in the transport of wood for construction purposes. In addition to these types, there existed a myriad of coasters and flotillas in the estuaries. In Provence the fleets plying the coastal waters around Marseilles were made up of *bateaux* (local boats), *bisques pontées* (decked), or *semi-pontées* (half-decked) and *tartanes pontées* (lateen coasters).[37]

The place of the French coasters in the intra-European maritime trade

During the 18th century, there was a considerable amount of trade between France, the Baltic countries, and Scandinavia. 18 to 21% of shipping entering the Baltic came from French ports, and seven to 10% of ships leaving were destined for France. However, French ships were virtually absent on the Northern routes. P. Bamford states that, between 1713 and 1780, for every 10 French ships entering the Sound, 500 English and 800 Dutch were passing through.[38] M. L. Pelus-Kaplan states that the average annual number of French ships passing through the Sound only came to 35 between 1710 and 1720. It even fell to 20 between 1720 and 1730, and then dropped below 20 ships until 1770. The absence of French shipping is even more dramatic given that exports from the Baltic tripled from 1720 to 1770, according to D. Kirby,[39] and S. E. Aström noted a "timber boom"—a doubling of the trade in pine destined for England between 1766–70 and 1786–90.[40] Although the Baltic had not become a market for French goods as Colbert had hoped it would, it had become an important market for re-exported colonial goods.

[37] G. Buti, op. cit.
[38] P. Bamford, op. cit.
[39] D. Kirby, op. cit., p. 365.
[40] S. E. Aström, op. cit.

The collapse in French shipping was the result of a complex process that started at the end of the 16th century. In 1766, a report from the Chamber of Commerce in Dunkirk stated that French merchants had finally understood that coastal shipping was part of an integrated global maritime strategy. "The Dutch owe a large part of their wealth and maritime power to coastal trade. Without any surplus at home to export, they decided to carry that of other countries. . . ."[41] The shipping and trading services of the Dutch and the large assortment of exports of the English were the bases of their respective commercial success. In addition, the English made use of their Navigation Acts to exclude other nationalities from their shipping market. Yet, the authors of these reports from Dunkirk emphasised the competitiveness of the Dutch coastal shipping fleet as the primary basis of their success. J. J. Bethmann, a German broker based in Bordeaux in the 18th century, repeats it when he writes, "Coastal shipping is a trade based on competition and French shipping is the most expensive of all."[42]

Three arguments are put forward to explain the Dutch superiority; 1) the *flûtes*, *galiotes*, and *koffs* the Dutch used had a draught appropriate to the Baltic; 2) the low cost of shipbuilding, and; 3) the low operating costs of the Dutch ships that were built to be sailed by a small crew. When Bethmann commented on the impossibility of foreigners competing with the Dutch in the Northern trade, he mentioned the implications of the French class system that necessitated an expensive number of ship's boys and apprenticeships aboard. These explanations for the Dutch superiority are further developed in two recent works by M. North[43] and D. Kirby.[44] North reproduces this statement from C. Wilson:[45] "Dutch ships are in a better state of repair, less expensive and safer," and "ships in good condition, under good command and with a good crew are efficient and

[41] We would like to thank Anne Moreau who finished her thesis on the coastal shipping fleets of the 18th century in Brittany at Solito (Université de Bretagne Sud) for sending us this report discovered in the *Archives Départementales de Loire-Atlantique C672.*

[42] Ch. Carriere, in *Histoire économique et sociale du Monde* P. Léon, ed., vol. 3, A. Colin, 1978, p. 197 cited by P. Butel, *L'économie française au XVIIIe siècle* (Paris: Sedes, 1993), pp. 149–150.

[43] M. North, op. cit. "introduction".

[44] C. Kirby, op. cit., p. 229.

[45] C. Wilson, *Profit and Power: A Study of England and the Dutch Wars* (London: Longmans Green, and Co, 1957), p. 111.

faster with fewer risks and consequently cheaper insurance."[46] Under these conditions, they out-competed the Hanseatic states in the transport of grain, wood, herring, and salt from the second half of the 16th century onward.

According to Kirby, French coastal shipping could not compete because the higher wages of the large crews contributed significantly to the higher operating costs, and because the French lacked sufficient financing due to the late development of systems of credit, while the Dutch ship building techniques gave the Dutch shipyards a dramatic advantage. In 1669, the construction of a *flute* in the Netherlands did cost 40% less than in England, let alone in France. In Saint Malo, at the time the main port for French ship-building, the Dutch superiority was clearly noticeable. A. Lespagnol explains that, up until 1670–80, the people of Saint Malo (Malouins) had the majority of their *flutes* built in the shipyards of the United Provinces, as shown by the inventory of vessels for the year 1664.[47] Although the Malouins controlled the route from Cadiz, they had ceded the wine and salt routes to the Dutch long before. And it was the Dutch who operated the trade between the Breton ports and Holland. No wonder, then, that the quartermaster Béchameil de Nointel remarked at the end of the 17th century, "It is true to say that the vessels of the Saint Malo merchants are almost never in Holland, the Dutch themselves carry the cargos that the Saint Malo merchants want to send there much more cheaply than they could do with their own boats."[48]

The French disappeared from the intra-European maritime trade routes in two stages. Around 1600, the French lost their foothold in short-haul European coastal trading—the old salt and wine routes between the vineyards in the Southwest of France, the salt marshes in Brittany, and the North Sea ports. It was around 1630 that the French also disappeared from the Baltic. From the second half of the 16th century, French coasters of, on average, 60 tons still frequented the ports of Narva, Riga, and Danzig, and during the time

[46] M. North, op. cit.

[47] A. Lespagnol, op. cit., p. 150.

[48] J. Beranger and J. Meyer, *La Bretagne à la fin du XVIIe siècle, after the report of Bechameil de Nointel* (Paris: Klincksieck, 1976).

of the corn crisis there were even more. The annual average number of voyages between 1562 and 1635 remained stable at a modest level of around 40 per year. However, at the beginning of the 17th century, the French fleet, with ships averaging 100 tons, could not keep up with the increase in tonnage of the Dutch or even of the English *flutes of* 200 tons or more. Around 1635, the volume of French shipping in Baltic ports fell sharply, and stayed at a low level until around 1670.

The Dutch monopolised the salt trade to the Baltic and the Flemish, English, and Germanic merchants took over the wine trade from the French. At the end of the 16th century, the trade between La Rochelle and the Northern countries also passed to the control of the Dutch and Zealanders, while England controlled its own trade with La Rochelle. In 1651 foreign ships (at an average size of 234 tons) represented 74% of the tonnage moored in the port of Bordeaux, and the myriad assortment of French coasters (at an average of 24 tons), made up only a quarter of the overall tonnage.

This foreign "conquest" raised concerns. In a memorandum written in 1624 to the town hall, the merchants of Rouen declared that, "our trade is being ruined mainly by foreign companies which are becoming familiar and taking a foothold in the town of Rouen." Lespagnol quotes a memorandum dating from 1645 written by the "elite merchants of the town of Nantes," expressing the same complaint. They wrote that, "The merchants and sailors have lost the sea routes through lack of work; we only see foreign ships and faces and mainly Dutch, English, Scottish, Irish and Portuguese. Every day families, factors and brokers arrive from these countries; it has become a habit over the last 15 to 20 years and they have taken the trade, commissions and contacts which the aforesaid inhabitants had with the foreigners." This pessimistic view regarding the foreign domination of the trade revealed, as Lespagnol writes, "the passive type of trade practised in the 17th century by the majority of port elites in Western France from Rouen to Bordeaux and from Morlaix to Nantes [the *Malouins* are an exception] who are generally happy to let the ships and merchandise come to them."[49] M. Morineau

[49] A. Lespagnol, op. cit., p. 155.

emphasised that, "the sailing ship itself is not the creator of wealth and the pilot of economic expansion" and "the sailing ship is not and was not the *primum mobile* of economic activity,"—suggesting that the concern for "trade" at the time, perhaps, prevailed over that for "shipping."[50] However, these port memoranda made clear that the foreign offensive was not just limited to maritime transport but was based on a global trade strategy that I. Wallerstein and J. Israel have clearly analysed.[51] Before Europe entered the second era of coastal shipping, during which colonial trade gave a new lease of life to the intra-European trade, French shipping in Europe was limited to the short-distance trade within just one coastal zone. French coastal shipping had been excluded from the long-haul routes.

Colbert's report to the First Trade Council on 4 August 1664 mentioned that the "Dutch and other foreigners" had taken over the maritime trade of the kingdom and stressed the importance of the connection between the trade with the colonies and the trade with Northern Europe. He wrote, "We could go and fetch [merchandise] from the West and East Indies and take [it] to the North, from where we shall bring back materials necessary for shipbuilding."[52] Winning back the coastal trade routes for the French flag was an important part of Colbert's programme. As the size of foreign shipping in the port of Bordeaux showed in 1651, the Dutch fleet could only cater to the large ports. It was not at all adapted to the needs of the intermediate and small ports—mainly due to the difficulties in accessing such harbours and because the loading capacity of the myriad smaller ports could not cope with the tonnage of the Dutch ships. This means that the policy of Colbert could only have been directed to the intra-European coastal trade, and, in particular to the Baltic trade. In fact, as M. L. Pelus-Kaplan writes, from 1671 onward, the *flutes*, some of Dutch origin, of the new French Northern Company created in 1669, went through the narrows of the Sound.[53] In spite of the fact that the initiative of Colbert seemed to have given an impetus to the return of the French flag in the Northern

[50] M. Morineau, "Au bord de la mer en Normandie [. . .]", op. cit., pp. 35–36.

[51] I. Wallerstein, op. cit., and J. Israël, op. cit.

[52] P. Clement, *Lettres, instructions et mémoires de Colbert*, (Paris: Imprimerie Impériale, 1861–1873), vol. II, 1st part, pp. cclxix and cclxx.

[53] M.-L. Pelus-Kaplan, "Navigation française et commerce français [. . .]," op. cit.

routes, the number of French ships were not as high as Colbert had expected, and, in addition, the Northern Company went very rapidly into deficit. The causes of this debacle are explained by M. Morineau, as he points to the fact that the market for French goods in the Baltic was limited, and that commercial success in the Baltic market depended on an intricate system of commercial exchanges.[54] As a result, the French presence in the Baltic vanished in the 1720s, in spite of the fact that the growth in the trade between France and its colonies could have increased the French commercial potential.

The War of the Augsburg League constituted a decisive turning point. That war resulted in the prohibition of French trade by the United Provinces in 1688 and by England in 1689. It caused a general paralysis of the intra-European trade. Under these circumstances, the defeat of the French navy at La Hougue in 1692 was a defeat in the full meaning of the word. Until the end of the 18th century, the French navy was driven from the Channel and North Sea, and the Count de Pontchartrain, Secretary of State for the Navy, had to end French participation in regular naval warfare. As an alternative, a strategy to use corsairs was initiated, with both private funds and state support. This strategy proved to be worthwhile, since it permitted the consolidation of new trends in trade capitalism in the West Indies, as well as in Asia.

This policy continued after the War of the League of Augsburg and the War of the Spanish Succession.[55] In fact, within the framework of monopolies and exclusion, the colonial trade could flourish as it was sheltered from foreign competition. The result was a massive redirection of French mercantile capital toward colonial trade and the withdrawal from the competitive intra-European trade. If the dominant image of coastal shipping in France is that of mediocrity in tonnages and investments, it is because the French coastal fleet was owned and operated by individual traders along the coast. That was also the case in the Baltic, but the long-haul European

[54] A. Lespagnol, "Guerre et Commerce maritime durant la phase initiale de la Seconde Guerre de Cent Ans, 1688–1713," *Impériale, Les Européens et les Espaces océaniques au XVIIIe siècle* (Paris: PUPS, 1997), pp. 83–98.

[55] Regarding this idea of the State-Trade compromise, see O. Pétré-Grenouilleau, "How did France enter and play its role in the Atlantic? State and maritime traders: from clashes to compromise, ca. 1580–1830," unpublished.

maritime trade routes were dominated by the large fleets from Holland, Denmark, Sweden, and England, as well as from Pomerania, Danzig, and the Hanseatic states.

The reports from the Chamber of Commerce dating from the second half of the 18th century show that the French were aware that having neither a trading network nor a fleet in the Baltic was a commercial handicap. In her thesis, M. Acerra has shown how dependent the French were on the Dutch and the English for the supply of naval stores for the French fleet.[56] At regular intervals, attempts were made at extending the exclusive monopoly of the colonial system to the trade with the Baltic, but all of these attempts failed.[57]

The increased trade with the colonies stimulated the intra-European trade. It strengthened the commercial links between the Baltic and the Mediterranean, and it changed the composition and value of the various exchanges along this route. Naval stores were worth more than cereals and herring, and the colonial goods were of greater value than alcohol and salt. French coastal shipping seemed unable to capitalise on the distribution of goods from the colonies and, instead, remained oriented towards the trade in foodstuffs and in proto-industrial textiles. Certainly, ships from Bordeaux, Nantes, and Le Havre carried colonial imports all over Europe, but the lion's share of this trade traveled on ships from Northern Europe.

[56] M. Acerra, *Rochefort et la construction navale française 1661–1815*, (Paris: Librairie de l'Inde, 1993), pp. 235–73.

[57] C. Haroche, *Joseph Delaville-Leroulx, merchant in Ghent (1777–1785)* (*MM, UBS*, 2001.) This research work was carried out from a basis of unpublished archives acquired by the Service Historique de la Marine de Lorient.

J. Delaville-Leroulx was going to settle in Hamburg to build up relations with the markets of Northern ports. He explains that he was acting on behalf of the State and a group of merchants, among whom were Le Couteulx de la Noray, Armand François Delaville, Perrier, Walwein, Mallet, Père et fils, Ribaud, and Levieux: "The government, desiring to establish French companies in the North and having written on this subject to all the French Chambers of Commerce, I have been chosen among the most distinguished merchants of the ports and by the government to form the company of Hamburg where I shall go [. . .] with half a million, four 300 ton ships and a naval commission." The project lasted a long time and Delaville-Leroulx came to settle in Lorient in the vicinity of the new Compagnie de Indes, created in 1785, and which amounted to the confiscation of trade outside the Ile de France by a politico-financial consortium.

During the years between 1850 and 1880, coastal shipping in Europe underwent important modernisation. On the one hand, steamers were introduced on routes between ports within the same zone, and, on the other hand, there was an increase in the number and the tonnage of the sailing fleet. Over time, the steamers took over, and there was a race to increase the size of the new generations of steamers on the great European trading routes. From the 1870s onward, the new vessels had similar characteristics to those of the larger ships that steamed all over the world. This transformation was accompanied by a re-arrangement of the coastal shipping routes. Regular freight services were established between the main European ports: Saint Petersburg, Hamburg, Rotterdam, Antwerp, Glasgow, London, Liverpool, Le Havre, Nantes, and Marseilles. Only coastal shipping that was capable of shifting from a regional to an international focus remained in business. The new coastal shipping routes mainly serviced ports that offered both European and transoceanic trade. These ports were able to adapt and invest in the necessary new infrastructure such as wet docks, loading bays and warehouses, handling equipment, quayside rail service, and the equipping of docks in major ports and rail links with the interior. While trade in French ports boomed, statistics for national coastal shipping under the French flag indicate stagnation. That means that French coastal shipping was largely excluded from the new trade.[58] The development of traffic in heavy goods was incompatible with the small fleets and small ports along the French coast. The railway replaced local coasters for

[58] A. Colin, *La navigation commerciale au XIXe siècle* (Paris: A. Rousseau, 1901).
Evolution of trade in the French ports (excluding national coastal trade)

1829	1.2	Million tonnes
1846	5.29	Mt
1869	13.5	Mt
1881	27.7	Mt
1895	22.0	Mt
1908	47.781	Mt

Statistics for national coastal trade

1830–1836	average 2.288 Million tonnes
1860	2.919 Mt
1865	2.223 Mt
1885	2.145 Mt
1895	2.872 Mt

collecting and redistributing goods to or from a large port. Local fleets of coasters were deprived of trade, and small ports disappeared from the map. However, the railway companies also gained the transport of heavy goods previously transported on sea. By using dumping prices on routes to and from seaports, the railways took part of the demand for transport away from national coastal shipping. The price of a ton of iron, which cost 32.85 francs for the journey Valenciennes-Périgueux, dropped to 16.85 francs on the Valenciennes-Bordeaux route. The crisis of 1850–80 signified the final death of the mediaeval model consisting of the traditional trade in salt, wine, and agricultural commodities. The old port complexes consisting of one main port surrounded by many small ports disappeared.

"For the maritime predominance of England," wrote A. Colin in 1901, "there are three main reasons," which are "its admirable industrial activity requiring imports of raw materials and exports of such large manufactured objects, its wealth in combustible coal which, given the development of mechanisation, has guaranteed its ships cargos for all the countries in the world, and finally, the almost total absence of any great cultivation of the land, forcing it to acquire provisions from outside the country of everything to meet the needs of its population. In these circumstances, it won't be long before there's a regular coming and going of ships."[59] The industrial goods changed the nature of coastal shipping, as these goods were not subject to seasonal variations. That made England and then Germany the dominant maritime traders in Europe. The French, however, had not many new products to offer, and that is why the French activities in coastal shipping remained limited. As in the past, the French developed alternative shipping on the transatlantic routes and the routes servicing the empire.

Conclusion

French coastal trade only succeeded in participating in the European coastal shipping routes between the 16th and the end of the 17th centuries. Except for the Saint Malo-Cadiz route, French coastal trade was limited to the lower levels of coastal shipping, such as

[59] A. Colin, op. cit., p. 192.

shipping within a coastal zone and local shipping. The exclusion of the French flag from intra-European trade by the Northern countries therefore took place well before Colbert started to develop the colonial links and before the rise of commercial capitalism. True, colonial trade reinforced the traditional trade flows in coastal shipping, but the French economy paid a high price for its dependence on raw materials for shipbuilding and did not take advantage of all the benefits of importing colonial goods, missing out on their re-export. The *Malouins* were able to take advantage of the Spanish lack of coastal shipping by providing the Spanish *flotas* with linen cloth, and thus captured a share in the "fabulous treasures" of the New World. We could reverse the argument by saying that the Northern countries knew how to take advantage of the French inability to link their colonial trade with the intra-European trade.

During the 19th century, French maritime trade tried to make trade with the empire and the transoceanic trade in general an alternative to coastal shipping in Europe. French coastal trade could not profit from the Industrial Revolution as it occurred late in France and in areas far removed from the ports. As a consequence, French coastal shipping kept transporting the goods that made up the coastal cargoes during the period of the *ancien régime*, such as food and textiles, and never went much further than one coastal zone. In sum, the French maritime sector seems to have been out of touch with the new realities of an industrial economy.

Part II

Regional and National Approaches

The First Players in the Colonial Adventure: Portugal, Spain, and the Netherlands

CHAPTER SIX

COLONIAL TRADE AND DEVELOPMENT: THE SPANISH CASE IN THE EIGHTEENTH CENTURY

Manuel Bustos Rodríguez

In this study, I propose to do two things: 1) study the relationship between colonial trade and economic development in Spain during the 18th century and 2) point out gaps in the research on this topic so that future scholars might investigate subjects heretofore unstudied and, thereby, advance knowledge in this field.

The traditional way of interpreting the role of colonies based on national historiography—at first as a justification for national pride and then, later, as a source of collective shame—has been replaced in the 20th century by a pragmatic and mainly economic approach. Among other things, this approach evaluates the hypothetical role of the colonies as a driving force in the economic development of the home country. This economic interpretation, far from being unique to the 20th century, takes up where some brilliant ministers and administrative employees (Uztáriz, Campillo, Patiño, Ward, Campomanes) in the Spanish governments of the 19th century left off.[1]

One of the more revolutionary contributions to this economic interpretation of the history of expansion and colonisation was the famous thesis by economist Earl J. Hamilton, published during the worldwide recession in 1929. Hamilton used a methodology that linked the development of European capitalism with the flow of precious metals coming to Europe from the New World. To do this, he created tables and graphs that are still reproduced today in reference works and textbooks.[2] He viewed the Spanish case as being

[1] See J. Muñoz Pérez, "Ideas sobre el comercio en el XVIII español," *Estudios Americanos*, Seville, XIX, 100 (1960).

[2] J. Earl Hamilton, "American Treasure and the Rise of Capitalism," *Economica*, IX (1929), pp. 338–57.

of particular importance, and dedicated a considerable part of his work to trying to explain why the social, economic, and even psychological structures in Spanish history differed from those in other countries.[3]

Hamilton's ideas were the subject of much criticism during the decades that followed the publication of his fundamental work.[4] However, his analyses have achieved their goal. Not only have they rekindled the debate about the effect of colonial trade on the homeland and, thereby, stimulated further scholarly research, but his theories have also contributed toward finding a global explanation for the great economic cycles Europe experienced between the 16th and 18th centuries. These cycles were, in the Spanish case, counterproductive to the modernisation of the country.

The study of the colonies and of their economic repercussions for Spain received great attention after the economic and political upheaval of the 1960s and the subsequent proliferation of universities and the concomitant increase in the number of professional historians. The important economic consequences of Spain's colonial endeavours, and their relationship to Spain's modernisation, were discussed again and again. Many of these works include cogent analyses at the regional and local levels, and make reference to the effects of the colonies on the economies of the different regions and areas that make up Spain. In view of this narrowed field of study, we intend to look into the mechanisms that linked the colonial economies to the different geographical areas within the nation state as a whole.

From the first moments of colonial expansion, the Spanish economy was particularly affected by the arrival of precious metals coming from the Mexican and Peruvian mines. The Crown, by establishing a monopolistic regime in America and excluding foreigners and its non-Castilian subjects, channeled the flow of silver and gold through

---

[3] J. Earl Hamilton, *American Treasure and the Price Revolution in Spain, 1501–1650* (Cambridge, Mass.: Harvard University Press, 1934).

[4] C. M. Cipolla, "La Pretendue Révolution des Prix" *Annales*, X (1955); I. Hammarston, "The Price Revolution of the Sixteenth Century: Some Swedish Evidence," *Scandinavian Economic History Review*, V (1957) pp. 118–54; J. Nadal Oller, "La revolución de los precios españoles en el siglo XVI," *Hispania*, XIX (1959), pp. 503–29; R. B. Outhwaite, *Inflation in Tudor and early Stuart England*, (London: Macmillan, 1969); M. Morineau, *Incroyables gazettes et fabuleux métaux. Les retours des trésors américains d'après les gazettes hollandaises (XVIIe–XVIIIe)* (Paris-Cambridge: Cambridge University Press, 1985).

one single port—first Seville, then Cadiz after 1717. This policy very rapidly made Western Andalusia the first region to experience the modern phenomenon of inflation—a phenomenon that several Spanish observers had already noted during the first half of the 16th century.[5] However, to focus an analysis only on the inflationary effects of silver and gold coming from the other side of the Atlantic ignores the complexities of the interaction between Spain and its American colonies.

In order to understand the impact the precious metals from the New World had on Spain, we need to know who the recipients of this wealth were. There were two distinct groups: 1) the Spanish Crown, and 2) individuals, whether native Spaniards or foreigners. These individual beneficiaries of the Spanish colonial presence in America were, apparently, a fairly diverse group. However, we now know that there were not as many beneficiaries as had originally been supposed.

We are still poorly informed as to the amount American precious metals made up of the total income of the Crown. The revenue from the duty on imported American goods and from the export of officially imported goods from Europe, along with "the old customs rights" tax should be included in estimates of the Crown's income, as well. Taxes and precious metals most likely supplied the state with about 40% of its revenue—a little more if we add the income from tobacco—at the beginning of the 1790s. In the short-term, the arrival of the fleet carrying treasure, especially in times of crises, gave the Crown the ability either to meet its most urgent expenses in wartime, or else to pay off other debts that could be deferred.

The Crown used part of its revenue to the benefit of the Spanish economy as a whole. For example, the Crown invested in improving the road network. However, in some ways, this investment benefited some sectors and regions to the detriment of others.[6] David Ringrose corroborates the fact that the Crown gave priority to investing in Madrid and its surrounding area, perhaps not surprisingly as

[5] See P. Vilar, "Los primitivos españoles del pensamiento económico: Cuantitativismo y Bullonismo" in *Crecimiento y desarrollo economiae historia: reflexiones sobre el caso español* (Barcelona: Ariel, 1974).

[6] J. Barbier and S. Klein Herbert, "Las prioridades de un monarca ilustrado: el gasto público bajo el reinado de Carlos III," *Revista de Historia Económica*, 3 (1985), pp. 473–95.

the court and government offices were located there. As a result, Madrid was very well connected to the agricultural markets in the interior.[7]

According to Hamilton, the riches flowing out of the Americas could have had some effect on the evolution of prices in Spain. However, it is less certain what role this American wealth played in the overall economy of the country as a whole—a country with precarious finances at best. Due to the monopolistic structure of the relations between Spain and its colonies, Atlantic Andalusia would have been the first recipient of any advantages to be gained by trade with the American colonies. Let us look at how this happened.

The Crown created the monopoly on American trade with two goals in mind: 1) maintaining control of the trade through the use of a single port, and 2) asserting Castilian rights over this lucrative trade. In practice, the assertion of Castile's exclusive rights was of limited importance. It was the maintenance of control over the American trade that was of primary concern to the Crown, at least until the liberalisation of this trade in the 1760s. The monopoly forced men and cargoes, travellers, and goods destined for America to register in the port established by the authorities as the monopoly headquarters—Seville from 1503 to 1717 and Cadiz between 1717 and 1778. From the time the single port monopoly was instituted, nobody could trade between Spain and the American colonies directly without passing through either of these two ports. Obviously there was a way around this monopoly—smuggling—which was no doubt quite frequent and often occurred with the connivance of the officials responsible for suppressing it. Castilian control over the American trade never really prevented the participation of the subjects of the old Kingdom of Aragon—comprised of Catalonia, Valencia, and Aragon—in the American trade, although, of course, it did place barriers in the way of trade with the Americas for the Aragonese.[8]

This restrictive legal framework is a factor which would determine, in a decisive way, Spain's benefits from its colonies. The merchants trading with the American colonies had to take the monopoly port system into account, either by carrying out their business within

[7] R. David Ringrose, *Madrid y la economía española, 1560–1850* (Madrid: Alianza, 1985), pp. 129–31.

[8] C. Martinez Shaw, "Cataluña y el comercio con América. El fin de un debate," *Boletín Americanista*, Barcelona, XXII, 1980 (30), pp. 223–35.

limitations set by the law, or else by breaking the law entirely and bypassing the official port. We are not in a position to measure, either wholly or partially, the amount of legal versus illegal trade. The documentation that does exist recording smuggling activities shows that as much as 60% of a load might not be registered. This leads us to believe that the illegal trade may well have surpassed the legal trade. In any case, the trade in contraband generally benefited foreigners—who were legally excluded from the American trade unless they had specific authorisation—more than it benefited the Spanish themselves. Although the Spanish contributed to bypassing the official port system and benefited from the contraband trade, they were not as dependent upon the smuggling of manufactured goods into the country as the foreigners engaged in this trade were.

It is simpler to measure the impact of the goods coming from the Americas on the Spanish economy—as long as these goods were not bypassing the official port—than it would be to measure this same impact on other countries that used multiple ports of entry. Consequently, the register of the *Casa de Contratación* (General Archives of the Indies: Register of Contracts) has enabled us to establish the volume of the official trade between Spain and its American colonies—although these sources tell us little about the goods traded and their origins until 1778.[9] These records show us that the 18th century was a century of global growth, though with some periods of decline. One cycle of stagnation coincides with the War of Spanish Succession. Following this war, there was another period of growth until the end of the 1740s. From then on, there was strong development until the 1770s, and then there was a period of reduced growth, followed by another strong period of growth—greater than that between the 1740s and 1750s. And, finally, there was a crisis until 1776. But what do these dates mean? Our interest in knowing the volume of trade between Spain and its American colonies does not extend beyond the desire to understand to what degree exports to the New World benefited Spanish economic development. To know this, we need to know the type of goods traded, where they came from, and where they were going.

[9] These are the sources used by Pierre and Huguette Chaunu for their study: *Séville et l'Atlantique, 1504–1650*, vol. 8; (Paris: Colin, 1955), and more recently, A. Garcia-Baquero, op. cit.

Unfortunately, until the introduction of the decree for free trade in 1778, only the volume (*ad valorem*) of the goods is indicated in the registers and, therefore, we do not know where they came from. Despite these limitations, however, we can deduce that Spanish products played a less important role in these parts than products from abroad. The Spanish products were, essentially, agricultural commodities and their derivatives such as brandy and wine, Basque iron—about 30% of which was destined for Cadiz in 1750—and other minerals. The products of foreign origin were precious metals and an enormous range of cloths and textile goods, which were mainly French, but also including some Flemish-Dutch, English, and German goods in varying proportions according to the period.

During the 18th century, commercial and financial transactions with America passed through the merchant community established in Cadiz. The majority of countries interested in the Hispano-American markets had a large presence in Cadiz, and these countries also maintained relations with the other provinces of Spain.[10] Even though the ports excluded from direct trade with the American colonies could use factors established in Cadiz, there is little information about how much and to what degree they used middlemen. One way to measure, at least approximately, the importance of each Spanish region in the American trade conducted through Cadiz is to calculate the percentage of registrations with the Cadiz Consulate. Using this method, we see that the Andalusians, Basques-Navarrese, and the Cantabrians had the highest number of members—71% of all those registered between 1730 and 1823—and those of Asturias, Castile la Mancha, Aragón, Extremadura, and the East (except Catalonia) were the least numerous.[11] However, not all the representatives were registered at the Consulate, and their presence in Cadiz did not necessarily mean that the profits acquired in Cadiz itself would have had an effect on the merchant's place of origin, since there is ample evidence that these merchants often preferred to invest in Cadiz or in the surrounding area.

---

[10] M. Gárate Ojanguren, "Comercio, burguesía y acumulación de capital en el País Vasco, 1700–1841," *Ekoomiaz*, 9 and 10 (1988), p. 52; there is more interesting information on the Catalans in C. Martínez Shaw, *Cataluña en la Carrera de Indias, 1680–1756* (Barcelona: Editorial Crítica, 1981), pp. 144–45.

[11] J. B. Ruiz Rivera, *El Consulado de Cádiz: Matricula de comerciantes 1730–1823* (Cádiz: Diputación de Cádiz, 1988), p. 40.

In general, there has been very little research about the networks through which capital (frequently in American silver currency) information, and experience in the mercantile sector was transferred from Cadiz or Seville to other areas of Spain.[12] The network could be relatively uncomplicated, but could also be indirect, going through numerous middlemen, and very complex. In almost all cases, the same land route network could have been used to bring together goods from other parts of Spain and abroad for export to the Americas. The analysis of legal documents is indispensable for researching these networks. Of particular use are wills, which give details of inheritances from several of the merchants established in Cadiz. These wills also detail the transfers of money from traders, living or dead, to their towns of birth or to other members of their families living outside Cadiz.

In other areas of Spain, familial ties and the bonds of "nationality" played a major role in the division of American profits. These profits were often used to endow some sort of organisation, such as contributing toward financing a church, convent, or chapel. They were also used to make investments in houses, land, and *objets d'art*.[13] Other times, the aim was to start up a business outside Cadiz or to participate in another, already established business. In order to know how the profits made in the "Carrera de Indias" affected the economic development of the Spanish regions, it seems important to establish what proportions of colonial trade was, in the end, invested in each region.

There has been practically no research into the way in which capital was channeled from the overseas trade through a complex system of payments via merchants, financiers, and entrepreneurs spread throughout Spain. Gradually, as old mercantilist principles regulating Spanish colonial legislation were dropped in the 18th century,

[12] A laudatory attempt to study the journey of American precious metals with the fleets to the Basque country by Basques and their onwards to Seville and Cadiz is found in L. García Fuentes, *Sevilla, los vascos y América (Las exportaciones de hierro y manufacturas metálicas en los siglos XVI, XVII y XVIII)* (Madrid: Fundación BBU, 1991), ch. IV.

[13] See for example M. J. Pascua, Sánchez, "Las fundaciones docentes en la España del siglo XVIII a traves los protocolos notariales gaditanos," *Gades*, Cádiz, 18 (1988), pp. 109–34, and "La fundación de la Casa de Viudas de Cádiz: El gesto caritativo de Juan Clat (Flagela), un comerciante de Damasco," in *La burguesía de negocios en la Andalucía de la Ilustración* (Cádiz: Diputación de Cádiz, 1991), ch. 2, pp. 283–97.

opportunities for a more direct participation in the American trade by the regions through their own ports were increasing, as were the possibilities for using the profits and mercantile experience gained in the American trade to the regions' own advantage. This process of the regionalisation of the American trade was long, gradual, and full of contradictions.[14] Concessions made to the French and English after the War of Spanish Succession resulted in a temporary and partial break with the monopoly port system. Later, the Crown gave increased opportunities for participation in the American trade to Spanish ports other than Cadiz and, consequently, to the hinterlands which supported them. Thus, San Sebastian, Barcelona, and La Coruña were given the privilege of dealing with the monopolistic trading companies—la Real Compañía Guipuzcoana de Caracas, created in 1728, and the Real Compañía de Barcelona in 1756. The Galician port of La Coruña was given the monopoly postal service to Havana and Buenos Aires in 1765. During the 1740s the temporary cessation of the fleet system and its substitution by free ships also meant greater flexibility for trade through Cadiz, which, on the whole, benefited the merchants.

The Real Compañía Guipuzcoana de Caracas has been the subject of various studies.[15] This was probably one of the mercantile groups that benefited most from the network of people and capital established between Cadiz and the North of Spain. Although the figures cannot be calculated with precision due to a lack of records, we know the company was successful in using its exclusive right to trade with Venezuela and to import cacao, cotton, indigo, and tobacco into Spain. Part of these imports were re-exported from Spain to other parts of Europe. Statistically, the amount of cacao imported by Spain grew from 3% to between 50 and 75% of the total Venezuelan cacao production, due to the rapid rise in demand when its consumption became fashionable.[16] In turn, the Compañía sent goods such as textiles (mostly of foreign origin), paper, wax, iron

[14] See A. J. Kuethe, "Los Borbones y el Consulado andaluz" in E. Vila and A. J. Kuethe, eds., *Relaciones de poder y comercio colonial* (Séville: Escuela de Estudios Hispano-Americanos de Sevilla, 1999), pp. 50–65, and G. J. Walker, *Política española y comercio colonial, 1700–1789*, (Barcelona: Ariel, 1979).

[15] R. Hussey, *La Compañía de Caracas*, (Caracas: Banco Central de Venezuela, 1962); and more recently, M. Gárate Ojanguren, *La Real Compañía Guipuzcoana de Caracas* (San Sebastián: Marcel Pons, 1990).

[16] R. Hussey, op. cit., pp. 80–89.

objects, cod, spices and agricultural goods, as well as olives, olive oil, vinegar, wines, brandy, flour, and dried fruit to Venezuela. Between the 1730s and 1780, the profits from this partnership were considerable. No doubt part of these profits were invested in San Sebastian, where the headquarters of the company were located, as well as in its hinterland in the Basque Country and Navarre. However, we still do not know the details of how this trade actually worked. In Navarre, for example, the merchants attempted to introduce their own brandy into the American markets using the services of the Compañía.[17] We do not know how much this capital generated in the Venezuelan trade contributed toward the development of the Basque economy, nor to what extent it helped to convert the region into a major centre of modern Spanish industrialisation.

The Compañía de la Havana was created in 1740 to organise commerce in tobacco.[18] The promoters and partners were mostly Basque, but we do not know to what extent the capital generated from their trade benefited the economy of the region. The company served as a bridge between the royal tobacco factory in Seville and the tobacco harvesters in Cuba, at least until the liberalisation of trade.

The Compañía de Barcelona built, at least partially, upon the Catalan tradition of sending merchandise to America—at first indirectly, then directly.[19] In addition to sending the traditional Catalan wine and spirits, the company also sent flour to the Caribbean and locally-produced textiles to all the colonies. Until the liberalisation of trade, nearly 82% of the Compañía's exports were spirits, wines, and flour and, consequently, the export trade of the region depended on these agricultural goods. Agricultural exports became the driving economic force of Catalonia.[20] Though the production and export of textiles was less important to the Catalonian economy than was agriculture, Catalan printed cotton cloth was once considered by many historians to be the driving force behind the development of Catalan industry.

---

[17] A. M. Azcona Guerra, *Comercio y Comerciantes en la Navarra del siglo XVIII* (Pamplona: Gobierno de Navarro, 1986), pp. 191–93.

[18] See M. Gárate Ojanguren, *Comercio ultramarino e Ilustración. La Real Compañía de la Habana*, (San Sebastián: Donostia, 1993).

[19] See C. Martínez, Shaw, op. cit.

[20] J. M. Oliva Melgar, *Cataluña y el comercio privilegiado con América. La Real Compañía de Barcelona a Indias* (Barcelona: University of Barcelona, 1987), pp. 269–70.

These privileged companies conducted an ever-increasing share of colonial trade. At the end of the 1750s and the beginning of the 1760s, the companies represented about 20% of total Spanish exports to the New World. Although they defied the Cadiz monopoly, they did not succeed in completely usurping its power. To what degree did they help develop the economies of the Basque and Catalan regions? These regions were later considered to be the most dynamic in Spain. In practice, however, none of the experience gained through the privileged companies succeeded in bringing about either a change in the production structure or any sort of truly significant economic development in these areas. The trade with the New World did, however, succeed in creating a series of initiatives, which, in the long-term, must have helped to create a better organisational infrastructure within the regions—an infrastructure that may well have helped their subsequent economic development.

The Galician port of La Coruña was the base for the "maritime mail," comprised of a series of fast and well-armed frigates. Although their objective was not commercial, they were used for the transport of merchandise such as Cuban sugar and Argentine leathers. The presence of these altered the town by transforming it into a small entrepôt, which received goods and merchants from bordering areas and, sometimes, in the case of the Catalans and Basques, from more distant areas. At the same time, local industries such as the production of fine linen for export developed quickly.[21]

The introduction of free trade had huge repercussions on the Spanish economy. The law allowing for free trade between the colonies and the various regions of Spain was promulgated on 12 October 1778 and was accompanied by an overall simplification of the system of trade.[22] Ports on both sides of the Atlantic were progressively incorporated into the framework of legal trade. However, certain significant ports, such as Valencia, were not authorised to participate in the American trade until later. The importance of this measure, which gradually broke the nearly three-centuries-long

[21] See L. M. Enciso Recio, *Los establecimientos industriales españoles en el siglo XVIII. La mantelería de La Coruña*, (Madrid: Ediciones Rialp, 1963).

[22] V. Rodríguez Casado, "Comentarios al Decreto y Real Instrucción de 1765 regulando las relaciones comerciales entre España y America," *Anuario de Historia del Derecho Español*, XIII (1936–1941); and J. Munoz Pérez, "La publicación del reglamento de comercio libre de Indias de 1778," *Anuario de Estudios Americanos*, IV (1947).

monopoly of a single port over the colonies, has been the object of some debate in the historiography of the post-1778 period.[23]

The visible result of such measures liberalising trade was the increased volatility of the Hispano-American trade.[24] This volatility also meant increased growth. Therefore, the Spanish authorities' expectations that growth would ensue from freeing up trade were not disappointed. However, the reasons for such growth are still debatable. It is, therefore, all the more surprising that the supremacy of Cadiz in the trade with the New World continued—76.4% for the period between 1782 and 1796, and 77% between 1797–1820.[25] More than 20% of trade to the Americas could and did leave Cadiz. The establishment of free trade also brought about changes in the networks and connections of regional and inter-regional trade, none of which are very well studied.[26]

A percentage of the merchandise exported from these ports came from other parts of Europe. We know, for example, that most of the exports from La Coruña in the 1780s were of European goods. Certain fabrics destined for the Americas were from outside Spain and, as the decree of 1778 permitted, were dyed in Spain. The same held true for flour, which was often milled from foreign wheat. Despite this re-export of foreign goods, estimates drawn from the official registers show that Spanish exports to the colonies increased from 38% registered in 1778 to 52% during the period between 1782 and 1786 and to 63% between 1797 and 1820. This increase is partly due to the fact that the availability of foreign merchandise in Spain gradually decreased and was exported directly, in ever increasing quantities, from the place of origin to Spanish America without passing through the Spanish ports.[27]

---

[23] The most significant examples of this are the important publications on the colonial trade and its effects on the Spanish ports and regions in the period after free trade, are to be found in the following notes. Most of its authors are grouped together in A. M. Bernal, *El comercio libre entre España y América Latina, 1765–1824*, (Madrid: Fundación Banco Exterior, 1987).

[24] John R. Fisher, "Imperial 'free trade' and the Hispanic Economy, 1778–1796," *Journal of Latin American Studies*, 13 (1981), pp. 21–56; and "The Imperial Response to 'Free trade': Spanish imports from Spanish America," ibid., 17 (1985), pp. 35–78.

[25] John R. Fisher, "El comercio y el ocaso imperial: el comercio español con Hispanoamérica, 1797–1820" in E. Vila and Kuethe eds., op. cit., p. 188.

[26] See D. R. Ringrose, *España, 1700–1900: El mito del fracaso*, (Madrid: Alianza, 1966), especially chapters 8 and 9.

[27] J. Fisher, "El comercio y el ocaso imperial," pp. 174, 184, and 187.

Research published in the last 20 years has been quite skeptical in its analysis of the repercussions of free trade on Spanish economic development as a whole, and on the particular regions specifically. At the same time, however, most of these recent analyses assert that free trade did stimulate Spain's overseas trade.[28]

Each region was affected differently by free trade with the Americas. To begin with, not every region had easy access to the sea. For example, the majority of the Castilian provinces were in the interior. Although the roads network was expanded, it remained insufficient to allow for the passage of significant quantities of goods for trade either to or from the American colonies. Other regions such as Navarre saw the same customs posts that had been established at their borders to protect their economy work to their detriment by obstructing the circulation of goods to their single port. Finally, a third group of regions such as Valencia and Bilbao, although they relied on their ports as an outlet for their goods, were not included in the initial free trade proclamation. The differences in factors—exportable goods, manufacturing industries, interested merchants, and ships—between the regions was also very evident after free trade with the colonies was declared. Let us now look at some of the better-studied regions.

In Galicia, there does not seem to have been a significant development in the regional economy linked to the American markets after the decree of 1778. La Coruña, the main port of Galicia, had fewer than 8% of its exports registered as being destined to Spanish America between 1780 and 1796 and, after 1796, no exports to the Americas were registered at all.[29] The region had to face much greater competition than it had previously, most of which was the result of free trade, which, consequently, reduced its economic strength.

[28] A good summary of this subject can be found in J. Fontana, *La economía española al final del Antiguo Régimen: Comercio y Colonias* (Madrid: Alianza, 1982), "Introduction", pp. xiii–xxxiv. The same basic message can be found in D. R. Ringrose, *España, 1700–1900*, op. cit.; J. M. Delgado Ribas, "El impacto de las crisis coloniales en la economía catalana," ibid, pp. 97–169, and, particularly "Comercio colonial y crecimiento economico en la España del siglo XVIII. Las crisis de un modelo interpretativo," *Manuscripts, Revista de Historia moderna*, Barcelona, 3 (1986), pp. 23–40; C. Manera Erbilla, "Manufactura textil y comercio en Mallorca, 1700–1830," *Revista de Historia Económica*, 6 (1988), pp. 523–55; L. Alonso Álvarez, *Comercio colonial y crisis del Antiguo Régimen en Galicia, 1778–1818* (La Coruña: Xunta de Galicia, 1986), and M. Gárate Ojanguren, "Comercio exterior en el País Vasco XVIII–XIX," *Historia Contemporánea*, 2 (1989), pp. 166–73.

[29] J. R. Fisher, "El comercio y el ocaso," p. 188.

Despite the opportunities that unprocessed raw materials offered to the region's industry, very little processing took place, and these materials continued to be exported in considerable quantities.[30] Agricultural exports from the region do not seem to have been able to compensate for this.[31] La Coruña continued to reinforce its position as a port for re-exporting American goods to other parts of Spain and Europe and as a port of call between Catalonia and the New World. This re-export and intermediary function might explain the dynamics of its economy, otherwise dominated by agriculture. Its industries, such as small textile mills and Sargadelos ceramics, had only weak links with the markets of the New World.[32]

The situation of Asturias, a neighbouring region, was not very different from that of Galicia. Between 1779 and 1783, those in charge of the Principality's general revenues recognised that trade with America brought in nothing to the customs and excise. Eventually, this situation improved, but the value and volume of trade continued to be weak. Lack of ships and of exportable surpluses from the region was the direct cause of this situation.[33] At the end of the 1780s and the beginning of the 1790s, the port of Gijón was responsible for only 0.3% of total Spanish overseas exports.[34] From then on, the Asturian merchants' connections with American trade and the capital that it generated were practically inexistent. Some retained a desire for ennoblement that they hoped could be attained through a connection with the New World trade, while others had important import businesses specialising in linen. But even in these cases, the American economy held little attraction for the Asturian merchant elite.[35] Nevertheless, one observer at the time recognised the concrete results the impetus of free trade had given to industry in the area. He noted the establishment of various factories in Gijón:

---

[30] P. Saavedra, "La renovación de los grupos burgueses en Galicia en la segunda mitad del siglo XVIII" in L. M. Enciso Recio, ed., *La burguesía en la Edad Moderna*, (Valladolid: Universidad de Valladolid, 1996), III, pp. 1366–67.

[31] L. Alonso Álvarez, op. cit., pp. 58–60 and 80–99.

[32] P. Saavedra, op. cit., pp. 1355–65.

[33] D. Peribáñez Caveda, *Comunicaciones y comercio marítimo en la Asturias preindustrial, 1750–1850*, (Gijón: Puerto de Gijón, 1992), p. 213 and "El comercio hispanoamericano a través de Gijón," *Bidea*, Oviedo (1989), pp. 722–24.

[34] J. Cuenca Esteban, "Comercio y Hacienda en la caída del Imperio español," in *Economia española al final*, op. cit., p. 402.

[35] B. Barreiro, Mallón, "La burguesía asturiana en el siglo XVIII," in L. M. Enciso Recio, op. cit., III, p. 1286.

beer, fine earthenware copies of Bristolware, stockings, and also the restoration of a leather factory that had been abandoned.[36]

After the liberalisation of trade, the growth of Santander, Cantabria's main port, was not so much due to the export of the region's goods to the American markets. Rather, it was due to the consolidation of its role as a re-exporter of goods from Spanish regions such as Viscaya and the Castilian countryside, as well as from other parts of Europe to the Americas, mostly the Caribbean. However, sparked by this trade and in response to American demand, an important industry for processing goods such as grain and, to a lesser extent, beer, leather, and glass grew up around the Santander-Reinosa axis in the 18th and 19th centuries. These activities were possible using capital earned from flour imported from the colonies by members of Santander's mercantile elite. This importation of flour was the most important activity in Cantabria in the 18th century.[37]

The Basque Country has traditionally been used as an example of the beneficial results of free trade. T. Guiard posited the thesis that free trade was very beneficial to the development of Bilbao, the commercial and financial capital of the Basque region during the last third of the 18th century. Previously, iron, which was exported to America from Bilbao, had been protected (in the Customs Excise Act of 1775) to avoid competition from iron produced in other European regions. To do this, a *veeduria* had been established in Cadiz, which was responsible for preventing any such European competition.[38]

In contrast to Guiard's theory, more recent research has highlighted how the delayed authorisation for direct trade with America forced Bilbao to use other intermediary Spanish and European ports for its exports.[39] This delayed concession for direct American trade also caused Bilbao to concentrate more on trade with Europe.[40]

---

[36] D. Peribánez Caveda, op. cit., p. 213.

[37] R. Maruri Villanueva, "La burguesía de Cantabria en el siglo XVIII (un perfil económico y social)," in L. M. Enciso, *La burguesía en la Edad Moderna*, III, p. 1286. See also Ramon M. Villanueva, *La Burguesía mercantil santanderina 1700–1850 (Cambio social y mentalidad)*, (Santander: Universidad de Cantabria, 1990), ch. I.

[38] T. Guiard y Larrauri, *Historia de la noble Villa de Bilbao*, (Bilbao: Ed. La Gran. Enciclopedia Vasca, 1971), vol. III.

[39] R. Basurto Larrañaga, *Comercio y Burguesia mercantil de Bilbao en la segunda mitad del siglo XVIII*, (Bilbao: Universidad del Pais Vasco, 1983), pp. 98–99.

[40] M. C. Gutiérrez Muñoz, *Comercio y banca. Expansión y crisis del capitalismo comercial en Bilbao al final del Antiguo Régimen*, (Bilbao: Universidad del Paris Vasco, 1994), p. 37.

Resorting to intermediary ports seems to have been a general tendency for the Basque ports, even after free trade had been granted. Moreover, there is no obvious link between the late development of the metallurgical industry and the commercial capital accumulated through exports to America.

However, it is often difficult to discern what possibilities were opened up for the Basque region after the end of the Cadiz monopoly. Consequently, recent studies have attempted to show that American trade was able to influence the modernisation of the Basque economy in a more subtle way. For example, through their experience in international trade throughout the 18th century, the merchants of Bilbao developed a powerful bank and an immense network of financial contacts between Europe and America, both basic elements for the development of a modern capitalist town.[41]

All in all, for the regional economies in the North of Spain, the benefits of participating in the direct trade with the Americas do not seem to have been particularly large from a commercial point of view, with the possible exception of Viscaya and Cantabria.

If we now look at the Mediterranean regions, we can see there is an obvious disparity. The port of Barcelona was the natural outlet for a large number of goods from the Catalan region—even though its participation in receiving exports from Spain to America, after free trade was instated, was limited: between 7 and 8% for the period between 1782 and 1796 and nearly 12% between 1797 and 1820.[42] The contribution of the Mediterranean ports in Spain to the exports destined for Spanish America also increased, including manufactured goods such as textiles, paper, and hats, as well as wine and brandy. These exports stimulated the development of the industries producing these products.

Taking these figures into account, we could contest the fact that profits from Catalan merchandise were greater than the costs arising from greater competition from imported goods immediately after free trade. Catalonia's volume of foreign goods increased, resulting in a fall in prices.[43] Anyway, the link between Catalan textile factories

[41] Ibid., p. 77.

[42] J. R. Fisher, "Imperial 'free trade . . .'," pp. 21–56, and "El comercio y el ocaso imperial . . .," p. 188.

[43] J. M. Delgado Rivas, "Política ilustrada, industria española y mercado americano 1720–1820," *Pedralbes*, 3 (1983), pp. 253–63; the thesis of C. Martínez Shaw, "El

and its naval industry and trade destined for America could reasonably be considered important factors in the development and modernisation of the Catalan economy, without even counting the value of the American finances received to shore up the region's balance of payments.[44]

This link between home industry and colonial trade did not exist to the same degree in the Valencia area, despite the great potential of the silk industry. The traditional analysis of the situation posits that the lack of commercial development was due to various causes such as a lack of port infrastructure, a small merchant class made up of many foreigners, and more conservative investment strategies.[45] However, a more recent study of the consular register showed the true value of the import trade via the port of Valencia. This trade was comparable to that of Alicante in the 1770s and 1780s, and was similar in development to that of Barcelona in the second half of the 17th century.[46] Similarly, the number of merchants involved in trade increased throughout the 18th century in Valencia, as it had elsewhere. Valencia's link with the silk trade is very clear. Moreover, the connection between the silk trade and the New World is very evident, even during the period of trade liberalisation.

In Mediterranean Andalusia, Malaga's dependence on Cadiz as opposed to Barcelona is shown in the royal registers and other official documents.[47] The royal registers show a limited participation in trade to Spanish America and confirm a dependence on Cadiz as opposed

libre comercio y Cataluña: contribucion a un debate," in *El comercio libre* op. cit., pp. 43–53, and A. García-Baquero, "Comercio colonial y producción industrial en Cataluña a fines del siglo XVIII," in J. Nadal and G. Tortella, eds., *Agricultura, comercio colonial y crecimiento económico en la España Contemporánea, Actas del I Coloquio de Historia Económica de España (Barcelona, 11–12 Mayo 1972)* (Barcelona: Ariel, 1973), pp. 268–94.

[44] C. Martínez Shaw, "El libre comercio y Cataluña," p. 51.

[45] See also the studies of García Bonafé: "El marco histórico de la industrialización valenciana," *Información Comercial Española*, Madrid, 485 (1974), pp. 137–38; J. A. Tomás Carpi, *La economía valenciana: modelos de interpretación* (Valencia: Fernando Torres, 1976), p. 45, and P. Molas, "Valencia i la Junta de Comerciantes," *Estudis 3* (Valencia: 1974), p. 107.

[46] Franch R. Benavent, *El capital comercial valenciano en el siglo XVIII* (Valencia: Universidad de Valencia, 1989).

[47] J. M. Delgado Ribas, "Cádiz y Málaga en el comercio colonial posterior a 1778," *Actas del II Congreso de Historia de Andalucía, siglo XVIII* (Córdoba, 1978), I, pp. 127–39 and A. Gámez Amián, "El comercio de Málaga con América (1765–1820). Una ocasión perdida," *Revista de Indias, IV*, 205 (1995), p. 638.

to Barcelona. However, the importance of the re-export trade from other parts of Spain, Europe, and the colonies is emphasised. There were positive effects on the production of some agricultural commodities such as wine and silk in Malaga's hinterland, but sugar cane, for instance, was a definite failure. The most powerful foreign merchants continued to depend on the exterior for their shipments. The volume of goods sent to America increased after the institution of free trade until about 1796, but after that the volume of trade declined and, in any case, most of the ships leaving for America came from Catalonia.[48]

The Mediterranean area, therefore, mainly benefited from the American markets through the port of Barcelona, which was linked to regional industries. Nevertheless, the real benefits of the American trade are debatable. In the other ports analysed, there were no such clear links with the American trade, nor were there links to the region's industrial development arising from the trade with Spanish America.

The case of Atlantic Andalusia is different because this region benefited directly from the monopoly on the Spanish-American trade. In the 18th century, Seville lost its position as the New World monopoly port and was converted into a distribution centre for commodities from a large surrounding agricultural area. Cadiz—much more cosmopolitan than Seville—took over the monopoly and, even after free trade with the Americas was liberalised, continued to retain its supremacy in this trade, far above the other authorised peninsular ports, holding 76–77% of all the registered exports during the period between 1782–1796 and 1797–1820.[49]

What became of the capital accumulated by this trade is somewhat obscure, however. This capital was enormously affected by a set of crises between 1796 and 1823, but little else is known about it. We can speculate that part of these funds, generated mainly by a foreign elite, must have been repatriated. Another part must have been invested in the Spanish regions whence the merchants in Seville and Cadiz had come. There is no doubt that a small part of the capital was put into secure investments of some sort or another, but

[48] A. Gámez Amián, Ibid., pp. 637–41 and 653–57.

[49] J. R. Fisher, "Imperial 'Free Trade'," pp. 21–56, and "El comercio y el ocaso imperial," p. 188.

very few companies were created to take advantage of the new political and economic situation created by free trade. Those merchants remaining in the Western area of Andalusia preferred seemingly safe investments such as land, houses, and securities, while others found a living in the sherry wine trade of the "Marco de Jerez." Sherry was transformed from a commercial to an industrial product in the mid-18th century. This shift was not only due to the trading centre created in the Bay of Cadiz, particularly after the decree of 1778, but also to those who returned to Spain following the loss of the American colonies.

For David R. Ringrose, the generally weak link between the Spanish regions—particularly those in the interior of the country—and the colonies explains why, with the exception of the port of Cadiz and its hinterland, the various regions seem to have been little affected by the crises at the end of the 1780s and at the beginning of the 19th century. These crises included first the English and then the Napoleonic blockade, as well as the loss of most of the colonies, and the subsequent breakdown in the Spanish imperial system. Economic activities that did not depend on the American markets took on a new importance. During the long period of wars, the important trade flow between both sides of the Atlantic continued in spite of the difficulties.[50] This point of view contrasts with that of J. Fontana concerning the collapse of Spanish foreign trade and the long depression from 1812–14 until the beginning of the 1840s.[51]

The figures regarding the transatlantic trade upon which the majority of studies are based do not include the impact of that trade on some fundamental elements of the Spanish economy. We have referred to the transfer of capital accumulated from trade with the Americas to various regions through complex intermediary networks. There is an enormous amount of work to be done on this subject. Researching these capital flows is a priority, as is research into the related biographies of the merchants involved in the mercantile associations trading with America. Moreover, there should be a formal reconstruction of the credit networks and the transfer of capital these merchants used.

[50] D. R. Ringrose, *El mito*, pp. 174–75.

[51] J. Fontana, "Colapso y transformación del comercio exterior español entre 1792–1827. Un aspecto de la economía del Antiguo Régimen en España," *Moneda y credito*, 115 (1970).

Certainly the late development of industry, and the modernisation of Spanish society in general, do not seem to point to Spanish America as a driving force for change in the home country. However, for the historian, research involves more than explaining the obvious main points. It means distinguishing, where sources and methodology permit, between the subtle processes of change and the continuity of institutions. There is still a lot left to be done—and we have the tools to do it.

CHAPTER SEVEN

PORTUGAL'S OVERSEAS TRADE DURING THE EIGHTEENTH CENTURY: A HISTORIOGRAPHICAL SURVEY

Niels Wiecker and Horst Pietschmann

Framework: The Iberian Atlantic

There have been numerous attempts since the 1950s to create a generalised interpretation of European expansion in the Atlantic and beyond from the 15th century. Following discussions at the International History Congress in 1955, Charles Verlinden enlarged upon the thesis of an Atlantic Civilisation in the 1960s to bring the different branches of the historiography of Western European "national" expansion under a single conceptual framework.[1]

Some years later Immanuel Wallerstein introduced the concept of what he called a "world-system."[2] Wallerstein used an approach based upon a posited "world-system," and his analysis tended to be based upon trade volumes and/or quantities in Early Modern transatlantic interaction. The criticism of this "global" approach, which emerged long before debates about "globalisation" became popular, pointed out the discrepancies between Wallerstein's theories and the actuality of the empirical findings of historians. This criticism implied that Wallerstein had stretched his theories beyond the limits of what available evidence would support.

At the beginning of the 1980s, Peggy Liss examined the complexity of historical developments in the Atlantic sphere in the 18th century, and formulated a network approach, using terminology based

[1] Cfr. Charles Verlinden, *Les origines de la Civilisation Atlantique: De la Renaissance a l'Age de Lumieres* (Paris: Neuchatel, 1966).

[2] Immanuel Wallerstein, *The Modern World-System*, 3 vols. (New York et al.: Academic Press, 1974). Essential for the present context are vols. 1 and 2. Cfr. also the interpretations of Wallerstein's "world-system" by Hans-Jürgen Nitz, ed., *The Early Modern World-System in Geographical Perspective* (Stuttgart: Steiner, 1993).

upon the concept of empire.[3] Liss' network approach reflected a methodological re-orientation that has been generally accepted since the 1980s, particularly in Anglo-Saxon research. As a consequence, the "Atlantic system" and its related research no longer concentrates as much on trade quantities but, rather, on the relations between the human participants in commerce on both sides of the Atlantic. To some extent, Liss' new focus, while still retaining the geographical expansiveness of earlier approaches, denoted a return to Verlinden's approach due to Liss' view of the Atlantic as an interconnected historical space. Her new Atlantic perspective was based on a far more reliable methodology than Wallerstein's since it did not focus on the flow of goods and quantities of precious metals but, instead, on the agents who set these streams in motion and organised, financed, produced, and consumed them.

The part played by Anglo-Saxon historiography in redefining historical viewpoints is also seen in the conclusions of much research done in the late 1980s and early 1990s. This research examined the English and Dutch influence in the North and Central Atlantic from the 17th century onward—a region that had heretofore been viewed through a French lens. This research showed that, during the 18th century, the English increasingly dominated this part of the Atlantic.

The "Iberian Atlantic" existed in the 15th, 16th, and parts of the 17th century—so much so, in fact, that German-language sources from seafarers in the second half of the 17th century still defined the Atlantic as the "hispanische see."[4] Yet, by the 18th century, the Iberian powers seem to have dropped out of sight in the historiography of the Atlantic. This perceived lack of Iberian involvement in the 18th century Atlantic might be due to the less-important role the Iberian colonial powers played in European politics during this century. Nevertheless, the Iberian Atlantic during the 18th century was vitally important to the European economy and, above all, to the developing European financial system.

[3] Peggy K. Liss, *Atlantic Empires: The Networks of Trade and Revolution, 1713–1826* (Baltimore: Johns Hopkins University Press, 1983), for a skeptical review of this book from the Brazilian perspective, see Kenneth R. Maxwell, "Portuguese America," in *The International History Review 6* (1984), pp. 529–50; this article is part of a collection of commentaries in the same journal all reflecting on Liss' "Atlantic Empires" from different viewpoints under the title *The Atlantic Empires in the Eighteenth Century*, pp. 507–680.

[4] Friedrich Martens, *Hispanische Reise-Beschreibung de anno 1671*, ed. by W. Junk, (Berlin: 1925), p. 10.

By the 18th century, the American empires of both Spain and Portugal had developed into considerable markets in their own right, with heavy demand for, and importation of, European goods. They were also the most important producers of precious metals. The mining of silver in the Spanish colonies and of gold in Brazil converted the Iberian colonies into economically potent regions with, concomitantly, a great deal of power, though they were still politically dependent on their respective motherlands.[5] Recent scholarly research has shown that the European powers became gradually more "Western" and more "Atlantic," implying that the colonial territories in America became both more attractive and more important to the "Old World."[6] Moreover, the Iberian Atlantic remained important in the 18th century because both Iberian kingdoms were able to overcome crises such as the Nine Years War and the War of Spanish Succession in the late 17th century, and were able to re-expand by building up their navies and extending their commercial activities.

Despite the importance within the wider European context that the Iberian Atlantic undoubtedly had, one can question the economic "success" of Iberian involvement in the Atlantic. For instance, why did neither Spain nor Portugal seem to profit from over three hundred years of overseas empire? Pieter Emmer has raised some important questions on this very issue, and argues that the way the Iberian expansion took place was not reasonable from an economic point of view.[7] He states that noneconomic motives were the main impetus for the Iberian expansion. While Emmer's thesis might hold true for the early phase of Iberian expansion, we remain convinced that transatlantic connections in the 18th century were primarily of an economic nature. This debate is one example of how the concept of the Iberian Atlantic requires more research in order to add data to the findings in the existing literature. We will comment on

[5] The abundant literature on the history of mining and commerce of precious metals in the Iberian colonies in America during Early Modern times cannot be presented in detail. For an excellent overview on the present state of research and most significant works, see the exhibition catalogue *El oro y la plata de las Indias en la época de los Austrias* (Madrid: Fundación ICO, 1999). The catalogue also includes literature on the post-Austrian period.

[6] Hans-Otto Kleinmann, "Der atlantische Raum als Problem des europäischen Staatensystems" in *Jahrbuch für Geschichte Lateinamerikas 38* (2001), pp. 7–30.

[7] Cfr. the article by Pieter Emmer in this book.

the literature for the case of the Portuguese Atlantic in the following pages.

Portugal and Atlantic Historiography

The term "Iberian Atlantic" was coined in the pioneer works of Pierre Chaunu and Frédéric Mauro, and studies of this region have been deeply influenced by these two scholars.[8] Both Chaunu and Mauro proved the Iberian dominance in the Atlantic area by providing impressive quantifying studies on ships navigation and the transport of goods. This dominance also positively influenced the flow of news and information, at least during the 16th century, as Renate Pieper has recently worked out.[9] For Portuguese activities during the 15th and 16th centuries, Vitorino Magalhães Godinho has added to our knowledge of basic economic history in a number of important publications that parallel those of Mauro.[10]

These fundamental works had great influence on later studies. Spanish research concentrated on commercial flows in Hispanic American port cities, on production of precious metals in the mining regions of Peru and Mexico and their influence on commerce, and, later, on commercial activities in different Spanish ports during the 18th century.[11] However, while Spanish historiography on the his-

---

[8] Pierre Chaunu, *Séville et l'Atlantique*, 11 vols., (Paris: Institut des Hautes Etudes de l'Amérique Latine, 1959); Frédéric Mauro, *Le Portugal et l'Atlantique au XVII*[e] *siècle (1570–1670); Etude économique* (Paris: S.E.V.P.E.N., 1960); (see also the slightly augmented Portuguese version: *Portugal, o Brasil e o Atlântico 1570–1670*, 2 vols.; (Lisbon: Estampa, 1989).

[9] Cfr. Renate Pieper, *Die Vermittlung einer Neuen Welt: Amerika im Nachrichtennetz des Habsburgischen Imperiums 1493–1598* (Mainz: von Zabern, 2000).

[10] Cfr. the new summary in the work by Vitorino Magalhães Godinho, *Mito e mercadoria. Utopia e prática de navegar. Séculos XIII–XVIII* (Lisbon: Difel, 1990). Godinho includes various of his earlier writings on the economic history of the Portuguese expansion in this monograph. One of the most important of these is surely *L'économie de l'empire Portugais aux XV*[e] *et XVI*[e] *siècles* (Paris: S.E.V.P.E.N., 1969).

[11] To get an impression of the literature on that topic which cannot be discussed here in detail see the study of Manuel Bustos Rodríguez in this volume and the exhibition catalogue already cited in note 6. We have to stress that Spanish historians focused on a single port also included an Atlantic perspective. For example the principal monograph on Spanish transatlantic commerce: Antonio García-Baquero González, *Cádiz y el Atlántico (1717–1778). El comercio colonial español bajo el monopolio gaditano*, 2 vols. (Sevilla: Escuela de estudios Hispano-America, 1976). It might have been the reawakening regionalism (or regional nationalism) in post-Franco Spain since the 1980s which caused a decline in Atlantic references in historical works and which led to a Spanish-focused historiography.

tory of the colonial empire long remained more or less restricted to the methodology established by Chaunu, Portuguese historiography took other routes.

Some excellent bibliographic overviews on European expansion were published at the end of the 1960s in the French series "Nouvelle Clio," covering the state of research at that time.[12] There have been fewer studies on Portuguese economic development and trade routes when compared with research concerning the Spanish colonial empire. Therefore, there is a dearth of studies covering the period of Portugal's re-emancipation from Spain after 1640.[13] Several synopses of the state of research in the 1970s exposed these gaps, especially since these omissions were only partially rectified much later by some broadly defined studies.[14] A fairly recent book by Frédéric Mauro and Maria de Souza documents the progress in research since then, though it excludes the Portuguese islands in the Atlantic and Portuguese Africa.[15] Another valuable introduction to recent research is the extensive anniversary publication dedicated to Mauro by his students and

[12] Frédéric Mauro, *L'expansion européenne (1600–1870)*. Deuxième édition revue et complétée. (Paris: Nouvelle Clio, 1967), vol. 27, including the bibliography for Portugal: pp. 72–76, and for Spain: pp. 77–84. Both cover the key readings concerning the metropoles and the colonies as well as the trade within the empires. The limited literature on Portugal's commerce in that period is reported in the work of Yves Bottineau, *Le Portugal et sa vocation maritime: Histoire et civilisation d'une nation*, (Paris: Boccard, 1977).

[13] The only exception is Charles R. Boxer, *The Portuguese Seaborne Empire, 1415–1825* (London: Hutchinson, 1969).

[14] Cfr. for example Val R. Lorwin and Jacob M. Price, eds., *The Dimensions of the Past: Materials, Problems, and Opportunities for Quantitative Work in History*, (New Haven, London: Yale University Press, 1972). While this collection contains a long article about Spain (Juan J. Linz, "Five Centuries of Spanish History: Quantification and Comparison," pp. 177–262) and two contributions about quantitative studies on colonial and contemporary Latin America, an article about Portugal is missing. Only John J. TePaske, "Quantification in Latin American Colonial History," pp. 431–76, includes in the 25-page bibliography at the end of his article some three pages on Brazil, pp. 473–76, covering works on commerce and navigation, the slave trade, trading companies, financial and fiscal system, prices, mining, agriculture, business and also demography. But most of the cited studies refer to very specific periods or regions, so on this basis it is impossible to reach conclusions. A research survey put together at the same time by the Comisión de Historia Económica del Consejo Latinoamericano de Ciencias Sociales (CLACSO) and various authors on the occasion of the International Congress of Americanists in 1970 in Lima confirms this conclusion, cfr. *La historia económica en América Latina*, 2 vols. (México: Sepsetentas, 1972).

[15] Frédéric Mauro and Maria de Souza, *Le Brésil du XVe siècle à la fin du XVIIIe siècle* (Paris: Sedes, 1997).

friends.[16] There are some comprehensive studies of Portugal's commerce with the Asiatic part of its empire; in particular, the works of Sanjay Subrahmanyam.[17] This trade region was administratively unified, which facilitates coherent investigation, despite the regional complexity, because the sources outside Portugal can be accessed more easily and studied more intensively.

Because the writing of Portuguese and Brazilian history has closely followed French trends in historical thought, quantitatively oriented approaches to the Iberian Atlantic decreased from the 1980s onward. The quantitative focus was supplanted by studies in the history of the mentality of merchants and similar new fields of investigation, which followed the lead of Michel Foucault. But gaps remained. For instance, the concepts developed by Jacob M. Price and others relating to the history of long-distance trade, and later employed to analyse commerce and commercial networks in the English-dominated Atlantic, have hardly been applied to Portugal and Brazil until recently.

A. J. R. Russell-Wood's *An Expanding World. The European Impact on World History, 1450–1800* had an influence on the general terminology used in the field of European expansion and Atlantic history, as well as on the larger debates under discussion since the 1990s. In its numerous volumes, the Atlantic plays an important role as an historical space, which is similar to the approach taken by Fernand Braudel to the Mediterranean.[18] Both works take these large oceanic spaces as a primary principle of study and as a framework for the organisation of the work as a whole.[19] Unfortunately, however, Iberian historiography and Iberian topics are underrepresented in the "*Expanding World*" series. This oversight is possibly due to linguistic reasons. For example, Iberian topics treated in the series tend to be investigated by English-speaking historians who are, possibly, not able to grasp all the nuances of, or insights in, the Spanish language. To what

[16] Guy Martinère, ed., *Le Portugal et L'Europe Atlantique, le Brésil et l'Amérique Latine.* Mélanges offerts à Frédéric Mauro. (Lisbon, Paris: Touzot, 1995); (Arquivos do Centro Cultural Calouste Gulbenkian, vol. XXXIV).

[17] For a summarised version with an extensive bibliography on this subject, see Sanjay Subrahmanyam, *The Portuguese Empire in Asia 1500–1700: A Political and Economic History* (London, New York: Longman, 1993).

[18] Cfr. Susan Socolow, ed., *The Atlantic Staple Trade*, 2 vols. (Aldershot: Brookfield, 1996); (*An Expanding World: The European Impact on World: History, 1450–1800*, vol. 9).

[19] Cfr. Pieter C. Emmer and Femme Gaastra, eds., *The Organisation of Interoceanic Trade in European Expansion, 1450–1800* (Aldershot: Brookfield, 1996); (*An Expanding World: The European Impact on World History, 1450–1800*, vol. 13).

extent these anthologies will really influence future scholarly debates is hard to answer.

Studies on the Portuguese empire such as those mentioned above are difficult to produce. There was a massive loss of source material during the Lisbon earthquake in 1755, which severely limits access to primary source documentation. Nevertheless, the earthquake alone does not explain the lack of studies for the years following the earthquake, when a large number of sources on commercial history can be assumed to have been produced under the regime of the Marques de Pombal. Another obstacle historians of Portuguese commercial history have to deal with is the sheer geographical area requiring attention, as the Portuguese empire had colonies or outposts spread throughout the world.

For example, the Portuguese islands in the Atlantic—Madeira, the Azores, and the Cape Verde islands—maintained independent inter-island shipping routes for trading and communication, while also sustaining direct shipping connections to Brazil and the Portuguese territories in Africa. In addition, there was direct navigation integrating slave trade centres along the African coastline with the ports of Brazil and those of Portuguese Africa.[20] So, in contrast to Spain—which, until the late 18th century, tried to concentrate the official trade in Cadiz on the European side, and a small number of central ports in America like La Havana, Cartagena de Indias, Porto Belo, and Veracruz—the circumstances for the Portuguese empire are different. Therefore, scholarly investigations must necessarily take into consideration a wider geographical space from which to examine streams of trade. In this respect, it is an important advancement that a directory of relevant sources regarding the history of Portugal, which lists records accessible in Portugal, Europe, America, Africa and Asia, is finally available.[21]

[20] For direct slave trading between Brazil and Africa, as far as it appears in the sources, cfr. the summary by Herbert Klein, *The Atlantic Slave Trade* (Cambridge et al.: Cambridge University Press, 1999), and also the published CD-ROM by Cambridge University Press by the same author. It contains all known slave trading ships in a huge database that allows detailed queries and is a valuable tool for historians investigating the slave trade. Cfr. in addition Pieter C. Emmer, *De Nederlandse slavenhandel 1500–1850* (Amsterdam, Antwerpen: De Arbeiderspers, 2000).

[21] Luis Miguel García Mora, *Fuentes manuscritas para la historia de Portugal. Guía de instrumentos de investigación.* (Madrid: Fundación Histórica Tavera, 1998); see also for Madeira the more detailed overview: *Documentação e arquivos insulares: actas do Seminário Internacional sobre documentação e arquivos insulares* (Funchal: Centro de Estudos de História de Madeira, 1999).

Illicit Trade and Portugal's Commercial Web

Another focal point in the study of the Portuguese Atlantic trade is the investigation of contraband. This part of economic history is frequently hard to investigate because of the lack of data, although, fortunately, there are studies about Brazil. Portugal, however, remains largely unresearched.[22] Moreover, there is an almost complete absence of studies about inter-Iberian naval commerce.[23] This represents a significant problem for meaningful research on the Iberian Atlantic. Oporto, Lisbon, and Cadiz were three of the most important Iberian Atlantic port cities, all of which were located either at expanded river-mouths or at wide bays that offered abundant opportunities for smuggling along the shores. A central element within the context of illicit trade is the differing alliances of Portugal and Spain. Portugal was strongly allied with England, while Spain maintained close ties with France. As a consequence, there was a strong English and French economic presence in Iberia, which is a fact that two recent monographs are dedicated to.[24]

However, commercial relations actually transcended the alliances' boundaries. To date, scholars have concentrated on economic affairs within the coalitions to the exclusion of merchants involved in inner-Iberian smuggling and trade. Moreover, English and Dutch commercial ships on the way to Asia also crossed the Central and South Atlantic, and their navigation routes passed the Portuguese possessions in America and Africa. Stops were made not only for trading,

[22] For a short but good guide to sources about contraband, see Ernst Pijning, "Fontes para a história do contrabando no Brasil: um balanço," in *LPH Revista de História* 7 (1997), pp. 41–55; for Rio de Janeiro see by the same author *Controlling Contraband: Mentality, Economy and Society in Eighteenth-Century Rio de Janeiro*. Ph.D. diss., Johns Hopkins Univ., 1997; the volume of contraband and its influence on late colonial Brazil has been debated recently in two statements published in HAHR 81 (2001) by Ernst Pijning, "A New Interpretation of Contraband Trade," pp. 733–38, and Jorge Miguel Pedreira, "Contraband, Crisis, and the Collapse of the Old Colonial System," pp. 739–44.

[23] One of the exceptions is Manuel Burgos Madroñero, "El comercio marítimo de la España de Carlos III con el puerto de Lisboa, 1763–1783," in *Actas del Congreso Internacional sobre Carlos III y la Ilustración*. vol. 2. *Economía y sociedad* (Madrid: 1989), pp. 425–64. For inland trade at the Spanish-Portuguese border see Miguel Angel Melón Jiménez, *Hacienda, comercio y contrabando en la frontera de Portugal. Siglos XV–XVIII* (Cáceres: Cicon, 1999).

[24] L. M. E. Shaw, *The Anglo-Portuguese Alliance and the English Merchants in Portugal 1654–1810*, (Aldershot, et al.: Ashgate, 1998); and Michel Zylberberg, *Une si douce domination: Les milieux d'affaires français et l'Espagne vers 1780–1808* (Paris: Comité pour l'histoire économique et financière de la France, 1993).

but also for ships to re-supply. This fact emphasises yet again the need for more research on the above-mentioned desideratum. Only when researchers have addressed these gaps in the research will it be possible to focus questions on an identifiable Iberian Atlantic system, or at least, on an Atlantic market area.

In spite of a lack of data, historians have more recently investigated and brought new insights to some crucial parts of the complex question of Portugal's Atlantic commerce. In particular, various facets of the commercial role of the Portuguese islands in the Atlantic have been examined in depth. The results are to be found in a set of published conference papers and several individual published articles.[25] Due to renewed interest in, and funding for, research on the Portuguese and Spanish Atlantic islands, there has been a rapid advancement in historical research into this long-neglected field.

Looking across the Atlantic toward Brazil, we see a distinctive Brazilian historiography. Brazilian historians have delved deeply into colonial economic history, and much essential information has come out of their research. They have given special attention to smaller coastal cities that have been neglected by European historians.[26] These ports were quite important in former centuries because Brazil's long coastline made it difficult for the central government to control and it was, therefore, vulnerable to smuggling and contraband trade. Thus far, Brazilian historians have largely ignored the former Portuguese colonies in Africa.

[25] See, for instance, Instituto Histórico da Ilha Terceira, ed., *Os Açores e o Atlântico (séculos XIV–XVII)* (Angra do Heroismo: IHIT, 1984); a series of conferences took place in the last decade both on the Azores and on Madeira and the conference papers were published. Unfortunately the proceedings are, in some cases, hard to find, cfr. João Marinho dos Santos, *Os Açores nos séculos XVe–XVI.* 2 vols. (Azores: Universidad dos Acores, 1989); Albert Silbert, *Uma Encruzilhada do Atlântico. Madeira (1640–1820).* (Funchal: Centro de Estudos de História de Atlãntico, 1997). Região Autónoma da Madeira, ed., *Slaves with or without Sugar: Registers of the International Seminar,* Funchal, 17–21 June 1996 (Funchal: Atlantic History Study Centre, 1996); Alberto Vieira, *O comércio inter-insular nos séculos XVe–XVI. Madeira, Açores e Canárias.* (Funchal: Atlantic History Study Center, 1987); Carlos Agostinho das Neves, *São Tomé e Príncipe na segunda metade do século XVIII.* (Funchal: CEHA, 1990); *História das Ilhas Atlânticas (Economia, Sociedade, Arte e Literatura).* 2 vols. (Funchal: CEHA, 1998); *O Brasil e as Ilhas. Actas do colóquio internacional.* (Funchal: CEHA, 2000).

[26] A. J. R. Russell-Wood, "Ports of Colonial Brazil," in Franklin W. Knight and Peggy Liss, eds., *Atlantic Port Cities: Economy, Culture, and Society in the Atlantic World, 1650–1850* (Knoxville: University of Tennessee Press, 1991), pp. 196–239.

The Present State of Research

What is the state of research regarding the economic impact of Portugal's overseas trade on the motherland itself? To summarise, there are five broad areas that have been most deeply investigated, though there is not always a strict delineation between these topics. They are: 1) the economic development of different regions; 2) the history of specific sectors; 3) the commercial traffic in specific goods or between particular ports; 4) the influence of politics on the economy in the age of Enlightenment; and, 5) the merchant elite.[27] Those readers familiar with Spanish historiography will recognise these categories from Spanish history. One of the major differences between Portuguese and Spanish historiography is, however, the lack of access to serialised commercial data for longer periods of time in Portuguese history, due to the Lisbon earthquake, as was mentioned above.

The Regional Approach

In European historiography since the mid-1970s, issues of regional concern have been extensively studied. Authors working on the history of Portugal and Spain largely followed the "Annales" school and, in particular, Emmanuel Le Roy Ladurie and Pierre Vilar.[28] The focus on the particular "home" region as a topic of research was, and still is, extraordinarily strong in these postdictatorial countries.

Since the 1980s, scholars have tried to evaluate the influence of Brazilian independence on the Portuguese economy.[29] Historians have

---

[27] For the historiography about commercial activities in the Portuguese colonial empire, see Artur Teodoro de Matos and Luís Filipe F. Reis Thomaz, eds., *Vinte anos de historiografia ultramarina portuguesa 1972–1992* (Lisbon: CNCDP, 1993); Moreover the website of the Comissão Nacional para as Comemorações dos Descubrimentos Portugueses (CNCDP) provides information on further readings: http://www.cncdp.pt.

[28] Cfr. Emmanuel Le Roy Ladurie, *Les paysans de Languedoc*, (Paris: Flammarion, 1969); Pierre Vilar, *La Catalogne dans l'Espagne moderne. Recherches sur les fondements économiques des structures nationales*, 3 vols. (Paris: Bibliothèque bénérale de l'École Pratique des Hautes Études, 1962); For the different traditions in regional history, see the comparison in Stefan Brakensiek and Axel Flügel, eds., *Regionalgeschichte in Europa. Methoden und Erträge der Forschung zum* 16. bis 19. Jahrhundert. (Paderborn: 2000), (Forschungen zur Regionalgeschichte 34).

[29] See for example, Miriam Halpern Pereira, "Portugal and the Structure of the World Market in the Eighteenth and Nineteenth Centuries," in Wolfram Fischer, R. Marvin McInnis, and Jürgen Schneider, eds., *The Emergence of a World Economy 1500–1914, Papers of the Ninth. International Congress of Economic History, Part I: 1500–1850.* (Stuttgart: Steiner, 1986) (Beiträge zur Wirtschafts- und Sozialgeschichte, vol. 33, I),

evaluated the exchange of goods, as well as the effect trade had on agriculture, industry, and finance. These historians also expanded their definitions of key terms. For instance, commerce was no longer understood as a mere exchange of goods between ports but, rather, as the interaction between distant regions with a variety of ties linking them. The importance of this broader approach cannot be underestimated, since it led to the introduction of investigations that also focused on the repercussions the colonial empire had on Portugal, a heretofore largely unstudied subject.

A parallel interest in the regional impact of commerce emerged among Brazilian historians.[30] For example, José Jobson de Andrade Arruda published an article in 1986 connecting commerce and its regional impact in Brazil. In the same year, two studies came out asserting that Brazil's commerce was separate from regional developments.[31]

The conception of what constitutes a "region" evolved. Smaller regional units received increasingly more attention. Important works were produced about the economic history of many different locations in 18th century Portugal. Quite recently, the Algarve was examined, as was the Alto Minho.[32] The monograph about the Algarve

pp. 279–300; another study in this context worth reading, is Jorge Miguel Pedreira, "La economía portuguesa y el fin del imperio luso-brasileño (1800–1860)," in Leandro Prados de la Escosura and Samuel Amaral, eds., *La independencia âmericana: consecuencias económicas.* (Madrid: Alianza, 1993), pp. 219–52; concerning the impact of trade on the colonies, two recent articles controversially discuss the state of Brazil's commerce before independence: Jorge Miguel Pedreira, "From Growth to Collapse: Portugal, Brazil and the Breakdown of the Old Colonial System (1760–1830)" in *HAHR* 80 (2000); pp. 839–64; and José Jobson de Andrade Arruda, "Decadence or Crisis in the Luso-Brazilian Empire: A New Model of Colonisation in the Eighteenth Century" in *HAHR* 80 (2000); pp. 865–78.

[30] Cfr. in the above cited Wolfram Fischer, R. Marvin McInnis, and Jürgen Schneider, eds., *The Emergence of a World Economy 1500–1914. Papers of the Ninth. International Congress of Economic History, Part I: 1500–1850* (Stuttgart: Steiner, 1986), (Beiträge zur Wirtschafts- und Sozialgeschichte, vol. 33, I): José Jobson de Andrade Arruda, "Commercial Trends within the Luso-Brazilian Empire: Brazil's Integration in the World Market," pp. 301–33, and Frédéric Mauro, "Structure de l'économie interne et marché international dans une époque de transition: Le cas dû Brésil, 1750–1850," pp. 335–50.

[31] For the single article, see note 31; the two articles were published in Maria Beatriz Nizza da Silva, ed., *O imperio luso-brasileiro 1750–1822* (Lisbon: Estampa, 1986), (Nova História da Expansão Portuguesa, vol. VIII), under the titles, "A produção económica," pp. 85–153, and "A circulação, as finanças e as flutuações económicas," pp. 155–214.

[32] Joaquim Romero Magalhães: *O Algarve económico, 1600–1773* (Lisbon: Estampa, 1993) (Histórias de Portugal 3); Fernando de Sousa and Jorge Fernandes Alves: *Alto Minho: população e economia nos finais de setecentos* (Lisbon: Presença, 1997).

is especially detailed and gives an impressive account of the multi-faceted interactions both within that region and with its neighbouring regions.

Most studies are dedicated to the study of Lisbon, and the city has been researched from various perspectives. For instance, the economic study of the city has ranged from detailed analysis of inventories to broader overviews of Lisbon's function as a financial centre.[33] This concentration on Lisbon is hardly surprising, but a more focused analysis of ports like Setúbal or Faro could be beneficial to the evaluation of Portugal's role in international commerce, since these were the transshipment ports from the Mediterranean to the North and Baltic Seas. For example, Spanish sources seem to suggest that Faro served as a substitute port for Cadiz during international conflicts, yet there is little research to prove this.[34]

The Portuguese Economy

There are a variety of articles on the Portuguese economy in general, as well as on particular commodities. Port wine is one example.[35] The export of port wine was of great importance for the Portuguese export trade, especially with England. Recent research emphasises the nexus between the trade in port wine and its production and marketing, chiefly in the Douro Valley.

Studies of other Portuguese products and industries cannot be presented in great detail here. For more information on industries and

[33] Cfr. Nuno Luís Madureira, *Inventários: aspectos do consumo e da vida material em Lisboa nos finais do Antiguo Regime* (Lisbon: unpublished MA thesis, Faculty of Humanities, ISCTE, 1989); Nuno Luís Madureira, "Crédito e mercados financeiros em Lisboa" in *Ler História* 26 (1994), pp. 21–43; Jorge Miguel Pedreira, "Tratos e contratos: actividades, interesses e orientações dos investimentos dos negociantes da praça de Lisboa, 1755–1822," *Análise Social* 31 (1996), pp. 355–79; Maria Manuela Rocha, "Actividade crediticia em Lisboa, 1770–1830," *Análise Social* 31 (1996), pp. 579–98.

[34] Cfr. the data for exports from Bilbao to international ports in Aingeru Zabala Uriarte, *Mundo urbano y actividad mercantil, Bilbao 1700–1810* (Bilbao: Biblioteca de Historia del Pueblo Vasco, 1994), pp. 679–768.

[35] For late 18th century, see Norman R. Bennett, "The Golden Age of the Port Wine System, 1781–1807" *International History Review* 12 (1990), pp. 221–48, which is based on the records of the British firm of Offley Forrester; see also by the same author "The Vignerons of the Douro and the Peninsular War" *Journal of European Economic History* 21 (1992), pp. 7–30; Bennett has also published a number of articles on the 19th century port wine trade; cfr. also Academia Portuguesa da História, ed., *O vinho na história portuguesa: séculos XIII–XIX* (Oporto: F.E.A.A., 1983).

products other than wine, the interested reader should refer to the existing overviews of the 18th century production of manufactured goods and trading practices. These works assert that groups of industries such as paper, glass, textiles, and iron were only loosely linked to European commercial activities. These goods were mainly exported to Brazil, while, in contrast, European regions imported products like oil, fruits, or salt. An earlier, but still pertinent, account of Portuguese exports is a work by Jorge Borges de Macedo, who used England as a point of reference for his interpretation of Portuguese economic history.[36] There is also a notable doctoral thesis written by Nuno Luis Madureira in 1997 that deals with these issues.[37] His outstanding analysis incorporates aspects of legalisation, accumulation of capital, industrial sectors, and regional viewpoints. In a similar study, Jorge Miguel Viana Pedreira includes the impact of trade with late colonial Brazil on the Portuguese economy.[38] These two works cover all aspects of the state of current research while also giving a reasoned analysis of the most important industrial sectors in Portugal.

The Gold Cycle

Gold from Brazil flowed to Portugal in abundant quantities in the first half of the 18th century, and has been well studied by historians since then. Brazilian gold was used to plug the trade deficit with England and other European countries, leaving very little in Portugal itself. The gold not only helped compensate for the Portuguese trade deficit, but also created a regional affluence in Minas Gerais, Brazil.[39]

Fortunately for historians, the gold fleets are well documented. In the study of the Brazilian gold boom, the quantitative approach used by Mauro and Godinho for the 16th and 17th century has remained in use among historians. One of the earlier articles on the topic was

[36] Jorge Borges de Macedo, *Problemas de história da industria portuguesa no século XVIII*, (Lisbon: Associação Industrial Portuguese, 1963) (2d edition, Lisbon 1982); in particular the maps and the appendix with sources are highly informative.

[37] Nuno Luís Madureira, *Mercado e privilégios: a indústria portuguesa entre 1750 e 1834*, (Lisbon: Estampa, 1997) (Histórias de Portugal 34).

[38] Jorge Miguel Viana Pedreira, *Estrutura industrial e mercado colonial Portugal e Brasil, 1780–1830* (Lisbon: Difel, 1994).

[39] Cfr. Charles R. Boxer: *The Golden Age of Brazil, 1695–1750: Growing Pains of a Colonial Society* (London: University of California Press, 1962).

Production of Gold in Brazil During the Eighteenth Century

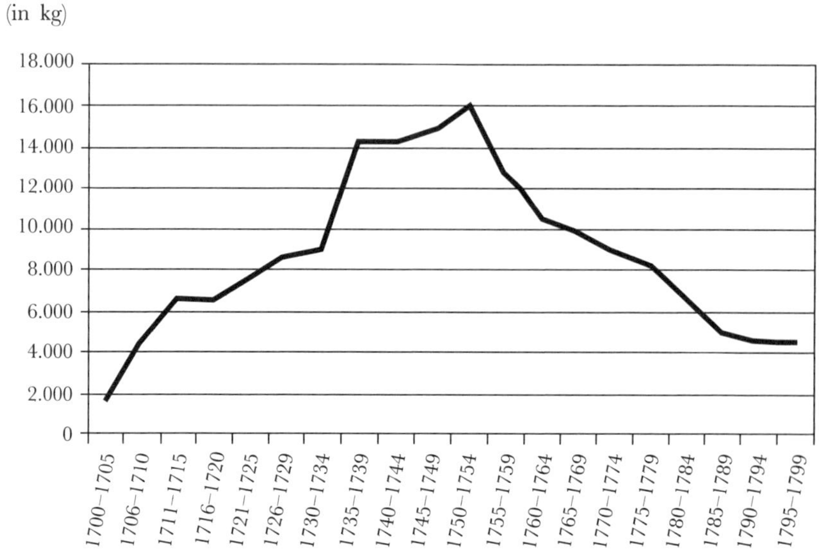

Source: Virgilio Noya Pinto, *O ouro brasileiro e o comércio anglo-português. Uma contribuição aos estudos da economia atlântica no século XVIII.* (São Paulo: Companhia Editora Nacional, 1979), p. 114.

written by Godinho, reflecting on the transition from the cycle of sugar to the cycle of gold.[40] It was not long after Godinho's seminal article that the interrelation between gold from the Portuguese colonies and imports of English manufactured goods became a focal point in research.[41]

One of the most detailed studies about Brazilian gold is by Virgílio Noya Pinto and, although it dates from the 1970s, it still continues to serve as a point of reference for scholars interested in the topic.[42]

---

[40] Vitorino Magalhães Godinho, "Le Portugal, les flottes de sucre et les flottes de l'or, 1670–1770" *Annales* 2 (1950), pp. 184–97, also published in Portuguese: "Portugal, as frotas do açucar e as frotas de ouro, 1670–1770" *Revista de História* 15 (1953), pp. 69–88.

[41] Charles R. Boxer, "Brazilian Gold and British Traders in the First Half of the Eighteenth Century" *Hispanic American Historical Review* 49 (1969), pp. 454–72; see also A. J. R. Russell-Wood, "As frotas de ouro do Brasil, 1710–1750" *Estudos econômicos* 13 (1983), pp. 701–17.

[42] Virgilio Noya Pinto, *O ouro brasileiro e o comércio anglo-português: Uma contribuição aos estudos da economia atlântica no século XVIII*, (São Paulo: Companhia Editora Nacional, 1979).

This is due not only to the data series it contains but also to the broad-based approach it takes, which allows for the analysis to incorporate goods other than gold. Moreover, Noya Pinto's work examines the commercial flows between Brazil, Portugal, and England. It is written from a "Brazilian" perspective, which, in effect, means that its argument starts—after a short introduction to Portugal's diplomatic and economic situation—with a substantial overview of gold mining in various regions of Brazil. It then looks at diverse Brazilian products like sugar, tobacco, dyewood, hides, and diamonds before turning its attention toward the Atlantic trade. To a large extent, Noya Pinto's monograph succeeds in combining the analysis of different commercial streams over an extended period of time. This work proves the previously held assumptions that gold was the most traded material and that England was the main trading partner. These ties between Portugal and England have been examined from many perspectives by a multitude of scholars, but, unfortunately, at the price of neglecting other trading partners.[43]

Pombal and His Political Economy

For the past few decades, historians have been investigating the relationship between politics and the economy. While this field of endeavour is not particularly new to the historiography of Portugal, there are still a number of unanswered questions that allow for present-day scholars to continue working in this area. The Age of Enlightenment is receiving particular attention, since it was during this time that economics began to be converted into an autonomous science. Moreover, it was during this period that the findings of this new science were implemented by politicians to directly intervene in economic affairs.[44]

The Marquês de Pombal was heavily involved in this sort of application of economic theory to political policy. In Spain, a number of enlightened contemporaries of Pombal's such as Campomanes, Aranda, and Jovellanos are given credit for the reform process. However,

[43] From the plentiful literature on Anglo-Portuguese relations, see H. E. S. Fisher, *The Portugal Trade: A Study of Anglo-Portuguese Commerce, 1700–1770* (London: Methuen, 1971).

[44] Cfr. José Luís Cardoso: *O pensamento económico em Portugal nos finais do século XVIII, 1780–1808* (Lisbon: Estampa, 1989).

Portuguese historiography tends to emphasise Pombal alone. The foundation of colonial companies under the Pombalian regime has been one focal point upon which historians have concentrated in an attempt to evaluate the connection between political action and economic theory.[45] Pombal's impact on the economy in Portugal has also been investigated in depth. Nevertheless, it is not easy to define either to what degree he influenced economic affairs in Portugal, or to state his motivations for his reform programme.[46] Certainly the central question of how far politics should and could control economic affairs remains under discussion by historians today. Thus, the characterisation of Pombal as a "paradox" still seems to be the most fitting description of the man and his legacy.[47]

Conclusion: Links Between Merchants and Merchandise

The final aspect we want to discuss is the historiography of the merchant elite and their commercial networks. Although European economic history initially concentrated on the quantities of merchandise being moved about, it has eventually evolved to include a social component. Merchant companies, merchant families, and merchant groups, mostly classified by their "nationality," became one of the most significant themes in European historiography. Because of their great economic importance, English merchants living in Portugal feature strongly in research on merchant groups in general in Portugal.[48]

---

[45] Cfr. Manuel Nunes Dias, "Os acionistas e o capital social da Companhia do Grão Pará e Maranhão Os dois momentos: o da fundação (1755–1758) e o da véspera da extinção (1776)" *Caravelle* 11 (1968), pp. 29–52; Manuel Nunes Dias, *Fomento e mercantilismo: A Companhia Geral do Grão-Pará e Maranhão* (Belém: Universidad Federal do Pará, 1970); António Carreira, *As companhias pombalinas de Grão Pará e Maranhão e Pernambuco Paraíba*, 2d ed. (Lisbon: Presença, 1982).

[46] Cfr. Madureira, Mercado (see note 38); Jorge Borges de Macedo, *A situação económica no tempo de Pombal, Alguns aspectos.* (Porto: Moraes, 1951) (3d ed. Lisbon 1989); José Viriato Capela, *Política, administração, economia e finanças públicas portuguesas, 1750–1820* (Braga: Universidad do Minho, 1993); L. M. E. Shaw, "The Marquês de Pombal (1699–1782): How He Broke Britain's Commercial Ascendancy in Portugal," *Journal of European Economic History* 27 (1998), pp. 537–54; for the post-pombalian era see the collected articles in Albert Silbert, *Do Portugal de Antiguo Regime ao Portugal oitocentista.* 3d ed. (Lisbon: Horizonte, 1981).

[47] Kenneth R. Maxwell, *Pombal, Paradox of the Enlightenment* (Cambridge: Cambridge University Press, 1995).

[48] Cfr. Shaw, *Anglo-Portuguese Alliance* (see note 25); Shaw proves that the English-Portuguese alliance already began in 1654 with an official contract when Portugal

More recently, investigations about other merchant groups have been produced, which illustrate the high degree of specialisation, commercial knowledge, and international linkages of these mercantile firms.[49]

Within this context of social and economic history, we want to draw attention to a series of works which can be of great significance for the concept of an "Iberian Atlantic" discussed at the beginning of this paper. As we pointed out, the underlying idea of the "Iberian Atlantic" is of a network in the Central and South Atlantic, with the Iberian Peninsula as the major hub. Future investigations into the social and economic history of this region will depend on detailed studies of traders in the Atlantic and their linkages to Portugal and Spain. A number of works have recently been dedicated to merchant elites in the Portuguese colonial empire.[50] There are, however, also studies about Portuguese merchants outside the Portuguese territories.[51] If this sort of data were to be coalesced, scholars might be able to verify or falsify claims that an Iberian Atlantic network did or did not exist.

Finally, to complete the Iberian perspective, a similar uniting of our knowledge about Spanish merchants is required. And, of course,

was seeking support shortly after the re-emancipation from Spain. Another interesting point is how the Inquisition intervened in economic politics; in this context, see also Shaw, "The Inquisition and the Portuguese Economy" *Journal of European Economic History* 18 (1989), pp. 415–31.

[49] See, for example, William Michael Donovan, *Commercial Enterprise and Luso-Brazilian Society During the Brazilian Gold Rush: The Mercantile House of Francisco Pinheiro and the Lisbon to Brazil Trade, 1695–1750* (Baltimore: Johns Hopkin University Press, 1991); Miriam Halpern Pereira, "Négociants, fabricants et institutions économiques au Portugal au debut de XIXe siècle" *Revue du Nord* 76 (1994), pp. 753–60; for the French community specialised in the books trade in Lisbon, see Francisco da Gama Caeiro, "Livros e livreiros franceses em Lisbao, nos fins de setecentos e no promeiro quartel do século XIX," *Anais da Academia Portuguesa da História* 26 (1980), pp. 299–327.

[50] See Elizabeth Anne Kuznesof, "The Role of the Merchants in the Economic Development of São Paulo, 1765–1850" *Hispanic American Historical Review* 60 (1980), pp. 571–92; Sanjay Subrahmanyam, "Staying on: The Portuguese of Southern Coromandel in the Late Seventeenth Century" *Indian Economic and Social History Review* 22 (1985), pp. 445–63.

[51] Jonathan I. Israel, "An Amsterdam Jewish Merchant of the Golden Age: Jeronimo Nunes da Costa (1620–1697), Agent of Portugal in the Dutch Republic," *Studia Rosenthaliana* 18 (1984), pp. 21–40; Rose-Blanche Escoupérié, "Sur quelques 'marchands portugais' etablis a Toulouse a la fin du XVIIe siècle" *Annales du Midi* 106 (1994), pp. 57–71; Nikolaus Böttcher, *Aufstieg und Fall eines atlantischen Handelsimperiums: Portugiesische Kaufleute und Sklavenhändler in Cartagena de Indias von 1580 bis zur Mitte des 17,* Jahrhunderts. (Frankfurt/M.: 1995) (Berliner Lateinamerika-Forschungen 4).

it is of vital importance to encourage research to collect information about Portuguese-Spanish commerce. The recent work by Christian Morrisson, Jean-Noël Barrandon, and Cécil Morrisson introduces a promising line of research since it departs from the study of the classical Brazil-Portugal-England route of gold export and import and looks instead at the influence of Brazilian gold in France.[52] Along with France and England, Spain should be a country examined by historians studying Portugal's European connections. We hope that one day we will be learning about the commercial routes between Portugal and Spain as we have already learned about Portugal and England.

In conclusion, let us say that these questions are related to the overall problem of the decline of both Iberian colonial powers. At the end of the 17th century, in the case of Portugal, Crown officers advised the king to transfer the centre of the Empire to Brazil, a proposal that was repeated several times during the 18th century.[53] Brazilian gold and Pombal's policies contributed to at least a kind of consolidation of Portugal's power during the 18th century. Spain, for its part, managed to consolidate its power thanks to the reform policies of the Bourbon dynasty. It is tempting, in light of these facts, to invert the dependency problem, and discuss the level of financial and economic dependency the remaining European colonial powers had on their own American colonies after the end of the Seven Years War. Recent evidence strongly suggests that the American colonies during the eighteenth century were far more important as political actors, despite their colonial status, than historiography has heretofore realised.

[52] Christian Morrisson, Jean-Noël Barrandon, and Cécil Morrisson, *Or du Brésil, monnaie et croissance en France au XVIIIe siècle* (Paris: Le Roy Ladurie Emmanuel, 1999) (Cahiers Ernest-Babelon 7). Michel Morineau, despite his well-founded criticism on the book, "Quodlibet: or brésilien, macroéconomie et croissance économique en France et en Angleterre au XVIIIe siècle" *Revue d'Histoire Moderne et Contemporaine* 48, 2/3 (2001), pp. 245–306, does recognise the general benefit of following the traces of Brazilian gold in France.

[53] Cfr. Kirsten Schultz, *Tropical Versailles: Empire, Monarchy, and the Portuguese Royal Court in Rio de Janeiro, 1808–1821* (New York: Routledge, 2001), "introduction."

CHAPTER EIGHT

THE DUTCH AND THE ATLANTIC CHALLENGE, 1600–1800

Pieter C. Emmer

How to profit from the Atlantic?

"Globalisation" is a term coined by journalists in order to impress people who don't know history. In spite of the fact that the term has no well-defined meaning, it is interesting to note that its impact on public opinion differs widely. In the Netherlands, "globalisation" is seen as a challenge providing the economy with new opportunities for export. In Germany, on the other hand, the term is used as a straw man by some members of the political elite in order to urge their voters to rally behind such long-fought-for achievements as the social welfare state and the 36 hour work-week. In reality, however, "globalisation" impacts only on a marginal section of most Western economies. The largest share of the GDP of most countries is either produced and consumed at home, or else generated by trading with countries nearby. The Dutch economy is a case in point, in spite of the fact that, in comparison with other developed countries, the percentage of its GDP generated by foreign trade is extremely high. Nevertheless, the Dutch could relinquish their trade with most countries in Africa and Asia if they increased their trade with neighbouring Germany by only 5%.

Did the situation differ when the voyages of discovery were undertaken? If anything, the world outside of Europe should have been even less important for Europe itself than it is today since the strong economies of Japan, the United States, Canada, and the oil-rich countries were still in the making. Between 1500 and 1800 most opportunities for economic growth for Europeans were situated right on their own doorsteps within their own continent—and only in certain parts, at that—and not overseas. Why, then, did Europe expand overseas so early and so rapidly, in spite of the exorbitantly high opportunity costs?

The high opportunity costs explain why European conquest, penetration, and trade remained marginal in Asia and Africa. In contacting these continents, Europeans concentrated on those goods and services that they could not produce at home, and the range of these was rather small. The most obvious and most unique product was slaves, for whom there existed no alternative in Europe.[1] Yet is seems very doubtful that any European power would have actually been willing to occupy parts of Africa in order to obtain slaves had they not been offered for sale by the Africans themselves. It is more likely that, in such a situation, Europe would have offered higher inducements to its own migrant labourers—of whom there were large numbers—to move overseas. Similar arguments can be developed concerning the goods imported from Africa and Asia. None of these goods were vital to the development of the economy, and none influenced the overall social welfare of Europe significantly.

In fact, it is rather puzzling why Europe was so keen on buying textiles in Asia. Most of these were made from cotton and silk and, had the Asians not offered such textiles for sale, Europe could have made—and indeed did make—perfectly acceptable alternative types of cloth. The answer must be that the simple laws of demand and supply had little to do with it. We cannot assume that one type of labour can easily replace another, and this also applies to textiles. When buying slaves in Africa, Europe had to pay the price for the self-imposed and virtually insurmountable barrier it had erected not to enslave its own inhabitants. In the case of textiles, Europe had to pay the price for the high barrier caused by the eclectic taste of its elites. Even today, textiles from elsewhere frequently seem to be at a premium in comparison with perfectly good, homemade textiles.

In view of these considerations, the trade with Africa and Asia between 1500 and 1800 might seem of marginal importance, as alternatives could have been made available. In any case, the trade did not warrant the large-scale occupation of parts of Africa and Asia. The Dutch East India Company (*Vereenigde Oost- Indische Compagnie* or VOC) did conquer some small enclaves in Asia such as the hinterland of Batavia on Java, parts of Ceylon, and a few of the smaller Spice Islands, but these colonising efforts remained limited. The only

[1] David Eltis, *The Rise of African Slavery in the Americas* (Cambridge: Cambridge University Press, 2000), pp. 57–84.

exception to this rule was the Dutch settlement colony at the Cape of Good Hope, and there is little doubt about the fact that large sections of the Cape settlement were a drain on the company's finances; i.e., they had been occupied without taking into account the opportunity costs. Time and again, the VOC tried to restrict the growth of the Cape colony, as the company had only initially envisioned it serving as a rest station for its ships *en route* to and from Batavia. Sailors who had fallen sick sometimes remained in the colony both on outward as well as inward voyages. In addition, the colony received some Huguenot settlers, though half the population consisted of Asian slaves, in spite of the company's decision not to allow slaves to travel with their masters from Batavia to the Cape. Slaves, the company believed, should be used in the more productive Asian trade centres, and sailors were in short supply on the company's ships.

For the VOC, the economic value of the Cape was limited. It produced foodstuffs for the ships, and exported some wine to Europe, which was not a unique product, while the remainder of the economy of the Cape was geared to subsistence production. Autochthonous demographic growth caused the number of settlers to increase rapidly, which, in turn, increased the need to occupy more and more land. The result was repeated warfare with the original inhabitants, the Khoi and San. Much to the chagrin of its directors, the VOC had to spend increasing amounts of money in defending its only de facto settlement colony. Had the company had its way, the Cape would have remained a small-scale rest and replenishment station with a few hundred settlers and not a growing colony with about 10,000 inhabitants around 1800 when the British took over.[2]

What applied to the Red Sea, the Indian Ocean, the Chinese Sea, and the Pacific, also applied to the European expansion in the Atlantic. Why should this ocean be more attractive to European traders, settlers, and investors than their own continent? The Atlantic offered few goods that could not have been obtained in Europe. The exceptions were precious metals, sugar, coffee, and tobacco. Because of their demographic decline, and because of their lack of know-how,

[2] Robert Ross, *A Concise History of South Africa* (Cambridge: Cambridge University Press, 1999), pp. 21–23 and J. van Goor, *De Nederlandse koloniën. Geschiedenis van de Nederlandse expansie, 1600–1975* (Den Haag: SDU, 1994), pp. 114–17.

the indigenous populations in the New World were not willing or able to offer most of these products for sale to the Europeans. This could have been a reason to leave the New World alone, as the barrier to profiting from the Atlantic was high: it involved not only trade, but also production. In fact, it seemed likely that the most promising production would have to take place in the tropics, raising the barriers even higher. Indeed, that is what happened with European penetration in Africa until the beginning of the so-called scramble in the 19th century.

Why were Spain and Portugal the first nations to take on the Atlantic challenge? Why did Iberian traders prefer to send ships across the Atlantic rather than to other parts of Europe, and why did the Spanish and Portuguese settlers move to the New World rather than to another part of the Old? Or to put it in economic terms: Why were the opportunity costs for the additional activities in Europe so high for the Iberians?

As far as trade was concerned, the answer must have been competition. There was room for Spanish and Portuguese expansion both in the Mediterranean as well as in coastal shipping to Northwestern Europe; but first Italian—and later, English and Dutch—shipping increased, not the shipping of the two Iberian nations. This means that sending ships to South America allowed the Portuguese and the Spanish to escape confrontation with their more efficient competitors in Europe. No wonder that, right from the beginning, shipping and trade with the Spanish and Portuguese colonies were protected against foreign competition. Yet, the commercial elite in both countries was unable to meet even this challenge of providing sufficient shipping. And, in the first decades of transatlantic trade, ships from other countries were already involved in the trade to the most rapidly expanding regions of Spanish and Portuguese America. Interloping was rampant in South America, and this practice was to continue through the following centuries.

As far as migration was concerned, it seems likely that, for the Spanish and, above all, the Portuguese, the barrier against settling in the New World was, indeed, lower than against migrating to other parts of Europe. The most ready outlet for the Portuguese, at least for the male part of the population, was becoming a sailor and, as we have noted above, the Portuguese fleet employed in European waters was not large. Alternatively, the Portuguese could have migrated to France or Italy, but, at the time, those countries themselves were sending migrants to other parts of Europe. Of course, Portuguese migrants could go to Spain as did so many migrants from France during the *Ancien Régime*, and that is what, in fact, happened. Yet, in view of the large number of Portuguese emigrants in Brazil, it seems strange that between 1500 and 1800 so few Portuguese migrated to other parts of Europe, with the exception of the Portuguese Jews. Either the Portuguese government restricted migration to destinations other than Brazil, or the migrants themselves were afraid to compete in the European labour markets.

The migration from Spain seems a more complex phenomenon, as Spain was sending migrants to its American colonies at the same time she was welcoming immigrants from other parts of Europe. This seems to suggest that either these two groups had different skills and could not be substituted for one another, or else there existed a geographical divide in Spain—and that this divide somehow made it easier for migrants in one region of Spain to migrate overseas than to move within Spain itself. Another possibility is that migration from Spain to the New World was not based on economic principles, but on government intervention, and that some groups of migrants had no choice but to migrate to South America.

As far as the economic activities in the Spanish and Portuguese colonies were concerned, only a relatively small percentage of these seemed to have yielded more than they would have had they been performed in Europe itself. The notable exceptions were the mining activities and the production of sugar, coffee, and other tropical cash crops. However, in order to obtain these products, the colonisation of both Spanish and Portuguese America could have been far less extensive and far less expensive than it turned out to be. That suggests that the major part of the Iberian expansion overseas was not based on a careful calculation of the opportunity costs, but rather on noneconomic considerations such as power politics, internal religious or civil strife, and missionary activities. The result of three centuries of Iberian colonisation seems to prove this point. Spain and Portugal were the first nations to respond to the Atlantic challenge, as they belonged to the most powerful countries in Europe. Around 1800, however, they both had lost that position and were numbered among the less developed countries in Europe.

How was the Atlantic challenge met by the other expanding nations of Europe: the Dutch, the French, and the English? Why did they decide to start trading with and migrating to Africa and the New

World rather than confine these activities to Europe? As far as trade was concerned, the situation for these newcomers in the Atlantic was certainly different from that of the two old ones. During the 17th century, the English, French, and Dutch were mainly active within Europe, and only in the 18th century did Britain's Atlantic trade surpass its European commercial activities. In 1700, 67% of British imports came from Europe and 23% from North America, the Caribbean, Africa, and the East Indies. By 1750, these percentages were 55% and 45% respectively, and in the years just before 1800, 42% and 58%. In absolute numbers, the value of all overseas trade had quadrupled: from nearly six million pounds in 1700 to nearly eight million pounds in 1750 and to nearly 24 million pounds during the last years of the 18th century.[3] The story of British exports looks very similar: in 1700, 85% of these exports went to Europe; in 1750, 77%; and in 1800, 30%. The value of British exports increased from 4.5 million pounds in 1700 to 18 million pounds around 1800. These figures indicate that the shift toward the Atlantic took place between 1750 and 1800, and that Britain's most dynamic Atlantic trading partners were the West Indies and North America, whose share in the export of British domestically-made products rose from 11% in 1700 to a whopping 56% just before 1800.

The Dutch remained much more oriented toward trade within Europe, in spite of some shift toward the Atlantic during the second half of the 18th century. Yet between 1600 and 1800, the European trade remained by far the dominant one: of the 100 ships leaving Dutch ports, about 80 had destinations in Europe and the Mediterranean, five sailed to Asia, and 15 had Atlantic destinations. In view of that, it seems reasonable to assume that Dutch shipping firms would not send their ships to Africa and to the New World had they earned less with these activities than with trading within Europe.

As far as trade in the Atlantic is concerned, there are two additional remarks to be made. The first concerns the slave trade. The number of slaves brought to the New World was partially inflated because of government subsidies. Toward the end the 18th century, the French slave trade was, in part, subsidised in order to secure

[3] Kenneth Morgan, *Slavery, Atlantic Trade and the British Economy, 1600–1800* (Cambridge: Cambridge University Press, 2000), p. 19 (table).

the continuation of the trade. In the Dutch case, the slave trade had to be exempted from the usual taxes on trading in the Atlantic and on the purchase of slaves.

Second, the profits made in the Atlantic trade and in shipping would certainly have been lower if there had been free competition. That free competition was severely limited because most of the trade and shipping connected with the plantations had exclusive links with a limited number of merchant firms in the mother country. These firms provided the planters with credit and, in return, the planter was forced to ship and market his products via that particular firm. In addition to these organisational limitations were the mercantile restrictions that were similar to the aforementioned restrictions placed by both the Spanish and Portuguese crowns that severely restricted international competition. Only Dutch ships were allowed to carry produce from the Dutch colonies in the Atlantic, and the same rules applied to the British and French colonies. Allowances were made for the fact that, in times of war, the shipping firms of the French and the Dutch could not always provide sufficient services, and special rules applied to British ships that originated in North America and provided the French and Dutch West Indies with foodstuffs. But trade and shipping in the Atlantic is a long saga made up of attempts to evade and restrict the market.

All of this contributed to the fact that Atlantic shipping was more voluminous than it would have been if these restrictions and subsidies had not existed. Yet, the British, the French, and the Dutch did not operate an exclusively Atlantic fleet like the Spanish and the Portuguese did, and they only sailed and traded in the Atlantic when these activities yielded more in the long run than did similar activities elsewhere.

As far as migration goes, the same situation applies. Britain again stands out as the major contributor to transatlantic migration both in absolute as well as relative terms. A large portion of the Dutch and French on the other side of the Atlantic were not really settlers, but migrants with the clear goal of eventually returning home. That raises the question of why the barrier to transatlantic migration was lower in Britain than in France, the Netherlands, and Spain and on a par with that of Portugal. Even if we allow for the fact that some groups of migrants such as prisoners of war, convicts, and religious refugees did not have a choice of destinations, we are faced with about one million migrants who left the British Isles to take up the Atlantic challenge rather than moving to some other destination on the European continent. In part, the geographical location of Britain must have played a role, as it was the only European region from which any migrant needed to make a sea voyage wherever he or she went. On the other hand, however, the relatively large and continuous migration of the English, the Scots, and the Irish to the New World was unique. Does that mean that of all the Atlantic powers, only Portugal and the United Kingdom made their Atlantic colonies attractive to migrants? Or were the populations of Portugal and England, Scotland, and Ireland more mobile to begin with, and is the transatlantic migration a spin-off of wide-scale internal migration?[4]

In comparison with Britain, Portugal, Spain, France, and the Netherlands seemed to have been the Atlantic losers. Britain is the only country to which the Atlantic made a difference in both the 18th and 19th centuries. In order to explain the divergence between the Atlantic powers in Europe, a comparison between Britain and the Netherlands seems most fruitful because the Atlantic trade of both countries developed so differently during the 18th century—in spite of the fact that, originally, both nations responded to the Atlantic challenge in similar ways as they had responded in Asia. Yet, toward the end of the 18th century, the Atlantic achievements of the Dutch and the British started to reveal a "big divide" and, after 1750, Britain's quantum leap in exports to the Caribbean and North America was unique. Why was this so?

The Dutch and British Economies at Home

The divergence of the Dutch and British experience in the Atlantic began at home. Economic growth in the Netherlands peaked between 1580 and 1620. After 1670 a period of stagnation set in lasting for about two centuries. This means that during the 18th century, the Netherlands had a stagnating economy at home when economic

[4] Nicolas Canny, "English Migration into and across the Atlantic during the Seventeenth and Eighteenth Centuries," T. C. Smout, N. C. Landsman, and T. M. Devine, "Scottish Emigration in the Seventeenth and Eighteenth Centuries," L. M. Cullen, "The Irish Diaspora of the Seventeenth and Eighteenth Centuries" and Nicolas Canny, "In Search of a Better Home? European Overseas Migration, 1500–1800" in Nicolas Canny ed., *Europeans on the Move; Studies on European Migration, 1500–1800* (Oxford: Oxford University Press, 1994), pp. 39–113 and pp. 263–83.

growth in the Atlantic increased dramatically. No wonder Adam Smith, writing in 1776, was of the opinion that the Netherlands had "acquired the full compliment of riches which the nature of its soils and climate and its situation with respect to other countries, allowed it to acquire." The Netherlands had accumulated so much capital that profits were driven close to zero, and the Dutch economy could advance no further.[5]

Let there be no misunderstanding: the achievements of the early and short-lived period of growth were impressive, even by modern standards. It was the first country to break the trend of lower real wages caused by rising populations and rising prices. After 1580 a widening difference between the real wages in the Netherlands and England developed which lasted until the middle of the 18th century. During the first half century after 1575, when the growth spurt set in, the nominal wage for unskilled labour increased from 0.28 to 0.73 guilders. As prices rose much more slowly, the increase in real wages was at least 50%! No wonder the Netherlands was flooded with migrant labour from abroad. There was little danger that these migrant labourers would bring down wages since their numbers were more than matched by the rapidly rising demand for labour—in spite of the opinion of Karl Marx that the Dutch Republic was the "model capitalist nation of the 17th century" and, thus, that, "by 1648 the people of Holland [were] more overworked, poorer, and more brutally oppressed than those of all the rest of Europe put together."[6]

The economic miracle at home took place well before economic opportunities in the wider Atlantic became attractive. Until 1650 the colonisation of North America was still a very slow and cumbersome affair, and, to an even greater extent, this was also the case in the Caribbean. The sea lanes were far from secure since piracy was rampant. The most promising Atlantic venture around 1600 was gaining legal or illegal access to Spanish and Portuguese Brazil, and that was what the Dutch did and continued to do. Around 1600, all settlement and colonisation schemes were British and French, not

[5] Jan de Vries, "Dutch Economic Growth in Comparative-Historical Perspective, 1500–2000" *De Economist*, 148/4 (2000), pp. 443–67, citation Smith, p. 451.

[6] Jan Lucassen, "Mobilisation of Labour in Early Modern Europe," in Maarten Prak, ed., *Early Modern Capitalism: Economic and Social Change in Europe, 1400–1800* (London: Routledge, 2001), p. 162.

Dutch. The break came during the 1620s when the Dutch tried to conquer part of Portuguese Brazil. This *volte-face* in Dutch Atlantic policies had disastrous consequences. Not only did the conquest and subsequent occupation of Northeastern Brazil deplete the coffers of the Dutch West India Company, but it also destroyed the illegal trade connections with the producers of sugar and coffee in Portuguese Brazil. Finally, in 1667, with the conquest of a major plantation colony in the Caribbean—Suriname—the Dutch begin to respond to the Atlantic challenge in ways similar to that of the other European nations.

However, the Dutch in the Atlantic remained "underprivileged" as none of its possessions ever produced the amounts of sugar, coffee, and precious metals that Spanish and Portuguese South America did, nor they experience the dramatic upswing of sugar production toward the end of the 18th century that British Guiana and Trinidad or French Saint-Domingue all had. As was the case in France after the loss of Canada and Louisiana, the Netherlands did not command a growing market in any of the settlement colonies.

After the fourth Anglo-Dutch War (1780–84), the differences between the Dutch and the British economy once again became evident when British trade in the Atlantic, and the slave trade in particular, grew more rapidly than did any other sector of foreign trade, while Dutch trade in the Atlantic stagnated, and the Dutch slave trade declined. The GDP per capita in the Netherlands peaked around 1650 and declined somewhat during the following two hundred years, while in the United Kingdom the GDP per capita was much lower than that of the Netherlands between 1500 and 1700, but almost doubled during the period 1700–1820. The same applied to the relative Dutch and British shares in European shipping tonnage. The Dutch share is estimated to have been 40% in 1650 and 12% in 1780; the British shares were respectively 12% and 26%.[7] On the surface, it seems as if the foreign trade of both countries moved in the same direction—i.e., away from Europe and toward the non-European world. However, the reasons for this shift were very different.

[7] Jan Luiten van Zanden, "Early Modern Economic Growth. A Survey of the European Economy, 1500–1800," in Maarten Prak ed., *Early Modern Capitalism: Economic and Social Change in Europe, 1400–1800* (London: Routledge, 2001), GDP p. 76 (table 4.3) and shipping tonnage: p. 82 (table 4.4).

In the case of the United Kingdom, the reorientation was caused by the Industrial Revolution, which encouraged the exportation of manufactured goods in exchange for the importation of foodstuffs and raw materials. The "Agricultural Revolution" in the United Kingdom allowed the country to double its population during the 18th century. The Netherlands, on the other hand, experienced a very slow increase in its population and did not industrialise until the second half of the 19th century. The increasing share of colonial products in Dutch trade was not a reflection of a new and innovative home economy but, rather, the opposite. It indicated that the Dutch had become less competitive in intra-European trade and that they had to retreat to an area where the competition was less fierce—i.e., by importing and exporting sugar, coffee, and cotton from their own West Indian colonies. Yet the Dutch share in the total volume of the trade in plantation crops declined. The value added in this trade was limited, and the colonial products were not paid for by new Dutch manufactures but, rather, by goods partly imported from Asia, and by the provision of services such as transportation and insurance. The Dutch had no equivalent to the rapidly increasing markets in the West Indies and North America.

Between 1750 and 1800, North America tripled their imports of British goods and the export of British domestic products to the West Indies increased five times during these 50 years. This seems to suggest that the mechanisation of British industry did help to increase Atlantic trade, as only merchants from Britain could offer an array of goods to satisfy the increasing purchasing power of the consumers in the British Atlantic. Textiles are a case in point because only Britain could provide textiles that were imported from India and from the European continent, as well as those made at home both in the traditional way and by mechanised mills. This unique supply survived the end of mercantilism in North America. "Given the superiority and cheapness of British articles over those manufactured by the Dutch and the French, it is not surprising that some American merchants maintained contacts with British firms during the War of Independence and that British manufactured products were so much in demand in the USA."[8]

Two products suffice to prove this point: sugar and cotton. During the course of the 18th century, the consumption of sugar in Britain

[8] Morgan, *Slavery, Atlantic Trade and the British Economy*, p. 66.

per head of the population was much higher and more rapidly increasing than anywhere on the European continent, indicating a link with the process of industrialisation.[9] In the Netherlands, the consumption of sugar per head of the population remained relatively low. Most refined sugar was exported. The production of, and the trade in, cotton is another indicator of economic modernisation. To a disproportionate extent, the cultivation of cotton in Suriname was in the hands of British planters. Cotton boomed during the British occupation of the colony (1798–1816), suggesting that this increase was a response to innovation in the British rather than in the Dutch economy because the cotton mills in the Netherlands had moved away from the cities and were not expanding. The rapidly rising quantities of imported West Indian cotton for export and of sugar for home consumption were indicators of Britain's economic progress. By the same token the absence of increased sugar consumption at home and of increased exports of cotton textiles produced in the Netherlands is indicative of the stagnation of the Dutch economy.[10]

The Volume and Impact of the Atlantic on the Dutch Economy

There have been a few attempts at calculating the volume of the Dutch share in the trade between Europe and the non-European world. Niels Steensgaard has suggested that the total value of all foreign

[9] D. Richardson, "The Slave Trade, Sugar, and British Economic Growth, 1748–1776," *Journal of Interdisciplinary History*, vol. 17 (1987), pp. 739–769.

[10] Jan de Vries and Ad van der Woude, *The First Modern Economy: Success, Failure, and Perseverance of the Dutch Economy, 1500–1815* (Cambridge: Cambridge University Press, 1997), pp. 490–504, 385–389 (sugar), and Stanley. L. Engerman, "Mercantilism and Overseas Trade, 1700–1800" in Roderick Floud and Donald McCloskey, eds., *The Economic History of Britain since 1700* (Cambridge: Cambridge University Press, 1994, 2d ed.), pp. 187–94. The declining Dutch share in the trade in sugar during the 18th century is mentioned in Gérard Le Bouëdec, *Activités maritimes et sociétés littorals de l'Europe atlantique, 1690–1790* (Paris: Armand Colin, 1997), pp. 131–41. A discussion comparing the rise of sugar consumption and industrialisation in Kenneth Pomeranz, *The Great Divergence: Europe, China, and the Making of the Modern World Economy* (Princeton: Princeton University Press, 2000) pp. 218, 274–75. The production and exportation of Suriname cotton is discussed in Alex van Stipriaan, *Surinaams contrast. Roofbouw en overleven in een Caraïbische plantagekolonie, 1750–1863* (Leiden: KITLV, 1993), pp. 141, 201. These Dutch cotton exports show up as imports into Britain in Seymour Drescher, *Econocide: British Slavery in the Era of Abolition* (Pittsburgh: University of Pittsburgh Press, 1977), p. 57 (table 12).

imports into the Netherlands around the middle of the 18th century amounted to 150 million guilders, of which 20–25% came from non-European trade. No allowance had been made for the sale, re-export and distribution from, to and via the Netherlands of colonial imports and exports from and to the neighbouring countries. For Britain around 1750, Steensgaard calculates the share of the non-European trade as a percentage of all trade at about 50%—twice as much as for the Netherlands.[11]

A second difference between the Dutch and British trade patterns which Steengaard's statistics bring to light is the fact that within British colonial trade the importance of America versus Asia can be set at 3:1, while that ratio is roughly 1:6 in the Dutch case. However, recently W. W. Klooster has pointed out that the volume of the mainly illegal Dutch trade with Spanish America has always been undervalued. In the existing literature, the export of cash crops from the Dutch plantations in the Caribbean supposedly constituted the lion's share of all Dutch Atlantic trade. Klooster's revisions suggest a 500% increase in the gross turnover of the Dutch Atlantic trade, increasing its value to about 10 million guilders. This means that the share of the total non-European trade to and from the Netherlands would come to 30–35% of the total Dutch trade and that the ratio between the American and Asian trades of the Netherlands can be set at 1:2 rather than at 1:6. And in 2003, Victor Enthoven suggested that the Dutch trade in the Atlantic might have been more important than the Dutch trade to Asia.[12]

De Vries and Van der Woude have recently recalculated a contemporary estimate of the Dutch National Income around 1800. They estimate a National Income of around 300 million guilders and suggest that all foreign and colonial trades (inclusive of banking) brought in 50 million guilders or about 18% of the total (30 million from the trade within Europe and 20 million from the

[11] N. Steensgaard, "The Growth and Composition of the Long-Distance Trade of England and the Dutch Republic before 1750" in James D. Tracy ed., *The Rise of Merchant Empires: Long-Distance Trade in the Early Modern World, 1350–1750* (Cambridge: Cambridge University Press, 1990), pp. 102–52.

[12] W. W. Klooster, *Illicit Riches: The Dutch Trade in the Caribbean, 1648–1795*, Ph.D. thesis, Dept. of History, University of Leiden, 1995, pp. 169–99. Victor Enthoven, "An Assessment of Dutch Transatlantic Commerce, 1585–1817," in Johannes Postma and Victor Enthoven, eds., *Riches from Atlantic Commerce: Dutch Transatlantic Shipping and Trade, 1585–1817* (Leiden, Boston: Brill, 2003), pp. 385–445.

Asian and Atlantic trades).[13] The combined figures of Steensgaard and Klooster suggest that the respective values of the European and non-European trades of the Netherlands had been 130 million guilders and 30 million guilders respectively (or roughly 4:1).

These figures indicate that the Dutch economy of the *Ancien Régime* was more dependent on foreign trade than virtually any other economy in Europe—except, perhaps Portugal. The mercantile sector was certainly less important to the economy of Britain than it was to the Dutch economy. Within the mercantile sector of Britain, however, the non-European trade, and especially the Atlantic trade, was twice as important as within the mercantile sector of the Netherlands. In addition to the rapid maritime expansion across the Atlantic, British ships also increased their share in the total tonnage in European waters. Between 1766 and 1776 the number of British ships calling at Saint Petersburg doubled. The percentage of imports from continental Europe and Ireland in total British trade might have declined from 67% to 42% (imports) and from 85% to 30% (exports) during the 18th century, but the trade increased in value from nearly four million pounds in 1700 to more than 10 million pounds in 1800 in imports and more than 3.5 million pounds (1700) in exports to almost 5.5 million (1800).

These developments seem to suggest that Dutch shipping and trade had to concentrate on its own West Indian colonies in order to replace lost markets in Europe, in spite of the fact that the transatlantic trade yielded lower incomes. Britain's trade, on the other hand, not only expanded in Europe but also—and to a disproportionate degree—in the Atlantic, suggesting that the transatlantic trade was the more profitable of the two.[14]

The economic histories of the Netherlands, Portugal, Spain, and France are killing fields for anyone trying to link industrialisation to foreign trade, let alone Atlantic trade. Stanley Engerman and David Eltis have pointed out that the contribution of the slave-worked Atlantic to the British economy was modest at best, suggesting that

[13] Vries and Van der Woude, *The First Modern Economy*, pp. 704, 705.

[14] P. K. O'Brien and S. L. Engerman, "Exports and Growth of the British Economy from the Glorious Revolution to the Peace of Amiens" in Barbara L. Solow ed., *Slavery and the Rise of the Atlantic System* (Cambridge: Cambridge University Press, 1991), p. 186 (table); Engerman, "Mercantilism and Overseas Trade," pp. 191, 192; and Le Bouëdec, *Activités maritimes*, p. 151.

the Industrial Revolution could not be directly linked to the increasing economic benefits derived from New World slavery.[15] Slavery-related activities might have been more important to the economies of Spain, Portugal, and the Netherlands than to British economy, but the industrialisation of all these countries took place after their involvement in the slave trade and in plantation slavery had ended. Anyone looking for a link between the contribution of the colonial periphery and investments in the Dutch economy in the 19th century will not point to the Atlantic or at the West Indies, but to Asia.

Between 1840 and 1870, the transfer payments generated by the forced cropping system ("cultivation system") on Java flowed into the public purse, and were used to increase government expenditure on the construction of waterways and of a new railroad system in the Netherlands. These transfer payments reached their peak in the late 1850s when as much as 23% of the yearly income of the Dutch state came from Java. However, that does not mean that the Javanese villagers were forced to finance the Dutch industrial take-off, as there was a gap of more than two decades between the end of the system of forced cropping on Java and the beginnings of Dutch industrialisation after 1890.[16]

In what way did the Dutch expansion in the Atlantic deviate from the British one?

Right from the start, the Dutch expansion into the Atlantic took a different course from the British one. First, the Dutch merchants broke the weakest link in the defences of the Iberian New World by illegally penetrating the production of, and the trade in, Brazilian sugar. Secondly, this peaceful, quiet policy of informal penetration was rather suddenly abandoned in favour of a full-fledged attack against Portuguese Brazil. The Dutch managed to conquer part of

[15] David Eltis and Stanley L. Engerman, "The Importance of Slavery and the Slave Trade to Industrialising Britain," *Journal of Economic History*, vol. 60/1 (March 2000), pp. 123–44.

[16] For a broader discussion of the contribution of the non-European world to the growth of the economy of the colonial powers: Stanley L. Engerman, "The Atlantic Economy of the Eighteenth Century: Some Speculations on Economic Development in Britain, America, Africa and Elsewhere" *Journal of European Economic History*, vol. 24/1 (Spring 1995), pp. 145–75, especially pp. 157–68.

the colony, but had to surrender it again only twenty years later. Between 1624 and 1654 the "Brazilian Adventure" cost the Dutch merchant community dearly.

While the Dutch were keeping the Iberians at bay in the South Atlantic, France and Britain used the opportunity to conquer a sizeable part of the Caribbean, where they started colonies of white settlers who produced tobacco for the export market. Their attempts at conquering Brazil lost the Dutch valuable time in obtaining their own Caribbean plantation colony. It was not until 1667 that the Dutch conquered Suriname, situated in Guiana on the South American mainland. A special limited company was created in order to defend and administer this colony since the Dutch West India Company (WIC) was in a state of virtual bankruptcy after the loss of Brazil. The weakened WIC no longer possessed enough resources to prevent the British from conquering New Netherland, the only Dutch settlement colony in the New World. This loss made the Dutch West Indian possessions dependent upon the British mainland colonies for the supply of many kinds of victuals.

That the role of the Dutch in the Atlantic deviated considerably from that of the other Atlantic powers can best be illustrated by examining the Dutch participation in the trade in sugar and slaves. The history of the Dutch slave trade is a history tainted with financial disaster. As early as 1640, the Dutch slave trade had become a losing proposition because the Dutch West India Company had delivered considerable numbers of slaves to the Portuguese planters in the Dutch part of Brazil without receiving the appropriate payments. The profitability of the trade seemed to have increased again after the Dutch stopped selling slaves in Brazil, and after they had found new customers among the planters in the British and French Caribbean. In their attempt at creating a "second Brazil," the Dutch merchants helped some of these planters to develop the cultivation of sugar cane, while others continued to grow tobacco, the main export crop at the time. Yet, it should be stressed that, almost from the very beginning in the early 1640s, the Dutch were not alone as the number of English slavers was rapidly increasing. Thus, the introduction of the Navigation Laws in 1652 did not revolutionise the Atlantic slave trade in the middle Atlantic as has been often suggested, but it did hurt the Dutch traders because they were no longer able to compete with the English slave traders in supplying European victuals and textiles, sugar refining equipment, and short-term credit.

By the early 1660s the English had succeeded in barring the Dutch from their Caribbean colonies, in spite of the protests of the planters. A decade later, a similar process took place in the French Antilles. Some smuggling continued, but it did not pay for the Dutch traders to extend credit to planters in those colonies where the government was keen on excluding them. Thus, their "second Brazil" was lost and, after the conquest of Suriname, the Dutch finally started to develop their own plantation colony and to intensify the illegal trade with Spanish America. That means that, for almost 50 crucial years, the British (as well as French) had been able to investment in plantation agriculture, which offered many more opportunities for future development than did the investments made by the Dutch during that period.[17]

A second deviation from the pattern of British activities in the Atlantic was the relatively large volume of the Dutch transit trade. Recent research has shown that the illegal trade to and from Spanish America, in addition to the transit trade to and from the French Caribbean, was worth more than the value of the Dutch plantation produce. The Dutch preference for the transit trade can be explained by the fact that it required much less investment than plantation agriculture. The drawback was, however, that the Dutch had no control over the volume, which differed widely from year to year.[18]

A third difference between the British and the Dutch experience pertains to the way in which both countries financed their West Indian activities. In the British case, there was a constant flow of monetary investments going to the plantations. Part of that money was the capital that a new planter took with him to the West Indies, and another part was provided by merchant houses that had specialised in the importation and sale of plantation produce and were used to advancing loans and mortgages to their customers.

Until 1750 the same pattern existed in the Dutch Caribbean, but after that year small groups of Amsterdam investors suddenly started to offer large mortgages to West Indian planters in Suriname as well as in the newly acquired British "Ceded Islands." As was the case elsewhere in Europe, Dutch investors suddenly moved away from

---

[17] P. C. Emmer, *The Dutch in the Atlantic Economy, 1580–1880: Trade, Slavery and Emancipation* (Aldershot: Ashgate, 1998), pp. 55–62.

[18] W. Klooster, *Illicit Riches-Dutch Trade in the Caribbean, 1648–1795* (Leiden: KITLV Press, 1998).

buying government bonds and other low-risk instruments of investment and started to put some of their money into high-risk "bubbles." In this case, the result of this investment bubble was disastrous. The amount of mortgages provided to the Suriname planters far exceeded the ability of the planters to pay the interest on these mortgages, let alone to pay back part of the principal. After 1773 this situation resulted in a wave of bankruptcies among the Suriname planters, and soon the majority of the plantations were owned by the investment funds that had showered such a large amount of mortgage funds on the planters in Suriname.

After 1776 the level of investment dropped dramatically, and this process of over- and under-investment severely hampered the expansion and modernisation of the Suriname plantations. As a result, some areas of Dutch Guiana could only develop their plantation sector due to the immigration of British planters, especially after the British takeover in 1796. In addition to slowing down the development of new plantation areas in Suriname, the lack of new investment capital also affected the buying power of the Dutch planters in the Atlantic slave market. Before the crash of the Amsterdam stock exchange, planters used bills of exchange drawn on the merchant houses-cum-mortgage providers in the Netherlands in order to pay the captains of the slave ships. That meant that slaving firms could obtain full payment for their slaves upon the return of the slave ship to its home port. After 1775 this method of payment came to a grinding halt, as most bills of exchange were no longer honoured and, as a consequence, the shipping firms themselves were forced to collect the price of their slaves in cash or in kind from the planters. It sometimes took years and years before a slave cargo had been paid in full. That explains why, after 1775 and again after the end of the fourth Anglo-Dutch War in 1784, the Dutch slave trade declined while the British slave trade experienced a dramatic increase in volume. In order to survive at all, the Dutch slave trade had to be freed from the usual taxes and levies.[19]

The continuous growth of the British slave trade was, in part, based on its superior productivity and, in part, on the way in which the slave traders were paid by those who bought slaves in the West Indies. In the Dutch case, the slave traders had to accept the bills

[19] Morgan, *Slavery, Atlantic Trade and the British Economy, 1660–1800*, p. 75.

of exchange directly from the planters, and these bills were drawn on the merchant house in the Netherlands that handled the commercial affairs of the planter. In the British case, the bills came from the agents of these metropolitan merchant houses residing in the West Indies. This provided the British slave traders with much more security than the Dutch slavers had. "By comparison with their French and Dutch counterparts, the Liverpool slave traders appear to have been much more independent of colonial credit and relatively unencumbered with the heavy indebtedness of the plantation economy."[20]

Yet, the buying power of the planters in the British Caribbean must have also contributed to the remarkably high profits in the British slave trade because the planters in the British West Indies enjoyed incomes that were, in part, based on the protective tariffs for their sugar in the British home market.[21] The British consumer not only bought more sugar, but also had to pay more for it than elsewhere. The figures are telling. In the 1720s Britain re-exported about 20% of its sugar to foreign markets and, during the last quarter of the 18th century, this percentage had fallen to less than 5%. The planters in the Dutch West Indies, on the other hand, did not receive such a subsidy and had to compete with the most cost-effective producers anywhere, resulting in relatively low profits in the slave trade as well as in plantation agriculture.[22]

In spite of the fact that the British investment policy in the West Indies had been much more even and continuous and, in spite of

---

[20] B. L. Anderson, "The Lancashire Bill System and its Liverpool Practitioners", in W. H. Chaloner and Barrie M. Ratcliffe, eds., *Trade and Transport: Essays in Economic History in Honour of T. S. Willan* (Manchester: Manchester University Press, 1977), pp. 59–97, especially p. 80.

[21] Stanley L. Engerman, "British Imperialism in a Mercantilist Age, 1492–1849: Conceptual Issues and Empirical Problems," *Revista de Historia Económica*, vol. XVI/1 (1998), pp. 195–231, especially pp. 206–7 "Thus the protective provision of the Acts [of Navigation] led to some redistribution from British consumers to planters in the British West Indies."

[22] Seymour Drescher, *Econocide: British Slavery in the Era of Abolition* (Pittsburgh, 1977), pp. 52–53; David Richardson in "Profits in the Liverpool Slave Trade: the accounts of William Davenport, 1757–1784," in Roger Anstey and P. E. H. Hair, eds., *Liverpool, the African Slave Trade, and Abolition: Essays to Illustrate Current Knowledge and Research* (Liverpool: Historic Society of Lancashire and Cheshire, 1976); p. 80 mentions a profit rate of 8%. That is more than double the rate of the *Middelburgsche Commercie Compagnie* operating between 1732 and 1803 according to Roger Anstey, *The Atlantic Slave Trade and British Abolition, 1760–1810* (London: Macmillan, 1974), pp. 38–57, especially p. 57.

the fact that the volume of their slave trade and of their plantation output increased toward the close of the 18th century, it was the British who took the step of abolishing the slave trade and of emancipating the slaves, not the Dutch. Of all the slave-trading nations in Europe, the Dutch could have abolished the trade with the least cost because it had virtually ceased to exist after the end of the fourth Anglo-Dutch in 1784. Yet, the official abolition of the Dutch slave trade was only legislated after Britain had brought pressure to bear on the Dutch government in The Hague, and when the trade was abolished the Dutch colonial officials in Suriname did not even fully comply with the law. Fortunately for the abolitionists, Suriname was not a colony with an expanding plantation sector, and the demand for slaves was only aimed at trying to avoid a further decline of the slave population.

The Suriname planters certainly had less buying power in the market for illegally imported slaves than their colleagues in Cuba and Brazil did, but between 1816 and 1826 many thousands of slaves were imported illegally. The number of illegally imported slaves fell far short of the number needed to halt the decline of the slave population, but Britain knew that in this case, it could put an end to this illegal trade. Moreover, the British ambassador in The Hague was able to force the Dutch government in The Hague into instituting a system of slave registration in Suriname, thereby effectively stopping further illegal imports in 1826. In that period, Brazilian and Cuban planters had so much buying power that they could have overcome this barrier. The same would have happened in Guyana and Trinidad had Britain not taken it upon itself to be stricter than any other nation in observing the end of the slave trade.[23]

Another difference between the British and the Dutch in the Atlantic can be found in North America. Britain succeeded in establishing a whole string of settlement colonies along the Eastern seaboard while, in contrast, the Dutch lost their only settlement colony as early as 1664. This development seems to underline the assumption that, from the middle of the 17th century, Britain's stake in the Atlantic economy was far greater than that of France and the Netherlands because of its North American settlement colonies. The

[23] Pieter C. Emmer, *Les Pays-Bas et la traite des Noirs* (Paris: Karthala, 2005), pp. 157–195.

economy of French Canada was too small to have had much of an impact. Yet, the per capita contribution of early North America to the British economy was probably less than that of the Caribbean, since the colonies in the Caribbean were more dependent upon Britain than the mainland settlements. Growth in the Caribbean meant an increase in trade and services from Britain, while growth in North America meant replacing Britain. In addition, it would be wrong to make the possession of settlements in North America an economic precondition for the growth of the West Indian plantation colonies. The Dutch, French, and British West Indies continued to grow rapidly after their link with the sister colonies in North America had been severed.[24]

The last unique feature of the Dutch Atlantic was the prolongation of the system of slavery until 1863. That continuation had various consequences. First of all, the continued "benefit" of slavery in Suriname did not lead to an increase in the total output of the plantations; it only prevented decline. Second, the Surname planters paid a price for the continued existence of slavery because they were forced to give in to metropolitan pressures to increase the food rations, to improve slave housing and the care provided to pregnant women and sick slaves. The longer slavery lasted, the more such amelioration policies could be realised. In the end, the slave system in Suriname might well have been unique because of the extensive protection granted to the slaves. Minimum standards for food, clothing, and housing, as well as a maximum number of working hours per week, had been laid down, and compliance with these regulations was enforced. The colonial government had even imposed regulations allowing the slaves to complain to authorities if the new regulations were not complied with. Plantations had to close down when they could not afford the costs of these improvements.[25]

During the post-slavery period after 1863, the Suriname planters underwent the changes that had occurred in the British Caribbean thirty years earlier. At first, most plantations were able to continue operating because the emancipation law stipulated that the ex-field

[24] The per capita value of the exports from Great Britain to British North America increased from only £0.90 to £1.20 between 1700 and 1770 according to John J. McCusker and Russell R. Menard, *The Economy of British America, 1607–1789* (Chapel Hill, London: The University of North Carolina Press, 1985), p. 280.

[25] Emmer, *The Dutch in the Atlantic Economy*, pp. 167–79.

slaves had to remain on the plantations during the apprenticeship period of ten years—not four as had been the case in the British Caribbean. In the Netherlands, there existed no influential abolitionist lobby capable of forcing the metropolitan government to abort the system of apprenticeship when it turned out to be less satisfactory than expected.

The belated slave emancipation in the Dutch colony could not prevent a repeat of the "flight from the plantations" elsewhere. At the time of slave emancipation in the British Caribbean, the abolitionists could still entertain the illusion that the liberation of the slaves would somehow coincide with an increase in income of both plantation owners and plantation workers. In the case of Suriname, virtually no one could have doubted that an alternative workforce had to be in place before the period of apprenticeship had ended.[26] The plantation sector in Suriname would have declined even more if it had experienced a similar gap in the supply of labour as in the British West Indies after 1838. After slavery had ended, the British planters continued to enjoy protective tariffs for their sugar. But they would have done even better had the British colonial officials turned a blind eye to the illegal slave imports and if the metropolitan government had put the supply of indentured labour in place before the end of the period of apprenticeship. The absence of illegal slave imports and the gap between the ending of slavery and the arrival of the first indentured laborers in the British West Indies again points to the British *Sonderweg*.

The same observation can be made regarding the market for colonial labour in Asia. As late as 1830, the Dutch instituted a system of forced cropping on Java that was based on forced labour. The Dutch could institute this system as late as 1830 because, by that time, the free labour ideology had not yet gained much popularity among the Dutch political elite. No doubt, a similar system of indentured labour would have greatly benefited the production of cash crops in India. However, this would have been unthinkable in view of the abolitionist ideology prevalent among the British population at large, and its self-imposed role as the foremost "moral" nation in the world. Without forced labour, the cultivation of sugar and cotton for export overseas at competitive prices in India was not possible, and India

[26] Ibid., pp. 143–65.

never managed to replace the West Indies. In contrast, by the early 1830s, Java already produced more sugar than Suriname. Similar systems of forced or semi-forced labour were used in the colonies of the other Continental colonial powers. The absence of forced labour in India once again demonstrates the British *Sonderweg*.

In the British case, the suppression of the slave trade, the subsequent abolition of slavery in the West Indies, and the aversion to the use of forced labour in India increased the costs of producing tropical export crops. Similarly, the ending of slavery in Suriname and the ending of the "cultivation system" in Java increased the costs of producing tropical cash crops. These abolitions and reforms constituted a triumph of the liberal ideology. Liberalism viewed a free labour market as the only viable labour supply system regardless of the circumstances. A system that was beneficial to Western Europe and North America could only be beneficial to the rest of the world. In the end (i.e., around 1870) even the Dutch yielded to this powerful ideology.

The Dutch in the history of the Atlantic

In what way does this information regarding the Dutch Atlantic affect our existing interpretations, which are mainly based on the British experience in this region?

First of all, the history of the Dutch Atlantic confirms the observation by Adam Smith that the wealth of the British colonies in the New World "in a great measure" was based on "the great riches of England, of which part has overflowed . . . upon these colonies."[27] The stagnation of the Dutch economy during the final decades of the 18th century had an immediate impact on its response to the Atlantic challenge. The Dutch slave trade was the only one to decline, and the number of non-Dutch planters in the Dutch Caribbean increased rapidly. The Dutch West Indies were outgrowing the Dutch metropolitan economy. The Dutch fell far short of exploiting their

[27] Engerman, "France, Britain and the Economic Growth of Colonial North America," in John McCusker and Kenneth Morgan eds., *The Early Modern Atlantic Economy* (Cambridge: Cambridge University Press, 2000), pp. 227–49, especially p. 231 (citation Adam Smith).

section of the Atlantic to the fullest, and for that reason the walls around their plantation colonies, built to guard against foreign exploitation, crumbled.

After the fourth Anglo-Dutch War, the Dutch plantation colonies increasingly accommodated the overflow in the British Caribbean. During the same last decades of the 18th century, the French and the British economies were expanding and that expansion was evident in the Caribbean, where Britain managed to expand sugar and cotton production in Trinidad and Guiana at a dazzling pace and where France made Saint-Domingue into the largest cash crop producer of the Caribbean. And, even between these two expanding nations, the difference in economic development at home showed up in the Atlantic: in order to match Britain's Atlantic achievement in relation to its population, France should have developed Louisiana into a second Saint-Domingue.

Second, the history of the Dutch in the Atlantic shows how a purely mercantile expansion in the Atlantic differed from a policy designed by a central state in shaping the foundations of a maritime empire. We tend to overlook differences in institutions, but the policy of the English state, headed by a central authority, was to direct shipping into trades that were relatively dangerous, and not to low-risk bulk trades. "Government action in the 1560s and 1570s helped to commit England to a relatively small fleet, relatively large ships, and relatively high costs of operating those highly defensible ships."[28] The Dutch had no such powerful government-cum-centralist policy, and this explains the lack of support for a continued presence in Brazil and North America. The Netherlands was not willing to match the defence efforts of its opponents. Their relatively low shipping costs were of no avail as the international market for logistics in the Atlantic declined in the course of the 17th century. Anyway, toward the end of the 17th century, the Dutch advantage in the productivity of maritime transport had been eroded.[29] In addition to this commercial decline, the Dutch lost out in power politics, since the

[28] Unger, "The Tonnage of Europe's Merchants Fleets," *The American Neptune*, 52/4 (1992), p. 259.

[29] David Eltis, *The Rise of African Slavery in the Americas* (Cambridge: Cambridge University Press, 2000), pp. 114–36.

Dutch state was extremely reluctant to spend money on expensive overhead costs such as defence. Only the British were able to build up a navy that not only could protect all of the British possessions in the Atlantic, but also could harm or take away the overseas colonies of Spain, France, and the Netherlands. What William III could achieve as king in Britain would have been impossible as *stadhouder* in the Netherlands.

Also the Dutch were simply unable to invest as much money in keeping their navy on a par with Britain because the British internal revenue system was far superior to that of any other country in Europe. Around 1780 the British Navy was made up of four times as many ships and men as the Dutch Navy.[30] The second best option for the Dutch in responding to the "Atlantic challenge" was their attempt to profit from their neutral position during the many wars of the 18th century. Britain, on the other hand, was able not only to severely damage its competitors in the Atlantic, but also to annex some of the most promising plantation colonies such as Guiana and Trinidad.

A second feature of early Atlantic history, which was uniquely British, was the supply of young, mobile people willing to work and settle overseas. Only Portugal seems to have duplicated the British experience in that respect. Without such a supply of settlers, the Dutch expansion in the Atlantic took on a different character. Most of the Dutch viewed their stay overseas as a period of temporary exile, comparable to making a long voyage on a ship. However, a caveat is in order here. It should be pointed out that the Dutch could command large numbers of young, mobile men to become sailors and soldiers overseas. Between 1600 and 1800, the Dutch East India Company was able to send more than one million of them to Asia, of whom only one third returned alive. These figures indicate that the Dutch excelled in sending men to the tropics on a temporary basis. Their system of recruiting poor, young, unmarried men from Scandinavia, Germany, and the North of France was unrivalled. That explains why Dutch merchants were so keen on exploiting the lethal trade niche with the tropical zones in Asia: they had

[30] Wolfgang Reinhard, *Parasit oder Partner? Europaïsche Wirtschaft und Neue Welt, 1500–1800* (Münster: Periplus-Texte, 1977), p. 122.

enough men. To "invest" these men in the Atlantic as settlers like the British must have been less profitable.[31]

A third observation regarding the general history of the Atlantic concerns the importance attributed to plantation colonies. In Britain these were viewed as "darlings of the empire," while in the Dutch experience the plantations colonies were viewed as generators of trade rather than as producers of tropical cash crops. The Dutch were keen on excluding foreigners from trading with the Dutch Caribbean, but they showed no interest in granting protection to their own products. The Dutch Republic did not have a "West Indian Interest" like Britain had. Of course, some will argue that in the Dutch system such a lobby was not a necessity since those merchants with West Indian interests also were in charge of the city, state, and national governments, while in Britain representatives of the landed interest were the dominant force in both government and parliament. This might be so, but the close ties between merchants and government officials or members of the legislative bodies in the Netherlands did not produce the beneficial policies vis-à-vis the West Indies that were prevalent in Britain. In Britain these links were organised individually, while in the Dutch case an all-embracing company was supposed to supervise these links. Over time, the situation changed, and in the 18th century free enterprise took over. Nevertheless, until the abolition of the sugar duties in 1846 British consumers were forced to subsidise the British Atlantic in a way unheard of in the Dutch case.

Last, but not least, attention should be paid to the differences between the Dutch and the British economies at home. These differences were of the utmost importance in explaining how the two countries met the Atlantic challenge after 1750. The Dutch case shows that Atlantic activities do not necessarily stimulate modernisation (and the same can be said of all other Continental powers with an Atlantic interest). In the case of Britain, the growing Atlantic activities coincided with the modernisation of the home economy. In the Dutch case, the growth of the Atlantic activities slowed down

---

[31] Jan Lucassen, "The Netherlands, the Dutch, and Long-Distance Migration in the Late Sixteenth to Early Nineteenth Centuries" in Nicolas Canny ed., *Europeans on the Move: Studies on European Migration, 1500–1800* (Oxford: Oxford University Press, 1994), pp. 153–91.

the decline of the home economy. This discrepancy makes a comparison between the respective Atlantic activities of Britain and the Netherlands increasingly difficult. The abolition of the slave trade and of slavery itself again exemplifies the British *Sonderweg*. It was the economic growth of the first Industrial Revolution that provided the abolition debate in Britain with a different basis from the debate in the Netherlands. The few Dutch abolitionists could not offer any alternative to the slave trade, and this same situation applied in the other Atlantic powers as well. Suppressing the slave trade and banning slavery would diminish their overseas trade, not reorient it, as Britain was able to do. The Industrial Revolution allowed Britain to respond to the Atlantic challenge as no other country was able to do.

The Big Two: France and the United Kingdom

CHAPTER NINE

BRITAIN'S EXPORTS AND THEIR MARKETS, 1701–1913

F. Crouzet

During the two centuries from 1701 to the First World War, British exports increased with amazing speed. At constant prices, they increased almost three-hundredfold. During the 18th century growth had been relatively slow—about 1.5% per year, on average. This growth increased markedly—to 3.6% per year, on average—during the 19th century. In both centuries, however, growth was irregular. For example, some "cycles" lasting about 40 years, during which growth and stagnation alternated, are discernable. This essay will specify the main regions to which the increasing flow of British goods was directed. Moreover, it will look at the changes in the relative importance of these goods, especially in the balance between European and non-European markets. An emphasis will be placed upon long-term trends rather than short-term fluctuations.

Only domestic exports of British goods and manufactures will be considered, and not the re-exports of colonial and foreign goods. Admittedly, these re-exports are relevant to the study of the relationship between Europe and the rest of the world, but they comprised only a part of gross British imports, and it is the role of domestic exports in British industrialisation that has been hotly debated, and with which this essay deals.[1] Unfortunately, the available statistical material is not consistent through the whole period surveyed in this essay. In the 18th century, English foreign trade statistics were compiled by the Customs Service according to the system of "official values"—i.e. at constant prices. Historians generally

[1] Moreover, the share of re-exports in total exports from Britain has changed over time. It was as high as a third in some periods during the 18th century (but smaller than in total French exports), and remained high during the French Wars, but it declined during the 19th century to under 20%. Most re-exports were products from British possessions (including India) and were sent to Northern Europe (see note 9).

agree that these statistics provide rough, but reliable, indices of the volume of exports. Moreover, until the 1780s, when average prices were stable, there was probably not much difference (plus or minus 10%) between the official values of exports and their market values. Later on, however, inflation and an upheaval in the price structure created serious gaps between official and market values. Fortunately, from 1796 onward (and with more detail available from 1814), statistics of "declared" or "real" (i.e. "current") values of exports become available and increasingly reliable. In addition, the late Ralph Davis re-valued exports at current prices for a group of three years in each decade, from 1784–86 to 1854–56.[2] Nonetheless, Tables 1 and 2, as well as other figures, only give an impression of the order of magnitude, and all percentages have been rounded off, in orders to avoid a misleading impression of accuracy (so they do not always add up to 100).

The 18th Century

Exports from England to continental Europe increased from the early 18th century to 1760 but fell sharply afterward. By 1772–73 (an important turning point, on the eve of the American Revolution), these British exports to continental Europe were not much higher than in 1700–01.[3] As exports to other continents had increased quickly, the share of continental Europe in England's total (domestic) exports fell from 82% in 1700–01 to 71% in 1750–51, and then collapsed to 41% in 1772–73. Continental Europe only contributed a 4% increase in English exports during those same seventy years.[4]

[2] R. Davis, *The Industrial Revolution and British Overseas Trade* (Leicester: University of Leicester Press, 1978).

[3] Actually, exports to Northern Europe had fallen, while those to Southern Europe had increased.

[4] This contribution is calculated according to the formula:

$$CE\ t_1\ \text{to}\ t_2 = \frac{EEt_2 - EEt_1}{ETt_1 - ETt_2} \times 100$$

CE = contribution of Europe to the increase in exports from the year t_1 to the year t_2;
EE = exports to Europe;
ET = total exports.

Table 1. Contributions by the main regions to the increase of total British exports: percent of the overall net increase (the – (minus) sign indicates a negative contribution)

	1	2	3	4	5	6	7
	according to official values			according to declared (current) values			
	1700–01 to 1772–73	1700–01 to 1789–90	1784–86 to 1814–16	1814–18 to 1842–46	1842–46 to 1869–73	1869–73 to 1909–13	1814–18 to 1909–13
Northern Europe	–8	10	30	21	36	25	29
Southern Europe	12	7	16	19	11	8	9
Europe	4	17	46	40	47	33	38
Ireland	15	13	8				
West Indies	19	15	16		1	–0,3	
Canada			7	–29	3	6	4
13 colonies United States	42	30	13	–16	16	–1	5
Latin America			7	24	9	13	12
America	61	45	43	–21	29	18	21
Africa	8	4	–0,3	12	2	12	8
Asia	13	20	3	60	15	27	23
Australasia				11	7	12	10

N.B.: Figures for 1700–01 are for England only, those of columns two and three are for Great Britain, the others for the United Kingdom (so that Ireland disappears). Northern Europe includes, *inter alia*, France, Austria-Hungary and Switzerland. Southern Europe includes the Ottoman Empire and North Africa; Africa is therefore South of the Sahara. The West Indies include both the British and foreign islands. Ireland includes the island of Man and the Channel islands.

Admittedly, in the 1780s, after the War of American Independence, sales to continental Europe recovered—in large part owing to the Anglo-French trade treaty of 1786. As a consequence, the contribution of Europe to the growth of total British exports between 1700–01 and 1789–90 reached 17%, a figure that is not negligible but remains modest. One must add that this recovery is one aspect of an overall change in the rate of growth in British exports after the American War of Independence. This growth was as spectacular as it was unprecedented. For example, from 1781 to 1792, the growth rate was 7% per year.

How, then, do we explain the "decline" in trade with continental Europe preceding this upsurge? Wars played some part, as they caused the temporary closure of some markets, for instance the Spanish one. But the main factor was that, until the 1780s, the penetration of continental markets, especially in Northern countries, by British manufactures—and particularly by woollens and worsteds, which were England's traditional export staples—became increasingly difficult. The reasons for this were the increased protectionism in several states (e.g., Spain, under Charles III), growing proto-industrialisation in several German regions and in Bohemia, and French competition in luxury goods. Moreover, about half of English exports to the important market of Portugal were actually intended for re-export to Brazil, and they suffered from the fall in the Brazilian gold production after 1760. Indeed, a significant share of English exports to the Iberian Peninsula was re-exported to America.

At any rate, the New World was responsible for most of the growth in British exports. The Thirteen Colonies were the leading market, especially as the population of these colonies increased ninefold from 1715 to 1790. Moreover, these colonies enjoyed one of the highest incomes per capita in the world. They consumed a wide range of British manufactures, so that the diversification of British industry was stimulated.[5] Admittedly, exports to North America suffered greatly from the American Revolution and the subsequent war, but once the new republic's economy had recovered from the fall in its national product caused by these hostilities, British sales to the United States increased sharply. In fact, they doubled from 1787 to 1791. As early

[5] And those manufactures were "middle class" goods, while the West Indies bought coarse textiles for slaves and luxuries for planters.

as 1789–90, North America (including the small Canadian market) was taking the same share of British exports as it had before 1775.

Nevertheless, the contribution of the British West Indies should not be overlooked: It made up 15% of the total increase in British exports between 1700–01 and 1789–90. The West Indian slave population rose sharply during the 18th century, and, consequently, the West Indies were selling to Britain growing quantities of sugar and other colonial produce. In wartime, moreover, the occupation of enemy islands opened up new markets to the British. Finally, the West Indies and North America made up—even after the independence of the United States—an integrated and multilateral commercial empire, so that exports from the American mainland to the Caribbean provided colonial and post-colonial North America with additional purchasing power with which to buy British goods. Altogether, there was an "Americanisation" of British exports. The share of British exports which went to the New World rose from 12% in 1700–01 to 38% in 1772–73 and to 35% in 1789–90. By 1805–06, British exports to the New World were to reach 50% of the total.

These figures support Ralph Davis's view that colonial trade was the major dynamic force in the English 18th century export trade. Moreover, there was progress—less striking, but substantial—in exports to other overseas areas. Exports to Africa were not large, but they were connected to the slave trade, the Atlantic system, and plantations in America. The East Indies, had for a long time imported only small quantities of British goods, but at the end of the 18th century, the East India Company succeeded in opening up a market for British goods in India, even though most of these exports were intended for European residents, as well as for its own armed forces. Asia contributed 20%—more than Europe—to the growth in total exports from 1700–01 to 1789–90. If Ireland, which, until 1800, was outside the British customs system, is also taken into account, it is clear that, during the 18th century, English exports were increasingly sent to markets that were "captive," either de jure (under the Navigation Laws) or de facto (the United States after independence), and that those markets, except Ireland, were outside Europe. These captive markets only received 19% of exports in 1700–01, but their share rose to 61% in 1772–73, and to 63% in 1789–90. They imported even higher shares of British exports during the Napoleonic Wars. It would be inaccurate to say that Britain turned away from

Europe or was pushed back by Europe (except during some years of war), but, rather, the expansion of Britain's trade came from its overseas "empire," in the broad sense of the word.

It must be added that cotton goods did not contribute significantly to the growth in exports before the 1780s. Earlier on, there had been balanced growth. There had been a relative decline in woollen goods, coupled by a marked increase in "other goods." These shifts reflected the broadening of the British economy and the widening range of its competitive manufactured goods. Nevertheless, the Industrial Revolution did not make any impact upon exports before the 1780s.

The 23 Years War

I shall be brief about the chaotic period of the French Wars, during which there were constant and complex short-run changes in the geographical distribution of British exports, as political or military developments suddenly closed or opened markets. However, the Wars did not prevent Britain's exports from growing—at an impressive rate of 6% from 1792 to 1802, and at a more restrained 3% from 1802 to 1814. This growth in exports was achieved thanks to a succession of transfers between the main trading areas of Europe and America.

The New World, and especially the United States, was the engine of growth in the 1790s. Then, at the turn of the century, there was a "return to Europe." Indeed, the years between 1798 and 1802 (not the 1780s, as it is sometimes said) were witness to an "invasion" of the European continent by British manufactured goods, mainly cotton yarn and cotton cloth. This invasion was due to lower prices resulting from technological progress. After a state of war had resumed in 1803, the United States again played a leading role in buying British exports, but diplomatic tension between London and Washington from 1807 onward, and the War of 1812, seriously disturbed Anglo-American trade. On the other hand, thanks to the Peninsular War, between 1808 and 1812, outlets opened in Southern Europe and Latin America for additional exports. After the collapse of Napoleon's "Great Empire" in 1813 and 1814, Northern Europe resumed its role as an important outlet for British exports.

Table 2. Shares of the main regions in total British exports (%)

	1	2	3	4	5	6	7	8
	according to official values				according to declared (current) values			
	1700–01	1772–73	1789–90	1814–18	1842–46	1869–73	1889–93	1909–13
Northern Europe	48	18	22	27	25	33	27	29
Southern Europe	34	21	15	19	19	13	11	10
Europe	82	39	37	46	44	46	38	39
Ireland	3	10	10					
West Indies	5	12	12		7	3	2	1
Canada				22	5	4	3	5
13 colonies	7	26	23	17	11	15	12	7
United States								
Latin America				6	10	9	11	11
America	12	38	35	45	33	31	28	24
Africa	2	5	3	1	3	2	5	8
Asia	2	8	15	7	17	15	20	21
Australasia					2	6	9	9

N.B.: Figures for 1700–01 are for England only, those of columns two and three are for Great Britain, the others for the United Kingdom (so that Ireland disappears). Northern Europe includes, *inter alia*, France, Austria-Hungary and Switzerland. Southern Europe includes the Ottoman Empire and North Africa; Africa is therefore South of the Sahara. The West Indies include both the British and foreign islands. Ireland includes the island of Man and the Channel islands.

If one attempts to draw a balance sheet of the "Twenty-Three Years War," using Ralph Davis's recalculated current values (and not the official values as mentioned above), the contribution of continental Europe to the increase in total British exports from 1784–86 to 1814–16 was 46%, while that of America was 43%. Moreover, according to both the current values of 1814–16 and the declared values of 1814–18, Europe and America received shares of total British exports that were quite similar—both imported around 40–45% of the total. There is a clear contrast with the "short" 18th century (until 1793), and a definite shift toward greater exports to continental Europe, thanks to the Industrial Revolution. Admittedly, the period between 1814 and 1818 were "post war" years, when stocks were sharply reduced in Britain and strongly increased on the European continent and in the United States. When cumulated additional exports to the main trading areas and their ratios to the grand total of cumulated additional exports which Britain achieved between 1783 and 1812 are calculated (this can only be done, unfortunately, in official values), the share of American imports is 60% (32% for the United States alone), so that America's role as an engine of growth appears decisive, especially as continental Europe's share was only 23%. Nonetheless, a partial reorientation of British trade toward Europe cannot be doubted, and one can risk the counterfactual statement that this shift would have been even more pronounced had the European continent not suffered through two decades of war.

19th-century markets

This new orientation was to be a lasting one. From 1814 to 1913, the growth of exports from the United Kingdom was staggering. For example, between 1814–18 and 1909–13 their value increased tenfold, their volume thirtyfold, and continental Europe was the leading market for British goods, importing around 40% of Britain's total exports.

Admittedly, from the end of the Napoleonic Wars until the 1840s, exports to Europe grew somewhat more slowly than total exports (and, indeed, fell up to the early 1830s). This stagnation in British exports to continental Europe resulted from the protectionist policies in place in most states on the European continent—protectionist policies sometimes labeled the "Second Continental Blockade."

However, a recovery took place in the latter part of the 1830s, thanks to exports of semi-finished goods, such as cotton, wool and linen yarn, pig-iron, and unwrought iron, all of which were capital-intensive, and all of which were products for which Britain had strong comparative advantages. Countries in continental Europe used these imports to make labour-intensive consumption goods, thanks to their lower labour costs. The contribution of continental Europe to the net increase in Britain's total exports from 1814–16 to 1842–46 was a substantial 40%.[6]

Among Britain's main trading partners, exports to Northern Europe had the fastest rate of growth—6.7% per year—during the years between 1846 and 1873. Its share in buying British exports rose from 25% in 1842–46 to 33% in 1869–73, and Northern Europe made the largest contribution—36%—to the increase in total British exports. When the rather modest exports to Southern Europe are added, continental Europe's contribution to British exports increases to 47%. This upsurge is to be explained, first of all, by the liberalisation of trade within Europe, thanks to the adoption of free trade by Britain itself, as well as to the Anglo-French trade treaty of 1860, and to the subsequent network of commercial agreements. In addition, the rapid industrialisation on the European continent, as well as the building of railways on a massive scale, opened up large markets to capital goods "made in Britain."[7]

After 1873, however, the onset of the "great depression," in addition to the continuing progress of industrialisation on the European continent (especially in Germany), the revival of protectionism, plus, according to many writers, a reduced competitiveness, all combined to slow down British exports to continental Europe.[8] Nonetheless, from 1814–18 to 1909–13, the contribution of continental Europe to the increase of Britain's total exports was 38%, of which 29% was destined for Northern Europe.

[6] Ratios for this period are peculiar, because of high "negative" contributions—i.e., a decrease in exports by the West Indies and the United States.

[7] During the period between 1814 and 1873, and especially from 1846 onward, exports of *all* the main categories of goods grew, while earlier on cotton goods had dominated. There was diversification of exports, which display a pattern of "balanced growth."

[8] From 1869–73 to 1909–13, the contribution of Europe to the increase of total exports was only 33%.

In this period, the Americas played a much smaller role in the growth of British exports than they had during the 18th century. Exports to the United States displayed a peculiar pattern, with sharp fluctuations and a low correlation to total British exports. After rising to a peak in the boom year of 1836, exports to the United States fell back to low levels in the 1840s. For example, their current value in 1842–46 was lower than it had been in 1814–18, so that their contribution to the increase of total exports was negative. Though the growth rate of British exports to the United States, at 3.9% per year, was lower from 1846 to 1873 than for total exports (5.7%), their contribution to the increase in exports between 1842–46 and 1869–73 was a significant 16%.

This was a swan song, however. British exports to the United States reached a peak in 1872 at 41 million pounds sterling, mainly due to the substantial sales of rails for transcontinental railroads, but they never again reached such a high level between 1874 and 1913, when their peak was at only 32 million pounds sterling in 1890. In 1913 British exports were valued at only 29 million pounds.[9] As a consequence, the contribution of the American market to the growth of total British exports from 1869–73 to 1909–13 was again negative (by a small ratio, admittedly) and, for the whole of the 19th century (here defined as the years between 1814 and 1913), it was an amazingly low 5%. The United States share in total British exports fell from 17% in 1814–18 to 11% in 1842–46. It went up again to 15% in 1869–73, but then fell to 7% in 1909–13. The rapid industrialisation of the United States, as well as their high tariff walls after the Civil War, was responsible for this remarkable relative decline in the import of British goods.

The relative decline in British exports to the United States was only partially compensated for by the rise in exports to Canada, which received 5% of total British exports in 1909–13, and contributed 9% to their rise from 1842–46 to 1909–13. The West Indies, the jewels of the 18th-century mercantilist empire, suffered an inexorable decline during the 19th century. Their share of total British exports fell from 14% in 1814–16 to 1% in 1909–13, when the

[9] On the other hand, British re-exports to the United States increased sharply from 1880 onward. For example, in 1901 and in the years 1911–13, their value was slightly higher than that of exports.

value of the British goods they received was lower than it had been in 1869–73. On the other hand, Latin America, which had been opened up to direct trade with Britain toward the end of the Napoleonic Wars, made a positive contribution to the increase in British exports during each of the three periods under discussion. During the whole period between 1814 and 1913, this contribution was 12%, while its share of total exports rose from 6% in 1814–18 to 11% in 1909–13. These ratios are neither insignificant nor particularly large. Actually, Latin American markets were small, and several factors limited their expansion. Most of the population in Latin America lived at subsistence levels, and demand for imported goods came mainly from the well-to-do in large towns, where markets were easily overstocked. Secondly, the purchasing power of the Latin American countries depended upon their export of only a few primary commodities, the prices of which fluctuated wildly, and, overall, fell. In addition, communications within Latin America were poor, and foreign capital was needed to improve them. Foreign investment for improving communications, as well as for other infrastructure projects, came in waves of boom and bust. Last, political instability prevailed. All these factors contributed to the volatile character of the trade relations with Latin America. All in all, trade with Latin America was risky, often not profitable, and altogether disappointing.[10]

The share of the Americas in total British exports, which had been 45% in 1814–18, fell to under one-third at mid-century, and to just under one-fourth on the eve of the First World War. Their contribution to the growth in exports over the 19th century was only 21%. An "Americanisation" of British trade in the 18th century has been mentioned earlier. I take the liberty of suggesting a process of "de-Americanisation" during the following century.

I put forward, with some hesitation, the word "Orientalisation," to describe the growth of 19th century exports directed toward a group of regions that included such diverse parts of the globe as Africa, Asia, and Australasia (exports to Australia became noteworthy during the 1830s). Actually, the Ottoman Empire (and North Africa),

---

[10] See D. C. M. Platt, *Latin America and British Trade, 1806–1914* (London: A. and C. Black, 1972), *passim*; and ibid., *Business Imperialism, 1840–1930. An inquiry based on British experience in Latin America* (Oxford: Oxford University Press, 1977).

which our tables include with Southern Europe, ought to be added to this group.

From 1814–18 to 1842–46 onward, exports to those three "continents" increased almost constantly at the rapid rate of 4.4% per year, while total exports only increased by 1.1% per year. Their absolute increase was equivalent to 83% of the total growth in exports, and Asia was responsible for 60% of that increase.[11] During the period between 1846 and 1873, the growth in exports was even faster—6.6% per year—but the contribution of these three regions to the growth in total exports was smaller—23%—because of the rapid increase in exports to Northern Europe, as well as because of the revival in the trade with the United States; however, it rose to 51% for 1869–1913. During the 100 years between 1814 and 1913, this contribution amounted to 41% of the total, of which 23% came from Asia and 10% from Australasia. The share of these three regions in total exports had only been 8% in 1814–18, rising to 22% in 1842–46, to 34% in 1889–93, and, eventually, to 38% in 1909–13.

Needless to say, this large section of the globe was not homogeneous. It mainly consisted of poor countries, such as India, plus some countries of recent settlement, such as Australia, New Zealand and, possibly, South Africa.[12] These countries differed from the "Third World" by their economic and social structure and by their rapid economic growth. Though Australasia greatly increased its share of British exports, Asia and Africa (i.e., the poor countries) were the largest customers. They received 20% of total British exports in 1842–46 and 29% in 1909–13. Moreover, Latin America and the West Indies were also poor, as was the Ottoman Empire, which we have included in the figures on Southern Europe. The whole group of poor countries is likely to have imported 29% of British exports in 1814–16, 48% in 1844–46, and over 41% in 1909–13.[13] However,

[11] See note 3.

[12] South Africa is an awkward case. It had a relatively large European population "of recent settlement" (which, however, only constituted a minority of the total population), plus a rapid economic growth in the late 19th century and early 20th century. Its PIB per capita (according to A. Maddison) was much higher than in the rest of Africa, but under half the West European level, and about the same as that of Latin America (which we consider "poor"). The difficulty is aggravated by the fact that exports to South Africa were a large and growing share of British exports to Africa South of the Sahara (57% in 1909–13). All things considered, however, we shall leave South Africa in Africa—i.e., among the "poor" countries.

[13] Davis's figures are used for 1814–16 and 1844–46. They include the Near East; the Ottoman Empire is not included in the 41% of 1909–13.

the share of British exports imported by the "advanced countries" and by those of recent settlement, which both can be considered relatively "rich" (i.e., Northern Europe, North America, Australasia), fell from 53% of total exports in 1814–16 to 43% in 1842–46, rising again to 58% in 1869–73, and, averaging 50% in 1909–13. Southern Europe, which was neither "advanced" nor "Third World," brings the total to 100%.[14] Between 1814 and 1913, the contribution of the poor countries and of the advanced and "new" ones to the increase in total British exports did not differ much, as they amounted to 40% and 50%, respectively.

Nonetheless, during the decades following the end of the Napoleonic Wars, British exports shifted toward underdeveloped regions.[15] A traditional explanation for this movement is that the warm climate and the low standards of living in Asia, Africa, and Latin America, when coupled with the increase in their populations, created an expanding demand for cheap cotton goods—which, for a long time, made up the bulk of their imports from Britain. Later on, there was a demand for capital goods, particularly for the railways. Another, and more sophisticated, explanation for this shift toward exporting to poorer regions is that British exports to poor countries were the dependent variable, and that they greatly increased from 1820 onward, owing to the growing consumption of those commodities in Britain and in other advanced countries of the imports into Britain of tropical commodities resulting from the rapid growth in population and income in the developed world. That resulted in an increase in the purchasing power of poor countries, and they spent it on imports from Britain.[16]

See also P. J. Cain and A. G. Hopkins, *British Imperialism: Expansion and Innovation. 1688–1914* (London: Longman, 1993), Table 5–2, p. 163: the share of "underdeveloped countries" in British exports is constant at 35–36%, from 1846–50 to 1909–13 (except in 1871–75, when it falls to 32%), but Latin America is not included in this group. If its share (roughly 10%) is added, the sum is close to our ratios.

[14] By 1909–13, Italy and Spain had converged somewhat with Northern Europe (but the latter includes Russia). So these percentages are quite rough. The ambiguous position of South Africa is discussed in note 12. Argentina might be excluded from the poor countries group. By 1913, its PIB per capita was over twice the Latin America average.

[15] But this was somewhat compensated for by the sharp relative decline of the West Indies.

[16] Actually, Britain had a large surplus in trade with poor countries, which was

Empire and exports

Now we turn to Britain's exports to its empire. First, it must be stressed that, between 1846 and 1860, there was a change from a mercantilist to a free trade empire—an empire that did not make up one discrete economic entity. Britain was open to goods from all countries, on an equal footing, and did not impose upon its possessions any special treatment in favour of its own goods. Admittedly, for a number of reasons, Britain remained, by far, the main supplier to her colonial empire, but the colonies were not "captive" markets anymore, in contrast to their status in the 18th century.[17]

From Table 3, it appears that, from the 1810s to the mid-19th century, the share of the British empire in Britain's total exports declined from roughly 30% to 25%. On the other hand, from the 1850s until the eve of the First World War, the empire's share of British exports exhibited cyclical fluctuations—fluctuations connected to the export of British capital.[18] The minimum share of British exports imported by the empire was 23% in 1871; the maximum was 39% in 1902. Still, the empire's share of British exports was slowly increasing, and after 1875 the ratio never fell below 31%. In fact, it reached 35% in 1909–13 (37% in 1913), which amounted to a 40% increase from 1869–73.

---

used to invest in these same countries and to make good the British deficit with the United States and Europe.

[17] Britain also had an "informal" empire in Latin America, in parts of the Ottoman Empire, and in China. Cain and Hopkins have shown that it was in the field of finance and services more than in controlling trade. It was also mainly a late 19th-century phenomenon. Anyway, it is not possible to estimate exports to such an ambiguous entity. Nevertheless, Latin America took 10% of British exports.

[18] Some other factors also played a role. The American Civil War contributed to an increase in the imperial share of exports (35% in 1863), but these fell afterwards because of the boom in exports to the United States and Northern Europe.

Table 3. Share of the Empire in Britain's total exports[19]

	All British Possessions	Five Dominions	All other possessions
1814–18	30%	6%	24%
1847–51	26	9	17
1869–73	25	11	14
1889–93	33	15	18
1909–13	35	17.5	17.5

However, this increase was mainly due to the increasing importance of the "colonies of recent settlement," which became self-governing dominions. The rise in British exports to these colonies started in 1820—21% of total exports to the Empire in 1827–30, 47% in 1854–57—they then stabilised, and increased again from 1895 onward until they reached 50% of the total in 1909–13, when their share amounted to 17.5% of total British exports. The new settlement territories had small but rapidly increasing populations, and they enjoyed high and rising incomes per capita. Australia was Britain's best customer in this group, but exports to South Africa had the fastest growth after diamonds and gold were discovered.[20]

On the other hand, the share of the possessions, which used to be called "colonies of exploitation," shrunk markedly, from one-fourth to under one-sixth of total exports. Even India, with 200 million inhabitants in 1820 and 300 million in 1913, only took in 10% of British exports in the 1850s and 12% in 1909–13—roughly the same ratio as its share in the world population. Nevertheless, India was the largest market in the British Empire, receiving one-third of all British exports to its colonies. The rest of the empire (the Dominions and India excluded) only received 5.6% of British exports in 1909–13.[21]

[19] Calculated from W. Schlote, *British Overseas Trade, from 1700 to the 1930s*, translated from the German by W. O. Henderson and W. H. Chaloner (Oxford: Oxford University Press, 1952), Tables 20a and 20b, pp. 160–62.

[20] From the 1810s to the 1850s exports to the "dominions" increased much faster than those to "other possessions." Later, the difference in growth rates was much reduced, but the "dominions" retained their advantage.

[21] Cain and Hopkins, Table 5.3, p. 164. The share of British Africa (South Africa excluded) was 1.7%, that of Germany was %.

It is surprising that the imperial share of British exports only rose by 40% from the mid-19th century to the First World War, and that so few exports went to the tropical colonies, while, during that same period, the British empire expanded rapidly (six million km^2 were added from 1870 to 1900). Obviously, the economic importance of the "New Imperialism" during the latter part of the 19th century was disappointing. One reason was the poverty that prevailed in almost all the territories that had been annexed. Foreign competition, especially for capital goods, also played a role after 1873—e.g., in Canada, which had the United States as a neighbour, and in South Africa. One must also mention the rise of a modern cotton industry in India that reduced the imports of British cotton goods. On the other hand, quantitative data suggest that imperial trade had counterproductive effects, and that British industrialists withdrew to imperial markets rather than fight their competitors. Indeed, the share of British textile exports that went to the empire increased after 1870 and reached 44% of their total in 1913. Likewise, the imperial share of exports of iron and steel manufactures was one-third of the total in the 19th century, and one-half in the early 20th century. According to A. Maddison, the growth rate of British exports, at constant prices, fell from 4.9% per year in the period between 1820 and 1870 to 2.8% from 1870 to 1913. Some decline in the competitiveness of British manufacturing cannot be excluded.

Conclusion

At each of the major stages in the development of British domestic exports (stages which were determined either by military and political disruptions or by marked changes in the rates of growth), progress was due to expansion of their markets in two, three, or four of the 10 great trading regions I have delineated. Among the continents, the Americas were the most important in the 18th century, but they declined in importance after the French wars despite the amazing economic growth of North America, and the concomitant opening up of Latin America. On the other hand, the role of continental Europe in absorbing British exports was minor until the French Wars but became important and stable from 1814 to 1913. During that same period Asia and Australasia made significant contributions to the growth of British exports. Altogether, the growth of British exports was unbalanced—from the point of view of their geographical distribution—during the 18th century and the early decades of the 19th century (particularly from 1814–18 to 1842–46; see Tables 1 and 2). However, growth became more balanced later—particularly in the 1850s and 1860s. There was some equilibrium between exports to European and non-European markets—to "poor" and "rich" countries, as well as between foreign and imperial markets. The British export trade was truly global, and this was unique when compared with the export markets of the industrial countries on the European continent which was mainly in Europe. Non-European markets were more important for Britain than for other European countries, including countries that also possessed colonies. After all, the British Empire had the largest territory and the largest population.

Note on sources

Statistical data used for establishing Tables 1 and 2 mainly comes from: B. R. Mitchell, with the collaboration of Phyllis Deane, *Abstract of British Historical Statistics* (Cambridge: Cambridge University Press, 1962), Tables 1, 2, 3, 10, 11, 12, 13, pp. 279–81, 282–83, 283–84, 309–11, 312, 313–27, 328–29.

B. R. Mitchell, *British Historical Statistics* (Cambridge: Cambridge University Press, 1988), has additional material in tables 2a, 15, pp. 452 and 496; but his table 16C (p. 500) does not separate exports and re-exports from 1854.

A. Maddison, *L'économie mondiale: Une Perspective Millénaire* (Paris: OCDE, 2001), has also been used: Tables F-1, F-2, F-4, pp. 377, 379, 380, and *passim*.

More details on some points are available in: F. Crouzet, *Britain Ascendant: Comparative Studies in Franco-British Economic History* (Cambridge and Paris: Cambridge University Press, 1990), chapters 6 and 11. F. Crouzet, "Towards an Export Economy: British Exports during the Industrial Revolution," in *Explorations in Economic History*, vol. 17, n° 1, Jan. 1980, pp. 48–93.

CHAPTER TEN

DO FRONTIERS GIVE OR DO FRONTIERS TAKE? THE CASE OF INTERCONTINENTAL TRADE IN FRANCE AT THE END OF THE EIGHTEENTH CENTURY

Guillaume Daudin[1] OFCE/Sciences Po

The world has been the frontier of Europe. The extension of the frontiers for both trading and settlement increased the opportunities for adventurous Europeans. The sectors linked to these seemingly ever-expanding frontiers were the most dynamic parts of the various national economies. During the 18th century, the French port cities provided ample proof of that dynamism. The trading activities of Nantes, Bordeaux, Marseilles and Rouen expanded much faster than did the rest of the French economy. However, France was merely used as a warehouse to stock goods en route between the West Indies and the rest of Europe. Hence, the usual trade theory would suggest that the French port-based maritime frontier was nothing more than an enclave of growth. But what of the profits that were made in this trade?

Many authors have asserted that the relations between European nations and the rest of the world played a decisive role in the "primitive accumulation" of capital during the centuries prior to the Industrial Revolution. The best known of these authors are Marx—even if the related chapter in *Das Kapital* makes only a passing mention of the European colonies—Eric Williams and, more recently, the World System School researchers such as Wallerstein, Frank, and

[1] This paper is an offshoot from the sixth chapter of my thesis, now published as a book: Guillaume Daudin, *Commerce et prospérité: la France au XVIII*[e] *siècle* (Paris: PUPS, 2005). The list of people that helped me writing it would make another paper. However, I have to mention and thank Nick Crafts, François Crouzet, and Antoine d'Autume. This paper specifically benefited from the comments by participants at the *Table Ronde sur le Commerce Colonial* in Lorient, France, in September 2001, at the 2002 all-UC conference in Economic History, and at the 2005 EHS conference in Leicester.

Amin, to name but a few.[2] Their statements are controversial. In particular, cliometricians have contested the economic importance of slave trading and plantation colonies for the English economy.[3] In fact, many economic historians would agree with Patrick O'Brien's view, as it is expressed in a paper written in 1982, that profits from the "periphery," or, approximately, the non-European world, were simply too small to have played a major role in European growth.[4]

---

[2] Karl Marx, *Le Capital: Critique de l'économie politique* (Paris: Giard & Brière, 1867 (1993)); Eric Wilson Williams, *Capitalism and Slavery* (New York: 1944 (1966)); S. Amin, *Accumulation on a World Scale* (New York: Monthly Review Press, 1974) Andre Gunder Frank, *World Accumulation, 1492–1789* (New York and London: Macmillan, 1978); Immanuel Wallerstein, *The Modern World System I: Capitalist Agriculture and the Origins of the European World-Economy in the Sixteenth Century* (New York: Academic Press, 1974); Immanuel Wallerstein, *The Modern World System II: Mercantilism and the Consolidation of the European World Economy 1600–1750* (New York: Academic Press, 1980); Immanuel Wallerstein, *The Modern World System III: The Second Era of Great Expansion of the Capitalist World-Economy, 1730s–1840s* (San Diego: Methuen, 1989). This list is not complete. Cf. François Crouzet, ed. *Capital Formation in the Industrial Revolution* (London: 1972, p. 8) for Williams's predecessors.

[3] Cf. R. B. Sheridan, "The Wealth of Jamaica in the Eighteenth Century," *Economic History Review*, XVII (1965); R. B. Sheridan, "The Wealth of Jamaica in the Eighteenth Century: A Rejoinder," *Economic History Review*, XXI (1968), 46–61; Robert Paul Thomas, "The Sugar Colonies of the Old Empire: Profit or Loss for Great Britain?" *Economic History Review*, 21 (1968); Stanley L. Engerman, "The Slave Trade and British Capital Formation in the Eighteenth Century: A comment on the William Thesis," *Business History Review*, 46 (1972); Philip R. P. Coelho, "The Profitability of Imperialism: The British Experience in the West Indies, 1768–1772," *Explorations in Economic History*, X (1973), 253–80; R. Thomas, and R. Bean, "The Fishers of Men: The Profits of the Slave Trade," *Journal of Economic History*, 34 (1974), pp. 885–914; David Richardson, "Profitability in the Bristol-Liverpool Slave Trade," *Revue française d'histoire d'Outre-Mer*, 62 (1975), pp. 301–308; Joseph E. Inikori, "Market Structures and the Profits of the British African Trade in the Late Eighteenth Century," *Journal of Economic History*, 41 (1981), pp. 745–76; William Darity Jr., "The Number Game and the Profitability of the British Trade in Slaves," *Journal of Economic History*, XLV (1985), pp. 693–703; Barbara L. Solow, and Stanley L. Engerman, eds., *British Capitalism and Caribbean Slavery: The Legacy of Eric Williams* (New York: Cambridge University Press, 1987); Joseph E. Inikori, "The Credit Needs of the African Trade and the Development of the Credit Economy in England," *Explorations in Economic History*, 27 (1990), pp. 197–231; David Eltis and Stanley L. Engerman, "The Importance of Slavery and the Slave Trade in Industrialising Britain," *Journal of Economic History*, 60 (2000), pp. 123–44.

[4] Patrick O'Brien, "European Economic Development: The Contribution of the Periphery," *Economic History Review* (1982). As an example of endorsement, cf. Paul Bairoch, *Mythes et paradoxes de l'histoire économique* (Paris: Recouverte, 1995), pp. 117–120. However, O'Brien himself has come back on some of his affirmations in this article. He now believes that maritime trade and associated conflicts were central in 18th-century economy.

To reach this conclusion, O'Brien computes the total British and European profits derived from all economic activities outside Europe during the late 18th and early 19th centuries. The first part of this essay applies O'Brien's method to the case of France at the end of the *Ancien Régime*. More precisely, it estimates the amount of profits coming from the "intercontinental sector," defined as including the intercontinental trade in goods and services, shipping, insurance, and production for intercontinental exports, as well as profits from intercontinental investments. In the second part, this essay compares the amount of profits coming from the intercontinental sector to a counterfactual situation in which the resources used in the periphery were instead invested in Europe's domestic economy. O'Brien's method of computing this potential investment in the domestic European economy has been criticised by Barbara Solow.[5] This essay follows her recommendations. Finally, this essay suggests an altogether different way to look at the importance of the intercontinental sector through the use of a growth theory concept: the notion of "heart of growth." The appeal of the frontier for entrepreneurs was more important for the whole economy than the aggregate profits it provided.

Measuring profits

Before we compare, we need to measure. My method for measure is presented here—more details are to be found in Daudin (2005).[6]

Profits from intercontinental trade

The total profits generated by intercontinental trade were equal to the amount of capital invested in intercontinental trade multiplied by the rate of the profits.[7] Suggesting a precise value for this rate of profit is very hazardous. Yet, after studying 43 sources and 400 profit reports, I feel confident enough to suggest that there was an

[5] Barbara Solow, "Caribbean Slavery and British Growth: the Eric Williams Hypothesis," *Journal of Development Economics*, 17 (1985), pp. 99–115.

[6] Daudin, *Commerce et prospérité.*

[7] Ibid., pp. 241–360.

annual rate of profit of 6.25% based on a three-year investment cycle, and, thus, a rate of profit of 20% during the entire three year cycle.[8]

To compute the amount of capital invested in intercontinental trade, we combine the available data regarding the export of goods (including specie) and the investment structure. The data available concerning the investment structure allow us to compute the share of goods in those investments. The product of the inverse of this share with the amount of exports is equal to the total amount of investment. In turn, this share allows us to compute the total amount of investment.[9] We employ Arnould's estimate of French trade at the end of the *Ancien Régime.*[10]

[8] Guillaume Daudin, "Profitability of Slave and Long Distance Trading in Context: The Case of 18th Century France," *Journal of Economic History* 64, no. 1 (2004), pp. 144–171.

[9] Daudin, *Commerce et prospérité*, pp. 191–240.

[10] Ambroise Marie Arnould, *De la balance du commerce et des relations commerciales extérieures de la France dans toutes les parties du globe particulièrement à la fin du règne de Louis XIV et au moment de la révolution* (Paris: 1791), Tables 1 and 2.

Table 1. Intercontinental French trade at the end of the *Ancien Régime*

	Iberian Empires	United States of America	West Indies	Africa (-) and Mascarene islands	Asia (-)	Near East and North Africa	Europe	Total
Imports (CIF)	0.0%	4.0%	31.3%	0.7%	5.7%	6.2%	0.0%	47.8%
Exports (FOB)	3.2%	2.1%	12.9%	3.7%	2.8%	3.4%	0.0%	28%
Re-exports (FOB) (only to Europe)	NA	NA	NA	NA	NA	NA	24.2%	24.2%
Total	3.2%	6.0%	44.2%	4.4%	8.5%	9.5%	24.2%	613,243,000 *livres tournois*

Hypothesis: 40% of French exports to Spain and Portugal were actually to their overseas empires.[11] The ratio of re-exports over exports is the same for the Near East and North Africa as it is for Europe. We have included specie exports to Asia.
CIF: Cost, Insurance and Freight. CIF prices are prices in the destination harbour.
FOB: Free On Board. FOB prices are prices in the departure harbour.
All goods in that table are valued at their prices in France.

[11] O'Brien suggests that 60% of English exports to Spain were actually to the Spanish colonial empire ("European Economic Development: The Contribution of the Periphery," p. 6). It is probable that the European Spanish market was more important for France than for England.

It is possible to compute the share of goods in investment thanks to the 125 ship investment accounts (called "*mise-hors*" accounts) from the 18th century. These accounts come from an article by Morineau and from various books by Dermigny, Meyer and Saugera.[12] As the following table shows, most of the data actually comes from Meyer and deals with the end of the *Ancien Régime*. Therefore, our period of interest is especially well-represented.

Table 2. Source and date of the investment accounts

Source	1729–1749	1757–1769	1770–1779	1780–1789	1790–1802	Total
Meyer		18	28	54	4	104
Dermigny				17		17
Saugera	1				2	3
Morineau	1					1
Total	2	18	28	71	6	125

The difference between outfitters and traders was not clear-cut in France: all investment accounts included both investment in shipping and investment in trading. Total investment can be broken down in four categories: ship outfitting, buying victuals, wage advances and the cargo.

The following table gives the synthesis of the share of the cargo in the total investment:

[12] Michel Morineau, "Quelques recherches relatives à la balance du commerce extérieur français au XVIIIe siècle: où cette fois un égale deux," in P. Léon, ed., *Aires et structures du commerce français au XVIIIe siècle* (Lyon: Centre d'histoire économique et social de la région lyonnaise, 1973), pp. 1–45; Louis Dermigny, *Cargaisons indiennes. Solier & Cie, 1781–1793* (Paris: S.E.V.P.E.N., 1960) (vol. 2); Jean Meyer, *L'armement nantais dans la deuxième moitié du XVIIIe siècle* (Paris: S.E.V.P.E.N., 1969); and Éric Saugera, *Bordeaux, port négrier: chronologie, économie, sociologie, XVIIe–XVIIIe* (Biarritz, Paris: J&D, 1995), pp. 240–242. More data is available in Daudin, *Commerce et prospérité*.

Table 3. The share of the cargo as a part of the total investment (by destination)

	West Indies and United States of America	Slave trade	India and China
Minimum	5.8%	15.1%	43.7%
Maximum	64.2%	90.9%	79.3%
Mean	38.4%	59.4%	62.3%
Median	40.2%	63.9%	65.9%
Confidence interval (95%)	34.3%–42.6%	54.6%–64.1%	54.4%–70.3%

Commissions are mentioned in some accounts, but they are actually part of the outfitters' remuneration rather than an investment, so are excluded. Miscellaneous costs—including stopover costs—are aggregated under the broad category of "outfitting." Specie is considered to be part of cargo.

We now have all the elements in place to compute the amount of profits coming from both the slave trade and the direct trade with the Western Hemisphere, South and East Asia. These trades amounted to 21.5% of the total intercontinental trade: i.e. 132 million *livres tournois*.

Using Table 3 and trade numbers—assuming the slave trade stands for all trade with Africa—one finds that exported goods constituted 45% of the total investment in trade and shipping. The capital invested each year in the slave trade and in the direct trade with Africa, the Western Hemisphere, and with South and East Asia was, therefore, equal to 225% (i.e. the inverse of 45%) of direct exports to Africa, the Western Hemisphere, and South and East Asia. Using the trade numbers already presented, we compute that this invested capital was equal to 297 million *livres tournois.*

The rate of profit from the full investment cycle was equal to 20%. Assuming that investment did not change from one year to the next, the profits of the outfitters and traders were equal to 59 million *livres tournois*, or 45% of the direct exports. The computation can be summed up as:

$$\begin{aligned} \textit{trade and shipping profits} &= \frac{\textit{profits}}{\textit{investment}} \times \frac{\textit{investment}}{\textit{value of exported goods}} \times \textit{value of exported goods} \\ &= 20\% \times 225\% \times 132 \textit{ million} \\ &= 59 \textit{ million} \end{aligned}$$

Intercontinental trade also included trade with the Near East, re-exports to Europe and exports to the Iberian empires through their home countries. Even if we suppose that the annual rate of profit was the same in these trades as in the ones we have just examined, it would still not be possible to simply transpose our previous computation for two reasons. First, the investment cycle was shorter. Second, non-French controlled part of that trade. For these reasons, we assume that profits in these trades were equal to 20% of the value of the goods exiting France, instead of 45% for direct exports.[13] The value of goods exported from France in these trades was equal to 189 million *livres tournois*. Hence profits amounted to 38 million *livres tournois*.

Other aspects of intercontinental economic relations

O'Brien includes insurance profits in the profits derived from the periphery. There is data on insurance for the first part of a trading voyage, i.e. from France to another continent. In La Rochelle, in peacetime, insurers were able to make a profit equal to 45% of the insurance premiums paid to them. The average premium amounted to 5.3% of the insured value.[14] However, traders usually did not insure their investment fully. The study of Solier's accounts reveals that ship losses entailed a loss of 20% on the operation: it follows that only 80% of the investment was insured. Other sources confirm this practice of "underinsuring." As was mentioned above, the value of the investment was 225% of the value of the exported goods. Hence, the value insured was equal to 180% of the value of exported goods. If the numbers from La Rochelle are an indication, premiums were equal to 9.5% of the value of the exported goods. Insurers' profits on the first leg on each trade voyage were, thus, equal to 4.25% of the value of the exported goods, or 3.7 million *livres tournois* at the end of the *Ancien Régime*. The computation can be summed up as follows:

---

[13] Daudin, *Commerce et prospérité*, pp. 374–75.

[14] John G. Clark, *La Rochelle and the Atlantic Economy During the 18th Century* (Baltimore: Johns Hopkins University Press, 1981), p. 21.

$$\textit{insurers profits} = \frac{\textit{insurers profits}}{\textit{premium}} \times \frac{\textit{premium}}{\textit{insured investment}} \times \frac{\textit{insured investment}}{\textit{total investment}}$$
$$\times \frac{\textit{total investment}}{\textit{value of exported goods}} \times \textit{value of exported goods}$$
$$= 45\% \times 5.3\% \times 80\% \times 225\% \times 132 \textit{ million}$$
$$= 3.7 \textit{ million}$$

For other types of intercontinental trade, we assume that the profits of the insurers in France amounted to 1.4% of the total amount of goods, equalling seven million *livres tournois*.

O'Brien includes three other forms of profits in his computation: income from capital invested directly in the periphery, profits made by providing services sold to the periphery, and profits made by producing goods sold to the periphery. Unfortunately, data on French investments in the periphery are lacking. It seems that France had invested mainly in the West Indies. Unlike the English experience, profits from the West Indian plantations usually benefited local planters rather than absentee owners.[15] As we have no reliable estimates, and because choosing another hypothesis would strengthen rather than weaken our argument, we assume that profits from production in the West Indies stayed on the islands themselves, and should not be included in the total French gains from its activities overseas.

Similarly, there is no direct data to study the sale of services to the periphery. Unlike England, France did not control a large part of the intra-Asian trade between countries in South and East Asia. More generally, services were probably, to a large extent, embedded in the commercial activity between France and the periphery. That means that the sale of services has already been taken into account in the preceding section: they do not need to be added again.

Finally, O'Brien suggests that the profits accrued to domestic producers on goods sold to the periphery were equal to 20% of their value. The same percentage can be applied to all intercontinental French exports. As a consequence, French producers made an annual profit of 34 million *livres tournois* on the exports of their goods.

The amount of profits from the periphery could be increased still further by including the profits garnered by the (French) suppliers of services used in France by the intercontinental traders. That would

[15] Wallerstein, *World system II*, pp. 167–71.

mean adding the profits made by bankers and by traders distributing imported goods in the domestic economy, the traders bringing goods to the harbours to be exported to other continents, the auctioneers and owners of warehouses, and so on. There are two reasons why this operation will be avoided. First, there is no information whatsoever available to provide a plausible indication of the income derived from the capital invested in these activities.[16] Second, the final estimate must be comparable to O'Brien's: the same limits on the inclusion of domestic activities in our calculations should be set than he as he does in his calculations.

Results

Three different calculations are summed up in the following table: 1) O'Brien's estimate for England in the late 1780s; 2) this article's estimate for France for the same period; and 3) for the sake of comparison, the results this article's method would yield if it were applied to England.

Our estimate of the total direct and indirect French profits from intercontinental trade at the end of the *Ancien Régime* is 142 million *livres tournois* (approximately 5.7 million pounds sterling). In view of the many uncertainties, this number should be seen as providing an order of magnitude only.

Our method "transposed" to England gives comparable results to those arrived at by employing O'Brien's method. The fact that O'Brien's numbers are lower can be explained by the exclusion of some indirect profits that were less important for France than they were for England.

[16] To some extent, the profit figure for domestic producers is itself uncertain. By choosing 20% we might have—like O'Brien and Thomas did—chosen a slightly high estimate. It is possible that it is high enough to actually include domestic service producer profits. However, unlike goods production, domestic service production was also associated with imports.

Table 4. Profits from intercontinental economic relations in France and England at the end of the 1780s (in million *livres tournois*)

	Our method applied to France	Our method applied to England	O'Brien's method applied to England
Total trade	613	502	502
Trade profits and commissions on trade and shipping	97	78	67
Profits on insurance	11	9	8
Profits from "colonial" production brought back to the metropolises			(12)
Profits from the intercontinental sale of services			(20)
Profits from making or growing domestic goods exported to the periphery	34	24	30
Total	142	111	105 (137)

In applying my method to England, I have treated relations with the Near East and North Africa the same way as direct intercontinental trade. O'Brien's trade numbers exclude New England, whereas our numbers on French trade include it. As we are not comparing English and French results, this difference is of little importance. Total French trade with the U.S.A. amounted to approximately 37 million *livres tournois*.

Direct role of profits in the domestic economy

Capital stock in the domestic economy and in the intercontinental sector

This raw amount of profits must be compared with the characteristics of the French economy. French national income was between five and six billion *livres tournois* in the late *Ancien Régime.* If one assumes that 60% of the domestic income went to labour, 25% to capital and 15% to land, total profits from intercontinental relations were between 9.5% and 11.5% of total income from investment.[17]

However, that does not mean that income from invested capital would have been 10% smaller had the intercontinental sector not existed. One needs to take into account the available alternative domestic uses of capital, following the recommendations of Barbara Solow. To do that, this article first measures the amount of capital in the intercontinental sector, as well as in the economy as a whole.

The amount of capital invested in the domestic economy

There are two methods for assessing total investments. The first method is the perpetual inventory method. It is based on estimates of past investments and of past depreciation, and is the method employed most frequently by historians. Bourguignon and Lévy-Leboyer have used it to compute the amount of fixed capital in France in 1820.[18] Feinstein has also used it to compute the amount of capital in Great Britain in 1760.[19]

However, this method presents two difficulties. First, it only provides an estimate of the amount of fixed capital, while it is probable that circulating capital was also an important production factor in the pre-industrial economies. Furthermore, this method gives no room for the information available on the income derived by investments. Rather than measuring the gross "accounted for" capital on

---

[17] See Daudin, *Commerce et prospérité*, pp. 397–402.

[18] François Bourguignon, and Maurice Lévy-Leboyer, *L'Économie Française au XIXe siècle* (Paris: Economica, 1985), p. 276. The basis of the computation is to be found in M. Lévy-Leboyer, "Les évaluations du capital français au XIXe siècle" *Pour une histoire de la statistique* (Paris: Institut National de la Statistique et des Etudes Economiques, 1976), pp. 393–416.

[19] Charles H. Feinstein and Sidney Pollard, eds., *Studies in Capital Formation in the United Kingdom, 1750–1920* (Oxford: Oxford University Press, 1988), p. 427.

which capitalists received income, the perpetual inventory method tries to measure the net productive stock of capital. Applying this method to France at the end of the *Ancien Régime* would yield an average profit rate of at least 7.7%.[20] This profit rate is much higher that the profit rate in the intercontinental sector: that result is not plausible.

The alternative perpetual inventory method computes the total amount of capital from the income derived from it. It relies on the future income expectations of the owners of capital.[21] Assuming that the rate of return on domestic capital was 4.5%,[22] the total amount of capital invested in the domestic French economy can be computed at between 27 and 32 billion *livres tournois*.[23]

The amount of capital invested in the intercontinental sector

Assuming that the return on capital invested in international trade came to 6.25%, 97 million *livres tournois* must have been the income derived from an investment of 1,552 million *livres tournois*. Capital invested in insurance is more difficult to compute. However, assuming the same profit rate, 11 million *livres tournois* was the income derived

[20] Cf. Daudin, *Commerce et prospérité*, pp. 402–403.

[21] Charles H. Feinstein, "Capital Formation in Great-Britain," in P. Mathias and M. M. Postan, eds., *Cambridge Economic History of Europe* (Cambridge: Cambridge University Press, 1978), pp. 28–96 and pp. 33–34 and Charles H. Feinstein, *Domestic Capital Formation in the United Kingdom* (Cambridge: Cambridge University Press, 1965), pp. 257–58.

[22] Farm rents seem to indicate that capita remuneration was between 3 and 4.5%. Cf. François R. Velde, and David R. Weir, "The Financial Market and Government Debt Policy in France, 1746–1793," *Journal of Economic History*, 52 (1992), pp. 1–39: they quote debates during the nationalisation of church goods—the remuneration was then fixed at a number between 3 and 3.5%—and different regional studies: Georges Frêche, *Toulouse et la région Midi-Pyrénées au siècle des Lumières (vers 1670–1789)* (Paris: Lujas, 1974); A. Poitrineau, *La Vie rurale en Basse-Auvergne au XVIIIe siècle* (Paris: Aurillac, 1965); P. de Saint-Jacob, *Les Paysans de la Bourgogne du Nord au dernier siècle de l'Ancien Régime* (Paris: Dijon, 1960). Remuneration of capital in *rentes* was close to 5% (cf. Gilles Postel-Vinay, *La terre et l'argent: L'agriculture et le crédit en France du XVIIIe au début du XXe siècle* (Paris: Albin Michel, 1997) and Philip T. Hoffman, Gilles Postel-Vinay, and Jean-Laurent Rosenthal, *Des marchés sans prix: Une économie politique du crédit à Paris, 1660–1870* (Paris: École des Hautes Études en Sciences Sociales, 2000)). We use an intermediate estimation of 4.5%.

[23] Here is the computation method in the case of the high hypothesis. The total French income was six billion. The domestic income was 5.76 billion. Capital remuneration in the domestic economy was 1.44 billion. That represented the remuneration of 32 billion *livres tournois* at 4.5%.

from an investment of 175 million *livres tournois*. Finally, assuming that the profit rate in the domestic economy was 4.5%, 34 million was the profit derived from producing exported goods. Thus, the grand total of all capital invested directly and indirectly in the intercontinental sector amounted to 2.5 billion *livres tournois* at the end of the *Ancien Régime*.

If there had not been any intercontinental trade . . .

Measuring the total amount of capital does not suffice to compute the amount of forgone income. One also needs to make additional hypotheses on the domestic economy. This article assumes that the relationship between outputs and inputs in the French economy could be represented by a Cobb-Douglas function.

The income from labour in intercontinental trade can be estimated to be about two-thirds of the income derived from investments and the total number of labourers involved in intercontinental economic activities to be between 120,000 and 170,000.[24]

All these hypotheses allow for the computation of two sets of numbers:

- The relative size of the intercontinental sector, broken down in capital and labour income;
- The relative income that would have been lost if the inputs used in the intercontinental sector had been transferred to the French domestic economy at the end of the *Ancien Régime*.

The intercontinental sector provided between 1.5% and 2% of additional income to the French economy at the end of the *Ancien Régime*.

This gain was distributed in an uneven way among the different inputs. First of all, the existence of an intercontinental sector had a negative effect on income derived from land, confirming the old assumption that trade prospered at the expense of domestic agriculture. However, the losses incurred by the landowners were more than compensated for in the total economy by the extra income gained by the owners of capital. Income derived from investment would have been reduced by 6.5% to 8% if the intercontinental sector had not existed. Capital owners were the largest beneficiaries of the intercontinental sector.

[24] Daudin, *Commerce et prospérité*, pp. 378–88.

Table 5. Static role of the intercontinental sector

	Total French income	Capital income	Land income	Labour income	Total British Income
Relative size of the intercontinental sector	4%–4.75% of GNP 9.5%–15% of industrial product	13%–15.5%	0%	2.5%–3%	7%–8% of GNP 23%–26% of industrial product
Lost income if the sector had not existed	1.5%–2%	6.5%–8%	-3%–-2.5%	0%–0.5%	

The role of profits through investment and growth

The intercontinental sector was small compared to the total French economy. Yet its existence had a redistributive role, mainly in favour of capital. Through this redistributive role, the intercontinental sector played a role in determining the rate at which capital was saved and invested. According to the authors cited in the introduction, the accumulation of capital was at the centre of economic growth, and, therefore, the role of intercontinental trade in economic growth through savings might have been important.

The role of intercontinental profits in French savings

The determinants of savings are central to the assessment of the role of French intercontinental profits in savings. One acceptable approximation is that differences in rates of saving between individuals can be explained by differences in the origin of their income. There are two reasons to make that assumption.

The first reason is that the origin of income gives a proxy of its repartition. This is important because rich people generally save more than poor people. Income from labour was distributed most equally and, therefore, less was saved. Income from capital was distributed most unevenly and, hence, more of it was saved. Income from land ownership was in between: distributed more evenly in France than in England, some of it accrued to poor people, but a much larger percentage benefited the rich.

The second reason for assuming that the origin of the income determines the rate of saving is that it might play a role in the behaviour of income earners with a similar income. A manufacturer and a landowner might have had the same income, but the manufacturer might be expected to exhibit more "capitalist" behaviour and consume less ostentatiously and, thereby, save more than the landowner.

Three saving rates compatible with estimates of past savings rates in England and France are suggested in the next table.[25]

According to these figures, the savings coming from the intercontinental sector amounted to 30 million *livres tournois* a year. Of these 30 million, 28 million *livres tournois* were income derived from

[25] For more details, see Daudin, *Commerce et prospérité*, pp. 413–16.

Table 6. Hypotheses on the relations between savings rates and the origin of income

Production factor	Share of income (France)	Share of income (England)	Hypothesis on saving rates
Capital	25%	35%	20%
Land	15%	15%	5%
Labour	60%	50%	2%
Total	100%	100%	France: 6.95% England: 8.5%

capital income and two million *livres tournois* from labour. The total yearly domestic savings amounted to between 350 and 420 million *livres tournois*. Intercontinental savings ranged from 7% to 8.5% of domestic savings. Taking into account the alternative use of production capacities, net gains were between 20 and 21 million *livres tournois* for capital income. Savings from labour income were not affected, while savings from land income were reduced by less than a million *livres tournois*. The whole net gain in yearly savings linked to the existence of an intercontinental sector thus ranged between 5% and 6.3% at the end of the *Ancien Régime* in France.

From savings to growth

The effect of these additional savings on the French rate of growth can be computed by using our hypothesis on French production capabilities. However, an additional hypothesis must first be made concerning the net capital accumulation and the capital/output ratio. The basis of this additional hypothesis is a comparison between the situation in England and France during the 19th century.[26] This comparison allows us to estimate that, in late *Ancien Régime* France, the net investment rate was between 2.4% and 3.9% and the net capital/output ratio was 2.5.

[26] Feinstein, "Capital Formation in Great-Britain"; N.F.R. Crafts, *British Economic Growth during the Industrial Revolution* (Oxford: Oxford University Press, 1985); Simon Kuznets, *Population, Capital, and Growth: Selected Essays* (London: Norton, 1974). Bourguignon and Lévy-Leboyer, *L'Economie Française au XIXe siècle*; Jean-Claude Toutain, "Le produit intérieur brut de la France de 1789 à 1982, série AF n° 15," *Economies et Sociétés, Cahiers de l'ISEA* (1987), 1–237.

If these numbers are accepted, a one-point variation in the saving rates increased the capital stock growth rate by 0.4 point. A 0.4-point variation in the rate of growth of the amount of capital in the economy increased the total income growth rate by one tenth of a point. Assuming that the gross French saving rate was 7% and that French real growth rate *per capita* was 0.6% at the end of the *Ancien Régime*, the elasticity of growth with regard to savings was 1.2. Thus, if the existence of the intercontinental sector increased savings by 5 to 6.3%, it increased the growth rate of the economy by a figure between 6% and 7.6% (i.e. between 0.036 and 0.046 points). If the size of this effect was constant from 1715 to 1790, the intercontinental sector increased GNP per capita in 1790 by 2 to 3%. This is higher than its static role, but still small.

A possible indirect role for profits

These numbers give a fair approximation of the role of intercontinental profits in late *Ancien Régime* France. The intercontinental sector was four times as important for growth as it was for total income. It was a dynamic sector that "pulled" the rest of the economy. Nonetheless, this direct role was relatively small. This is not surprising. Most individual sectors seem small when compared with the overall economy.

Actually, even if the profit figures were not as small as this paper suggests, the notion of an intercontinental sector "irrigating" the rest of the economy with its capital contradicts the basic motivation for making investment decisions—profit. If the intercontinental sector offered higher profits than the domestic economy, why would the intercontinental traders (we will use the term as a short-hand for all the actors in intercontinental trade) have transferred their capital from this sector to other ones?

A sector attracting capital rather than redistributing it

Limits in the movement of capital from the intercontinental sector

In France, as in Great-Britain, intercontinental traders were involved in industrial investment. In Scotland, tobacco traders played a role in mining, the iron industry, linen production, and in the cotton sector.[27] In Nantes, especially before the Seven Years War, international traders and their capital were important in the textile industry, in glass making and in the indigo industry.[28] Nevertheless, there is no indication that intercontinental traders invested more in industry than other categories. In Scotland, their capital was only invested in 17% of cotton firms.[29] This proportion of investment, in fact, might not have been very different from their share in total savings.

One can surmise that intercontinental traders invested less in domestic industries than did other actors. In the case of Nantes, Pétré-Grenouilleau reminds us that after the "starting" period of industries, intercontinental traders had a tendency to withdraw their capital.

> All in all, two phases can be distinguished. The first one is contemporaneous with the birth of large colonial trade: the trading community tried then to create the industrial fabric that was to complement its own speculations (sugar factories and calicos). The second phase starts very early, probably even before the mid-century. It is characterised by a clear withdrawal. This withdrawal became obvious just before the Revolution.[30] (my translation)

Boulle notes that, even before the Seven Years War, intercontinental traders did not invest outside of Nantes. He remarks that "the range of investments from Nantes was limited." He underlines that, around the mid-century in Le Havre, capital was moving from industry to trade rather than the reverse.[31] Bairoch, too, points out that, even when traders invested in industry, they did not invest in the important or decisive sectors driving the Industrial Revolution.[32]

---

[27] T. M. Devine, "The Colonial Trades and Industrial Investment in Scotland, c. 1700–1815," *Economic History Review*, 29 (1976), pp. 1–13.

[28] Pierre H. Boulle, "Slave Trade, Commercial Organisation and the Industrial Growth in 18th century Nantes," *Revue française d'histoire d'Outre-Mer*, 59 (1972), pp. 70–112.

[29] Devine, "The Colonial Trades and Industrial Investment in Scotland, c. 1700–1815," p. 10.

[30] Olivier Pétré-Grenouilleau, *L'argent de la traite: milieu négrier, capitalisme et développement: un modèle* (Paris: Aubier, 1996).

[31] Boulle, "Slave trade," p. 98; Boulle, "Marchandises de traite et développement industriel dans la France et l'Angleterre du XVIIIe siècle," *Revue française d'histoire d'Outre-Mer*, 62 (1975), pp. 309–330, (pp. 320–321).

[32] Paul Bairoch, "Commerce international de la révolution industrielle anglaise," *Annales E.S.C.* (1973), pp. 541–571, (pp. 547–9).

Intercontinental traders were, quite simply, behaving like most other people would have under the same circumstances. They would rather invest in activities they knew already and had mastered than in other sorts of endeavours. This preference for the known did not necessarily exclude some asset diversification, including investment in emerging industries. Yet, this diversification was directed toward industrial firms located nearby, and to firms in which there was a potential for vertical concentration allowing for the utilisation of knowledge and social networks already accumulated in intercontinental trade.

Movement of capital and people to the intercontinental sector

The intercontinental sector both tended to keep its capital to itself and attracted people from the domestic economy. This attraction of people was also an attraction of capital: when someone moved into the intercontinental sector, he took his store of financial, human and social capital with him.

The origins of 166 Nantes families involved in colonial trade in the second half of the 18th century are available.[33] The local bourgeoisie had been at the centre of the late 17th century expansion, but it did not represent more than 9.4% of the trading families in the second half of the 18th century. Most immigrants were traders from the domestic economy. Pétré-Grenouilleau remarks that, out of the 92 traders whose fathers' profession is known, 59 came from trading families. Migration from other French ports—like Bordeaux or maritime Western France that sent penniless nobles or families ascending the social ladder—was the exception rather than the rule.

In Marseilles, the number of *négociants* increased from 275 at the end of the 17th century to 450 around 1750 and still further to 750 at the end of the *Ancien Régime*. *Négociants* from outside Marseilles were 18.7% of the total at the beginning of the century, 24.6% at mid-century and 46.3% at the end of the *Ancien Régime*. The Solier, whose activity has been studied by Dermigny, are a good example of the migrating movement.[34] As Carrière said: "The migration curve closely follows the expansion curve, and that is to be expected." (my translation).[35]

---

[33] Pétré-Grenouilleau, *L'argent de la traite*, pp. 18–41. Dermigny, *Cargaisons indiennes*

[34] Dermigny, *Cargaisons indiennes*.

[35] Charles Carrière, *Négociants marseillais au XVIIIe siècle*. 2 vols. (Marseille: 1973), pp. 265 and 280–81.

In La Rochelle at the end of the *Ancien Régime*, only 58% of the ship outfitters came from the town itself or its neighbouring regions of Aunis, Saintonge, Guyenne and Gascoigne. In Lorient at the same time, 63% of the ship outfitters did not come from the town itself but, rather, from the neighbouring dioceses, especially Vannes. In Bordeaux, "the majority of the ship outfitters were strangers to the region: Protestants from Languedoc, Catholics from Bretagne and Bayonne, or foreigners like the Bethmann from Frankfort."[36] In the 17th century, "the Saint-Malo capitalist centre was [. . .] the heir of the Vitry centre;" and "the Saint-Malo trading group was open [. . .] it became larger throughout the 17th century by attracting dynamic elements from the cities and ports in its attraction zone."[37]

The importance of migration to the trading centres is beyond dispute. Its motivation was probably the following: migration was an important stage in the individual accumulation of financial, social and human capital. When the situation of domestic traders was such that they faced decreasing returns in local activities, one can assume that they often also had enough knowledge and social connections to change the scale of their activity and continue their accumulation of capital in the intercontinental sector.

The intercontinental sector: a plausible heart of growth?

The "heart of growth"

To understand what positive role the intercontinental sector could play in domestic growth despite that fact that it attracted and kept for itself capital and entrepreneurs, one can use a neo-classical growth model.[38] *Per capita* economic growth, if there is no technical progress or institutional change, can only come from capital accumulation. In order to generate growth, the society has to forego part of its

[36] Cf. quoted by Pétré-Grenouilleau: D. Bouniol, "Étude sociale des armateurs Rochelais membres de la Chambre de Commerce dans la seconde moitié du XVIIIe siècle" (Maîtrise: Université de Nantes, 1972); X. Moutet, "Négociants et armateurs de Lorient au XVIIIe siècle" (Maîtrise: Université de Nantes, 1974); Paul Butel, *Les négociants bordelais, l'Europe et les îles au XVIIIe siècle* (Paris: Aubier, 1974), p. 16.

[37] André Lespagnol, *Messieurs de Saint-Malo: Une élite négociante au temps de Louis XIV* (Rennes: Presses Universitaires de Rennes, 1997), p. 88.

[38] Robert Solow, "A contribution to the theory of economic growth," *Quarterly Journal of Economics*, 70 (1956), pp. 65–94. On growth models in general, cf. Robert J. Barro, *La croissance économique* (Paris: Economica Parution, 1995) (1996).

present consumption in order to increase production and consumption in the future. Decreasing marginal returns to capital limit this process. Each additional accumulated unit of capital increases future production by a smaller quantity than the amounts accumulated before. Over time, the gains from capital accumulation decline and, as a result, the speed at which capital is saved will be reduced. At some point, the gains from capital accumulation are equal to the cost of forgone consumption. This will lead to a halt in growth as the economy reaches its long-term production level. In order to explain the continuation of growth beyond that point, it is necessary to introduce an exogenous phenomenon such as technical progress. That is why this neo-classical growth model is called an "exogenous" growth model.

However, it is also possible to construct a growth model that does not need an exogenous factor in order to explain sustained growth. Since the mid-1980s, new research on such growth models has been concerned with activities that have declining returns for private actors and non-decreasing returns for the society as whole. An example would be research and development of various technologies. "AK" models use an alternative approach.[39] They posit an economic sector in which capital returns are constant. In order to avoid increasing returns to scale, which—without externalities—would predict that no competitive equilibrium can exist, capital must be the only input such a sector uses. Regardless of its size, this sector allows the economy to escape declining returns. That is why it is termed a "heart of growth."[40]

---

[39] Paul Romer, "Increasing Returns and New Developments in the Theory of Growth," in W. A. Barnett, ed., *Equilibrium theory and applications* (Cambridge: Cambridge University Press, 1989).

[40] The "heart of growth" notion has been introduced by R. Rebelo, "Long-Run Policy Analysis and Long-Run Growth," *Journal of Political Economy*, 99 (1991). The Lucas model is another example of a heart of growth: Robert E. Lucas, "On the Mechanics of Economic Development," *Journal of Monetary Economics*, 22 (1988). For a general study, cf. Jérôme Glachant, "Les théories de la croissance: fondements et implications," (Doctoral dissertation, University of Paris I, 1994), and Jérôme Glachant, "Croissance et structure du système productif dans une économie log-linéaire," *Annales d'économie et statistique*, 39 (1995). Actually, the assumption that the rate of capital accumulation in the intercontinental sector is constant is not a necessary condition for continued growth as long as we assume that this rate is always higher than in the domestic economy.

Under these conditions, growth is accelerated in the medium run. Even if no capital is invested yet in the "heart of growth" sector, the knowledge about its existence encourages capital accumulation. The usual transition mechanisms in a neo-classical growth model, where capital accumulation is slower and slower till it stops will be not apply. Furthermore, if a heart of growth sector exists, growth can continue unabated in the long run. As long as each additional input of capital can be used in that heart of growth, it will not suffer from declining returns.

However, this model has an unwanted property: even if, in the medium run, the existence of a heart of growth accelerates the development of the non-heart of growth sectors, in the long-run, it non-heart of growth sectors will stop their development as soon as the return they can offer to capital equals what the heart of growth sector can offer. The heart of growth will grow in an autarchic way, and finally dwarf the rest of the economy. This will be avoided if the non-heart of growth offers something that cannot be provided by the heart of growth, for example consumption goods. In that case, capital accumulation in the heart of growth cannot not be an end by itself. The development of the other sectors of the economy is indispensable if the owners of capital want to enjoy the result of their savings.

The profit rate of the intercontinental sector was higher than in the rest of the economy, and it attracted investments: that corresponds to the definition of a heart of growth sector for the French economy during the period of the late *Ancien Régime*. However, if the capital accumulated in the intercontinental sector was not recycled in the rest of the economy through consumption, it would have been simply an enclave, with no link to French development as a whole.

Why the French port cities were not enclave economies

This risk was mitigated by the consumption habits of the members of the intercontinental sector. It appears that they were using a steady share of their income to consume domestic French products. In fact, it is ironic that this consumption pattern should be presented as a good thing. The consumption habits of French traders have often been criticised, and many authors who compare the relative industrial backwardness of France to the rapid industrial progress of England have blamed the lack of capitalist thriftiness of the French bourgeoisie. Hoselitz claimed, for example, that every Frenchman aspired to become a *rentier*.[41] Taylor and Léon cited the taste for *offices* and land.[42] These swallowed the capital of intercontinental traders and prevented its use in the more dynamic sectors of the French economy. This was also exposed by Colbert and Necker, maybe somewhat hypocritically, as they knew the State's finance depended in part on the income from *offices* sales.[43]

Recent research on individual ports—Bordeaux, Nantes or Saint-Malo—seems to contradict this traditional view. *Rentes*, land and *offices* were not the "grave" of capital from the dynamic sector of the economy, and, instead, should be treated just like other consumption goods. It is, after all, to be expected that status goods were an aim of the accumulation of riches—either for oneself or for one's children.[44] Moreover, the tendency towards conspicuous consumption was not exclusive to French trading communities. As Crouzet remarks, "[in England] the dream of every enriched trader was to become a *country gentleman*" (our translation).[45] Conspicuous consumption neither inhibited the drive to obtain wealth nor did it infringe on the autonomy of the merchant world.

---

[41] Cf., for example: Bert F. Hoselitz, "Entrepreneurship and Capital Formation in France and Britain since 1700," in M. Abramovitz, ed., *Capital Formation and Economic Growth (Conference Proceeding, NY, 1953)* (Princeton: Princeton University Press, 1955), pp. 291–337 (p. 105). This particular thesis "that broadly overestimates the importance of the State in the creation and the funding of industry" (François Crouzet, "Angleterre et France au XVIIIe siècle: analyse comparée de deux croissances économiques," in M. Margairaz, ed., *Histoire Economique: XVIIIe–XXe siècles* (Paris: Larousse, 1966 (1992)), pp. 323–353, p. 341, note 2) is disputable. Nevertheless, the idea remains.

[42] George V. Taylor, "Noncapitalist Wealth and the Origin of the French Revolution," *American Historical Review*, 72 (1967), pp. 469–496 (pp. 473–474, pp. 477–479, p. 485); Pierre Léon, "Les nouvelles élites," in Braudel and Labrousse, eds., *Histoire économique et sociale de la France* (Paris: PUF, 1970 (1993)), pp. 601–650 (pp. 632–634, p. 642).

[43] William Doyle, *Venality: The Sale of Offices in Eighteenth-Century France* (Oxford: Oxford University Press, 1996), p. 20, and Jacques Necker, *De l'administration des finances de la France* (Paris: 1784), III, p. 149.

[44] Butel, *Négociants bordelais*, pp. 325–364. Pétré-Grenouilleau, *L'argent de la traite* (pp. 126–27 and 128–129). Lespagnol, *Messieurs de Saint-Malo*, pp. 735–772. Olivier Pétré-Grenouilleau, *Les négoces maritimes français, XVIIe–XXe siècle* (Paris: Belin, 1997), pp. 96–101.

[45] Crouzet, "Angleterre et France au XVIIIe siècle: analyse comparée de deux croissances économiques," pp. 339–343.

Beside status goods, the community of intercontinental merchants in France had a taste for a large number of consumer goods produced in France such as textiles, foodstuffs, furniture, domestic services, and housing. This shows that the intercontinental port cities were linked to the French domestic economy by the consumption patterns of their merchants. These port cities were supplied by their hinterland, especially in low-value goods, but also by the rest of the country.[46] During the 18th century, the link between the dynamic maritime cities and the domestic economy was never severed in the same way that it now is in some developing countries in which rich elites consume mainly imported goods.

The existence of these links was enough to prevent the intercontinental sector from becoming an enclave. Thus, it is plausible that it played a positive role as a heart of growth sector. It is difficult to measure how large this role was. However, one can venture to suggest some possible numbers based on the simulation of a heart of growth model.[47] These numbers are given as an illustration of the potential effect of the intercontinental sector: the complexity of the computation warrants additional research in a forthcoming paper. According to a first back-of-the-envelop computation, it seems that, without the intercontinental sector being a heart of growth, French stock of capital would have been nearly 30% smaller, French growth per capita would have been 0.21 percentage points smaller (one-third of total growth), and French GDP would have been 8% smaller. These numbers are larger than the preceding ones, but not by an absurd amount.

---

[46] Thomas Le Roux, *Le commerce intérieur de la France à la fin du XVIIIe siècle: les contrastes économiques régionaux de l'espace français à travers les archives du Maximum* (Paris: Nathan, 1996) gives maps of Nantes's supply areas.

[47] The model is presented in Guillaume Daudin, *Commerce et prospérité*, pp. 534–543. A forthcoming paper will deal with the formal side of this simulation. For information, here are the hypotheses: share of capital in domestic income = 25%; preference for the present = 4.5%; rate of profit in the intercontinental trade sector = 6.5%; income per head in 1715: 135 *livres tournois*-1790; income per head in 1790: 205 *livres tournois*; domestic capital stock per head in 1715: 500 *livres tournois*-1790; domestic capital stock per head in 1790: 1015 *livres tournois*; intercontinental sector capital stock per head in 1790: 85 *livres tournois;* no intercontinental sector in 1715 (this is obviously an exaggeration); a scaling factor (I in the model): 1. Based on that, one can compute the inter-temporal consumption elasticity that is compatible with the model, the starting and the finishing conditions, which is equal to 7. More details are available directly from the author.

Conclusion

The aim of this paper was to contribute to the debate on the role of overseas expansion, and, more particularly, on the role played by the profits from intercontinental trade in the growth of capital in the domestic economy in Early Modern France. O'Brien's method leads to a measure of the profits linked to intercontinental trade of 142 million *livres tournois*. Their direct role in the domestic capital accumulation could only have been limited, as the intercontinental sector was small when compared with the entire economy. Less than 7.5% of French growth can be explained by the capital accumulated in the intercontinental sector. Maybe a change of perspective is necessary. Instead of looking at how the intercontinental sector supplied the rest of the economy with capital, it might be more fruitful to look at how investment in the intercontinental sector encouraged the accumulation of capital in the domestic economy, as it offered a way out of declining returns for successful entrepreneurs that did not trap them in an enclave economy. A tentative measure of the size of this effect can be proffered: even if the effect on GDP is only 8%, it is three to four times as large as what is found by other methods. If this suggestion is right, the frontiers of the expanding European economy might have been more important for the hopes and the dreams they generated than for the capital they directly provided.

CHAPTER ELEVEN

COLONIAL TRADE AND ECONOMIC DEVELOPMENT IN FRANCE, SEVENTEENTH TO THE TWENTIETH CENTURIES

Olivier Pétré-Grenouilleau

The old and always lively debate on the role of the periphery in the development of the centre, or more precisely, of the colonial world in the rise of the West, is for the most part focused on the Old World, particularly Great Britain, the pioneer of the Industrial Revolution. France, much less studied in this debate, constitutes just as interesting a case study, due to the length of time it was involved in the colonial world—from the last third of the 17th century to the second half of the 20th—its role in European politics, and the nature of its development process. The possession of the important colony of Saint-Domingue, coupled with the size of its colonial trade, made France a colonial power on par with England at the end of the *Ancien Régime*. France was also the second nation of Western Europe to industrialise. Finally, only France and England out of all the Western European nations, experienced a more or less continuous development process. Spain and Portugal's economic development, for example, stagnated from the 17th century onwards, with neither country industrialising until the late 19th century, and, even then, only modestly. Likewise, the Netherlands, also a colonial power, suffered from static growth and late industrialisation.

Colonial trade can mean two very different things. On the one hand, it can mean the established trade with a nation's own colonies. On the other hand, it can refer to trade with the colonial world in general which, at certain historical moments, meant most of the world outside Europe. In this essay, I will be referring to France's trade with its own colonies. I shall try to differentiate between growth, meaning a purely quantitative expansion, and the idea of development, defined as a quantitative *and* qualitative process creating new synergies and favouring the combined expansion of several economic sectors.

Studies of the links between colonial trade and development generally start with three factors of analysis: 1) the outlets offered by the colonies for goods from the home country; 2) the raw materials imported from the colonies; and, 3) the profits from colonial trade and their possible reinvestment in the home economy. I think we should add a fourth factor of analysis, specifically; 4) the role of colonial trade in the processing and finishing of the tools necessary for the shift from merchant to industrial capitalism. Nor should it be forgotten that the expansion of one economic sector, for example that of a port or a port's hinterland, is not necessarily synonymous with national economic growth.

The essay presented here in no way aims to bring ready-made answers to this prickly and complex problem of the relationship between colonial trade and economic development. In presenting the pieces of the puzzle, and by insisting on a variety of ways of analysing the diverse factors comprising colonial trade, this essay is an attempt to highlight the variety and the complexity of the interactions to be taken into account when analysing the influence of colonial trade on the economic development of the home country, while also making some preliminary conclusions about how much, in fact, this colonial trade did, or did not, factor in to France's economic development. To do this, I have selected three periods of time: 1) the beginnings of France's colonial trade, between 1660–1720; 2) the consolidation and restructuring of this trade, from the 1720s to 1792; and, finally, 3) the development of a "second" French colonial system following the French Revolution, from the end of the 18th century to the middle of the 20th century.

The Beginnings of French Colonial Trade, 1660–1720

The presumed importance of the role played by colonial trade in France's economic development is due, in part, to the way in which historians have tended to view French trade before the advent of colonisation. This pre-colonial trade has long been interpreted as unimportant, fragile, technologically backwards, and inward-looking.[1]

[1] On this question, see O. Pétré-Grenouilleau, *Les négoces maritimes français XVIIe–XXe siècle* (Paris: Belin, 1997), ch. 1–3.

Therefore, many historians have viewed the expansion into colonial trade as little short of a miracle, and as a revolutionary process allowing growth in whole sections of the economy, and as a result, the development of French capitalism in general. I believe, however, that this interpretation lends undue significance to the role of colonial trade in France for the following reasons; 1) nascent capitalism and trade networks were already in place prior to the beginnings of colonial trade; 2) the technical infrastructure was already in existence and was often adapted by those involved in colonial trade with little alteration; and, 3) it was disproportionably the ports and their hinterlands, and not the nation as a whole, that were strongly affected by colonial trade. I will elaborate on these points below.

Nascent capitalism and trade networks

Colonial trade did not awaken and modernise a slumbering trade sector. On the contrary, colonial trade was, itself, the result of a cumulative process lasting several centuries. In order to understand this development, we must go back to the 15th century.[2] Economic growth within the Kingdom of France began to accelerate after the Hundred Years War. Ports such as those of the Basse-Seine, Bordeaux, and Brittany were again in French hands by the end of the 15th century, and, with the cessation of hostilities, were able to increase the volume of their foreign trade. The trade conducted through these ports has often been described as "passive" because French merchants were generally content to be the middlemen between local producers and foreign merchants dealing in the purchase and international transport of local foodstuffs. But this description of passivity ignores very important developments in the formation of trade networks.

For example, in Nantes, the wine trade was the result of many small merchants bringing in one or two cargos and then joining together in order to charter ships. This was also the case for Bordeaux, whilst at La Rochelle, merchants joined together to underwrite loans to farmers who, in turn, sold grape futures, usually in June. In this way, the merchants of La Rochelle benefited from advantageous prices while stocking up on merchandise to sell to foreigners in

[2] For more substantial on this, see Pétré-Grenouilleau, *Les négoces maritimes français*, pp. 9–84.

October or November. Meanwhile, protected by local privileges resulting from the rights given to Mediaeval towns, a bourgeoisie began to develop.

Moreover, at the beginning of the 16th century, fisherman, merchants, and sailors all became involved in long-distance ocean fishing, as well as in the illicit trade with the Iberian colonial empire. This trend towards more distant trading ventures then accelerated during the second half of the 16th century. Together with the traditional Mediaeval trade in wheat, wine, salt, oils, and textiles which linked Northern and Southern Europe, new trading opportunities were developed. For instance, cod fishing grew exponentially.[3] In Africa and America, exploration led to the pursuit of new sources of wealth.

Rouen and the Norman ports of Saint Malo and La Rochelle figured most prominently as the recipients of this increased foreign trade. Slowly these ports, or, more specifically, the merchants working through these ports, began to integrate themselves into the Iberian trading networks. In fact, once the merchants became involved in foreign trade, the heretofore nascent capitalism became self-perpetuating. This demonstrates that, far from being archaic, France's precolonial trade laid an important foundation upon which France could build when constructing its own colonial trading endeavours.[4]

Although France's entry into the colonial system was slow in comparison to the Iberians, it was not as delayed as that of the English or the other Northwestern European countries.[5] France's delayed

---

[3] The historians of industrialisation use the term "leading industry" (*industrie motrice*) for a sector of activity capable of bringing growth to a part of the economy. We could use "growth trade" *trafics porteurs* to describe speculation bringing growth to the maritime economy.

[4] Referring to this, P. Léon and C. Carrière said that "spatially cramped, passive in great measure" it was the reflection of a "capitalism poor in men and means" in F. Braudel and E. Labrousse, *Histoire économique et sociale de la France* (Paris: P.U.F., 1993), II, p. 188. In the same collection (I, p. 357), R. Gascon gave one part the title "le retard français, essai d'explication." Using this sort of analysis, A. Lespagnol wrote in his thesis: "it was at the turn of the Seventeenth and Eighteenth centuries . . . that French merchant capitalism, *for long dawdling and drowsy* . . . really made its entrance on the world stage" in *Messieurs de Saint-Malo, une élite négociante au temps de Louis XIV* (Rennes: *P.U.R.*, 1997), p. 13. However, his whole thesis shows to what degree the Saint Malo trade was "mature," as far as commercial techniques from the 17th century were concerned. On this subject, see Pétré-Grenouilleau, "Dynamique sociale et croissance. A propos du prétendu retard du capitalisme maritime français," *Annales, Histoire, Sciences Sociales*, 1997, 6, pp. 1263–74.

[5] The synchronism between the rise of the English West Indies from 1660 and the rise of French colonial trade under Colbert is revealing. At the beginning, Dutch

entry into the colonial system might well be because other, more traditional and safer, trade continued to be economically viable. On the eve of the 17th century, it was motivation and not the means that were lacking for colonial trade. Ambitious merchants, often on a modest scale, led the way and invested in the new trade routes of the time. But the wealthier merchants with greater capital at their disposal still hesitated to commit themselves.

Technical infrastructure

In addition to the existence of nascent capitalism and merchant and trade networks, as was seen above, historians have another reason to doubt that colonial trade was of particular importance to the economic development of France. Whether it was the type of mercantile fleet, the means of payment for marine operations, or even insurance methods, the technical infrastructure to facilitate colonial trade was in place well before France entered the trans-Atlantic colonial trade.

Let us look at the case of the mercantile fleets. With entry into the trans-Atlantic colonial trade came a real, marked increase in the number of ships within each category of vessel. Tonnages increased continually throughout the 18th century. Nevertheless, other than the construction of ships for the slave trade and for long voyages to the Indian Ocean, it was only during the Industrial Revolution that progress in ship-building became truly spectacular.[6] Moreover, no

penetration into the colonial Atlantic was certainly much more spectacular than French attempts, but it ended in progressive and bitter failures (in Brazil, North America, and the West Indies). The lesser degree of French operations is explained at the beginning by the lack of economic inducements in the West Indies (before the sugar revolution), by the fact that many merchants preferred to continue investing in safer and sufficiently profitable trade, and that, for a long time, the state had preferred to try to snatch the wealth of the Iberian empire by piracy and freebooting, rather than developing the West Indies.

[6] The fact that the state had to subsidise the French slave trade while Santo Domingo was bursting with energy may seem paradoxical. In fact, there are three reasons for this: the first, a determining one, is that the price of slaves sold by the French slave traders was above that of the captives offered by foreign, particularly English, traders. This price is explained by technical reasons (number of crewmen, etc.) where D. Eltis stopped in his *The Rise of African Slavery in the Americas* (Cambridge: Cambridge University Press, 2000), but also by the limits imposed by the French government and companies with a monopoly on the private slave trade. The second reason is that the colonisers often preferred to buy their slaves secretly from

matter what the period, increases in tonnages generally follow commercial imperatives, not create these imperatives. The technology existed to build ships with greater tonnage, but it was pragmatic business interests which determined whether or not they would actually be built.

The same holds true for port infrastructure. The first great construction works often date to the 16th century. From then on, improvements or extensions were rare. Heavy investment was nearly always postponed. Nantes preferred to continue to extend its entry harbours closer to the mouth of the Loire. Whereas wet docks were built from the 18th century at Liverpool and Bristol, it was not until the end of the 19th century that the French traders demanded the same after their ports became nearly inaccessible to foreign ships with large tonnage. Vast sums of money were then expended in the restructuring of ports—to no avail, however, because French ports never made up the advantage they had lost. In addition, at the beginning of the 20th century, port capacity was well below new international standards.

Lastly, most of the commercial techniques used in the maritime trade of the 17th through 19th centuries were already clearly identifiable at the turn of the 16th and 17th centuries. For instance, family-run trading companies, with sleeping partners and a share system of financing, instruments for credit, and maritime insurance were already in existence well before the advent of colonial trade. Colonial trade led to nothing more than superficial modifications to the basic business techniques already in place.

Regional port strategies

In the 16th century, Bordeaux was able to benefit from the profitable wood from Toulouse before it was replaced by colonial indigo. Its long-famous wines and the wealth of its agricultural hinterland meant it had available exports, and it was through trade with the West Indian islands that this port entered the trans-Atlantic colonial trade.

foreign traders. This became very common in wartime, when the French slave trade was almost totally interrupted. Therefore, between the interests of the colonisers, those of the ship-owners and the mercantile state, negotiations never ceased. The third reason is that, in order to compensate for the progressive opening up of the French islands to foreign trade, the state gave the French slave merchants tonnage payments in 1784, then a premium per head imported into Santo Domingo in 1786.

It was not until the 1740s that the slave trade began to attract its ship-owners, and, after 1763, for the slave trade to flourish. It was during the second half of the 17th century, when the Atlantic trade was well established, that Marseilles, traditionally oriented towards the Levant, chose to "Westernise" part of its trade. During the 16th century, La Rochelle's merchants had been very involved in deep sea fishing ventures. With the rapid rise in colonial trade in the 18th century, it was Canada which appeared to offer La Rochelle's merchants the best opportunities for growth. However, in 1763, France lost this colony; hence a reorientation of their commercial ventures to the slave trade.

Lastly, let us look at Nantes. Iberian merchants settled there from the mid-16th century, and it was the headquarters of the *Compagnie des Indes* until 1733 (when it was transferred to Lorient), as well as playing a large role in the trade in slaves destined for the islands. Without an agricultural hinterland as rich as Bordeaux, Nantes chose to concentrate on the slave trade, which it dominated during the first half of the 18th century.[7]

A second stage in the development of regional ports began in the 18th century, when fierce competition and the quest for market share led to a new hierarchy amongst the ports themselves. Four of them stood out: Nantes, Bordeaux, Marseilles, and Rouen-Le Havre. These ports came out ahead because they had concentrated their "leading trade" in the rapidly developing West Indies, in contrast to those ports specialising in piracy or the North American trade, which declined in importance. Nantes, Bordeaux, Marseilles, and Rouen-Le Havre were also able to capitalise on general shifts in the urban landscape at the time. In France, and in Northwestern Europe generally, the 18th century was a time when large towns became areas of regional attraction, and when national markets were beginning to form or consolidate. The time of port enclaves open to the ocean, merchant city states, and trading posts was in the past. Some ports

[7] Nantes's share of the French slave trade was 75% in 1707–11 and 63.3% between 1712 and 1721. That of the Breton ports (including Nantes) was respectively 80% and 74.6%. Whereas Nantes's share then declined until the middle of the century (without descending below 48–50%, however), that of the Breton ports remained steady: more than 80% between 1722 and 1731 and more than 60% thereafter. See Pétré-Grenouilleau, *Nantes au temps de la traite des Noirs* (Paris: Hachette, 1998), ch. 1–2.

with sufficient means to start with, such as those listed above, were able to capitalise on this shift.

At least two main points can be extrapolated from this glance at the conditions prior to, and during, France's entry into the trans-Atlantic colonial trade. The first is that French trade was not dependent upon the expansion of colonial trade for growth. In fact, French entry into colonial trade was only made possible by the experience its merchants gained in other trading enterprises. Secondly, although the national and international context was propitious, French entry into the trans-Atlantic colonial trade was, above all, the result of regional trading strategies. That is an essential point to bear in mind when we analyse the links between colonial trade and development. France's entry into the trans-Atlantic colonial trade was certainly not the nation's first foray into international trade, nor, necessarily, its most important. Nevertheless, this colonial commerce developed rapidly. What was the nature of this development, and what was its impact on the national economy? This is what we must now try to define.

The Consolidation and Restructuring of Colonial Trade, the 1720s to 1792

The archival material relating to colonial trade for the period between the 1720s and 1792 is fairly continuous, though there is a break in available documentation between the years 1781–1786. The proliferation of available quantitative data coincides with the end the first stage of the development of colonial trade at the end of the 17th century. This explosion in available material for the 18th century can, at times, be misleading. Historians are apt to overlook the very real developments in colonial trade during the 17th century due to a wont of resources which, in turns, leads them to lend undue importance to the progression made in the 18th century. For example, the figures for the balance of trade analysed by Arnould (1791) do not always appear entirely credible, exaggerating "certainly the extent" of the growth in trade, notes P. Léon.[8] As J. Meyer wrote, the whole ability of the historian consists in reconstructing fragile data into an exact order of size by collecting and rearranging often very diverse information.[9]

---

[8] In F. Baudel and E. Labrousse, *Histoire économique et sociale de la France*, II, p. 500.

[9] Ibid., Some "very heterogeneous, even incomplete elements" were combined,

This reconstruction of fragile data from diverse information is especially difficult when comparing the first and second stages of French colonial trade. For example, it is extremely difficult to compare in any way French trade before the great boom in colonial trade in the 18th century, with what came after. Prior to the take off in colonial trade, French trade was cantered on Europe and focused on agricultural commodities such as wheat, wine, and salt. In the 18th century, it expanded to encompass trans-oceanic routes, and dealt in tropical products of greater value, the increasing distribution of which was synonymous with an evolution in consumer tastes and fashions.

Inexorable, though irregular, growth in foreign trade

Between 1716 and 1720 and the average for the years 1787–1789, the increase in total trade (in millions of *livres tournois*) would have been 567% according to the balance of trade and 394% according to Arnould. It would have been between 302% and 412% for European trade and between 836% and 1310% for colonial trade (where P. Léon includes the East Indies trade). The volume of foreign trade rose almost continuously. From these figures, one gets the impression that French foreign trade in the 18th century was nothing short of miraculous.[10] However, we must remember three things: 1) the boom in French foreign trade in terms of average progress rates is very small; 2) that this growth in foreign trade in gross value

wrote P. Léon, because "the percentage of error" appeared "constant, relatively weak and having only a little influence on the movements of the whole." We should note, however, following F. Crouzet and P. Verley, that the data in the *Balance du Commerce* have often aroused an exaggerated mistrust and that the quality of the document "is not inferior to English data of the same period" (Verley, *L'échelle du monde. Essai sur l'industrialisation de l'Occident* (Paris: Gallimard, 1997), p. 439). On the condition that one only takes the statistics seriously from 1726 onward to eliminate a very possible under-evaluation at the beginning (according to D. Landes) and the effects of monetary fluctuations.

[10] There are unending possibilities for quotations from studies developing this idea. "Ah! How wonderful France was at the time of slavery!" notes M. Morineau, before adding: "not being said aloud, the exclamation gushes forth jubilantly from the innermost depths of their sensitivities and can be clearly guessed in the essays of many historians moved by the splendour of the islands in the 18th century and the exuberance of the colonial trade which fed off it" ("La vraie nature des choses et leur enchaînement entre la France, les Antilles et l'Europe, XVIIe–XIXe siècle," *Revue Française d'Histoire d'Outre-Mer*, 1997, 314, pp. 3–24; quotation p. 3).

must be compared with the price increases;[11] 3) the growth rates are very irregular. It is erroneous, therefore, to assert that growth for the whole of the 18th century was uniformly spectacular.

According to P. Butel, based on Bruyard, a first levelling off was reached between 1736 and 1740 when, during each of these years, the total value of foreign trade reached over 200–205 million *livres tournois*. Progress was steady until 1749–1755 when it reached 486.1 million.[12] Interrupted by the Seven Years War, growth continued afterwards but more slowly until the 1770s when, on average, it did not reach 600 million yearly. There was a boom following the American War of Independence which lifted French trade to its highest levels yet.[13] In less than 10 years, from a level lower than 600 million pounds, it exceeded the thousand million mark due, particularly, to the increase in the price of colonial foodstuffs and to the rise in new products like coffee and cotton. Between 1716–1748, exports reached 4.1% of GNP, then fell to only 1% from 1749–1778 and rose slightly to 1.4% thereafter. The inputs of colonial trade alone attained 5.7%, 3.5% and 2.1% in these years, respectively.

One notices very quickly that the growth attained in the 18th century, at first glance so spectacular, essentially occurred in only two periods at each end of the century—1716–1748 on the one hand, and 1778–1792 on the other. These periods are at either end of a much more moderate period of growth between 1749–1778. If one goes further and compares the rates of growth of foreign trade of these periods with those of other sectors, or even with the French economy in general, it can be seen that only the first phase—1716–1748—is notable for its vigorous average growth rate.[14]

[11] P. Butel estimates that in constant price, the increase in volume of foreign trade was "at least between 1 and 3" between 1716–20 and 1784–88 See: *L'économie française au XVIIIe siècle* (Paris: Sedes, 1993), p. 68.

[12] "In less than twenty years, from 1736–40 to 1749–55, trade was to double . . . its value, going from 278.4 million to 486.1 million and in the middle of the century this value represented more than three times that of the first years of Louis XV's reign" (P. Butel, *L'économie française*, p. 82).

[13] According to Butel (*L'économie*, pp. 81–82), the average value of foreign trade would be 155 million *livres* in 1716–20. It reached more than 244 million in 1736, 342 in 1741, and went from an average of 278.4 million in 1736–40 to 486.1 million in 1749–55. In 1760, at the lowest point of the Seven Years War, it dropped again to less than 292 million, only to rise again to 444 million in 1763 and 555 in 1764. In 1784–86, it reached 1.062 million, thus exceeding England (775 million).

[14] C. Keyder and P. O'Brien estimate the average annual rate of growth in production in France to be 1% between 1701–10 and 1781–90 which, in detail, is

It should be noted that the strong rates of growth attained in the 18th century, apparently so exceptional, are very often less than those for the 19th century which is generally presented as the century of decline for French trade.[15] The extreme relativity of judgements concerning the "wonderful 18th century" appear greater when one considers that the performance of French trade in the years 1716–1748 can be explained, in part, by the quite low level it started from at the end of the 17th century. Moreover, West Indian trade was by no means the only cause of progress. In fact, as P. Butel has shown, this progress stemmed from the fact that the French were "the main vendors of manufactured articles on the Iberian market," that they "also dominated the markets of Italy and the Levant," and that, in Northern Europe, they played an important role in the re-exportation of colonial goods.[16] This strong growth was, therefore, due to the combination of previously well-launched, colonial trade—a third of the total value of imports, and a fifth of exports—and partly due to the continuance of traditional European trade.[17]

This combination of the expansion of both the colonial and the intra-European trade is the hallmark of the 18th century. The 18th century was also marked by the "Americanisation" of French foreign trade, meaning the progressively increasing importance of colonial commerce to its foreign trade. However, it is important to put this "Americanisation" into perspective. On the one hand, French foreign trade in the 1780s was not any more structurally based on the trade with Africa and America than it had been before, and, on the other hand, because France remained solidly attached to the

0.6% for agricultural production and 1.9% for industrial production. Between the end of Louis XIV's reign and the Revolution, the rate of growth of traditional textile manufacture was above 1.5%. It was 2.4% in metallurgy (for iron) and 2.3% for coal mining (Butel, *L'économie*, p. 66). P. Léon (in F. Braudel, *Histoire économique et sociale*..., p. 521) arrives at estimates similar to those of Marczewski, concerning the average annual rate of growth for the century of the cotton industry (3.81%), coal production (3.8%), and cast iron (1.9%).

[15] Between 1820 and 1892, the value of French foreign trade went from 733 million francs to 7.465 million, which is a 10.5-fold increase. Between 1815 and 1875 exports in volume grew at the average annual rate of 4.56% (3.01% before 1840, 6.03% from 1845 to 1865).

[16] Butel, *L'économie*, p. 68.

[17] In value, according to the data supplied by Butel (*L'économie*, p. 88), trade with Africa and the American colonies represented 11.6% of French imports in 1716 and 33.8% in 1754—which, for exports, gives 4.2% and 14.9% respectively.

continent with 74% of total trade being intra-European in 1726 and 63.2% in 1775, while even the colonies' share of France's trade was 25.6% and 36.6%, respectively.[18] We should add that, according to P. Léon, France still received as many raw materials—19.4% in 1716 and 20.3% in 1787—but ordered increasing amounts from Europe—83.7% in 1787.[19]

The idea of an "Americanisation" of French foreign trade should not lead us to forget the importance of France's relations with Europe. Moreover, there is still very little known about overland trade due to the lack of quantitative data and particularly due to insufficient research—a lack of knowledge that skews figures and analyses in favour of colonial trade. Some of the fragmentary data describe this overland trade as "not negligible," despite transport costs being very clearly in favour of maritime transport at the time.[20] This same lack of data applies to the contraband trade to certain European countries, particularly England, which remains largely unstudied although it, too, was most likely not small.[21] All these gaps in our knowledge had led to the inevitable reduction of the share of France's trade allocated to the European trade.

So to what do we owe these fabulous figures reached on the eve of the Revolution, when the value of foreign trade exceeded a milliard *livres tournois*? This rise is due, in part, to the dramatic rise in colonial foodstuffs at a time when other prices tended to fall.[22] In

[18] The growth in value of colonial goods was spectacular. Reaching their best secular level, notes Butel, they represented on average 320.2 million *livres* in 1788–90. But in relative value, the percentages reached at the end of the first half of the 18th century hardly rose afterward, remaining around levels already reached (41.6% for imports in 1772, but only 31.8% in 1787; dropped to 10.4% for exports in 1772 and rose again to 17% in 1787 (P. Butel, *L'économie* . . ., p. 88). Unlike Butel's data, P. Léon's include trade with India; they reflect the idea of a decrease since imported colonial goods went from 30.2% in 1716 to 24% in 1787.

[19] Léon, in F. Braudel and E. Labrousse, *Histoire économique et sociale*, pp. 507–9.

[20] Jean-Pierre Hirsch, *Les deux rêves du commerce. Entreprises et institutions dans la région lilloise* (Paris: EHESS, 1991), shows the liveliness of trade along the border with Austrian Flanders, where "merchandise from the whole of France came to be traded for merchandise from the islands and abroad, supplied by Flanders and Austrian Brabant." (pp. 172–73).

[21] Russian correspondence from London, quoted by F. Braudel, shows that in 1787, two-thirds of French trade to England was smuggled.

[22] The example of the price of wheat, often used as a good indicator, is particularly clear. The trend was downward between 1770 and 1787, and in 1780, a lower level was reached than in 1753. Textiles, another key industrial sector, also

addition, this rapid rise is attributable to the re-export of colonial goods arriving in France from other locales in Europe—more often than not without being processed. In 1716, this colonial re-export was worth 17.7% of foreign trade. It reached 33% in 1787.[23]

Growth after the American War of Independence was also limited by the deterioration of the French situation in the non-colonial markets. At the end of the century, Spain, Italy and the Levant were less important than before. The German States, as well as the other Northern European countries began to play a more considerable role in French foreign trade.[24] Nevertheless, competition became more and more stiff, and a good part of this trade to Northern Europe was controlled by foreigners, and was based on re-export of colonial foodstuffs.[25] Finally, whereas industrial products represented two thirds of the value of English exports, they only accounted for two fifths of French exports.[26] Growth in foreign trade after 1786 was

fell between the end of the 1760s and the beginning of the 1780s. Prices then rose again for several years, though remaining lower than those around 1765, before again falling steeply (Butel, *L'économie*, pp. 50, 70).

[23] P. Butel, *L'économie*..., p. 87. This is when the rate of growth was highest. In Bordeaux, between 1728–30 and 1788–89, the rate of growth in re-exports (particularly sugar, coffee, and indigo) was on average 6.5% a year. P. Léon (in F. Braudel, *Histoire économique et sociale*, p. 507) notes that 73.8% of sugar imported to Bordeaux between 1721 and 1778 was re-exported. The figures are more or less the same for coffee. In Rouen, he adds, 34% of sugar coming from the West Indies was re-exported between 1728 and 1733, the percentage then increased spectacularly: 74% for 1763–69 and 67% for 1772–76. In Marseilles, "the proportion of coffee re-exported reached 100% in 1786." The size of these re-exports obviously poses a problem, all the more so since, from the end of the 17th century, the state tried to encourage the national refineries (the first refineries were founded even before the West Indian "sugar revolution"—at Bordeaux in 1630, La Rochelle between 1654 and 1658—using sugar from Morocco). In the next century, a large industrial complex based on sugar extended along the Loire between Nantes, Angers, Saumur, and Orleans. However, the interests of the ship-owners did not always coincide with that of the manufacturers but, above all, domestic consumption was insufficient because the French used much less sugar than the English.

[24] "Germany," writes Léon, was a "real gold mine for national trade." The increase in trade in that direction reached 715% "in an area which must cover a good part of Central even Eastern Europe." Braudel, *Histoire économique et sociale*, p. 505).

[25] On the eve of the Revolution, writes Butel, 60% of the value of goods exported to "Germany" and to Northern Europe from France were goods made in France, but this was a recent expansion, after the American War of Independence (*L'économie*, pp. 92–93).

[26] It is true that wines and spirits, classed as "agricultural goods," could be related more to "manufactured" goods than to raw materials. Significant to the French, they were secondary to the English, excluding beer. On this subject, see J. McCusker,

much less spectacular that it appeared, and was very largely dependent on the French part of Saint Domingue. This trade with Saint Domingue did contribute to ensuring a positive trade balance.[27] It also led to high profits, as well as the arrival of precious metals in France, which, in turn, stimulated commerce.[28] But it seems unlikely that it was a driving force in the economic and, in particular, the industrial growth of the country.

We have seen that, although far from being negligible, the data available can only supply us with an idea of size relative to commercial growth. This data would have to be of surgical precision to measure the role of colonial trade in the national economy because at that level of analysis, a variation of one or two decimals can change everything. Moreover, it is untenable to try to distinguish between two very highly interlinked trades—the colonial trade on the one hand and general foreign and domestic trade on the other

"The business of distilling in the Old World and the New World during the seventeenth and eighteenth centuries; the rise of a new enterprise and its connection with colonial America," in J. McCusker and K. Morgan ed., *The Early Modern Atlantic Economy* (Cambridge: Cambridge University Press, 2000), pp. 186–224.

[27] L. Meignen has shown that the apparent deficit of French foreign trade at the end of the old regime should be qualified. In eliminating the financial inputs and outputs from the official figures, and integrating colonial trade with home trade, we see a small surplus in foreign trade. This surplus was gradually reduced and the remaining part of his study indicates the extreme fragility as well as the adverse effects of the colonial trade ("Le commerce extérieur de la France à la fin de l'Ancien Régime: déficit apparent, prospérité réelle mais fragile," *Revue Historique de Droit Français et Etranger*, 1978, pp. 583–614). It will also be noted that trade surplus has never alone been a sign or factor of a healthy economy. In 18th century France (where it is explained by the increase in colonial re-exports), as in that of these last few years (where it has been partly the effect of the decline in domestic consumption), it reflects as much the weaknesses of the national economy as its strengths. If the trade balance is the essential criteria of a country's wealth, one must consider the U.S.A. today as belonging in the category of the most deprived nations. We must therefore be wary of illusions created by reading economic indicators from too commercial a point of view.

[28] With regard to the "enormous" sums of money received by France, from Central and Northern Europe, and "more so Spain and the Spanish-American world from which it drained its piastres," Léon writes that it was thought of more as "merchandise;" a "merchandise indispensable to new transactions, because a large part of the sums entering the country escaped in the direction of the Levant and even more to the Far East, to pay for the "return" trade. Silver money also leaked with increasing fervour in the direction of Geneva, Piedmont, the North and particularly the Mediterranean" (in F. Braudel, *Histoire économique et sociale*, pp. 512–13). It is due to Spanish *piastres* that the people of Bordeaux succeeded in making their way into the slave trade markets of East Africa during the last third of the 18th century.

hand. Therefore, it seems to me that we must be very circumspect with conclusions drawn from the available data. It is not statistically possible to establish anything other than probabilities as far as the relationship between colonial trade and national economy. Nevertheless, we can assert that the image of foreign trade constantly and ever more rapidly beating its own records due to the virtually revolutionary dynamism of colonial trade corresponds very little to reality. Once measured in constant price and compared to other sectors of activity, colonial trade can be broken down into a succession of periods of growth of variable intensity—growth which is much more moderate than is generally imagined. Without denying the evidence—the leap forward made by French foreign trade over the course of the 18th century—we can only say, however, that the importance of the colonial sector was minimal.

The ability of French foreign trade to stimulate and truly lead the rest of the economy seems only to have been perfectly obvious during a quite short period between 1716–1748, well before the time when it could have influenced France's Industrial Revolution. The further one progresses into the 18th century, the more the relativity of the "Americanisation" of French external trade is clear, the more its fragility is obvious, and its ability to be the driving force of an Industrial Revolution becomes more doubtful.[29] Furthermore, let us remember that, out of the 320.2 million *livres* (on average) of colonial trade in the years 1788–1790, 232.5 million were imports. The colonies only constituted a small outlet for domestically-produced goods. This was partly due to the small size of the French colonies.[30]

---

[29] Industrial expansion (term to be distinguished from that of "Industrial Revolution") benefited, writes Butel (in *L'économie*) "from the increase in demand for credit worthiness, itself linked to the rise in population," the French population went from around 21.5 to 26 million between 1701–10 and 1781–90 (+28%); another estimate gives the following figures: 21.5 million in 1700 and 28.1 in 1790 (+31%). It was also facilitated by the progress in the opening up of French society to the markets. Finally, the role of the intra-European market, although little studied, must not be forgotten.

[30] In 1760 the various European colonies were populated by 27.1 million inhabitants; 65.9% lived in the Spanish colonies, 12% in the Dutch colonies, 10.3% in the British colonies, 6% in the Portuguese colonies and only 2.2% in the French colonies, according to B. Etemad, *La possession du monde. Poids et mesures de la colonisation*, (Bruxelles; Complexe, 2000), p. 183. Th. M. Doerflinger notes that "the exports to the Antilles surged ahead during the final decade of the old regime, from a record of 45 million *livres tournois* in 1779 to 79 million in 1787." He explains this by "the concurrent rise in the population of the French West Indies," which was itself due

It is also partly due to the absence of a colonial settlement that had a high demand for manufactured products, such as the thirteen colonies of America.[31]

From the evidence available to us, it seems clear, then, that colonial trade cannot be considered as an essential factor in the progress of the national economy, and even less so as *the* main stimulant to the industrial boom. Commenting on the assumption that sugar played an important role in the accumulation of capital, D. Eltis writes very rightly that, in England at the end of the 18th century, there were a good 50 or so activities likely to do as well.[32] In France, as in England, you cannot always see the woods for the (colonial) trees.[33] Therefore, rather than looking at the national level or at a level more or less derived from the sectors of activity, we should turn more to a regional scale, particularly that of the ports and their hinterlands. It is when looking at ports and their hinterlands that we can see how the French colonial trade functioned. Likewise, it is only on this scale that, though difficult, it is truly possible to compare a large number of variables. In fact, studies of the Industrial Revolution increasingly tend to ascribe industrialisation to regional factors.

---

to the massive introduction of slaves ("The Antilles Trade of the Old Regime: A Statistical Overview," *Journal of Interdisciplinary History*, 1976, VI-3, pp. 397–415, quotation p. 402).

[31] According to Butel (*L'économie*, p. 87), France exported 42.7 million manufactured goods in 1716 (including 34.5 of textiles), and 180.4 million in 1787. At this date, the colonial world (meaning not only limited to the French colonies) absorbed 56 million, equal to 32%. The percentage was therefore decreasing (and not increasing) in relation to 1716 (36.7%). The colonial world as a whole did not achieve more than Italy (32%), less than Spain (37%), and much less than Germany (60%, particularly due to silk goods).

[32] The profits "in the case of the slave trade and sugar are sometimes seen as making the vital contribution to the pool of savings funding the British Industrial Revolution. However, there must have been at least fifty industries with the potential to produce gross profits equal to or similar to sugar, and hundreds more that could have done so in combination with related activities. . . . In terms of gross profits, it is not at all clear why slave trading or the larger sugar business should be singled out," D. Eltis, *The Rise of African Slavery in the Americas*, p. 271.

[33] Coal mining progressed "by at least 700 to 800%" over the whole of the 18th century, writes Léon (in F. Braudel, *Histoire économique et sociale*, p. 521). The production of cast iron increased to 200% and iron to 300%. It should be noted that this real increase in *production* is as significant as (if not more so than) the increase in value of colonial trade stimulated by the rise in price of tropical commodities.

The Importance of Regional Trade

Two observations about ports and their hinterlands can be made in relation to the role of significant colonial trade: 1) this type of trade can favour a reticulate type of development model; 2) it does not only stimulate one activity, but, rather, affects a broader area which increasingly acquires specific characteristics compared with the exterior. The most spectacular example of this by far is Bordeaux and its mostly rural hinterland which was greatly stimulated by the growth of commercial, particularly colonial, trade, as shown by P. Butel.[34] In 1789, Bordeaux made nearly as much from exports—102 million *livres tournois*—as from imports—146 million, essentially comprised of re-exported colonial foodstuffs.

This amazing feat, almost unique in France, is partly explained by the agricultural potential of its hinterland, as well as by the extensive networks built up with Northern European regions importing colonial goods.[35] These two factors were already in play before Bordeaux entered colonial trading circles. Moreover, although exports from Bordeaux to the West Indies grew over the course of the century throughout, they were far from constituting Bordeaux's only outlet. For example, Brittany itself received more wine than did the island colonies.[36] Finally, the price of this type of development was

[34] "To lessen the importance of colonial trade does not seem to be a realistic point of view. In order to trade, merchants needed supplies of food, flour, and wine and manufactured goods, the production of which brought life to entire regions, not only in the port hinterlands but far into the interior." This phrase taken from *L'économie française au XVIIIe siècle* (Butel, p. 69), and here used generally, corresponds perfectly to the case of Bordeaux.

[35] Doerflinger notes that Bordeaux exported, relatively, no more goods to the West Indies than Nantes or Rouen. He writes, "the growth of Bordeaux's Antilles sector . . . seems to have occurred independently of, not in concert with, the development of exports to the Antilles." This is perhaps going a little quickly, because Bordeaux exported goods from its hinterland, which was not always the case of other ports which had to import some of the goods exported from the islands. In addition, not exporting any more than the others, Bordeaux could perhaps do so at a lower cost. The role of its hinterland must therefore not be forgotten. The establishment of privileged links with the Northern countries from the 17th century must also be taken into account; they greatly facilitated the re-exportation of colonial commodities transiting through Bordeaux. From this, the "good fortune of Bordeaux" no longer remains a "riddle" as described by Doerflinger ("The Antilles Trade," p. 415).

[36] Butel notes that (among the other export markets) the West Indian market absorbed 27,700 barrels of wine from Guyana in 1787–89. But the home wine

the virtual non-existence of an industrial factory or infrastructure worthy of the name in Bordeaux. This explains why François Crouzet saw in Bordeaux's 18th century development one of the main reasons for the decline of Southwestern France in the next century.

In 1789, Marseilles made 81 million *livres tournois* from exports and 149 from imports, equalling 230 million total. If this is added to the value of Bordeaux's trade—248 million—we come to a total of 478 million pounds, nearly half the value of the total French foreign trade of the time. Marseilles exported much less than Bordeaux, but it did supply a not inconsiderable quantity of manufactured goods for export.[37] They mostly went to the Mediterranean, particularly to the Levant, rather than to America, which served more as a crutch for the industrial sectors in decline than as a stimulating and innovatory factor.[38] In Nantes, prosperity based on the colonial trade fed a whole network of outer ports and secondary ports, such as Paimboeuf, Pornic, and Le Croisic. This prosperity attracted a rising elite to the town from a large part of Western France, so stimulating social mobility. However, many goods exported for the slave trade, in fact, came from purchases made outside the area, despite the progress of the textile industry, particularly for the manufacture of printed calico. In Rouen, as P. Boule[39] has shown, the rise of the textile industry precedes and explains that of the slave trade, not the reverse.[40]

market, particularly Brittany, by ship took far more, with an average of 53,000 barrels from 1782 to 1787 (*L'économie*, pp. 72–73).

[37] In 1787 the Aix-en-Provence region exported 18 million *livres tournois* of manufactured goods (soaps, hosiery, earthenware etc.), which placed it second for regions exporting this type of product, behind Brittany (20.3 million with its cloth). However, to this must be added the exports from the Montpellier region (particularly sheets), which were worth 17.2 million *livres* and were exported through Marseilles, definitely the main port for the export of French manufactured goods.

[38] This was the case for candles, the outlets in the religious communities of Provence declined, or even of the hat trade, in part ruined by the effects of the plague in 1720 and the closing of the port.

[39] Boulle, "Marchandises et développement industriel dans la France et l'Angleterre du XVIIIe siècle," and "Slave Trade, Commercial Organisation and Industrial Growth, in 18th-Century Nantes," in *Revue Française d'Histoire d'Outre Mer*, 1975 (pp. 226–27, pp. 309–30), 1972 (214, pp. 70–112).

[40] Here I limited myself to the main French ports (Bordeaux, Marseilles, Nantes, and Rouen), but the conclusions that could be drawn for numerous others would not necessarily be any different. In Dunkirk, writes Butel (*L'économie*, p. 73), "the records of the century were made in 1788 and 1790." They were essentially due to colonial *imports* (average value of trade was 320.2 million *livres*, of which 232.5 were imports).

These examples show that colonial trade contributed to the reinforcement of regional specialisations which had often already been established. As such, the evolution of the port hinterlands seems to conform perfectly to the way in which the French economy in general evolved during the 18th century. As D. Weir has shown, it progressed less due to technological processes and large accumulations of capital than through better integration of its markets and by progress in regional specialisation.[41] This again minimises the influence of colonial trade. As an important factor in a reticular system of growth, it particularly encourages the old established tendencies. On a regional scale, therefore, colonial trade does not fill any really revolutionary role in the development of the French economy.

As T. Leroux has shown, it was the sectors most committed to colonial trade with the New World that, at the end of the 18th century, were the most poorly linked to the national market economy. Only Marseilles, through the Rhone corridor, was linked with the Paris region, whose area of influence continuously spread.[42] In addition, in the 18th century, at the time when the growth in colonial trade was at its height, the maritime regions of Western France, despite being the most involved in this trade, were beginning to be overtaken by the increasing vitality of the interior and Eastern France. In fact, P. Léon wrote that, up until near the end of the 18th century, in spite of certain uniformity in the industrial infrastructure, it was Western France that was the wealthy part of France, but that the distribution of productive strength began to change from Colbert's time onwards. This shift toward the interior and Eastern France appeared to speed up after 1760."[43] In fact, it was notable that, since colonial trade really took off, the differential in industrial vitality not involving the Western seaboard continued to rise at a rate corresponding roughly to that of progress in colonial trade!

This is support, not for the idea of a colonial economy alone leading the rest of the economy, but in favour of a much more probable hypothesis; affirmation of a long-term, major dualism between two types of sectors, not always closely linked together. On the one

[41] D. Weir, "Les crises économiques et les origines de la Révolution française," *Annales E.S.C.*, 1991.

[42] T. Le Roux, *Le commerce intérieur de la France à la fin du XVIIIe siècle* (Paris: Nathan, 1996), particularly p. 292.

[43] In F. Braudel, *Histoire économique et sociale*, pp. 525–26.

hand, the interior and Eastern France resolutely opening up to the processes leading to the industrial era; on the other, the French Western seaboard increasingly locking itself into a type of development which was both peripheral and artificial, and based more on trade than on production. Furthermore, even before the end of the *Ancien Régime*, certain ports began to feel the perverse effects of this type of development. Such was the case of Saint Malo, where the rise of the mercantile elite was not sufficiently compensated for by the arrival of newcomers. It was also the case in La Rochelle where traders had already begun to feel the pressure of living in a city lacking a real hinterland.[44]

The peripheral nature of this type of development can also be seen when looking at capital. In fact, most studies indicate that the world of trade functioned very largely in harmony with what could be called 'relational capitalism'.[45] Capital required for fitting out the ships was found by appealing to those who were directly interested it its success such as ship-owners, other traders, and captains, as well as by looking to those in the family circle and other personal contacts. A large part of the capital required for long distance expeditions was, therefore, generally raised within the port hinterlands. The rest could come from quite far away, from other large towns of the Kingdom, or even from abroad, without leaving the existent trade networks *per se*. In contrast to England, where the banking system was more developed, it appears that French colonial trade did not attract much capital from outside the mercantile world.

The only cases available for studying this phenomenon are in the financial sector and are both limited in time. They concern the 17th century in particular, when the State often greatly encouraged financers to invest in charter companies. This is also the case for the slave trade in La Rochelle during the last third of the 18th century. No doubt due to subsidies given by the State, which contributed to making the slave trade seemingly more viable, the share of Parisian cap-

[44] For Saint Malo, see Pétré-Grenouilleau "Dynamique sociale et croissance," pp. 1272–73. With regard to the trade of La Rochelle, J. M. Deveau writes: "too confined within the town boundary, it was not able to find a solution of substitution" in *La traite rochelaise* (Paris: Karthala, 1990), p. 310.

[45] For a more substantial development of this concept, see Pétré-Grenouilleau, "Les négoces atlantiques français: Anatomie d'un capitalisme relationnel," *Revue du XVIIIe siècle*, 2001 no. 33, pp. 33–47.

ital in local slave ships increased significantly although still remaining much smaller than that of local investors.[46] In all, either one opened up to more diversified environments while remaining on a regional, or even local, scale, or one drew on areas geographically further afield but socially more limited.

The result of this was that major profits—those from trade being greater than those of minor shareholders, as indicated by Guillaume Daudin—were eventually divided among a relatively limited number of people, the majority of whom were located within the port hinterland itself.[47] There was, therefore, trading elite in existence. This phenomenon was apparent in the formation of a small patrician class, as well as through the very distinct increase in the number of people belonging to the mercantile middle classes. The way both the elite and the rising mercantile middle class invested their profits from the colonial trade has often been criticised. Extravagant investments, the purchase of land, and the pursuit of ennoblement were often seen as signs of an "aristo-tropism" and as proof of "treason" on the part of the merchants who, it was said, would not hesitate to leave trade once their fortune was made. These reproaches, in fact very largely exaggerated, should not allow us to forget that the merchants' attitude was perfectly rational, even though social logic and the logic of power sometimes went against economic logic by turning some capital away from productive investment. Controlling part of the economy of their region, the different port traders generally directed their profits either back to trade itself, or else towards increasing their social, cultural and symbolic capital. Financial involvement with industry, which could have encouraged diversification of the regional economic fabric, was much less attractive.[48] Also, as

[46] The share of Parisian capital in the slave shipping of La Rochelle went from 4% before 1763 to 12% after 1785. In 1784 the state decided to allocate a subsidy to ship owners in relation to the declared tonnage of the ships. Two years later, it awarded another relating to the number of slaves disembarked at Santo Domingo. An essay for a *maîtrise* on the Nantes slave trade between 1789 and 1793 shows that, of a sample 156 slave ships, 87% of the people participating in the financing were market traders. 12.8% were non-merchant individuals. Among the latter, only two people were from outside the city; they were Parisians. On the role of finance in the 17th century, see Pétré-Grenouilleau, *Les négoces maritimes français*, p. 41.

[47] G. Daudin, *Le rôle du commerce dans la croissance: une réflexion à partir de la France du XVIIIe siècle*, thesis, Paris I, 2001.

[48] On social and cultural aspects of the trading world, see Pétré-Grenouilleau,

L. Meignen rightly points out, the "great ports of the kingdom are like *islets of development*,"—or, better yet, of growth—but not of "centres of development."[49]

It has long been thought that the "late development" of the Atlantic seaboard compared with the Northern and Eastern regions began in the industrial era. It has also been argued that it was the Wars of the Revolution and the Empire, and the break up of trade relations with the colonies that led to the ruin of certain manufacturing sectors on the Atlantic seaboard which were dependent on the colonies. However, it appears to me that the difference in development between these regions of France is rooted earlier in time. It seems that the greater the increase in the growth of the Atlantic ports was, the more the difference in the regions was accentuated, particularly during the second half of the 18th century. This is not really surprising. First of all, colonial trade was particularly important to the Atlantic ports, notably Nantes and Bordeaux.[50] Secondly, generated by, or attracted to, the dynamism of local and regional capital, the expansion of the Atlantic hinterlands was particularly advantageous to the local trading elite. Diverting local capital to social, economic and symbolic end of no productive use, this merchant elite reinforced an artificial and peripheral development model, mostly based on the rise of colonial trade and becoming increasingly distinct from the rest of the Kingdom. Therefore, there were certain undesirable effects in terms of development resulting from colonial trade which are just as important, if not more so, than the positive effects generated in terms of growth.

Les négoces maritimes français, pp. 92–101, 141–45; *L'argent de la traite. Milieu négrier, capitalisme et développement: un modèle* (Paris: Aubier, 1996) ch. II and *Nantes au temps de la traite des Noirs* (Paris: Hachette, 1998), pp. 226–41. On the links with industrialisation, see *Les négoces*, ch. 6. The expression "manufacture is nothing, selling is everything," in P. Barbéris, *Le monde de Balzac* (Paris: Arthaud, 1973), p. 227, summarises quite well the state of mind of the merchants and their reticence to invest durably in industry, considered by them to be something auxiliary to trading.

[49] L. Meignen, "Le commerce extérieur de la France," p. 603.

[50] Doerflinger notes that "Rouen, Nantes, Bordeaux and Marseilles controlled approximately 78% of the West Indies trade in 1730, 84% in 1753, and 98% in 1778." But the "West Indies trade was the commercial backbone" of Nantes and Bordeaux, "while Rouen and Marseilles, fundamentally oriented towards Europe and the Mediterranean, respectively, depended far less heavily upon trade with the Caribbean" ("The Antilles Trade of the Old Regime," pp. 400, 408).

Undesirable effects of colonial trade

Growth from colonial trade also masked a certain number of undesirable effects on the maritime economy. Before entering the trans-Atlantic colonial trade, France had played a considerable role in deep sea fishing, while ships from Normandy left to venture along the African coasts. However, between long distance and coastal commerce, there was a level missing in French trade, particularly since the end of the 18th century and the decline of the Breton fleet—that of international shipping. This lack has often been described as due to the high price of ship building. However, no study based on comparative statistical data has ever been able to demonstrate that this was an insurmountable problem for the French. Furthermore, there is no reason why the French would not know how to build bulk carriers for seagoing navigation when they already knew how to build ocean going vessels. A more likely reason for the lack of international vessels is the fact that French crews were often more numerous, and comprised of more officers, than were the crews of other nations, all of which costs more. I think that when the French entered the trans-Atlantic colonial trade, they voluntarily abandoned European seagoing navigation since they had not been well-positioned in for several decades, anyway. Moreover, it was quite simply more profitable and easier to concentrate on colonial trade, which was a reserved trade benefiting from many State subsidies. The "compromise" established at the end of the 17th century between the State and the mercantile world would, in the end, weigh very heavily against them in the 19th century (see Le Bouëdec's article in this volume).[51]

The French more or less abandoned deep sea fishing in the 18th century, before again investing in it after the second half of the 19th century. In order to become "the greatest re-exporter of colonial goods in Europe," France had to, once again, concentrate the majority of its maritime routes on the colonial world.[52] The development of its colonial trade was made to the detriment of all other trade

[51] See Pétré-Grenouilleau, "How did France Enter and Play in the Atlantic? State and Maritime Traders: From Clashes to Compromise, 1580–1830," in H. Pietschmann, ed., *History of the Atlantic System* (Hamburg: Vandenhoek & Ruprecht, 2002), pp. 279–293.

[52] Butel, "France, the Antilles and Europe," p. 159.

routes.[53] The trade with Asia, a source of large profits, was also connected to colonial trade—textiles from India for the slave trade, slaves for the Mascarene Islands, etc. This colonial trade was not only a weak link in times of war. It also depended on the hazards of production in the West Indies, and on control of the markets for redistribution in Northern Europe. The development of the French islands had reached its limits during the last decades of the *Ancien Régime*.[54] Merchants from English North America and, later, from the United States invaded the Antilles markets from 1770 to 1780. At the same time, "England regained a place among European markets for the re-export of Antilles sugar."[55] The situation was, therefore, in jeopardy even before the beginning of the French Wars.

Another negative effect of colonial trade on the economy of France should be pointed out: the high cost of acquiring and maintaining the colonies. The returns in colonial commodities should be weighed against the investments made in the colonies to the detriment, as A. Young once noted, of agricultural development in the many port hinterlands. The cost of the navy required to maintain relations between the home country and its colonies must also be taken into account. Moreover, the enormous sums absorbed by colonial wars, particularly by the American War of Independence, contributed to an increase in the State's budgetary deficit, which, in part, led to the meeting of the States General and, thereby, the beginning of the French Revolution which would, in part, slow down the economic expansion of the country. Furthermore, noting the chronic deficit in France's trade balance with certain European states, M. Morineau has put forward the hypothesis that the gaps were filled by money spent by the French armies on campaign: "in other words, and

[53] According to Butel, in millions of *livres tournois*, the growth of the French colonial trade was 119% between 1730 and 1740, 71.7% between 1740 and 1754, and 76.7% between 1765 and 1776. For the other trade, the figures are the following: Northern trade 107.6%, 109.4%, and 55.4%; Dutch trade 29.3%, 15.9% and –16.15%; Spanish trade 43.1%, 14.4%, and –6.1%; Levant trade 331%, 29.7%, and 17.3% ("France and the Antilles," p. 163).

[54] The reports concerning the islands written during the years 1785–89 certainly insist on the great prosperity present, but note the problems which became ever more apparent. These included a lack of economically viable land for clearing, an excess of deforestation and consequent erosion and flooding, and many examples of less-than-productive, or even abandoned, plantations (L. Meignen, "Le commerce extérieur de la France," p. 603).

[55] Butel, "France, the Antilles and Europe," p. 172.

bluntly, it was the French themselves through their taxes who paid for the sugar in Berlin and the coffee in Vienna."[56]

As has been proven above, the growth from colonial trade was partly artificial, too decentralised, and ultimately marginal in relation to the rest of the economy to have acted as a lever for development in 18th century France. In fact, the trade surplus and the importing capacity of the country pushed merchants into purchasing outside goods the country which they then also wanted to sell abroad. Hence, colonial trade did not stimulate either domestic production or trade. Finally, an imbalance in the economic structure of the country was created. France became too used to acquiring its wealth from abroad and neglected its national production, which was less rapidly economically viable, and subject to European competition. This can be seen regarding the merchandise used by the slave merchants of Saint Malo, the majority of which was imported from abroad.[57] Of course, all this tends towards reinforcing the importance of agriculture in the country.[58] During the last fifteen years of the *Ancien Régime*, the percentage of manufactured and hand made goods of the Kingdom's exports went down. This all happened in France at a time "when techniques had been confirmed . . . and King Cotton had already changed textile production in Great Britain."[59]

[56] M. Morineau, "La vraie nature des choses," p. 18.

[57] "To guarantee more than 13 million *livres* of exports for Guinea, 5 million *livres*' worth of goods—36%—had to be imported. Ropes and food were entirely of French origin, alcohol, and miscellaneous goods were 90% and metals 85%. However, pipes and tobaccos were entirely imported, and arms, mostly powder, were 65% of French origin. Textiles, the value of which reached 7 million *livres*, were more than 52% foreign" A. Roman, *Saint-Malo au temps des négriers* (Paris: Karthala, 1981), p. 81.

[58] France exported a total of 1.066 billion *livres tournois* during the period 1787–89. Agricultural products and unprocessed raw materials represented 724 million *livres*. This phenomenon, writes L. Meignen, "is a sign of weakness in an economy . . . which does not transform the raw wealth taken from its soil or imported as much as it might. Only merchants get rich" ("Le commerce extérieur de la France," pp. 597, 602).

[59] In 1775–77, finished objects represented almost 45% of exports. In 1787–89 the percentage fell to 34.6%. Textiles, "which supplied more than a third of the exports," declined from 34.9 to 26.1%; "nevertheless this sector is considered . . . as the leader of the first Industrial Revolution" (L. Meignen, "Le commerce extérieur de la France," pp. 613–14). It should be noted that in 1680 France was the first European supplier of textiles to Spanish America, with nearly 40% of the market. At this time, Breton cloth sold equally well in England; and in 1701, the English manufacturers rose up against French imports of woollen goods which they saw as "disastrous" competition.

The French tendency to direct their production to luxury or semi-luxury articles such as silk and fashion items also seems to begin at the end of the 18th century, and not only from the 1820s–1830s, as P. Verley asserts in his *Echelle du monde.*[60]

The Second Colonial System, 1792–1960

Two ideas have dominated French historiography on the end of the *Ancien Régime.* The first is that of a latent crisis in the colonial system, which explains the revolutionary eruption of modern capitalism. The second is that of a trading sector completely wiped out by revolutionary and imperial upheavals. Both theories assert that a unique French colonial system would be founded on a totally new basis at the turn of the nineteenth and twentieth centuries. It is true that there is nothing in common, on a territorial level, between the few colonies held by France at the end of the 18th century and the immense colonial empire which it administrated in 1914. Nevertheless, there is more continuity than rupture between the two systems. There are definitely different boundaries between the two systems, but they both have rather similar logic. Generally, France went from the old exclusivity of trade to a quite similar concept called "reserved trade with the colonies." I think it is important to emphasise this continuity on an ideological level. In fact, this ideological continuity partly explains how the second French colonial system was understood and managed and through that, how it could or not have been economically viable.

From one colonial system to another, 1792–1880

The idea of a colonial system in crisis even before the Revolution, then wiped out by it, is partly sound, though certain caveats must be made. The second half of the 18th century until the 1840s was

[60] The decline in exports of French cloth to Spain can be seen from 1760, and the decline in exports of cloth from Languedoc to the Levant and the Barbary Coast after 1780. After the American War of Independence, the only encouraging point in the textile sector—apart from the reliance on the reserved market of the colonies—was the increase in exports of "fashion" textiles and "silks" to the German states.

a time of restructuring rather than a revolutionary break with the past.[61] Therefore, we have to view the role of the French wars of Revolution and Empire as a digression from, rather than a complete break with, the past. This is evidenced by the fact that colonial trade started up again after 1815, that it found new markets from the 1840s onwards, and that it survived until the 1890s more or less completely intact, and remained in some form or another until the second half of the 20th century. It is therefore difficult to accept the idea that colonial trade was dead in 1792.

Although the colonial maritime trade was brutally interrupted, resulting in a "pastoralisation" of the Gironde hinterland, as F. Crouzet described it, as well as the collapse of industries dependent on the colonial trade, these events did not succeed in totally destroying the colonial trade.[62] From the French foothold in Europe, a new type of foreign trade took shape, directed more towards the continent of Europe itself.[63] Most able traders continued working and, beyond engaging in piracy, they continued to explore new trading routes, particularly to the new nation of the United States. Some trading dynasties collapsed, particularly the oldest ones, but other more recent ones were sometimes very successful. Finally, a number of fortunes were temporarily protected by the purchase of land or property. In 1815, there was still a powerful trade sector, though certainly not in as good shape, nor comprised of the same traders as it had prior to the Revolution. This sector capitalised on the return to peace. Since a trade sector did, in fact, survive the upheavals

---

[61] On these questions, see Pétré-Grenouilleau, *Les négoces*, pp. 126–69 and "Pour une histoire du négoce international français au XIXe siècle: Problèmes, sources et perspectives," *Revue d'Histoire du XIXe siècle*, 2001.

[62] On this subject, see Cl. Cailly, *Mutations d'un espace proto-industriel: le Perche aux XVIIe–XIXe siècles* (Paris: Fédération des Amis du Perche, 1993). On Nantes, see Pétré-Grenouilleau, *L'argent de la traite*, pp. 168–69.

[63] French foreign trade had reached a milliard *livres tournois* at the end of the Old Regime. It dropped to 553 million francs in 1798, to rise again to 938 million in 1806. At this date, 477 million were made on imports and 456 on exports. Germany, Holland, Spain, and Portugal played an important role then, as did the United States, through the intermediary of which the colonial goods continued to arrive. There were then many fluctuations (705 million in 1810, 585 in 1812, 585 in 1814, 838 in 1818), before a drop that continued until 1825 when, with 1.201 million, the level before the Revolution was reached and exceeded. Figures taken from E. Levasseur, *Histoire du commerce de la France. Deuxième partie, de 1789 à nos jours* (Paris, A. Rousseau, 1912), pp. 19, 97 and following.

of the revolution and the Empire, it might have been expected that these traders would try to take advantage of a return to order and integrate themselves into new trading routes. However, attempts at exploration of new routes and markets were limited, and only began to grow from the 1840s onwards.

Meanwhile, trade based on the routes, markets, and commodities prevalent before the Revolution began again, and the merchants tried to make it last as long as possible. This was very clear under the Restoration with the renewal of a slave trade, although illegal, linked to the re-activation of the sugar networks with the French West Indies and the setting up of new ones, particularly with the Spanish-American colonies. Here and there, particularly in Nantes, the capital of the illegal French slave trade, this continuance of older patterns of trade played an important role in the regional social dynamics, and made some families rich. This tendency to look towards the past, rather than the future had a few causes. First of all, it was the result of the profound psychological shock provoked by the revolutionary and imperial periods during which a whole generation of traders saw their dreams of success shattered.[64] As a reaction, the end of the *Ancien Régime* was seen as a golden era and idealised, meaning that merchants then attempted to revive the routes and markets common during the pre-Revolutionary period. Only Le Havre was somewhat immune to this romantic idealisation of outdated markets due to the influence of capitalists from outside the city, most of whom were Parisian or English.

Trade for the period between 1815–1840 was also influenced by a totally different context. On the national level, conservative pres-

[64] Brought to light by a pioneering article by Y. Renouard ("La notion de génération en histoire," *Revue Historique*, 1953, 1, pp. 1–23), the operating value of the generation concept has been vigorously defended by A. J. Tudesq, *Les grands notables en France 1840–1849. Etude historique d'une psychologie sociale* (Paris: *P.U.F.*, 1964), and clearly illustrated by J. F. Sirinelli, *Génération intellectuelle. Khâgneux et Normaliens dans l'entre-deux-guerres* (Paris: Fayard, 1988). Following the example of these authors, the concept of generation was not only conceived as an age classification. It defines a group of men who, faced with a common experience, developed comparable attitudes or behaviour. This implies that the marker "events" (in the broader sense) can introduce elements of convergence or lasting differences within the milieu. I entirely agree with A. J. Tudesq when he wrote, "as a research hypothesis, 'generation' can give to social history what the notion of 'cycle' gave to economic history . . .; it must allow social history to pass from static study of social structures to moving studies of social psychology," (*Les grands notables*, pp. 101–2).

sure groups agreed on the necessity for a protectionist system favouring colonial production. On the international level, the great plantation system experienced renewed vigour with the rise of Cuba, Brazil and Réunion. This survival of this backwards-looking colonial trade should also be seen in relation to the modernisation of the country's economic and mental structures—a modernisation that was slower and more incomplete than that of England, particularly within trading and maritime circles, but in existence nonetheless. Therefore, the years between 1792–1880 were in no way "a waste of time." The old colonial system was virtually wiped out, whereas the new one was only just beginning to develop, but a whole system of thought, partially inherited from the Enlightenment, and the mercantilist system was reconstituted. Thereafter, the conversion of the Republicans to the idea that colonisation was beneficial led to a vigorous renewal of the French colonial process at the end of the 1880s.[65]

What are the consequences of the progressive renewal of French colonial trade on an economic level? The table below shows some elements of an answer to this essential question.

Here we can see that colonial trade's share of total French trade was modest under the Restoration—only around 10% of the total. Moreover, we can see that it was only with the help of trade with Algeria that foreign trade under the July monarchy held any sizable proportion of the total. Algeria was the first and, perhaps, the only settled colony France had, the size of which increased continuously and even exceeded that of all the other colonies combined under the second Empire.[66] Some reorientation towards Senegal and, particularly, to the Indian Ocean and the island of La Reunion can also be seen—movement which reinforces changes begun during the second half of the 18th century. The first half of the 19th century in France was characterised by a renewal of traditional colonial trade which limped along. A second phase was entered with the second

[65] On this theme, approached within the framework of Black Africa, see "Cultural Systems of Representations, Economic Interests and French Penetration into Black Africa, 1780–1880," in Pétré-Grenouilleau, ed., *From Slave Trade to Colonisation. Europe and the Colonisation of Black Africa (1780s–1880s)* (London: Routledge, 2004).

[66] In 1846 Algeria made 110.5 million in general trade (total of the other colonies 174.3) and 98.5 in special trade (against 146.4). In 1869 the figures are respectively 215 (against only 205.6 for the other colonies together) and 193 million (against 180.7).

Share of colonial trade in total French foreign trade

Year	Imports general trade*	Imports special trade*	Exports general trade*	Exports special trade*	% of colonial trade in g. t.	% of colonial trade in s. t.
1829	62.2+ (616)♣ 10%♦	55.7+ (483)♣ 11.53%♦	66.7+ (608)♣ 10.97%♦	63+ (504)♣ 12.5%♦	130.9+ (1224)♣ 10.69%♦	118.7+ (987)♣ 12%♦
1846[1]	89.8+	71.3+	84.5+	75.1+	174.3+ (2437)♣ 7.15%♦	146.4+ (1772)♣ 8.26%♦
1869[2]	122.6+ (4009)♣ 3%♦	119.5+ (3153)♣ 3.79%♦	83+ (3994)♣ 2%♦	61.2+ (3075)♣ 1.99%♦	205.6+ (8003)♣ 2.56%♦	180.7+ (6228)♣ 2.9%♦

* values are expressed in millions of francs, + indicates the value of colonial trade, ♣ total value of foreign trade, ♦ expresses the share of colonial trade in total foreign trade

Source: Data calculated from information supplied by E. Levasseur, *Histoire du commerce de la France, Deuxième partie de 1789 à nos jours* (Paris: A. Rousseau), 1912.

[1] In 1846, the colonies' share was 11.58% for general trade and 13% for the special trade if Algeria is taken into account.

[2] In 1869, with Algeria included, the colonies' share was 5.11% of the general trade and 5.81% of the special trade.

Empire. No longer was there a half-hearted attempt at the renewal of colonial trade but, rather, a real collapse in its total share of French foreign trade to between 3% to 5% of the total, as evidenced by the data for 1869. Finally, with the colonial conquests under the Third Republic, the Empire's share in French trade rose again from the beginning of the 20th century. In 1913, colonial trade comprised about 11% of total foreign trade—imports and exports combined—which is practically the same as it was in 1829.

Several conclusions can be drawn from this rapid analysis. The first is that the prodigious increase in territory of French colonial possessions between 1815 and 1915, apparently did not lead to any revolutionary change as far as French foreign trade was concerned. The share of colonial trade in French foreign trade collapsed under the second Empire at a moment essential for growth and modernisation of the country's productive capacity. The increase in domestic demand due to progress in the economic unification of national territory, and a foreign trade very largely oriented towards the wealthy countries of Europe were, therefore, much more important than relations with the colonial Empire. Hence, it is clear that colonial trade for the entire first half of the 19th century played only a very secondary role in the economic development of the country. Lastly, on the level of the domestic French trade generally, and the maritime trade in particular, the results are even more mixed. On the one hand, the secondary importance of trade with the colonies for the national economy did not prevent some merchants from becoming richer. On the other hand, the inability of merchants to secure a share in the competitive markets meant that French trade, in fact, was limited to territories under France's direct control. Thereby, France moved from the old exclusive system to the system of "reserved trade."[67]

Regional Trade During the Second Phase of Industrialisation, 1880–1940

France changed between 1815 and 1940. The country opened up to industry. From the second half of the 19th century coal was the primary import for nearly all the French ports. France's entry into the second phase of industrialisation led to a need for raw materials and, consequently, to an increase in production markets, as well as a concomitant expansion of new areas directly connected to European markets, all of which meant an increase in international trade. Motivated by this increase in the volume of international trade, and by the growing importance of raw materials and industrial products, the second phase of the Industrial Revolution led, in turn, to numerous innovations in shipping. Specifically, iron then steel hulls were developed, there was a greater specialisation in the sort of ships built, and a spectacular increase in tonnage and speed. The ports had to be adapted to these shipping innovations by digging deeper access channels, increasing handling equipment, and by expanding

[67] The reasons for the downgrading of our merchant navy should be researched within a series of interacting elements—among these some played a determining role: the weakness of the players (merchants, state, pressure groups) and the limits imposed on French maritime expansion by an original model of industrial development. All led to reinforce certain established specialisations or tendencies and finally, to reduce the already limited range of possibilities for expansion of the maritime trade.

the size of storage facilities. At the same time, attitudes in the trading sector changed. In Nantes and Bordeaux, for example, the railway, which hardly aroused any enthusiasm at the beginning, suddenly became interesting to merchants. It was the same thing for industry itself, which the ship owners and merchant traders had always regarded as an auxiliary to trade. From then on, they understood that, to attract trade and maintain good profits, they either had to be capable of processing imported heavy goods on the spot or else of sending them on rapidly by rail. From the end of the 19th century, many traders saw the railway and industry as absolute necessities for their survival.

As a result of this industrialisation, the colonial share of French foreign trade made a great leap forward. As a rule, in the ports, colonial trade did not create industry but, along with other sectors, it contributed towards strengthening the development of industries. Depending on the specialisation of the port, colonial trade played a more or less important role. For example, Nantes was the sixteenth largest French port in 1870, but rose to sixth place in 1903. Its strong industrial growth was mainly based on the metallurgy industry—and industry that expanded rapidly due to ship-building and the expansion of food industries such as canning and biscuit making. Although not insignificant, real colonial trade did not play a truly decisive role.[68] It was more or less the same everywhere else. The increase in port trade was mostly caused by the growth in trade between industrialised countries. The case of Le Havre is a little different. As the primary port for the importation of American goods, particularly cotton, and of many tropical foodstuffs, its trade was more influenced by, and dependent upon, colonial trade. However, Le Havre was more of a transit port, particularly onwards to Rouen, for colonial merchandise rather than a place for processing it. Moreover, there are few detailed studies to measure the share of colonial trade in the industrialisation process. The only case where colonial trade really plays an important role in the industrialisation process is in Marseilles, where the "Glorious Forty Years" (1840–1880)

[68] Regarding Nantes, also Bordeaux, see H. Bonin, Pétré-Grenouilleau, "De-industrialisation and Reindustrialisation: The Case of Bordeaux and Nantes, in F. Amatori, A. Colli, N. Crepas, eds., *Deindustrialisation and Reindustrialisation in 20th century Europe* (Milan: Franco Angeli, 1999), pp. 233–62.

were analysed in detail by Xavier Daumalin.[69] Some of Marseilles' riches came from its privileged links with Algeria and the Far East via the Suez Canal, as well as its relations with West Africa. However, these relationships reinforced rather than created a local industrialisation process.

France, the Empire and the National Economy, 1880–1960

In 1960, in his *Mythes et réalités de l'impérialisme colonial français*, H. Brunschwig, suggested that only a few civil servants, soldiers and businessmen had in fact benefited from a colonial expansion which, after 1880, had been both costly and useless for the country. This was then confirmed by several important studies, among them X. Daumalin on Marseilles and J. Marseille at a national level.[70] The history of the links between France, its second colonial empire and the national economy is, therefore, relatively well-known. However, it should be remembered France entered into colonial ventures very slowly at the end of the 19th century. Many liberals in France pointed out that what was won in Africa or Asia due to the reserved markets was lost elsewhere in more lucrative competitive markets. Part of the nationalist Right thought that France should not invest too much in this Empire because it would risk compromising the essential effort of countering Germany's hold on Alsace and Lorraine. Leaders of the Socialist and Communist left at the beginning of the 20th century saw in the colonial venture another misappropriation of large amounts of capital and a new form of Capitalist exploitation. The majority of the French population seemed little concerned with the Empire, one way or another. This was illustrated by the comment made in 1905 by the young minister for the colonies,

[69] X. Daumalin, *Marseille et l'Ouest Africain: Cycle des oléagineux, attitudes coloniales, capitalisme portuaire, 1841–1956*, thesis, Marseille, 1992. The essential points are explained in *Histoire du commerce de Marseille*, 8 (Marseille: Chambre de Commerce et d'industrie, 1992). See also X. Daumalin and O. Raveux, "Marseille 1831–1865: Une révolution industrielle entre Europe du Nord et Méditerranée," *Annales Histoire Sciences Sociales*, 2001, 1, pp. 153–76.

[70] X. Daumalin, *Marseille et l'Ouest Africain*; J. Marseille, *Empire colonial et capitalisme français. Histoire d'un divorce* (Paris: Seuil, 1984). More recent works confirm these points of view. See, for example, C. Hodeir, "Le grand patronat colonial français face à la décolonisation, 1945–1962: problèmatiques, sources, conclusions," *Outre-Mers, Revue d'Histoire*, 2001, 330–331, pp. 129–42.

Etienne Clémentel, when he said, while holding a map of French colonial possessions before him, "colonies (. . .) I did not know there were so many".

Nevertheless, at least a large portion of the business world believed in the Empire. In fact, the colonies provided outlets—13% of exports from France in 1913—and raw materials—9.4% of domestic imports in 1913, but 95% of the imports of goods benefiting from preferential customs' rates such as whole grain rice, caster sugar and table wine in 1906.[71] The Empire ascended to the second place amongst France's trading partners and, through both good and bad years, did not drop below third place before the First World War. It played the role of regulator and shock absorber in times of difficulty. It contributed less to the increase in growth than to slowing down the decline. A more detailed analysis of sectors of activity and types of industry confirms this idea. In 1913, when the whole Empire absorbed only 11.4% of French exports, it was predominant in a small number of sectors: 67.6% of French exports of refined sugar, 65.1% of soaps, 41.4% for tools and metal items, 35.9% for cement and 33.1% for cotton fabric. The Empire, a reservoir for the country's agricultural raw material, received a part of these raw materials once they were processed. Generally, the more a sector found itself in difficulty, the more it turned towards the Empire. Take, for example, cotton; the Empire absorbed 90% of exports between 1939 and decolonisation. These troubled sectors, often far from being leaders—cotton was 1.6% of total French exports in 1958 and 0.6% in 1970, for example—could slow down their decline by taking advantage of the reserved outlets. However, having these reserved outlets also contributed to delaying these industries' modernisation. For the more mature, leading sectors—metallurgical, chemical, and electrical industries—the Empire only played a backup role limited to times when other, more competitive markets, receded. The rest of the time, they did most of their business with the industrialised countries.

The Empire also attracted capital. It was the third most popular destination outside of France in 1914. This was due to profitability

[71] The Empire's share in French imports reached its highest level in 1938 concerning agricultural raw materials (71.2%). This was the case for the mining and metal raw materials in 1949, with 21.4% (5.6% in 1938), and in 1958 for phosphates, with 97.2% (42% in 1938).

and rates of profits exceeding those obtained by companies working in France and in other areas outside France. This capital was spread out, particularly in Indochina and Algeria, but not as much in sub-Saharan Africa. The concentration of capital was also clear with regard to the companies concerned, since a large part of the profits only benefited a very limited number of companies: in 1929, the top 10 made 39% of the profits declared by 132 companies and the share of the top 10 reached 50% in 1958. Up until the Depression of the 1930s, the development of the Empire particularly benefited traditional industrial capitalism. It encouraged the continuation of a dual French economy—an economy shared between the large and the small-to-medium sized companies—and delayed the breakdown of family-run businesses in the production system. The Empire acted as a crutch for traditional, industrial capitalism.

With the 1930s crisis another phase began. Between 1927 and 1938 overseas exports fell by 65.8% whilst those to the Empire dropped by only 1.7%. This was particularly the case with the cotton industry.[72] Nevertheless, in a changing world, the Empire represented a stable element and the French began celebrating imperial grandeur. It was a time when, whilst denouncing colonial exploitation, the S.F.I.O. (*Section française de l'internationale ouvrière*) gave itself the objective, not of putting an end to it, but of making it an instrument of progress for the population concerned. In 1937, Maurice Thorez, speaking for the French communist party, declared that "the right to divorce does not signify an obligation to divorce." Six years earlier, the Colonial Exhibition had received nearly three million visitors. In 1939, 40% of the French declared themselves ready to fight rather than leave any part of their colonial possessions to others. The same state of tension was noted after the Second World War, when France began to imagine how it was going to regain its lost status as a great world power. In 1949, 81% of the French thought it was in the interest of the country to have colonies. This opinion

[72] The phenomenon was not general, as show by the example of the Nantes biscuit industry, which refused the opening onto the African markets. Used to a wealthy clientele and proving to be racist, the foreign trade manager of the LU company declared on 4 February 1931 that in these countries "the success of sales does not lie so much in the quality of the product as in the presentation, to which the lazy consumers, overcome by the climate attach a great price" (Departmental Archives of Loire-Atlantique, 18 JJ 445).

came more from the working classes than the employers in agriculture, trade and industry, however.

It is clear, then, that a rift was appearing between, on the one hand, politicians attached to the Empire for ideological reasons and, on the other hand, the economic sector which was beginning to think that the Empire was too expensive, and that it would be better to encourage modernisation of the country in order for it to enter into the new European economic community.[73] In France, as was the case in Great Britain as well, the facility existence of colonial markets contributed towards the diversion of funds and, therefore, the delay in the development of economic sectors more oriented towards internal growth or to trade between developed countries. Also, in the 1950s, when an increase in domestic consumption encouraged the establishment of new types of economic regulations, both these countries experienced serious difficulties adapting. In France, rather than a crutch, the Empire began to act like a ball and chain which was difficult to get rid of. Only a man like De Gaulle, who symbolised national *grandeur*, could then persuade the country to accept decolonisation without giving the impression of betraying it too much. "Algeria costs more than it brings in," he proclaimed at a press conference in April 1961. It was, therefore, "a fact, [that] decolonisation is in our interest, and consequently our policy."

Conclusion

At the end of our analysis—an analysis that should be continued by others—three points can be emphasised: 1) the first is that the French State has, more often than not, seen the colonies as an instrument of prestige and power rather than as an economic tool to be developed. The effects of colonial trade on the national economy appear to be very mixed, sometimes leading undeniably to phases of growth on a regional level but often, as well, to many adverse effects on development. Chronologically, the periods when colonial trade played an important rather than a peripheral role were, in the end, not

[73] Progress in mass consumption (guaranteed minimum wage, extension of union rules, credit, etc.) lifts the constraints on the foreign outlet, at a moment when agreement to new forms of production and sales liven international competition, and where the necessary restructuring of the economy requires massive investment.

particularly frequent; 2) the second point is that the periods during which French foreign trade really broke records was the turn of the nineteenth into the 20th century, and not in the 18th century.[74] Therefore, the conditions for development and underdevelopment most likely did not originate in the mercantile era; 3) in France, colonial trade hardly seems to have played the revolutionary role that some would like to assign to it by transposing upon France the judgements made on England. It was because they were already "mature" that the French merchants could enter the colonial venture at the end of the 17th century, and it was then within a more or less "reserved" and, therefore, less competitive colonial sector. The same holds true for the links between colonial trade and national development. France is a long way from having been transformed by its colonial possessions.

[74] O'Brien, "European Economic Development: The Contribution of the Periphery," *The Economic History Review*, 1982, 1, pp. 1–18, quote pp. 1–2.

The Baltic Region or the Curious Virtues of the So-Called Unequal Exchange

CHAPTER TWELVE

THE NORTH: A STAKE IN EUROPEAN ECONOMY

Pierrick Pourchasse

Maritime trade between Northern and Western Europe has made up an important portion of the entirety of European trade from 1000 AD to the present. Very early on, the Baltic zone specialised in the export of agricultural and forestry-related products. Foreign trade not only became extremely important, but it also had a positive influence on the production of all sorts of other goods in the area. The Vistula basin became a regular and vital supplier of cereals to markets in Holland and Portugal—regions in which there was often a cereal shortage—as well as in other regions which periodically suffered from a shortfall of cereals. Wood and wood products from Livonia and Finland, metals from Sweden and Russia and textile fibres from Lithuania and Byelorussia made it possible for Western industries, particularly shipbuilding, to develop. According to Pierre Jeannin, "*at that time, there probably did not exist anywhere else in the world, such a strong yet concentrated movement of raw materials.*"[1] For the Dutch, who had monopolised trade with Western Europe between the 16th and the first half of the 18th centuries, trade with the Baltic was called the "mother trade," due to its great importance for Dutch commerce and shipping.

Trade with Northern Europe, however, was always unbalanced because the Nordic countries were not major consumers of Western manufactured goods. As Michel Morineau has written, "*in response to the need to import and to live through exporting more, . . . the imbalance became a main motivation and, all things considered, was responsible for a high level of employment in shipping and in the general trade.*"[2] Consequently, during

[1] P. Jeannin, "Les comptes du Sund comme source pour la construction d'indices généraux de l'activité économique en Europe (XVe–XVIIIe)," *Revue Historique*, 1964, vol. 88, p. 62.

[2] M. Morineau, "Le commerce de la Baltique dans ses rapports avec le commerce hors de la Baltique (du milieu du XVIe siècle à la fin du XVIIIe siècle" in

the 18th century, Northern Europe became more and more open as a market for Western goods and colonial merchandise.

Before talking about the "North," however, it is necessary to define exactly what is meant by this term which, of course, depends on the geographical situation of the country concerned. With regard to France, this definition varies, and some authors include the United Provinces and Britain.[3] In this study, we will keep to the limits fixed by the royal administration at the beginning of the 18th century. In 1716, the French monarchy had set up an inventory listing the balance of trade with various states. Merchants were obliged to declare to the tax office all the merchandise they were either sending abroad or receiving from abroad. Originally, the category of the "North" in the Trade Balance List covered the countries along the Baltic coast, including Norway, an integral part of the Danish-Norwegian kingdom, as well as the Hanseatic towns on the North Sea, with the markets of Hamburg and Bremen being the most important. Several modifications were made during the 18th century, however. One after the other—Denmark in 1733, Sweden in 1734 and Russia in 1744—countries were taken out of the general statistics for the North and trade with these countries fell under different headings. In 1779, during the reforms instituted by Necker, the classification of the Nordic countries was seriously modified, and Prussia and the Hanseatic towns were, from then on, listed under new headings.

This study focuses on 18th century France, with the Breton economy supplying most of the examples that will be used. It deals with the basic character of the trade with the North, both imports and exports, as well as the rivalries between the three great European powers at the centre of this trade—rivalries characterised by the weakness of the French, and the British rise in power at the expense of the Dutch.

The Interactions of Antwerp and Amsterdam with the Baltic Regions, 1400–1800 (Leiden: Nijhoff, 1983), pp. 35–42.

[3] F. Braudel and E. Labrousse, eds., *Histoire Economique et Sociale de la France* (Paris: Presses Universitaires de France, 1970), p. 194.

Trade with the "North"

The balance of trade

In an interesting article, Pierre Jeannin has studied the place of Nordic markets in French overseas trade in the 18th century, using data supplied by the Balance of Trade List figures.[4] This source is somewhat unreliable as the aim of the List when it was initially put together was to show a surplus of trade in France's favour. It has been heavily criticised, particularly for the way the List evaluates the merchandise. For example, the prices enumerated on the List did not correspond to market prices, especially for colonial commodities. Nevertheless, the List does show the major trends in international trade. An analysis of the Balance of Trade List shows that Northern Europe represented an essential element in the trade circles of the Kingdom of France.

Figure 1. The North's share in all European trade (excluding the Levant) according to the trade figures

	IMPORTS	EXPORTS (re-exports included)
1721–1740	7,4%	8,2%
1761–1780	11,8%	21,3%

The French economy developed throughout the 18th century, as did the value of trade with the North. Only periods of conflict created breaks in the rise in trade. Imports from the area designated by the term the "North" increased respectively from 275% between the years 1720–1730 and 1748–1758, and from 408% between 1720–1730 and the decade 1770–1780 (average values). The progression in exports was even more spectacular, with increases of 556% and 888% for the same years respectively. The most spectacular increase came from Russia with 1005% and 1290% increases in exports and imports between the years 1744–1753 and 1771–1780, respectively. The

[4] P. Jeannin, "Les marchés du nord dans le commerce français au XVIIIe siècle" in P. Leon, ed., *Aires et structures du commerce français au XVIIIe siècle* (Lyon: Centre d'histoire économique et social de la région lyonnaise, 1975).

number of goods destined for Sweden (+ 864% between 1734–1743 and 1771–1780) rose more rapidly than did the purchase of Swedish goods in France, which only progressed by 284% during these same periods. In the case of Denmark, the increase in imports and exports was lower than for Sweden and Russia, but, nevertheless, were quite high—282% and 287%, for the decades 1733–1742 and 1771–1780, respectively.

Although, throughout the course of the 18th century, the categories of the Balance of Trade list were redefined to make it possible to distinguish Denmark from Sweden and Russia, we are unable to do the same for trade with the Hanseatic towns, Poland and Prussia, even though the latter countries and towns were among the most active in Baltic trade. Although France bought ever more raw materials from the far North (Russia and Sweden), the majority of exports was made to countries which were not differentiated in the Balance of Trade. According to P. Jeannin, "this 'North,' surely more than half of which means Germany."[5] More precise information from the Balance after the Necker reform confirms Germany's position. In the three years of 1787, 1788, and 1789, the trade conducted by the Hanseatic towns represented 37% of French imports and 70% of exports for the whole of the North.

However, these figures should be put into perspective. The expansion of trade between France and the Baltic is partly explained by

Figure 2. Balance of Trade with Russia (1744–1780)

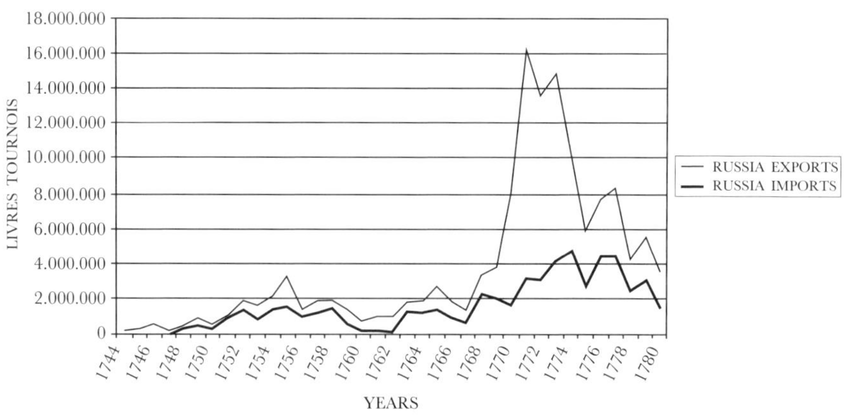

[5] P. Jeannin, "Les marchés du nord," op. cit., p. 69.

the decrease in the importance of the Dutch middlemen. Trading circles had less recourse to indirect import through the Dutch and, therefore, "direct import into France grew more rapidly than the volume of international East-West trade."[6]

The Balance of Trade with the different countries or groups of this area seems to have been constantly in France's favour, sometimes by very large amounts. This problem has been studied by Michel Morineau in several articles which raise a number of questions of great interest.[7]

Exports

The North was an essential outlet for the French colonial trade and constituted a "real gold mine" for the Trade Balance.[8] The whole *raison d'être* for French sugar cultivation and export was its re-export and, in peacetime, France greatly dominated the European market.[9] In Nantes, the re-export figures for sugar were regularly above 80% of the imports (88.4% in 1740, 89.3% in 1774). For both the great colonial ports of Bordeaux and Nantes, the North, particularly the Hanseatic towns and Holland, constituted the main clients for French colonial merchandise. Between 1774 and 1880, 34% of exports from Bordeaux went to Hamburg.[10]

Exports to other Baltic countries were not insignificant, even though the figures were much lower. Between 1775 and 1780, 3.6% of exports from Nantes went to Denmark, Sweden and Russia. These figures are explained by Denmark and Sweden's possession of their own colonies, as well as by the weak Russian market for luxury goods.

Although colonial exports were of very high value, wine production must not be forgotten, since wine was part of the cargo of the majority of the ships leaving France for the Northern countries, all

[6] Ibid., p. 70.

[7] M. Morineau, "La vraie nature des choses et leur enchaînement entre la France, les Antilles et l'Europe (XVIIe–XIXe siècle)," *Revue Française d'Histoire d'Outre-Mer*, 184, 1997, n° 314, pp. 3–24.

[8] F. Braudel and E. Labrousse, *Histoire Economique et Sociale de la France*, op. cit., p. 505.

[9] R. Stein, "The French Sugar Business in the 18th Century: A Quantative Study," *Business History*, 22–1980, p. 11.

[10] P. Butel, "La croissance commerciale bordelaise dans la seconde moitié du XVIIIe siècle," (Lille: University of Lille, 1973), p. 244.

Figure 3. Sugar Exports from Bordeaux and Nantes (in thousands of pounds)

	Bordeaux		Nantes	
	To Holland	To the North	To Holland	To the North
1741–3	6	11	11	3
1751–3	12	19	11	9
1764–5	9	27	11	5
1774–6	28	33	12	8
1788	46	32		

Source: Robert Stein, "The French Sugar Business in the Eighteenth Century: a Quantitative Study," *Business History*, 22, 1980, pp. 1–17.

of which were large-scale consumers of wine and brandy. "In 1750, the combined purchases of the Hanseatic countries, Danes, Swedes and Russians exceeded that of the Dutch. The main reason was the great flow of direct trade between France and the different countries of the North."[11] From the 17th century onwards, wines from the Rhine lost their predominance in the Baltic and, in the 18th century, most imports came from France.[12] Although Bordeaux and Cette (Sète) were the main ports for export, the Nantes region had a developed wine production facilities from the end of the 17th century. The Dutch, interested in all wines, had been the catalysts for the local agricultural community to shift from producing cereals to wine.[13] The Nantes region produced large quantities of brandy, all the more so since competition from "the countries upstream was not to be feared because of the duty that was levied at the Ingrandes customs."[14] Nantes production acquired a great reputation: "At Bremen, brandies from Nantes, Cognac and St. Jean are the most demanded of (French) products."[15]

[11] M. Morineau, "La balance," op. cit., p. 207.

[12] J. M. Bizière, "Le commerce de vins aux pays baltiques, 1553–1657," *Scandinavian Economic History Review*, 2, 1972, pp. 121–32.

[13] R. Dion, *Histoire de la vigne et du vin en France des origins au XIXe siècle* (Paris: Flammarion, 1959), p. 426: "local wines which up till then were not part of the export trade except through smuggling, since their value was too low to justify the expense of a long voyage, did not interest them any less than the high quality wines traditionally destined for distant markets."

[14] Ibid., p. 426. "Under the influence of the Dutch, distilling wine . . . became a country activity taking its place as one of the normal jobs following the wine harvest."

[15] P. Voss, *Bordeaus et les villes hanséatiques, 1672–1715*, 2 vol. (Bordeaux: Université de Bordeaux, 1995), p. 184.

The Northern countries used great quantities of salt to preserve fish. "Salt was a key product of maritime trade. The organic link between navigation and transport of salt was so narrow that salt was sometimes used as a standard when the commercial tonnage of a new ship was to be determined."[16] For most of the 18th century, French salt was pre-eminent in the exports to the Baltic. Transport was a large part of the cost of salt, itself a low-value product, and France had the advantage of its position, being much closer to the Baltic markets than its Spanish, Portuguese and Italian competitors. After a change in French exports from the Bay of Bourgneuf to the Aunis marshes in the 15th and 16th centuries, Brittany again was the leading exporter of salt by around 1710 and remained so for most of the 18th century.

Imports

The coastal area of North Brittany had a favourable geographical situation for the cultivation of flax. Having been an important manufacturing area during the 17th century, the region specialised in providing thread for the rich "*Crées*" and "*Bretagnes*" industry. Local flaxseed was, unfortunately, of poor quality, because it weakened rapidly and had to be replaced regularly (at least every three years) to prevent the flax from degenerating. The producers had to import foreign seed. The different varieties of flaxseed from Kurzeme and Livonia (Rakitzer, Drujana and Marienburg), much sought after for their quality and their yield, were to become a heavily traded item between Brittany and the Baltic.[17] Virtually all the seed that arrived in the ports on the North coast of Brittany came from the port of Libau in Kurzeme.[18] A study of the minutes of the Leon officials at Saint-Pol who checked the quality of the seed on its arrival in the

---

[16] P. Jeannin, "Le marché du sel marin dans l'Europe du Nord du XIVe au XVIIIe siècles," in M. Mollat, *Le rôle du sel dans l'histoire* (Paris: Faculté des Lettres et Sciences Humaines de Paris, 1968), p. 78.

[17] H. Sée, "Le commerce de Morlaix dans la première moitié du XVIIIe siècle d'après les papiers de Guillotou de Kerever," in J. Hayem, *Mémoires et documents pour servir à l'histoire du commerce et de l'industrie en France*, 9° série (Paris: Hachette, 1925), p. 186. "Seeds of Zealand are less valued in Brittany and are sold at a lower price there than the cereals from Riga and Libau."

[18] J. Tanguy, *Quand la toile va. L'industrie toilière bretonne du XVIe au XVIIIe siècles* (Rennes: Éditions Apogée, 1994), p. 29. "Of the 281,332 barrels surveyed, 91.6% had been loaded at Libau, 5.2% at Memel, 2.3% at Riga, and 0.1% at Königsberg."

port enabled Jean Tanguy to count 211 ships which had carried flaxseed to Roscoff between 1700 and 1783.[19] The total number of boats was much greater, since we found 152 ships destined for Roscoff in a survey carried out on the figures from The Sound Toll over a period of twenty years. The import of foreign seed, which made Breton production dependent on foreign countries, was the subject of much criticism. Research, such as that done by the *Société d'Agriculture de Bretagne*, was done on production processes so that native linen could be regenerated *in situ*.[20] However, the results were not particularly promising, and foreign seed continued to be imported until the end of the 18th century.

Of all the goods imported from the Baltic to France, forest products were the most prevalent, as well as being of greatest value.[21] The requirements for wood were considerable, especially for construction, coopering and ship-building. For the latter activity, forest products were the main raw material and "Prussian wood," the name given to the wood from the Baltic ports, was famous for its quality and strength.[22] Despite the State's pre-emption rights for French forests, their production was insufficient and the quality poor. Also, masts and planks from the North were strategically important products for the Navy in times of war. The merchant navy also had to be supplied with forest products from the "North."[23] Other goods necessary for shipbuilding, for example, Swedish tar and pitch—both of superior quality—were very sought after for caulking ships as well as for protecting rope. They were brought regularly to all the shipbuilding ports, particularly Brest and Lorient.

Roe, used as bait for sardine fishing, "was supplied by Norway—10–12,000 barrels a year, and the price of this item, which had become a necessity for the Breton fishermen, had increased regu-

[19] Ibid., p. 143.

[20] H. See, "Le commerce," op. cit., p. 185, "The cultivation of linen will only ever be precarious as long as we have to bring the seeds from abroad."

[21] P. Jeannin, "Les marché du nord," op. cit., p. 59.

[22] Memorandum from Arnoul (1720): "The aforesaid ship will be entirely built of good new wood from French oak. Both decks will be edged with planks two inches thick from Prussia, the fo'c'stle behind of one and a half inches, that in front of an inch and a quarter." Quoted by L. Roblin, *Le commerce de la mer: Nantes 1680–1730*, thesis (Paris IV, 1987), p. 154.

[23] P. W. Bamford, "French shipping in Northern European trade, 1660–1789," *The Journal of Modern History*, vol. XXVI, September 1954, n° 3, pp. 207–19.

larly due to the lack of competitive sales. The total value of Norwegian roe sold in Brittany can be estimated at more than 400,000 pounds a year, paid for by the national fisheries, to sustain a foreign industry. Roe is the egg of cod, and sardine fishing was dependent on Norwegian cod fishing: a break in trade with this power could eliminate sardine fishing in France which was, in fact, limited by the quantity of roe available at the time and which was only about 15 thousand barrels a year (. . .) up to the present, the catch of only one Norwegian port (the port of Bergen) has provided nearly all the supplies necessary for sardine fishing in France and Spain."[24]

As well as these above-mentioned goods which were necessary for various activities and industries, the role of the "North" in times of corn crises must not be forgotten. Polish trade depended on the export of cereals, which were its only source of foreign revenue. The quantity exported remained small compared to total production. J. Topolski calculated that, during the 17th century, between 4% and 5% of Polish cereal was destined for export outside the Baltic.[25] The figures for the 18th century are certainly much lower due to the development of agricultural production in Western Europe. Danzig, supplied by the immense basin of the Vistula, was the great entrepot for cereals being exported to countries in permanent deficit such as Friesland, Sweden, Norway, or to countries temporarily affected at various times by corn crises like France and the Iberian Peninsula. In the 18th century, when the situation was critical, France relied upon foreign wheat from the Amsterdam market, England or from the Baltic ports. The number of ships passing the Sound freighted with cereals shows the irregularity of demand from the Northern countries.[26] Although Brittany was one of the richest French provinces in cereals, it was not, however, protected from corn crises. The sudden appearance in the Sound Toll's accounts of massive imports of cereals destined for France and, particularly, for Brittany, is proof

[24] A. N., F/12/1838 pêches maritimes; 1773–1787, Pêches maritimes XVIIIe siècle; encouragements pour la préparation des rogues de Pêche française, Versailles 7/2/1788.

[25] J. Topolski, "La Baltique fut-elle responsible de la regression économique en Pologne au XVIIe et XVIIIe siècles?," Colloqium 'La mer baltique, zone de rencontres et d'affrontements,' Strasbourg, 1978, p. 15.

[26] P. Jeannin, "Les comptes," op. cit. "The Sound statistics act as a thermometer which rises when a Western economy is sick."

of the acuteness of the crises of 1724–1725[27] and 1751–1752 in the province.[28] During the second half of the 18th century, French imports of Nordic grain increased. "From 1751 to 1780, the Tables (of the Sound Toll) recorded about seven times more grain destined for France than during the previous thirty years."[29] However, the importance of these imports must not be exaggerated. They were small in comparison to the total consumption of grain in Europe. J. A. Faber gives the example of the years 1640–1649 when average annual imports, around 100,000 lasts, would have fed at least a million people.[30] As far as France was concerned, the total imports of rye and wheat between 1721 and 1783 were 70,174 lasts.

Internationalisation of trade

Integration of the North into the European economy

The Baltic world was not uniform, and the different areas of production did not supply the same commodities. There was a clear specialisation by regions. Cereals mostly came from the Vistula basin, hemp and flax from Russia, flax from Kurzeme, Byelorussia and Lithuania, and iron from Sweden and Russia. All the Northern countries exported wood, but the regions were specialised: Brandenburg and Poland produced mainly oak pieces, particularly staves for barrels and planking for ships, while Livonia, Estonia and Byelorussia,

[27] H. Sée, "Le commerce Saint Malo au XVIIIe siècle d'après les papiers des Magon," *Mémoires Hayem*, 9, 1925, p. 41. "The harvest is poor as it was in 1724–5: the situation has become so critical that a decree of the council of 1724 allowed trading between provinces. The bushel of wheat in Brittany will soon be up to 7 pounds . . . As far as wheat is concerned, Magon thinks that it would be better to order it from Dantzig where it is cheaper. But since wheat has gone up in price in Poland, Laurencin puts all his orders through Holland."

[28] A. D. I. V, C 1652. 1751: "Wheat has shed little straw; not a quarter of the previous year." 1752: "Harvest so poor that imports are necessary in the dioceses of Saint Malo, Saint Brieuc, Tréguier and Léon" Quoted by J. Meyer, *La noblesse bretonne* (Paris: S.E.V.P.E.N., 1966), p. 528.

[29] P. Jeannin, "Les marches du Nord," op. cit., p. 62.

[30] J. A. Faber, "Structural Changes in the European Economy During the 18th Century as Reflected in the Baltic Trade," in W. G. Heeres, L. M. J. B. Hesp, L. Noordegraaf, R. C. W. van der Voort, eds., *From Dunkirk to Danzig* (Hilversum: Verloren, 1988), p. 84.

the largest wood producers of the Baltic area, specialised in masts. Finland produced thick planks and beams which, according to the trade gazette (1766), were much sought after because "they are made of a kind of yellow fir which lasts a very long time." Sweden exported little wood, preferring to keep its production for home consumption, and, finally, Norway exported few "high quality" products but, rather, supplied particularly medium and small masts, billets and beams as well as narrow planks.

In fact, export was vital to the economy of different countries. During the 17th century, Western Europe represented up to 85% of Russia's foreign trade.[31] During the 17th century, the different countries set up rigorous management of their production. Sweden organised the spatial management of its production with the so-called *Bergkollegium* which meant that there was a policy of production units being spread throughout the territory to avoid depleting the forests. In Poland, the basis of the wealth of the great estates lay in cereal production. Polish magnates sought to keep a large part of the revenue from agriculture for themselves by seeking to make full use of the *corvée* system. The result of this agrarian policy was the enslavement of the rural population, a situation that lasted until the 19th century.

The importance of the Dutch

The Dutch were the first to benefit from the growth in trade between the Baltic and France, and so strengthened the position of their fleet. Between 1748 and 1758, their ships represented 41.2% of Baltic-French navigation. This development can be, in part, due to fundamental changes in the Dutch role in European commerce from the 1740s onwards. Amsterdam lost control of the production and processing of goods essential to international trade, and the Dutch commercial system evolved towards one based on intermediary service, such as the transporting of merchandise for other countries.[32] France purchased fewer goods from Holland, but, instead, brought them directly from the North by ships flying the Dutch flag. The

[31] A. Maczak and H. Samsonowicz, "La zone baltique; l'un des elements du marché européen," *Acta Poloniae Historica*, XI, 1965, p. 96.

[32] J. Israël, *Dutch Primacy in World Trade, 1585–1740* (Oxford: Oxford University Press, 1989), p. 399.

steady decline in Dutch shipping passing through The Sound—50% at the beginning of the 18th century, 40% during the 1740s, and 30% in the 1750s—was, essentially, due to a large decrease in the number of voyages to or from Amsterdam.[33] On the contrary, the Dutch seem to have strengthened their position in foreign markets, particularly in France, in the first half of the 18th century. In 1784–1785, the Dutch were still involved in 18% of French trade with the North, as opposed to 15% for Denmark, 15% for Eastern Friesland and 14% for Sweden.[34] The merchants and agents of the United Provinces were present in all trading areas. The Dutch community, which had fled Nantes at the end of the 17th century, was set up again under Louis XV, and participated in the development of the town. Holland supplied various goods for the slave trade; "to encourage this trade, the merchants of the United Provinces had factors and representatives in the market place . . . They imported a great diversity of goods, as much from their own country as from Sweden and Norway."[35]

Although the importance of the Dutch merchant navy's relations with the North declined in the second half of the 18th century, Amsterdam's financial role remained dominant; "it is particularly credit, generally agreed by the rich bankers of Amsterdam who accept bills of exchange drawn with them from every corner of Europe, which maintains it in its old position of international importance."[36] French trade with Northern Europe was organised around the Amsterdam market. The purchases of the *Compagnie des Indes* were carried out by the intermediary of a Dutch agent, even though the company had privileged, and, sometimes, exclusive suppliers in other Northern countries. The latter endorsed the bills of lading after a theoretical verification of the ships' cargos. Payments for goods were

[33] J. T. Lindblad, "Structural changes in the Dutch trade with the Baltic in the 18th century," *Scandinavian Economic History Review*, 1985, 38–2, p. 193.

[34] Hans Chr. Johansen, "How to Pay for Baltic Products?," in W. Fischer, R. Marvin McInnis, and J. Schneider, eds., *The Emergence of a World Economy 1500–1914, Part I Beiträge zur Wirtschafts- und Sozialgeschichte*, vol. 33–1, 1966, p. 138.

[35] J. Mathorez, "Notes sur la colonie hollandaise de Nantes," *Revue du Nord*, 1913, "Goods using slavery do not only come from the North. Apart from national production, the Nantes traders get their supplies from many foreign countries, for example India and its cotton fabrics."

[36] J. G. Van Dillen, "Amsterdam, marché mondial des métaux précieux," *Revue Historique*, CLII, 1926, p. 199.

carried out by Dutch middlemen: "payment for wood from Prussia supplied by Delattre, the King of Prussia's advisor, was done by bill of exchange drawn on Hornecca Hoguer of Amsterdam."[37]

The Scandinavians, particularly the Danes, also took advantage of the French weakness in the North to develop their maritime activities. Dan Andersen counted 168 Danish ships at Cette and Marseille during 1785.[38] These ships were particularly active in war time, and used their neutrality to trade between the French ports. Then, in peace time their competitiveness enabled them to continue and develop this trade abroad.[39]

An economically viable trade

However, trade with the North was a lucrative business. Studies on trade profits in Baltic commerce showed a high rate of profit—higher than other branches of European trade and only slightly less than for colonial trade in its early days. This is the reason why the Hanseatic towns, the Dutch and the English fought fiercely for its control.[40] Economic historians of the 18th century knew that trade with the North was an important source of profit. Dutch profit was "ordinarily around 100%, not including the first profit made on the transport from France to Holland. So a Dutch vessel of 200 tons sent to Riga, loaded with two-thirds salt and one-third wine, vinegar and brandy, traded these goods with a 200% profit. If it returned with a cargo of hemp, pitch and tar which it traded in France, the profit exceeded 100%."[41]

The average value of the Dutch flûtes and galliots was between 30,000 and 40,000 florins (between 67,500 and 90,000 *livres*).[42] The

[37] G. Le Bouëdec, "Les approvisionnements," op. cit., pp. 387–88.

[38] Dan. H. Andersen, *The Danish Flag in the Mediterranean Shipping and Trade, 1747–1807*, Ph.D. thesis, University of Copenhagen, 2000.

[39] Johansen, "Den danske skibsfart i sidste halvdel addet 18 arhundrede," *Erhvervhistorisk arbog*, 1975.

[40] M. Bogucka, "The role of Baltic trade in European development from the XVIth to the XVIIIth centuries," *Journal of European Economic History*, vol. 9, n° 1, 1980, p. 12.

[41] Departmental archives of the Gironde, C 1639, memorandum of 1733 (quoted by P. Butel, "Bordeaux et la Hollande au XVIIIe siècle, l'exemple du négociant Pellet," *Revue d'Histoire Economique et Sociale*, 45, 1967, p. 62).

[42] P. Butel, *La croissance commerciale bordelaise dans la seconde moitié du XVIIIe siècle*, Thesis (Lille: University of Lille, 1973), p. 292.

price of the cargos paid by the *Compagnie des Indes* lead us to believe that, according to the return trips to the Baltic (the cargos of salt paid less than colonial products, but allowed a faster turnaround), the capital value of a ship was recovered in between four to eight voyages in peacetime—two to three years—and in three voyages in time of war—one and a half years. The rapid payment of the cargo was a considerable advantage for shipping going to the North when compared to colonial trade. In Lorient, maritime transport expenses were generally paid for by the *Compagnie des Indes*. Amsterdam played the role of financial relay for the company by paying the captains for the balance of cargo transported: "in 1752, Jean Dorts of the *Jeune Allard* only received a part payment of 702 *livres*; the remaining 10,893 *livres* were paid on his return to Amsterdam."[43] The Dutch were everywhere, whether organising the transport or controlling the financial operations with the North.

The rise of England

England gradually became the most important purchaser of goods from the North. In the 18th century, more than half of Swedish iron exports were destined for England. While the Dutch balked at abandoning the White Sea route, the English took the initiative and transferred the intense activity that they had had in the port of Narva since the end of the 17th century to Saint Petersburg.[44] The first ship from Saint Petersburg registered in the Sound Toll Accounts passed in 1710. The ship was on its own and under the English flag. In 1715, there were 59 ships—47 were English and 10 were Dutch. A series of treaties and commercial advantages, such as authorisation to pay customs duty in Russian currency when other foreigners had to pay in silver *thalers* which were undervalued,[45] confirmed the dominant position of the British merchants in Russian foreign trade.[46] A system of advance payments enabled the British traders

[43] G. Le Bouëdec, *Les approvisionnements de la Compagnie des Indes (1737–1770). L'horizon géographique lorientais*, Thesis, Université de Paris IV, 1982, 2 vol., p. 387.

[44] P. Jeannin, "En Europe du Nord, sources et travaux d'histoire commerciale," *Annales Economies Sociétés Civilisations*, 4, 1968, p. 852.

[45] I. de Madariaga, *La Russie au temps de la Grande Catherine* (Paris: Fayard, 1987), p. 506.

[46] Journal Général de France, 1785, pp. 90–91: "The Russians invariably paid

to reserve local production at particularly advantageous prices. In the second part of the 18th century, England acquired nine-tenths of the iron, between two-thirds and three-quarters of the tallow and between three-quarters and four-fifths of the flax and hemp exported from Saint Petersburg.[47] The rate for Russian raw material was fixed by the volume of British purchases. In 1755, the French Consul, Hanssen of Elsinore declared that, "the hemp is very expensive in relation to the large quantities the English are always selling."[48] However, the Dutch retained their dominant position in the port of Riga.

England sought to increase its imports and decrease its exports to reduce the deficit in its trade balance. In the first part of the century, the great majority of British ships went into the Baltic in ballast, as

Figure 4. Average annual number of passages through the Sound for ships going East

By area of loading

Century	Dutch Republic	Scandinavia, Germany	England and Scotland	Others (*incl. France*)	Total
second half of 16th	986 (55%)	418 (22%)	126 (7%)	369 (19%)	1899
first half of 17th	1188 (55%)	398 (29%)	203 (10%)	319 (16%)	2038
second half of 17th	822 (50%)	388 (24%)	181 (11%)	243 (15%)	1634
first half of 18th	722 (40%)	408 (23%)	310 (18%)	301 (17%)	1741
second half of 18th	877 (28%)	931 (29%)	742 (23%)	626 (20%)	3176

Source: J. A. Faber, "Structural Changes . . .", op. cit., p. 90.

90 copecks for the rix-dollar, the English 120–125 copecks and the French 140–145 copecks. The copeck was worth about 12 French deniers, which made 100 copecks 7 *livres* 5 *sols tournois*. On the other hand, Petersburg only exchanged with Amsterdam; there, due to loss in exchange, the rouble was only worth 36 to 39 sluyvers, around 3 livres 18 sols to 4 livres 5 sols tournois." Quoted by P. Dardel, *Navires et marchandises dans les ports de Rouen et du Havre au XVIIIe siècle*, Ports-Routes-Trafics XI, Paris, 1963.

[47] A. Attman, *Dutch Enterprise in the World Bullion Trade 1550–1800* (Gothenburg: Acta Regiae Societatis Scientiarum et Litterarum Gothoburgensis, 1983), p. 70.

[48] AN, AE, B1 481 reg. 1, Elsinore.

the main import product (by volume) was French salt from the Atlantic coast. From the second half of the 18th century, British salt production, which was mined on an industrial basis in Cheshire, eventually took over the Northern markets to the detriment of its competitors. In 1787, England exported 43.5% of the salt which entered the Baltic, which was two and a half times the French export to the same regions. New England became a producer of strategic materials for shipbuilding without, however, displacing the Nordic products. A pamphlet from 1768 showed this British decision: "We have decided to compete with the Polish in their function as labourers working for the Dutch . . . And at the same time we shall allow our brothers, the Irish, to replace the Danes as cowherds for the Dutch."[49]

In war time, British industry had few problems in finding supplies of products from the "North." Convoys regularly passed through The Sound. British ships waited in the *Kattegat* for the frigates responsible for convoying them safely home. Sometimes the English merchant ships formed their own convoys. Fleets were made up of 15 to 20 armed vessels accompanied by several others which were unarmed. These vessels, with reinforced hulls—the canon of an average frigate could not do them much harm—were steered and armed in such a way that made attack very difficult. In case of an attack, "they defended themselves from the captain's cabin which is vast. As in an impenetrable entrenchment, it is closed on the side facing the main mast with very thick planks of musket-proof oak with slits through which they fire continually with heavy musketry using shot which destroys everyone on board the vessel before they themselves can be harmed. Thus, our most powerful corsairs who know these vessels never stop."[50] War also enabled the British to develop their exports, so Hamburg, for instance, was deprived of French colonial goods, and was, instead, supplied by England.

France and the North

In 1782, Coquebert de Montbret exclaimed: "what fatality separates us from the North, whereas we know how to open up the most bar-

[49] Quoted by I. Wallerstein, *Le mercantilisme et la consolidation de l'économie-monde européenne* (Paris: Flammarion, 1984), pp. 366–67.

[50] AN, AE, B3 418. Memorandum from Frammery dated 6 July 1779.

barous and the bleakest of countries."[51] The Sound Toll's accounts clearly show this lack of French enthusiasm for the North.

The absence of the French flag

Figure 5. French shipping and Baltic trade

	France-Baltic			Baltic-France		
	Total	France	%	Total	France	%
1720–1730	2137	114	5,3	1231	117	9,5
1748–1758	3392	34	1	2686	38	1,4

These rather unexceptional figures are indicative of the decline in French shipping to the North in the 18th century. From the Sound Toll Accounts, Edmund Cieslak has calculated that, from 1716 to 1783, ships under the French flag transported 2.2% of French imports to Danzig—as opposed to 51% ships under the Danzig flag—and 3.7% of exports—as opposed to 37.3% of ships from the Polish port.[52] M. L. Pelus remarked that, in previous centuries, serious crises coincided with a greater presence of French ships in the Baltic.[53] In the 18th century, this was no longer the case. For instance, during the corn crisis of 1751–1752, only one French ship took delivery of cereals in the North.

Why this weak French presence? Many explanations have been put forward. According to Pierre Dardel, French sailors feared sailing the Baltic, as it was a very dangerous sea that they did not know.[54] To resolve this problem, and to create a new merchant navy destined for the North, a memorandum written in 1756 suggested

[51] D. Ozanam, *Claude Baudard de Saint-James, trésorier Général de la Marine et Brasseur d'Affaires (1738–1787)* (Geneva: Droz, 1969), p. 115.

[52] E. Cieslak, "Sea borne trade between France and Poland in the XVIIIth century," *Journal of European Economic History*, vol. 6, n° 1, 1977, p. 53.

[53] M. L. Pelus, "Crises de subsistances et 'commerce du Nord' dans la seconde moitié du XVIe siècle," in M. Balard, J. C. Hervé and N. Lemaitre, eds., *Paris et ses campagnes sous l'Ancien Régime, Mélanges offerts à Jean Jacquart* (Paris: Publication de la Sorbonne, 1994), pp. 241–250.

[54] P. Dardel, "Les relations maritimes et commerciales entre la France notamment les ports de Rouen et du Havre et les ports de la mer baltique de 1497 à 1783," *Annales de Normandie*, 1969, p. 52.

employing Dutch captains and sailors from the North.[55] However, between 1788–1790, when the war between Russia and Sweden paralysed trade in the Eastern Baltic, large numbers of French ships passed through the Sound—100 in 1789.[56] The reason for this relative lack of French interest in the North was not the French sailors, who were already used to facing such distant and fearful seas, but was the more generalised disinterest the French had for everything concerning trade in the North.[57] French ship owners did not send ships to the North, and merchants were used to letting foreign ships ply the trade between France and the Baltic. The main reasons for the French loss of interest in the North were, essentially, their lack of organisation and their lack of competitiveness in comparison to their Dutch and Scandinavian competitors. These latter nations had well-established networks for the purchase of goods. For example, at Riga, the best masts were destined for Holland and England. Moreover, the management of trade—representatives, agents and brokers—with ships adapted to the conditions for sailing and trading in the North—shallow draught ships with back loading scuttles for the transport of very long masts were necessary—and the availability of a very efficient financial system were simply not present in the French commercial system. The French merchants obviously preferred their goods to be transported by foreigners, and, thereby, increase their own profits rather than to lose money by using the national fleet.

French attempts to open up to new markets, particularly in Russia, were a failure. In 1723, the voyages of three French ships to Saint Petersburg ended in a 40% loss of capital for the first ship, 20% for the second ship, and the third had to be sold on its return to France in order to pay the crew.[58] The merchants were responsible for the failure of these voyages, due to the absence of preliminary contacts with the local agents, which forced the captains to sell off their mer-

---

[55] Quoted by A. Kraatz, *La Compagnie Française de Russie. Histoire du commerce franco-russe au XVIIe–XVIIIe siècles* (Paris: François Bourin, 1993), p. 165.

[56] H. C. Johansen, "French Trade with the Baltic area in the late 18th century," paper presented at the Congress of the International Association of History of the Northern Seas, Tvärminne, 1979.

[57] A. M., C954, Letter from M. de Castries to M. de Sourdeval dated 11 September 1765: "Among the seventeen French ships that arrived in Amsterdam in 1781, several came in ballast or with goods of little value and others left our ports in ballast." (Quoted by H. Sée, "Les relations," op. cit.)

[58] AE/M D/7 folio 8, Memorandum from Drouet dated March 1728.

chandise at low prices. The ship owners who risked setting out for the Baltic considered this enterprise as a rather less than heroic gesture—so much so that, during the 18th century, when the widow of a foreign merchant asked for citizenship in Le Havre, she played on her "devotion to French trade interests through the shipment she had sent to Russia and the Northern countries and . . . the losses that she had made there."[59] The last great French attempt of the century took place in 1785, when, stimulated by Marshall de Castries, Claude Baudart de Saint-James financed a new company called the "*Compagnie française du commerce du Nord.*" To lower costs, the ships were bought in Stralsund and in Stockholm and the crew, as well as the captains, were recruited in Hamburg. Despite the seriousness of his organisation, the constitution of a network of agents in the North, the capital invested and the number of ships involved, the activities of the Company only lasted three short years. The directors blamed "the manoeuvring it suffered at the hands of the Dutch who, fearful of seeing most of their trade with France fall into the hands of dangerous competitors, sacrificed considerable sums of money to beat their rivals. They offered to transport goods at prices lower than those of the *Compagnie du Nord*, even lower than those they demanded before its creation."[60]

Many merchants considered the Dutch as "the natural enemies of all trading peoples" and made suggestions to supplant Amsterdam in the trade with the North.[61] From 1701 onwards, a proposal from the Trade Council, inspired by English navigation laws, demanded that "foreigners cannot bring merchandise to France which is not of their local production, that it should come directly from the country where it is produced firsthand and not after being warehoused . . ."[62] In 1762, the French agent in Danzig tried to persuade the Ministry at Versailles to purchase the wood necessary for the navy directly from Danzig rather than getting it through a Dutch middleman.[63] The *Compagnie des Indes* was reproached for purchasing through

---

[59] P. Dardel, "Les relations maritimes," op. cit., p. 54.

[60] D. Ozanam, Claude Baudard . . . op. cit., p. 99 and foll.

[61] AN Marine, B VIII–475, C 53 n° 22 (quoted by W. Kirchner, "Relations économiques entre la France et la Russie au XVIIIe siècle," *Revue d'Histoire Economique et Sociale*, XXXIV, 2, 1961, p. 160.

[62] A. D. I & V. C 754.

[63] E. Cieslak, "Sea borne," op. cit., p. 58.

middlemen, who supplied them with commodities of inferior quality and at a higher price.[64] However, although the *Compagnie des Indes* signed contracts with French merchants (with Grou and Michel of Nantes and Goossens of Paris, to name a few), they always went through Amsterdam. The merchants, in spite of their recriminations, could not do without their Dutch middlemen. In 1729, Guillotou of Morlaix wanted to create a company to import flax seed from Livonia. He suggested that Widow Labat and Son of Amsterdam, his best Dutch client, should participate in the project. He wrote, "I have the honour of offering you a voyage to Libau. The merchandise which is in demand there is wine, brandy and salt and the return cargo will be flax seed which is sold at a better price there than in Riga."[65] In 1788, Paimboeuf, to open up to other markets, sent a memorandum to the King with the aim of, "encouraging the establishment of Dutch families who would like to settle in Paimboeuf to trade directly with the colonies."[66]

The failure of French ship owners to trade with the North is due to this lack of persistence, and to the absence of a real determination to penetrate a new market. As for the other trades in which France was well placed, for example the colonial trade, they seemed to be looking to make a "killing" and the initial losses in the Northern trade seemed to discourage their initiatives. Building a network of representatives and gaining the confidence of foreign clients was a slow process, and did not bear fruit for several years. It seems the French did not want to rise to the challenge, and preferred to direct their activity to the protected trade with the colonies.

The French network

The French merchant communities in the Northern towns were small compared to the Dutch or Germanic communities settled in the French ports. On the other hand, the Huguenot communities who had emigrated from France formed real networks and family ties

[64] M. D. A.A.E., France, 2012, folio 23, Memorandum on trade with the Northern powers by Mr. Jodin of Geneva.

[65] H. Sée, "Le commerce de Morlaix dans la première moitiçé du XVIIIe siècle d'après les papiers de Guillotou de Kerever," in J. Hayem, *Memoires et documents pour servir à l'histoire du commerce et de l'industrie en France*, op cit., p. 186.

[66] A.D.I & V, C 1584 (quoted by H. Sée, *Mémoires Hayem*, 9, 1925, p. 221).

between French agents and agents on the foreign markets were very important and were frequently utilised for trade. Paul Butel has shown that the Protestants from Guyana made up the majority of emigrants to the commercial areas of the North and, rightly, thinks that, "one of the main factors for Bordeaux's power can be seen in the family ties between the Bordeaux ship-owning community and trade in the great markets of the North."[67] The French were not absent from trade with the North, but, although the solidarity engendered by family origin was very strong, these trading houses were very international. One of the main representatives for the *Compagnie des Indes*, the Testas family of Amsterdam who were originally from Bordeaux, was very much integrated into the Dutch merchant elite and a large part of its activity was directed towards colonial trade with the Dutch West Indies.[68] Some of the great fortunes of the "Northern" ports were the result of this Huguenot emigration. Jean Bedoire, originally a wigmaker from the Saintonge, settled in Stockholm around 1665 where he became a copper and iron merchant. His son became one of the richest men in Sweden by exporting Swedish metal, particularly to France (he was the exclusive supplier of the *Compagnie des Indes*) and by importing wine and salt.[69] The companies His and Boué were among the most important merchants in the town of Hamburg. However, not many French émigrés made their fortune. In Saint Petersburg, the three French companies active during the second half of the 18th century, Godin, Michel and Raimbert, lacked a solid financial basis, and were unable to undertake large operations and, therefore, could not prosper. The merchant Michel, son of a French emigrant to Saint Petersburg, specialised in retailing luxury goods to ladies from the high society for whom he made frequent trips to France. In 1778, Consul Lesseps noted that, "Michel's profits were always low but it was only known after his death; as for Raimbert (representative for the *Compagnie des Indes*), he was not very rich either."[70]

[67] Butel, *La croissance commerciale*, op. cit., p. 545.
[68] Ibid., pp. 542–43.
[69] G. De Faramond, "Des relations commerciales inégales des origins à 1914" in M. and J. F. Battail, eds., *Une amitié millénaire, Les relations entre la France et la Suède à travers les âges* (Paris: Beauchesne, 1993).
[70] W. Kirchner, "Relations économiques entre la France et la Russie au XVIIIe siècle," *Revue d'Histoire Economique et Sociale*, XXXIV, 2, 1961.

France had consular agents in the main ports of the North to help and protect French merchants and sailors, and to supply information to Versailles about trading and the political life of the different countries of the North. However, these officials did little to improve France's place in the Nordic markets. One of the weaknesses of the French consuls in the Northern ports seems to have been their weak commercial influence compared to their foreign counterparts. In Marseilles, the main port for Danish shipping in the Mediterranean, first Sollicoffre, then Ployard, both members of influential Protestant families in the town, were named consuls of the Scandinavian kingdom.[71] In Bordeaux, the representative for the Court of Vienna was Jean-Jacques de Bethmann, one of the richest merchants of the great Aquitaine port.[72] France rarely chose local consuls. One of the few exceptions was the French consulate in Elsinore which, during the first half of the 18th century, was entrusted to the Danish merchant, Hanssen, who was very interested in developing trade with France, particularly with his brother, the consul for Denmark in Bordeaux. His successor, de Brosseronde, had great difficulty in maintaining the links with France since, not speaking the local languages, he had little contact with the local merchants.

Difficulties in wartime

French vessels, few even during peacetime, were totally absent in wartime. In 1778, it was with stupefaction that the Consul of Elsinore saw a ship from Saint Malo arrive which to him, "seemed to have furiously ventured" into "an English ants' nest."[73] France, whose navy was in a weak position in the seas of Northern Europe, left the control of the North Sea to its British rival. The French corsairs were certainly present, but their few successful raids had only a limited effect on English trade. Besides, it was very difficult for these corsairs to find refuge in a Danish or Norwegian port where the local authorities were uncooperative.

---

[71] Ployard's brother, the Danish consul in Marseilles, was also consul of the Scandinavian kingdom in Tunis.

[72] W. Henninger, *Johann Jakob von Bethmann 1717–1792* (Bochum: Kaufmann, 1993).

[73] AN, AE, B1 481, folio 150.

Neutral vessels had the responsibility of transporting strategic goods for the French navy. To escape the British controls, they had several bills of lading. For example, in August 1757, Jan Hylkes of Makkum in the Netherlands had two identical bills of lading in his possession, one destined for St. Sebastian and Bilbao, the other for Lorient. The neutral vessels took advantage of their position, and the price of freight greatly increased in times of conflict. In 1782, freight for the journey between Riga and Nantes reached 28,000 florins, more than double the freight costs between Riga and Amsterdam.[74] On the Lorient-Riga line, the price of freight increased by about 45% between 1755 and 1757 in Lorient, and by more than 100% after 1760. The neutral ships were not afraid of being taken by the British. Although English justice was strict, it was also independent, and had a greater sense of ownership than French justice. In 1797, a ship owner from Trondheim stated that there was no reason to take out insurance against being taken, since the insurers never paid without long discussions. The only ones to fear were the English, but they paid damages if the cargo was confiscated and, for this reason, the value of the cargo was artificially increased in the official papers and the charter party.[75]

During times of conflict, the French arsenals were regularly deprived of masts, tar and pitch—all of which were highly strategic goods for its royal navy. During the American War of Independence, the ships loaded with masts destined for France were captured in great numbers by the British and the Dutch ships responsible for transporting them. They left them at Amsterdam or at Texel, where the merchandise accumulated on the quayside. Since transport by sea was impossible, the Minister of Sartine decided to send the masts waiting for delivery in Holland overland. By following various canals, rivers, and roads, the masts were brought to the mouth of the Loire, which was the end of their journey. At the end of 1781, nearly 2000 masts were loaded at Paimboeuf and delivered to the King's arsenals. They took more than six months by this route to arrive at their destination, whereas it only took 10 days by sea.

---

[74] P. Butel, *La croissance*, op. cit., p. 292.

[75] H. Berg, *Trondhjems Sjofart under Eneveldet, 1600–1814* (Trondhjem: Trondhjems Sjøfartsmuseums Årsskrift, 1938–41), pp. 219–20. Quoted by Andersen, op. cit., pp. 21–22.

Measures taken too late

The king was conscious of the weakness in French navigation in the North. For example, the naval authorities had great difficulty in finding ships' masters with experience in the Baltic in 1733, when France decided to send a squadron to Poland to support the election of Stanislas Leszczynski, or again in 1734 when the French went to help Danzig under siege by Russian troops.[76] Although some agreements were made with the Baltic powers in the first part of the 18th century, the French power only really worried about the situation in the last years of the *Ancien Régime*. The Council law of 1784 gave a six month franchise for stocking merchandise from the North brought by French vessels and exempted provisions from all export duty in the ships destined for the North. A series of subsidies according to the ship's home port completed this measure which was aimed at encouraging French shipping in the Baltic. In 1784, the French government signed a trade agreement with Sweden, and obtained the warehousing franchise in Gothenburg in exchange for an island in the Caribbean. A few years later, in 1787, a trade treaty was agreed with Russia putting French merchants on an equal footing with their foreign competitors. These different measures seem to have born fruit, but hardly had time really to improve the French position before the Revolutionary Wars.[77]

Figure 6. Number of French ships passing through the Sound between 1784 and 1795

(In both directions)

1784	1785	1786	1787	1788	1789	1790	1791	1792	1793	1794	1795
25	20	19	35	64	110	122	91	25	0	0	0

A total of 511 of which 65% was destined for, or leaving from, St. Petersburg.

[76] A. N., Marine, B2, volume 293 (ff. 589, 689, 712), volume 295 (ff. 317, 322, 405, 488), volume 356 (ff. 28, 30, 41) (quoted by Cieslak, "Sea born," op. cit., p. 54).

[77] Butel, "Le traffic européen de Bordeaux, de la guerre d'Amérique à la Révolution," *Annales du Midi*, 78, 1966, p. 59. Hans Chr. Johansen, "French Trade with the Baltic in the late 18th Century," unpublished, p. 13. For Butel, the measures taken by the French authorities encouraged the French traders to fit out their ships for Russia. Johansen thinks that the war between Russia and Sweden, which reduced the number of ships available in the Baltic zone and the high French demand for cereals, can explain this large increase in French shipping passing the Sound.

France did not really have the will to invest in the North. The French merchants did not give themselves time to construct solid networks of representatives in the different Baltic ports. The State, aware of these weaknesses, took positive measures, but much too late. French trade was no doubt too concentrated on the protected links with its colonies, and ignored an activity of prime importance to its economic activities.

On the other hand, throughout the 18th century, the British State had a growing interest in questions of trade, and sought to help its entrepreneurs by giving them possibilities for increasing their profits. The British trade with the "North" was an example of this desire for economic expansion. The regulations on shipping, trade treaties, and the system of convoys, to name but a few, gradually enabled England to gain control of the trade with the North and, therefore, to supply without difficulty the industrial sectors of prime importance to the British economy, such as shipbuilding and the metal industry.

CHAPTER THIRTEEN

DENMARK-NORWAY, AFRICA, AND THE CARIBBEAN, 1660–1917: MODERNISATION FINANCED BY SLAVES AND SUGAR?*

Dan H. Andersen

Introduction

The importance of the slave trade and the colonial goods produced by slave labour has been debated intensively, but usually the focus has been on Britain. Britain was the first industrial nation, Britain was big, and Britain mattered. But there are more small states than big ones, and their colonial experience is important, not least of all because their experiences force us to consider the development trajectories open before and during the Industrial Revolution. The colonial experiences of these smaller states leads to the question: Were colonies necessary, or even beneficial, for modernisation and industrialisation?[1]

---

* Note about currency and measures. The Danish rixdollar specie had a silver content of 25.281 grams. One commercial last is about 2.6 tons. The rixdoller used here was the current rixdollars which had a lower silver content. One rixdollar = six marks = 96 skillings. Usually the exchange rate was about five rixdollars to one £. One *tønde* liquid (barrel) was about 139 litres.

The term *Denmark* will denote the whole conglomerate state. *Denmark proper* denotes Denmark itself.

[1] The international literature on colonial trade is immense, but some prominent contributions, which have inspired the structure and arguments of the present article are: Eric Williams, *Capitalism and Slavery* (New York: University of North Carolina Press, 1944); Stanley L. Engerman, "The Slave Trade and British Capital Formation in the 18th Century: A Comment on the Williams Thesis," *Business History Review* 46, 1972; Patrick O'Brien, "European Economic Development: The Contribution of the Periphery," *The Economic History Review* XXXV, no. 1, 1982; Barbara Solow, "Caribbean Slavery and British Growth: The Eric Williams Hypothesis," *Journal of Development Economics* 77, 1985; William Darity Jr., "British Industry and the West Indies Plantations," in Joseph E. Inikori and Stanley L. Engerman, eds., *The Atlantic Slave Trade* (Durban and London: Duke University Press, 1992); P. K. O'Brian and Stanley L. Engerman, "Exports and the Growth of the British Economy from the Glorious Revolution to the Peace of Amiens," in Barbara Solow, ed., *Slavery and the Rise of the Atlantic System* (Cambridge: Cambridge University Press, 1991); Joseph E.

This article will seek to answer two questions relating to Danish colonial trade and economic development in the 17th and 18th centuries. The first question concerns how big, in terms of both money and work force, was the section of the economy that dealt with the production, transport and processing of colonial products, specifically slaves and sugar? The second question asks whether this sector was especially dynamic and what, if any, were the substantial spill over effects from it into other sectors? Basically, then, this article will seek to assess if it is possible to assign a role to colonies and colonial trade in the modernisation and industrialisation of a minor state like Denmark-Norway, or, rather, was its modernisation and industrialisation the result of factors to be found exclusively on the European continent?

The years around 1840 witnessed a major shift in the Danish economy, when per capita growth doubled from 0.6% in the decades 1820–1840 to 1.4% in the decades 1840–1910. Substantial Danish grain exports to Britain began in the late 1820s after a long post-war depression, and Denmark is traditionally considered an example of agricultural export-led growth, which stimulated industries and services linked to agriculture. A newer interpretation does not deny the importance of agriculture and exports, but emphasises the importance of endogenous factors such as institutional prerequisites, a growth enhancing ideology, and human capital working hand in hand with agricultural exports. Industry and services were not only pulled along by agriculture, but also helped to create the conditions and responses that allowed Danish farmers to capture the British market, first for grain and later for bacon and butter.[2]

The economic expansion from 1840 cannot be directly linked to colonial trade. The Danish slave trade had been banned in 1792, though there was a 10-year grace period, and the sugar plantations on the Danish Caribbean islands had been severely hit by falling prices from 1817/18 coupled with a series of bad harvests. Any qualitative and quantitative changes caused by colonial trade will have to be located in the preceding century, especially the decades prior

Inikori, "Slavery and Atlantic Commerce, 1650–1800," *The American Historical Review*, vol. 82, no. 2, 1992. Otherwise only works directly relevant to this paper will be mentioned in the footnotes.

[2] Ole Hyldtoft, *Danmarks økonomiske historie 1840–1910* (Herning: Årchus, 1999), pp. 9–25.

to Denmark's entry into the Napoleonic Wars in 1807. Here Danish shipping and trade, both European and colonial, experienced a huge expansion, partly fuelled by the European wars.

The main focus of this chapter will be on Denmark proper, as most of the benefits of colonies accrued to the metropolis, but the 18th century Danish state constituted an economic unit, and attention will also be given to the effects of colonial trade on the core provinces of Norway and the German Duchies. In a backward economy dominated by agriculture and a militarised public sector, a comparison with total national income will make the contribution of any other sector or trade seem insignificant and will underestimate long-term dynamic effects. Therefore, a comparison will be made with Danish intra-European shipping and trade.

The grand strategy of the Danish Empire

The geographical and political area under study is the old conglomerate Danish state and the "Empire" which, by the mid-18th century, had reached its maximum extent, however modest in comparison with the empires of other European nation. The core territories were the twin kingdoms of Denmark and Norway and the Duchies of Schleswig and Holstein. Norway was lost to Sweden in 1814, and the Duchies were lost to the emerging German state in 1864. In the North Atlantic there were the Faeroe Islands, Iceland and Greenland. These were areas belonging to the Danish or Norwegian kings from the Viking age. In the case of Greenland there had been a hiatus between the extinction of the Norse settlements about 1500 and the resumption of colonisation in 1721.

The Danish tropical empire consisted of three small territories. In Asia, the Danish king acquired Tranquebar on the Coromandel Coast of India in 1620, and, by 1800, the territory of Tranquebar was 56 square kilometres with three large and a score of smaller villages. The capital of Tranquebar had about 5000 inhabitants. There were also small trading stations along the coast, the most important of them being Serampore in the Bengal region.

In Africa the Danes had taken possession of an area on the Western coast of Africa in present day Ghana in the 1660s. However, the area under Danish control fluctuated, depending on the Danish ability to both manoeuvre in the power struggle between the African tribes, as well as to deal with the competition between the European fortresses on the coast.

In the New World, three islands in the Caribbean were taken over. Uninhabited St. Thomas was acquired by the Danes in 1666. St. John was captured in 1718, despite British and Spanish protests, and, finally, the fertile island of St. Croix was bought from France in 1733. These islands are presently known as the US Virgin Islands. Their total surface area is 333 square kilometres.

In addition to these aforementioned territories, Denmark, like other European states, had a trading station in Canton. Moreover, on various occasions there were attempts to colonise the Nicobar Islands in the Sea of Bengal.

In terms of size the Danish colonial possessions were modest, but they were partially interconnected. Guns from Denmark, textiles from India and cowries bought in the Maldives and shipped via Tranquebar and Copenhagen to Africa, bought the slaves that fuelled the production of sugar on the Caribbean plantations.[3] Danish colonial and trading policies exhibit some of the same traits as those of bigger states. Initially, semi-official chartered companies administered the colonies and had a monopoly on shipping and trade. Later, attempts were made to tie the colonies to the metropolitan state in a closed mercantilist system. When shipping and trade expanded, and the necessary skills and experience—not the least of which was navigational—had been obtained and absorbed, the state took over the administration of the colonies and shipping, while trade was gradually opened to private interests.

The Danish colonial system was never totally closed and linked to Denmark exclusively in a purely mercantilist fashion. The colonies were small and Denmark was not an important power in European politics. Thus the success and, indeed, the survival of the Danish colonial system depended very much on the ability to exploit the local political and economic environment *and* Denmark's freedom to manoeuvre in European politics. Much of the Asian trade was financed by illicit British capital, and Chinese tea was transported from

[3] Per O. Hernæs, *Slaves, Danes, and African Coast Society* (Trondheim: University of Trondheim, 1995) (reprint 1998), pp. 173–74. Erik Gøbel, "Danish Trade to the West Indies and Guinea, 1671–1754," *Scandinavian Economic History Review*, vol. 31 (1983), p. 30. Ole Feldbæk, *Dansk søfarts historie 3. 1720–1814. Storhandelens tid.* (Copenhagen: Gyldendal, 1997), p. 43.

Copenhagen to the Channel Islands and the Faeroes to be smuggled into Britain.[4] Danish slavers did not confine themselves to buying slaves from the Danish possessions in Africa, and, for instance, the Danish island of St. Thomas in the Caribbean also functioned as an entrepot for the re-export of slaves. In the Danish Caribbean most of the planter-class was foreign-born. The produce of the islands—mainly raw sugar—had, by decree, to be transported to Copenhagen, but on occasion the rules were relaxed, and there was an intensive legal and illicit trade with the American continent from the islands. During the European wars Copenhagen became an entrepot for raw colonial products of foreign origin, most of which were re-exported to the Baltic, Sweden and the Dutch Republic.

Denmark's dependency on its freedom of manoeuvre in colonial and commercial policy was amply demonstrated during the years between 1660 and 1720 and again from 1720 to 1807. In 1660, the Danish state emerged from the devastating wars with Sweden with a sharply reduced territorial base, massive demographic losses, and huge war debts. Further wars with Sweden between 1675–79 and from 1709–1720, the necessity for alliances, economic constraints, and the Dutch economic and military dominance all worked in unison to limit Denmark's ability to implement more independent economic policies.[5] In this period, the connection with the African and Caribbean possessions was maintained in various ways, but was of slight if any importance. But, after 1720, Swedish expansionist aims had been curbed, and the Dutch were no longer able to obstruct a fully mercantilist Danish policy. Between 1720 and 1807 Denmark was at peace, apart from brief wars or skirmishes with Russia in 1762, with Sweden in 1788 and with Britain in 1801. Danish neutrality was combined with a policy of commercial expansion during the wars between the great powers of the 18th century. Thus the

[4] Ole Feldbæk, *India Trade under the Danish Flag 1772–1808. European Enterprise and Anglo-Indian Remittance and Trade* (Odense: Studentlitteratur, 1969); H. S. K. Kent, *War and Trade in Northern Seas. Anglo-Scandinavian Economic Relations in the Mid-eighteenth Century* (Cambridge: Cambridge University Press, 1973), pp. 112–129. Kaare Lauring: Kinahandelen, "et spørgsmål om finansiering," in Hans Jeppesen et al., eds., *Søfart. Politik. Identitet* (Helsingør: Handels og Søfartsmuseet på Kronborg, 1996).

[5] Henrik Becker-Christensen, *Protektionisme og Reformer, 1660–1814.* Dansk Toldhistorie II (Copenhagen: Toldræsen, 1988); Niels Steensgaard, "Slotsholmen og verdenshavet. Kan adelsvældens og enevældens Danmark placeres i det kapitalistiske verdenssystem?" in Hans Jeppesen et al., eds., *Søfart*, op. cit.

islands in the Caribbean were used as platforms for the legalisation and re-export of French and Dutch colonial goods, and the Danish flag was used to cover the cargoes and capital of merchants from the belligerent states. It is within this context that these holes in the colonial system must be seen. They were the result of the weakness of the imperial powers, but were also part of a policy designed to exploit to the fullest possible extent Danish neutrality and freedom from engagements in European politics.[6] The purchase of St. Croix from France in 1733 was an early example of this policy. The real price was not the stipulated 750,000 livres (= 164,000 rixdollars), but, rather, a benevolent Danish neutrality during the War of the Polish Succession.

From the 1740s, the merchant marine under the Danish flag began to expand, and in Danish historiography the period from the mid-18th century to 1807 is usually described as a period of flourishing trade. By 1785, a French report estimated the Danish merchant marine to be the third largest in Europe after the British and the French.[7] A point of debate is whether this expansion was solely based upon Danish neutrality during the European wars, which enabled Danish ships to take over the markets of the states at war, or, perhaps, was the outcome of more "natural" economic factors such as low costs and a favourable geographical location at the entrance of the Baltic.[8]

There has been no comprehensive study of the impact of colonies and colonial trade on Danish economic development in terms of capital formation and modernisation. Admittedly, there is a scarcity

---

[6] The weakness of Denmark as an imperial power is emphasised in Neville A. T. Hall, *Slave Society in the Danish West Indies* (Baltimore: Johns Hopkins University Press, 1992), pp. 1–33.

[7] Ruggiero Romano, "Per una Valutazione delle Flotta Mercantile Europa alla Fine del Secolo XVIII," in *Studi in onore Amintore Fanfani*, V. (Milano: Giuffrè, 1962).

[8] Hans Chr. Johansen, "Den danske skibsfart i sidste halvdel af det 18.århundrede," *Erhvervshistorisk årbog*, 1975. See also, "Danish shipping services as a link between the Mediterranean and the Baltic 1750–1850," in L. R. Fischer and H. W. Nordvik, *Shipping and Trade, 1750–1950* (Pontefract: University Press, 1990), and "Scandinavian shipping in the late Eighteenth Century in a European perspective," *Economic History Review* Vol. XLV, nr. 3 (1992). Ole Feldbæk: "Eighteenth Century Danish Neutrality: Its Diplomacy, Economy and Law," *Scandinavian Journal of History* 8 (1983). Dan H. Andersen and Hans-Joachim Voth, "The Grapes of War: Neutrality and Mediterranean Shipping under Danish Flag, 1747–1807," *Scandinavian Economic History Review* no. 2, vol. 48 (2000).

of primary source material. Accounts and copybooks from non-chartered shipping companies are rare, but the larger problem is the lack of even semi-reliable year-by-year trade statistics for Denmark-Norway in the 18th century. This lack of statistics makes it impossible to establish precise annual imports and re-exports of sugar from the Caribbean islands and Copenhagen and to then compare sugar with other exports. It is necessary, therefore, to use a more circuitous route and employ various forms of contemporary data to establish proportions between various trades and sources of income for Denmark.

Slaves and Sugar

Initially, Denmark's African and Caribbean possessions were administrated by a semi-official chartered company created in 1671 and known as the Danish West India and Guinea Company (*Vestindisk-Guineisk Kompagni*). In 1754, the state bought out the shareholders, took over the administration of the colonies in Africa and the Caribbean and then opened trade to all private interests in Denmark, Norway and Schleswig.[9]

Africa and the slave trade

By a royal resolution in March 1792 the Danish slave trade was forbidden from 1 January 1803 onwards. This decade-long grace period was designed to allow the plantation owners to "stock pile" the slave population on their estates in the Caribbean, after which time it was hoped that the slave population would be self-reproducing. The period after 1792 was consequently a very active one in terms of slave exports, and, indeed, some re-export of slaves took place after 1802.

The surge in slave exports after the acquisition of St. Croix in 1733 is obvious, as is the feverish activity after 1792. Up to the 1730s, the slaving expeditions were an important element in Danish Caribbean trade, but, as the production of raw sugar for shipment to Denmark grew, ships in the triangular trade constituted a decreasing proportion of the total trade. There was a total of about 3,000

[9] In 1764 trade was extended to Holstein.

Table 1. Distribution of Danish slave exports 1660–1806

	Total	Annual average
1660–1733	17,200	236
1734–1765	15,500	500
1766–1792	31,250	1,202
1793–1806	33,500	2,577

Source: Per O. Hernæs, *Slaves, Danes, and African Coast Society*. (Trondheim: University of Trondheim, 1995), reprint 1998, p. 232.

voyages between Denmark and Guinea/the Caribbean between 1747 and 1807, and fewer than 200 of them sailed in the triangular route.[10]

No comprehensive attempt has been made so far to establish whether the Danish slave trade was profitable. There is a general consensus that it was certainly not highly profitable, and in some periods may indeed have been loss making.[11] Some contemporaries certainly thought so. In 1727, the influential Copenhagen merchant and manufacturer Fredrik Holmsted, who was one of the main share holders in the Danish West India and Guinea Company, suggested that the company give up the slave trade entirely because it was not profitable. In 1765, a private company was granted the slave trade monopoly in return for taking over the administration and the costs of the fortresses, but in spite of various concessions, the company folded in 1776. The Slave Commission, created to assess the economic repercussions of abolition, more or less dismissed the economic importance of the slave trade *per se* in its report in 1791. Essentially, the fact that slave prices in the Caribbean were too low, mortality among Danish sailors too high, and the state subsidised the trade by paying the administrative costs of the forts made the Danish slave trade unprofitable.[12]

At this point we need to consider the question at hand, which is not whether the slave trade brought large profits, profits or even

[10] Per O. Hernæs, *Slaves, Danes*, op. cit., p. 242. Erik Gøbel, "Danish Trade to the West Indies and Guinea, 1671–1754," *Scandinavian Economic History Review* vol. 31 (1983), p. 25 (note 14) and p. 48.

[11] Svend Green-Petersen, "The history of the Danish Negro Slave Trade, 1733–1807," *Revue Française d'histoire d'outre-mer*, vol. LXII, 1975, pp. 209–15.

[12] Ole Justesen, "Kolonierne i Afrika," in Ole Feldbæk and Ole Justesen, *Kolonierne i Asien og Afrika* (Copenhagen: Politiken, 1980), p. 361. Hans Chr. Johansen, *Dansk økonomisk politik i årene efter 1784. Bd. 2. Krigsfinansieringsproblemer 1789–93* (Aarhus: Universitetsforlaget i Aarhus, 1980), p. 62.

losses, nor whether private profits outweighed public expenses, but, rather, whether it had a significant impact on Danish economic development. A total of a few hundred shipments and less than 100,000 slaves over a century and a half can hardly by themselves have contributed to Danish economic development and the capital formation to any significant extent.

We can look for dynamic effects from the selection of goods brought to Africa on Danish slavers. Many of the goods were bought in other European countries, but a substantial part of the cargoes were Danish-made firearms, which were an important Danish asset in the competitive environment on the African West Coast. Annual sales of Danish guns were close to 1,700 pieces in the 1750s, increasing to about 3,000 at the end of the century. At the same time the price of slaves rose relative to that of guns.[13] Increased output at one gun factory, however, can hardly be considered important from a quantitative or qualitative/dynamic point of view. It is more worthwhile to look at the output side and examine the contribution of the plantation economy in the Caribbean and the sugar refineries in Denmark.

The Caribbean and the sugar plantations

Sugar production on the Danish Caribbean islands was fairly modest until the acquisition of St. Croix in 1733. The surface area of St. Croix was much larger than that of St. Thomas and St. John (213 square kilometres out of a total of 333 sq. km for all the islands) and was more suitable for sugar cultivation.[14] In recognition of this fact, the Danish government created a division of labour between the islands in which St. Croix was the sugar producer, and St. Thomas and St. John were made free ports in 1764 and 1767, respectively, in order to capture the Caribbean transit trade. During the great European wars this strategy proved extraordinarily successful. When land on St. Croix was cleared, production, incomes, and land prices, increased greatly.

[13] Per O. Hernæs, *Slaves, Danes*, op. cit., p. 374.

[14] The description of the islands and the economics of the plantations is from P. P. Sveistrup, "Bidrag til de tidligere dansk-vestindiske Øers økonomiske Historie, med særligt henblik på Sukkerproduktion og sukkerhandel," *Nationaløkonomisk Tidsskrift* 80 (1942), pp. 65–183.

Table 2. Production, value and net profit of sugar plantations on St. Croix, 1786–87 and 1797

	Production 1755 = 100	Value of plantations (mill. rixdollars)	Profits from plantations (mill. rixdollars)
1755	100		
1770	1133		
1781	1667		
1786	1107	6.82	
1792–95	1247		1,8
1797		23.28	
1800	2167		

Source: Sveistrup, pp. 126–131, 136, 146–148.
Note: West Indian rixdollars have been converted to Danish at the rate of 80 Danish rixdollars to 100 West Indian. Value includes lands, buildings and slaves. Net profit is an average of 1793–96. Interest is not included.

A value of 23 million rixdollars and profits of up to two million rixdollars were huge sums for the time, as the combined GNP of Denmark, Norway and the Duchies may have been a little over 100 million rixdollars, and the annual budget of the Danish state balanced at about eight million rixdollars.[15] But a number of factors speak against these profits having played an important part in Danish capital formation. The 1790s were very good years for the planters, as the Revolutionary Wars and a slave rebellion on French St. Domingue raised sugar prices — a rise which was immediately reflected in land values. Debts were huge and, by the end of the century, equalled somewhere between 40–60% of the total value of the plantations. In fact, many planters seem to have lacked capital to such a degree that it was a normal practice for the state to issue them bills of exchange secured against the coming harvest.[16] Debts, fluctuating harvests and sugar prices when combined with conspicuous spending posed barriers to savings. Finally it is one of the curious aspects

[15] By comparison it has been estimated that in the last years of *l'ancien régime* the French Caribbean colonies had an annual net profit of 100 mill. to 125 mill. livres annually (= 20–25 mill. rixdollars) and that the plantations on St. Domingue were worth 1,488 mill. livres (= 298 mill. rixdollars). See Robert Stein, "The French West Indian Sugar Business," in Hilary Beckles and Verene Shepherd, eds., *Caribbean Slave Society and Economy* (New York: Ian Randle, 1991), p. 99 and footnote 30.

[16] Sveistrup, pp. 128–29.

of the Danish Caribbean colonies that the planter class was a heterogeneous group with Danes being in the minority. During the pioneer years when St. Croix was cleared and settled, it proved impossible to attract many Danes, though land was available at very low prices. The consequence was that a cosmopolitan society dominated by British planters developed on the islands. These planters had commercial and family links to the rest of the Caribbean as well as to the American continent. Therefore, the vast majority of planters did not settle down in Denmark or invest their accumulated funds in Danish industry or agriculture.[17]

Denmark, the sugar refineries, and re-export of sugar

A sugar refinery was established in Copenhagen in 1662, but, in spite of various privileges granted to it, production was too small to cover even the modest levels of Danish consumption.[18] A second refinery started operations in 1704, but Denmark's participation in the Great Nordic War of 1709–20 had a detrimental effect on raw sugar imports as well as on many other import commodities. Sugar shipments from the Caribbean islands did not meet domestic consumption. Between 1671, when the Danish West Indian and Guinea Company was formed, and the 1740s, the annual number of expeditions heading to Africa and the Caribbean was usually fewer than five, and never more than ten. Only from the 1730s onwards did the situation improve. The government initiated a strongly mercantilist policy, including huge duty increases on foreign refined sugar which, in practice, led to the virtual prohibition of its legal import. At the same time, Danish Caribbean production of raw sugar rose markedly after the acquisition of St. Croix in 1733.

After 1750 the first refineries were created in Norway and in Denmark outside Copenhagen, and by 1770 there were 10 refineries outside Copenhagen, but they were mainly used to meet domestic

[17] On the issue of the national composition of the planter class see among others Jørgen Bach Christensen, "Jord, slaver og plantere. Kolonisamfundet på St. Croix 1742–1804," in Peter Hoxcer Jensen, et al., *Dansk kolonihistorie. Indføring og studier* (Århus: Universitetsforlaget i Aarhus, 1983), pp. 137–51.

[18] The standard work about the Danish sugar production is P. P. Sveistrup and Rich Willerslev, *Den danske sukkerhandels og sukkerproduktions historie* (Copenhagen: Gyldendal, 1945).

consumption. The big refineries, the processing of sugar for export, and the re-export of foreign raw sugar all remained in Copenhagen in the period of expansion from the 1750s onwards. By 1770, there were 15 refineries in Copenhagen, and by 1798, 12 were in existence. The number in Schleswig and Holstein increased drastically, and around 1800 there were 13 refineries. The total workforce for all sugar refineries at the turn of the century was about 500.[19]

The transport of raw sugar from the Danish Caribbean islands to Denmark, mostly directly to Copenhagen, was the exclusive right of ships flying the Danish flag. When transports begin in earnest, the number of voyages mirror two aspects of the commercial life of the Danish Caribbean islands between 1733 and 1807:

1) The rapid rise in sugar production after 1733;
2) The islands' function during European wars as a funnel through which the produce of the French islands (and, after 1780, the Dutch islands) was transported to Copenhagen, from whence it was re-exported to the Baltic, Sweden and the Dutch Republic.

The graph exhibits a strong upward trend combined with very volatile fluctuations. The smaller variations are associated with market and harvest fluctuations. The larger ones are obviously linked to the European wars. Denmark did not gain much from the Seven Years War in 1756–63 when Britain was able to maintain naval superiority and implement the "Rule of 56," which prohibited neutral ships from sailing to colonies such as those of the French, which they were forbidden to frequent in peacetime. But the War of American Independence was the catalyst for several boom years during which Denmark was able to exploit its neutrality to an unprecedented extent. The spike in 1781 and 1782 was caused by the Dutch entry into the War in 1780.[20] During the Revolutionary and Napoleonic Wars double the number of sailings occurred when compared to peace-

[19] In 1798 there were 260 people employed in the refineries in Denmark proper. Sveistrup and Willerslev, op. cit., p. 79. At the same time a total of 36 employees in five refineries in Flensburg produced refined sugar worth an estimated 290,000 rixdollars. Ulrike Albrecht, *Die Gewerbe Flensburgs von 1770 bis 1807* (Neumünster: Wachholtz, 1993), p. 245.

[20] The Danish exploitation of neutrality under very favourable conditions is analysed in Ole Feldbæk, *Dansk neutralitetspolitik under krigen 1778–1783* (Copenhagen: Shirting, 1971). This work contains an English summary.

Graph 1. Passports issued for ships destined to the Danish Caribbean and West Africa, 1750–1806

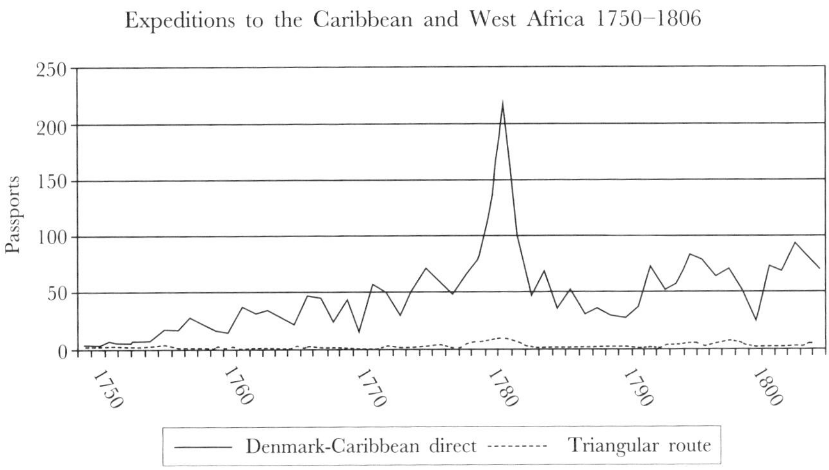

Source: Erik Gøbel, personal communication.

time years, but they were still nothing approaching the extraordinary years 1781 and 1782. The slump in 1801 was due to Denmark's brief war with Britain that year.

Not all of the raw sugar was transported to Denmark, and at times less than half the Caribbean colonial production came to the metropolis. Some was sent to the American continent to buy supplies of timber, staples, and provisions, but the planters also sent substantial shipments of raw sugar to Amsterdam to pay their debts to their Dutch creditors. In 1770 and 1777 regulations were tightened to ensure that raw sugar from the Danish Caribbean was transported to Copenhagen, and in 1786–87 the Danish state bought the planters' debt from their Dutch creditors.

To estimate the role and value of sugar in the Danish economy we must distinguish between the output of refined sugar, most of which was consumed domestically, the export of refined sugar and syrup, and the re-export of raw sugar.

The impact of the sugar imports on the Danish economy

Between 1764 and 1778 the average annual auction value of raw sugar imported into Copenhagen was 0.5–0.75 million rixdollars. Freight, duty and various commissions may have constituted 15–20%

of this amount. Once in Denmark the value of the raw sugar doubled, so production value was 1–1.5 million rixdollars, and the average annual net income in Denmark from raw sugar imports amounted to 600,000–900,000 rixdollars.[21] By 1798 the volume of production was probably double that of 1770.

Since domestic consumption in Denmark itself increased substantially though smuggling, especially in the early period, it is difficult to assess the increase in imports by looking at consumption figures. An estimate suggests an increase in per capita consumption from a few hundred grams in the 1740s to 1.5–1.75 pounds in 1770 to perhaps 2.5 pounds by the turn of the century. This quantity of consumption was far behind the British level of over 16 pounds in the 1770s, but was on par with what the French were consuming. It reflects the fact that Danish tea and coffee consumption had not spread much beyond the wealthier members of society in Copenhagen and the other major cities.[22]

The impact of the export of processed sugar on the Danish economy

About 40% of the production volume was exported. This, however, was less as a proportion of value because a disproportionate amount of exports were in the form of cheap syrup.

The impact of the re-export of raw sugar and other colonial products on the Danish economy

Though the government tried to help promote the export of processed sugar with various subsidies, the most important export was the re-export of raw sugar and other colonial products, especially during the great European wars. During the War of American Independence, for instance, Danish imports of raw sugar and other colonial prod-

[21] This is based upon an analysis of the data in Sveistrup and Willerslev, op. cit., pp. 50–60 and 87–88. In June 1781 freight was about two skillings per pound raw sugar sold at about 10 skillings. Freights usually doubled during a war, so I have assumed average freight to be 1 skilling during peace years when the auction price was about 5 to 7.5 skillings per pound. In 1770 a contemporary estimated value of total Danish sugar production to be about one million rixdollars which fits my calculation pretty well. Sveistrup and Willerslev, op. cit., pp. 87–88.

[22] Sveistrup and Willerslev, op. cit., pp. 96–98. Ralph A. Austen and Woodruff D. Smith, "Private Tooth Decay as Public Economic Virtue: The Slave-Sugar Triangle, Consumerism, and European Industrialisation," in Joseph E. Inikori and Stanley L. Engerman, eds., *The Atlantic Slave Trade*, op. cit., pp. 187–88.

Table 3. Annual export values of refined sugar and syrup from Copenhagen, 1763–1794 and 1804

	1000 rixdollars
1763–69	79
1770–77	196
1778–82	231
1783–89	262
1790–94	214
1804	476

Source: Sveistrup and Willerslev, pp. 110, 124.
Note: The export values are artificial values lower than the real selling price on the foreign market. The number for 1804 is from an independent calculation by the Copenhagen merchant Pierre Peschier using market prices, so the increase is overstated.

ucts rose drastically. This dramatic increase was especially evident after the Dutch entered the War in 1780 and the usual transit island of St. Eustatius was conquered by the English in February 1781. Denmark was now the only neutral European state with possessions in the Caribbean, and in 1782 and 1783 the import of colonial products (mainly raw sugar, but also coffee) rose to an estimated value of 4.3 and 4.5 million rixdollars. These products were imported into Copenhagen and mostly then re-exported. These commodities were the products of the French and Dutch Caribbean possessions, which were exported through Danish St. Thomas and St. John, which had been made free ports in 1764 and 1767, respectively. In the boom years, products from the Caribbean constituted no less than 40% of Copenhagen's imports — and most imports into the rest of Denmark went through the capital. Though re-exporting colonial goods cannot have generated the same value as processing raw sugar did in Denmark, the country managed to earn some money from freights and commissions, and during the wars the price of freighting goods doubled or, in some cases, even trebled.

After the declaration of peace in 1783 and the realisation of accumulated stocks, the value of raw sugar re-exports declined steadily to a low of 56,000 rixdollars at official values in 1790. The outbreak of war in 1793 brought about some increase in the export of processed sugar, but the main increase was, once again, in the re-export of foreign raw sugar and colonial products coming from St. Thomas and

St. John. As graph I indicates, the volume of imports and, therefore, re-exports was not on the same scale as in 1781 and 1782, but raw sugar valued over two million rixdollars was re-exported in 1804.[23]

To conclude, the "Americanisation" of the imports and, indirectly, the exports from Denmark itself in the decades prior to 1807 was the result of two different developments. The first was "normal" commercial activity in times of peace and war. The Danish sugar industry provided for increasing domestic demand and had some refining capacity left over to allow for the export of processed sugar from Copenhagen. From 1770 to 1807 the annual average value of production was one to two million rixdollars, while the exports of refined sugar and cheap syrup were probably worth between 200,000–500,000 rixdollars, and the re-export of raw sugar in peaceful years equalled about 200,000 rixdollars, but was very volatile. The total value added of sugar production for Denmark, including freight and commission, may have been in the range of 0.5–1.5 million rixdollars.[24]

Secondly, the Danish colonies fulfilled a "scavenger" function during the great European wars. The free ports of St. Thomas and St. John were platforms for the transportation of French and Dutch colonial products to Copenhagen covered by the neutral Danish flag. This activity depended upon political circumstances, not the least of which was the efficiency with which the British controlled the seas during any given time. During some years, such as during the War of American Independence and the series of wars from 1793 onwards, the value of this extra re-export of French and Dutch raw sugar and colonial products was probably two to four million rixdollars, but this amount was heavily dependent upon political and military developments. The value added from freight, commissions, and duties was around 0.5–1 million rixdollars, and possibly more in good years.

[23] Sveistrup and Willerslev, op. cit., pp. 62–63 and 124.

[24] Income from customs on St. Croix should perhaps be included, but the Danish state had expenses from bailing out investors in Caribbean speculations during the War of American Independence, planters defaulting on the Dutch debt it had taken over in 1786–87 and from naval escorts during the wars. These are difficult to estimate and I have assumed duties and expenses cancelled each other.

Intra-European trade and shipping

In order to determine the importance of colonial trade and the accompanying sugar refineries compared with other trades and exports, some benchmarks have to be established. Denmark-Norway's most important exports were Norwegian timber and fish. The Norwegian surplus and the Danish deficit were compensated for by the export of grain from Denmark to Norway. During the second half of the 18th century income from shipping became increasingly important. Thus comparisons are made with:

a) population and GNP;
b) value of the Danish grain harvest and export;
c) Norwegian timber and fish exports;
d) size of the merchant marine and the income from intra-European shipping;

a:

Table 4. Population (in 1,000s) and GNP (in millions of rixdollars)

	Denmark	Norway	Duchies	Total
Population 1769	835	727	553	2,115
Population 1801	926	883	604	2,413
GNP 1785	49	23	32	104

Source: Population 1801: Hans Chr. Johansen, *Dansk økonomisk politik i årene efter 1784*, op. cit. Vol. 1, p. 68; Ulrich Lange, ed., *Geschichte Schleswig-Holsteins* (Neumünster: Wacholtz, 1996), p. 287. GNP: Sv. Aage Hansen, "En disputats om dansk økonomisk politik i årene efter 1784," *Nationaløkonomisk Tidsskrift* 106 (1968), p. 190.
Note: Population figures are fairly accurate, the GNP-calculation is a very tentative first and so far only attempt.

b:

Table 5. Grain harvest of Denmark proper and exports (mainly rye) to Norway and abroad, 1730–1804

	Harvest (barrels)	Annual average Export (barrels)	Value of export (in 1,000s of rixdollars)
1730–40		295,509	450
1736–44		309,475	700
1750	5–6 mill.		
1752–54		524,272	860
1762–65		316,973	1,080
1766–68		384,047	1,660
1775–84		522,243	1,720
1793		570,768	2,610
1794		592,209	2,840
1796		696,308	2,740
1798		566,744	2,570
1800	8–9 mill.		
1802–4		801,850	6,880

Sources: Amounts: Søren Bitsch Christensen, *Monopol, Marked og Magasiner*. Unpublished PhD. thesis, University of Århus, 2001, pp. 142–164 and bilag 3. Values: Most of the grain was rye, so amounts are multiplied with average annual sales prices for rye from Danish manors published in Dan H. Andersen, Mette Ehlers and Erik Helmer Pedersen, *A History of Prices and Wages in Denmark, 1660–1800. Vol. 2: Prices and wages in Danish estate accounts* (Copenhagen: Schultz Grafisk, 2004). See also http//www.danishpricehistory.com. For 1802–04 prices have been established from corresponding increases in the assizes for rye. To get CIF prices, 25% has been added to the Denmark sales prices cover commissions and freight. See Søren Bitsch Christensen op. cit., pp. 428–29. Values are rounded up or down to nearest 10,000.

c:

Table 6. An estimate of the value of Norwegian timber and fish exports in 1805

(million of rixdollars)

	Timber	Fish
1805	4.5	2.7–3

Annual average number of cargoes with Norwegian timber and fish, 1800–06

	Timber	Fish
	1871	394

Source: Ståle Dyrvik, et al., *Norsk økonomisk historie 1500–1850* vol. 1 (Oslo: Universitetsforlaget, 1979), pp. 160, 177–78. Axel Lindvald, "Bidrag til Oplysning om Danmark-Norges Handel og Skibsfart 1800–1807," *Historisk Tidsskrift* 1917, pp. 474–477.
Note: It is not stated whether values are FOB or CIF prices. Of timber exports about 5% were to Denmark proper. Of fish exports only small amounts went to Denmark proper, apart from 1802 and 1803, when 9 and 8% respectively were destined for Denmark proper.

England was the main recipient of Norwegian timber exports.

Table 7. An estimate of the annual average of Norwegian timber exports to England (official values), 1752–1800 (in 1,000s of rixdollars)

	I. Official values
1752–54	365
1762–64	355
1772–74	350
1782–84	345
1792–94	590

Source: Birgit Nüchel Thomsen and Brinley Thomas, *Dansk-engelsk samhandel* (Århus: Universitetsforlaget, 1966), p. 51.
Note: The official values are based upon a list of prices from 1694. Values can only be used to show changes in amounts.

d:

Size of the merchant marine under the Danish flag, 1800–1807

No. of vessels >10 lasts (26 tons)	2,400
Tonnage in commercial lasts	120,000–136,000
Crews	16,700–21,400

Average annual arrivals in European ports, 1800–1806

	Arrivals	Tonnage (commercial lasts)
	4,503	230,450

Source: Axel Lindvald, "Bidrag til Oplysning om Danmark-Norges Handel og Skibsfart 1800–1807," *Historisk Tidsskrift* 1917, pp. 422 and 470–71. Crews are rounded up or down to nearest hundred. One last was about 2.6 tons.

The size of the merchant marine under the Danish flag trebled between 1750 and 1800, and most of these new vessels were employed in foreign shipping. The Iberian Peninsula and the Mediterranean became especially important areas of operation after the conclusion of peace treaties with the North African Barbary States between 1746–1753.

Table 8. Income from shipping (all vessels >10 lasts)[25]

	Gross income in millions of rixdollars (annual average) Estimate I		Estimate II	
	1750–70	1800	1750–70	1800
Peace	1.5–2			
War	3–3.6	9–10		8.8–9.5

Source: As above and sources for table 8. See also footnote 25.
Note: Freights from shipping outside Europe are included, but constituted a very small part of the total.

[25] Estimate I: Based upon a contemporary estimate in 1770 that annual gross income for a ship operating in the Mediterranean during a war, was 4,000 rixdollars, during peace 2,500. It has been assumed that each passport issued for the Mediterranean represents one year, including time laid up during winter. Dividing with total tonnage for the Mediterranean, gross income is 66 rixdollars per last during war, 37 rixdollars during peace. These numbers have been multiplied with an assumed average tonnage 1750–70 of 50,000 lasts to get total gross income during war and peace.

Table 9. Income from shipping to the Mediterranean

	Average annual departures	Annual average gross income (1,000s rixdollars) Estimate I	Estimate II
1747–55	86	190	
1756–63	171	680	
1764–77	120	300	
1778–83	280	1,100	
1784–92	270	675	
1793–1806	562	2,800	2,600

Source: Lars N. Henningsen, *Provinsmatadorer fra 1700-årene* (Flensburg: Rosenkilde og Bagger, 1985), pp. 111–114. This work has a German summary. Ole Ventegodt, *Redere, rejser og regnskaber* (Flensburg: Rosenkilde og Bagger, 1989), pp. 34–39 and 190–238. This work has a German summary. Dan H. Andersen, *The Danish Flag in the Mediterranean. Shipping and Trade, 1747–1807*, Unpublished Ph.D. thesis, University of Copenhagen, 2000. Appendix C and database on CD-ROM. See also footnote 25.

Note: Departures 1772–77 are interpolated numbers, as the registers have been lost.

Conclusion

In some ways the Danish trade experience in the second half of the 18th century mirrored that of Britain. Foreign trade increased much more than did either the population or domestic production. Likewise, in Denmark and in England, the import, processing and re-export of colonial goods comprised an increasing proportion of all imports and exports. Moreover, in both Denmark and in England, these activities were centred in the capital city. But here the similarity ends. Danish shipping increased more than did shipping in any other European country, with the possible exception of Sweden-Finland, and it was probably the Monarchy's most important source of foreign currency. This type of shipping was not based upon domestic production and imports, but, rather, on transporting the goods of

Estimate II: The accounts of two Flensburg ships in European shipping for the years between 1793 and 1806 show gross income of 65 and 77 rixdollars per last respectively. The same procedure as above has been applied using 70 rixdollars per last, but only for the the years 1793–1806. See also Ole Ventegodt, *Redere, rejser og regnskaber*, op. cit.

other states. Shipping benefited from, and much of colonial trade depended upon, a very special set of circumstances created by Danish neutrality during the almost continuous warfare in the last decades of the century. The "colonisation" of Danish imports was very much a wartime phenomenon. When the Napoleonic wars ended, so did the role of Copenhagen as a centre of the redistribution of colonial goods. The importance of sugar and other colonial goods in the Danish economy dwindled. The Danish colonies probably only managed to break even financially in the mid-18th century, and it was most likely only the War of American Independence and the Revolutionary and Napoleonic Wars that helped these colonies to contribute in any significant sense to the Danish balance of payment. And, even in the best of times, the colonial sector did not contribute on the scale that European trade and shipping did.

Here we must address the "small ratio" argument, which is also at the centre of the discussion on the British slave trade and the contribution of colonies to British industrialisation.[26] In Denmark-Norway, the sector engaged in the transporting, processing and re-exporting of colonial goods at first sight seems small. In most war years the colonial sector's contribution to GNP was less than 2% and in most peace years less than 1%. Shipping and the export of the country's own products like grain, timber and fish was more important than slaves and sugar. But apart from the above-mentioned products, no other non-agricultural sector in the Danish economy generated the income and foreign currency that sugar and colonial goods did at the end of the 18th century.

Furthermore, a modern sugar processing industry was established which met domestic demand and won markets abroad. Colonial trade and the processing of colonial goods were *the* most important trade and industry in Copenhagen. In the last decades before 1807, the annual value added in Denmark from the processing and re-exporting of raw sugar was 1–2.5 million rixdollars. In addition, the export of refined sugar made an important contribution to the Danish balance of payment.

Some historians have argued that Denmark-Norway could have shifted domestic capital, investment and demand to sectors or products other than colonial goods. After all, sugar was a luxury product

[26] Cf. footnote 1.

of no great nutritious importance at the levels consumed. However, much of domestic demand would have been covered anyway from smuggling, and we may ask: what other sectors and what other products could the nation have turned to? Sugar was the only industrialised product that Denmark itself could offer abroad.

We do not in Denmark-Norway find a link between colonial trade and industrialisation, such as some historians have discovered in the case of Britain. The export of manufactured goods to the colonies did not compensate for a lack of domestic and European demand, especially for textiles. There was some export of Danish comestibles, textiles, and guns to Africa and the Caribbean, but the Danish textile industry was neither important nor competitive. It is also difficult to find any sort of ripple effect that the sugar industry had on the economy at large. The Copenhagen merchant houses dominating colonial trade did invest in the sugar refineries, but apart from those investments and the occasional manor or two, they usually reinvested their fortunes in shipping and trade, not manufacturing. Danish industrialisation only started in the next century with advances in the 1840s, 1870s and 1890s.[27]

It is difficult to find permanent effects on the Danish economy from colonial trade because the period in which Denmark's trade was Americanised was so short and based upon exceptional circumstances. The move towards dependence upon American goods was halted by Denmark's entry into the Napoleonic Wars on the French side in 1807, while seven years of war against Britain erased most of the fortunes and other financial gains made from shipping and trade. During the war, the merchant marine, worth perhaps 10 million rixdollars, was lost, and hyperinflation was endemic. The State declared bankruptcy in 1813. After the conclusion of peace, trade and shipping had to be reorganised along new lines due to the loss of certain markets, not least of which was the Norwegian market, because Norway had been lost to Sweden. The great merchant houses in Copenhagen one by one succumbed to post war depression, loss of markets, and the State's deflationary policy. These were exactly the houses that had run the colonial and overseas trade which, for a brief time, had made Copenhagen a centre of North

[27] Ole Hyltoft, *Københavns industrialisering 1804–1914* (Herning: Systime, 1984), pp. 53–60.

European colonial exchange. Their accumulated skills and fortunes were lost.

Colonial trade and shipping proved a welcome help to the Danish economy in the decades prior to 1807; a time during which agricultural reforms and increased defence expenditures sucked up huge amounts of capital. Apart from the establishment of a modern sugar industry (and we should not forget that Sweden, which did not have colonies, also developed a sugar industry) colonial trade and shipping did not transform the Danish economy or society.

The logic of small power colonialism and imperial retreat

Why would an underdeveloped state on the European periphery acquire colonies in Africa and the Caribbean? And why did it hold on to them with great tenacity even though it took a century before they showed a profit? Why did Denmark not use its small tropical possessions as stepping-stones for imperialist ventures during the 19th century, a time during which vast areas of the world fell under European sway, either directly or indirectly? Instead, Denmark sold Tranquebar in 1845, the African possessions in 1850, and the islands in the Caribbean in 1917. In all three cases, the Danish government had made several previous attempts to offload the properties.

Let us try to reconstruct the rationale for Danish involvement in Africa and the Caribbean during these centuries, based on the assumption that the structures of the *longue durée* will have shown some continuity. In the 17th century, Denmark-Norway was territorially huge, but economically underdeveloped. It was predominantly agricultural and far behind advanced states like the Dutch Republic, France and England. It did, however, have important assets. These assets included a huge military apparatus, not least of which was a powerful navy, unchallenged absolutism and political loyalty or outright docility among the populace, a fairly efficient and cheap administrative system, experience with controlling and administering a vast territory, including its overseas possessions, and, through the German Duchies and Hamburg, contact with ethnic and religious networks and the more advanced economies in Europe. From 1720, the Danish state could add another asset to this list: freedom from European engagements and Dutch pressure. These assets, when combined, were ideally suited for colonial ventures. Even if these ventures did not pay off in the short or even in the long run, the monetary investments in them were minimal, and the resources employed were ones that the Danes had in relative abundance. The benefits to be had from the colonial ventures were those that were lacking in Denmark at the time. For instance, the domestic production of high value goods and the influx of foreign currency from exports or import substitution were to be gained from colonial enterprises. By having monopoly access to colonies, Denmark might entice foreign merchants with skills and capital to settle in Copenhagen. Benefits accrued to the capital, where the governing elite could profit financially by investing in colonial ventures, while letting the State bear the brunt of the expenses by using its diplomatic and military resources.

In the 19th century these conditions no longer applied. Trade was liberalised, monopoly access to colonies was less important, and the price of colonial goods fell. In a much more peaceful international climate, Denmark could no longer profit from neutrality. Furthermore, the loss of Norway and the relative shift in military strength in favour of the great powers had made the military assets of Denmark disappear. Absolutism was increasingly challenged from within, and the emerging middle class of farmers wanted low taxes, economic liberalism, and had no sentimental feelings for their colonial possessions. The Danish colonies were too small to have an economy of scale, and there was no sizeable class of colonial officials allied with colony trading companies to push for expansion.

After a quarter of a millennium colonies had become peripheral, both to the Danish economy and in the national consciousness.

CHAPTER FOURTEEN

GREAT POWER CONSTRAINTS AND THE GROWTH OF THE COMMERCIAL SECTOR: THE CASE OF SWEDEN, 1600–1800

Leos Müller

Introduction

The importance of foreign and, especially, colonial trade on the development of Early Modern economies is one of the classic questions in economic history. It has been considered on the global level, on the systemic level, and on a national economy level. The prevailing wisdom regarding the influence of colonial trade on the development of Early Modern economies has, basically, shifted from seeing commerce as one of the decisive factors in capitalist development to seeing it as a quite marginal and insignificant factor. The question has been discussed from a multitude of angles: the different aspects of trade, the different theoretical starting points, the points of industrial development and so on.[1]

[1] It is not necessary to go into detail about the comprehensive literature concerning this debate. I will—on the global or systemic level—stress at least the importance of the Sweezy-Dobb debate, and the subsequent Robert Brenner debate. In Rodney Hilton, ed., *The transition from feudalism to capitalism* (London: Macmillan, 1978); T. H. Aston and C. H. E. Philpin, eds., *The Brenner Debate. Agrarian Class Structure and Economic Development in Pre-Industrial Europe* (Cambridge: Cambridge University Press, 1985) and the recent debate on the dependency theory, Immanuel Wallerstein, *The modern world-system.* 3 vols. (New York: Academic Press, 1974–89). For criticism of Wallerstein's view, see for example, P. W. Klein, "Dutch capitalism and the European world-economy," Maurice Aymard, ed., *Dutch capitalism and world capitalism. Capitalisme hollandais et capitalisme mondial* (Cambridge: Cambridge University Press, 1982); Patrick O'Brien, "European Economic Development: The Contribution of the Periphery," *The Economic History Review* 1982/1; see also Stanley L. Engerman, "Mercantilism and overseas trade, 1700–1800," in Roderick Floud and Donald McCloskey, eds., *The Economic History of Britain since 1700*, volume 1: 1700–1860 (Cambridge: Cambridge University Press, 1994), pp. 182–85; recently also David S. Landes, *The Wealth and Poverty of Nations. Why Some Are So Rich and Some So Poor* (New York: Abacus, 1999).

The Dutch Republic, Great Britain, France, Spain, and Portugal have received most of the scholarly attention regarding the development of their national economies. The reasons for this intense interest are clear; their colonial empires and, consequently, their colonial commerce on the one hand, and the obviously spectacular economic developments in Britain and the Dutch Republic on the other hand. Sweden, the focus of this essay, has been touched upon in this context. However, attention has mainly centred on its military role in the 17th century, or on its position as a raw-material supplier to the core states. Despite these interesting roles that Sweden played in the Early Modern period, the question of Sweden's economic development is not the focus of these studies.[2]

Swedish economic historians of the Early Modern period mainly paid attention to the study of relations between the state and the economy, the agricultural sector, and the iron industry. In general, domestic and foreign commerce have not been seen as very significant factors in Sweden's economic development. Nevertheless, iron exports attracted some historical attention, mainly due to the importance of the iron industry. Iron production and exports are viewed as an early market sector in Sweden's economy.[3]

Paradoxically, on the other hand, historians have long seen foreign trade as the driving force behind both Sweden's industrialisation in the late 19th century and the country's modern economic growth. The export boom in sawn timber, and, later, in pulp and paper seemed to provide investment capital for domestic industries. Contacts with international markets promoted the introduction of new technologies and the rapid increase in productivity. In a few decades, this made Sweden one of the richest countries in the world.[4] Recently, this so-called "export model" has been criticised by pro-

---

[2] Jonathan Israel has paid a lot of attention to Sweden's role in the Dutch economic development. J. I. Israel, *Dutch Primacy in World Trade, 1585–1740* (Oxford: Oxford University Press, 1989). See also, Jan de Vries and Ad van der Woude, *The First Modern Economy. Success, Failure, and Perseverance of the Dutch Economy, 1500–1815* (Cambridge: Cambridge University Press, 1997).

[3] Lars Magnusson, *Sveriges ekonomiska historia* (Stockholm: Prisma, 1996), pp. 131–45.

[4] In 1870–1900 the Swedish national product increased on average by 2.5%, 1900–1930 by 3%. This was relatively very high economic growth. Ragnar Bentzel, "Svensk ekonomisk tillväxt 1870 till 1975," Erik Dahmén and Gunnar Eliasson, eds., *Industriell utveckling I Sverige. Teori och verklighet under ett sekel* (Stockholm: IUI, 1980), p. 159.

ponents of the "domestic market model". These historians stressed, instead, the role of institutional change, agricultural development and the growth of the domestic market.[5] This model stresses that Swedish development was a slow step-by-step transition of the economy. There is an obvious similarity of arguments between the Swedish advocates of the domestic market model and critics of dependency theory.

In comparison with the Dutch Republic, Britain, France, or even Denmark, Sweden has never been a true colonial power. Nevertheless, in the course of the Early Modern period, Sweden had colonial ambitions. It had colonies, chartered companies, and took part in overseas trade. In the second half of the 18th century, foreign commerce increased in significance. I will pay some attention to Sweden's colonial endeavours and look at the significance of colonial or, more exactly, long-distance trade. However, it should be stated at the outset that Sweden's colonial ambitions failed quite quickly. Moreover, Sweden's colonial trade was almost invariably insignificant. Sweden's colonial adventures should, therefore, be viewed as an historical curiosity.

Seventeenth-century Sweden, even if it is regarded as a great power in military terms, was geographically situated on the European periphery, and commodity exchange between Sweden and the key markets in Europe—the Dutch Republic or England—followed the classical pattern of exchange between periphery and core. Sweden supplied the more developed economies with raw materials and imported refined and high-value goods, capital and know-how. But Sweden's economic development did not follow the path of economic dependency and underdevelopment that was the fate of many of the colonies. Instead, by 1800, Sweden became a well-integrated and quite sophisticated part of the West European and Atlantic economies. Why did Swedish economic history differ from the model proposed by the dependency school of development history? What role did foreign commerce play in Sweden's case? What role did Sweden's ability to carry out its own economic policy play in its development? These are the questions which I aim to discuss in this essay.

[5] Lennart Schön, *En modern svensk ekonomisk historia. Tillväxt och omvandling under två sekel* (Stockholm: SNS, 2000) pp. 34–37. Schön himself is perceived as one of the foremost advocates of the domestic market model.

Sweden's foreign trade and the state's revenues

By 1600 Sweden was one of the largest European states. However, a tiny population of around one million people inhabited this vast territory.[6] Swedish agriculture could not feed more. The climate of the Swedish empire was simply not favourable for agriculture and, as agriculture was the basis of any traditional economy, Sweden was relatively poor. Sweden was geographically situated on the periphery of Europe, distant from the rich and densely populated states. Sweden's geography can be seen as a comparative disadvantage for commercial development and integration.

On the other hand, at least two important comparative advantages should be mentioned. First, Sweden had supplies of high quality copper and iron ore and seemingly endless supplies of timber. These resources could potentially be converted into cash, if there was outside demand for metals, timber and timber products. Furthermore, the Swedish empire was situated relatively favourably, with a long coastline and major commercial links throughout the Baltic and North Seas. The possibility of direct maritime links to Western Europe has to be seen as a key precondition for the exploitation of Swedish resources and for the country's commercial integration within the West European and Atlantic economy.

It should be emphasised that these two comparative advantages—resources and transport—were also important preconditions for the Swedish export boom in the late 17th century. This export boom was based on both resources—sawn timber, paper and pulp—and low transport costs, since all of the timber products could be shipped by sea. Additionally, the iron and machinery industries, which were dependent upon the excellent iron ores that were available in Sweden, were important sectors for industrial transition.

However, around 1600, these comparative advantages were very marginally exploited. The Swedish state followed the classical logic of feudal states at this time; a logic in which status and power were equal to the size of both the population and of agricultural pro-

[6] Of course, it is impossible to get an exact figure for the population of the Swedish empire in the 17th century. The estimates vary widely, due to areas incorporated or lost, due to the disastrous impact of wars on the population and due to the lack of any demographic statistics. For discussion of this subject and for the comparison of accessible figures see Jan Lindegren, *Maktstatens resurser* (manuscript), Uppsala, 2001, pp. 16–19.

duction. To increase its status and power, Sweden, the logic followed, had to expand into more densely populated and richer territories on the other side of the Baltic Sea. Indeed, Sweden was very successful in this feudal expansion. Between the years 1560–1660 Sweden expanded to the detriment of Russia, Poland, Denmark and the German Empire. Yet this expansive policy required much more manpower and money than the core lands of Sweden and Finland could provide. One way to increase the state's resources was more efficient taxation and more extensive use of manpower. And the Swedish military state was a very successful machine in this sense.[7] Nevertheless, this more efficient exploitation of the population did not solve Sweden's shortage of cash. Therefore, foreign trade appeared to be a very useful option.[8]

During the course of the 1620s and 1630s a new commercial policy was implemented which aimed to increase export revenues and trade duties. The state revenues from the 1630s testify to the importance of commerce-related income. In 1633, customs duties made up about one-fifth of all state revenues. However, it should be stressed that the situation in 1633 was exceptional, due to the importance of the Prussian ship tolls. These duties, imposed on the grain trade in Danzig, made up almost 19% of the state revenues in 1633. Such a high percentage was an exception. And, Sweden only kept the Prussian tolls between 1628 and 1635.[9] Nevertheless, these duties were a potential source of cash. In the following decades Sweden strongly promoted the export of its own commodities, especially bar-iron and copper. In the period between 1661–1670, customs duties rose to about 615,000–800,000 rixdollars.[10] As Table 1 shows, in

[7] According to calculations made by the Swedish historian Jan Lindegren, the Swedish state received regularly in the first half of the 17th century revenues of about 1–1.1 million rixdollars, which is estimated at about 40–45% of the total agricultural surplus production in Sweden and Finland, to compare with Denmark's 25 per cent. Lindegren, *Maktstatens resurser*, op. cit., p. 109.

[8] In the late 16th and early 17th centuries there was striking difference between Sweden and its enemies (Denmark, Russia, Poland) in exploitation of international trade flows. For example, Denmark made the Sound Toll one of the most important revenues sources. The share of the duties in the Danish state revenues was about one-third in 1642. Lindegren, *Maktstatens resurser*, op. cit., p. 110.

[9] Einar Wendt, *Det svenska licentväsendet i Preussen 1627–1635* (Uppsala: Almquist & Wiksul, 1933).

[10] Georg Wittrock, *Karl XI:s förmyndares finanspolitik* (Uppsala: Akademska Bokhandeln, 1914–17), pp. 471–72 (vol. 1), pp. 421–22 (vol. 2).

1677, customs duties already made up over 800,000 rixdollars of the total state revenues of 5.3 million rixdollars. This figure does not include customs duties in the Baltic provinces and the German territories. These customs duties are the best testament to the rapid increase in foreign trade.

Characteristics of Sweden's foreign trade between 1600 and 1650

The available figures concerning Sweden's foreign trade testify that there was a rapid increase during the 17th century. Between 1613 and 1660, Swedish exports rose tenfold, from about 250,000 to 2.5 million rixdollars.[11] Most of the increase is related to iron and copper exports, which were the two key staple commodities. An analysis of Stockholm's foreign trade from 1600 to 1650 shows that the combined share of copper and iron made up, on average, 81% of all exports.[12] This figure is quite representative for all Swedish trade,

Table 1. Sweden's state revenues 1633 and 1677

Year	1633 Rixdollars	1633 Percent	1677 Rixdollars	1677 Percent
Ordinary and extraordinary revenues	1,803,792	55.3	1,471,765	27.7
Customs and excise	22,040	0.7	808,796	15.2
Prussian tolls (Danzig and Pillau)	614,000	18.8	0	0
Loans	59,384	1.8	770,437	14.5
Subsidies	400,000	12.3	750,000	14.1
Baltic provinces and Pomerania	364,236	11.2	758,034	14.3
Other income		0	760,333	14.3
Total	3,263,452	100	5,319,365	100

Source: S. E. Åström, "The Swedish Economy and Sweden's Role as a Great Power 1632–1697," in Michael Roberts, ed., *Sweden's Age of Greatness, 1632–1718* (London: Macmillan, 1973), pp. 82–83 (table 7)

[11] Lindegren, *Maktstatens resurser*, op. cit., p. 111, see also Bertil Boëthius and E. F. Heckscher, *Svensk handelsstatistik 1637–1737* (Stockholm: Stockholms Stadsarkiv, 1938).

[12] Åke Sandström, *Mellan Torneå och Amsterdam. En undersökning av Stockholms roll som förmedlare av varor i regional och utrikeshandel, 1600–1650* (Stockholm: Borås, 1990), p. 313.

due to Stockholm's role as Sweden's major entrepôt. In the mid-17th century, Stockholm controlled about 70%–80% of Sweden's exports and imports. The following analysis of the structure of Swedish trade is based on figures for Stockholm.[13]

The most significant long-term shift was the transformation of the iron trade. The volume of iron exports increased from about 17,000 ship-pounds in the 1610s to between 100,000 and 150,000 ship-pounds—about 13,000 to 20,000 tons—in the peaceful decade of the 1660s, and continued to grow at a slower pace during the remainder of the century.[14] The quality of the exported iron changed too. In the early 17th century, Sweden exported mainly low-value pig iron. In the 1640s bar-iron became the major export item, but was joined by ironware, guns and steel as important export products. Perhaps the most dramatic change during this time period, however, was the shift in export markets. In 1600, the majority of Stockholm's iron went to Danzig and Lübeck—the old Hansa towns. By 1650, the major destination was the Dutch Republic, where about 50% of the iron was sent. England also became a significant buyer of Stockholm's bar-iron.[15] Sweden moved from the orbit of the Hansa towns into the orbit of the Dutch and English staple markets.

Copper exports also rose rapidly after 1613, and they reached an average annual volume of 10,000 ship-pounds—or about 1,300 tons—by around 1620. But exports fluctuated a great deal in the following years, as did copper prices on the Amsterdam market. Copper was a unique commodity, due to its limited number of suppliers. Therefore, attempts were made to monopolise supplies by both the Swedish state and the Dutch entrepreneurs, Elias and Pieter Trip.[16] Not surprisingly the state and its chartered Copper Companies lost. Despite the volatility of exports and prices, copper continued to play

[13] There are some scattered published data on Sweden's foreign trade in the 17th century, in Boëthius and Heckscher, *Svensk handelsstatistik*, op. cit. But the best structural analysis of Swedish foreign trade has been made in Stockholm's trade statistics (tollage books, customs books etc.), see Sandström, *Mellan Torneå och Amsterdam*, op. cit.

[14] The unit ship-pound (*skeppund*) was used in the Swedish metal exports (1 ton = 7.5 ship-pounds).

[15] S. E. Åström, *From cloth to iron. The Anglo-Baltic trade in the late 17th century*, 2 vols. (Helsinki: Societas Scientiarum Fenniea, 1963–65), p. 35, and Sandström, *Mellan Torneå och Amsterdam*, op. cit., p. 326.

[16] P. W. Klein, *De Trippen in de 17e eeuw. Een studie over het ondernemersgedrag op de Hollandse stapelmarkt* (Assen: Nederlandse Economische Hogeschool, 1965), pp. 327–73.

Figure 1. Iron exports from Stockholm, 1615–1694 (in 000 ship-pounds)

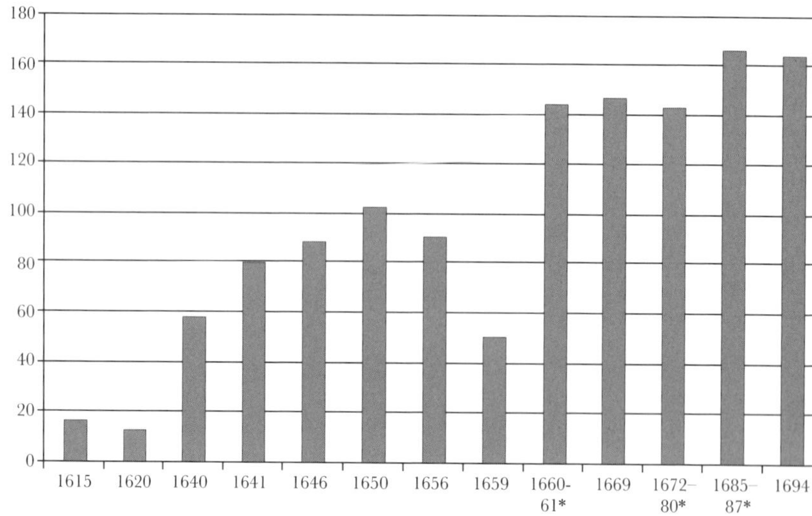

Source: K. G. Hildebrand, *Fagerstabrukens historia. Sexton- och sjuttonhundratalen* (Uppsala: Almquist & Wiksell, 1957), p. 36 (*1660–61, 1672–80, 1685–87 average annual exports). See note 14.

an important role in Sweden's finances until the mid-17th century. Even if the volumes of exported copper were much lower than the volumes of bar iron, the export values of iron and copper remained comparable.

The expansion of Sweden's metal industries and the accompanying exports could not have been accomplished without co-operation between Dutch entrepreneurs and the Swedish state. Dutch interest in Sweden was rooted in changed conditions of commerce. During the course of the Thirty Years War, the Dutch lost their traditional suppliers of iron in Germany and Spain, and Sweden became a welcome substitute. Sweden could provide cheap labour, high-quality iron ores, timber for charcoal, water energy, and, also, exclusive trading privileges. On the other hand, Sweden lacked capital, industrial and technological know-how and the necessary commercial networks. The Dutch entrepreneurs could provide these. The Dutch entrepreneurs who settled in Sweden usually had special advantages in their business. For example, Louis de Geer, the most successful Dutch entrepreneur in Sweden, came from iron-producing Liege.[17]

[17] Maj-Britt Nergård, *Mellan krona och marknad. Utländska och svenska entreprenörer inom*

The Momma brothers, who were immigrants investing specifically in the copper and brass industries, came from Aachen [Aix-la-Chapelle], the traditional centre of copper and brass industries.[18]

Little by little, Dutch entrepreneurs took over the key iron-works, mines and factories. They invested heavily in the modernisation of production. They brought in skilled Walloon, German and Dutch labourers. And the Walloon immigration left a particularly significant mark on communities in the iron-producing areas in Sweden. Yet, all this growth would have been impossible without an intricate web of commercial links, credits, and family relations between Amsterdam and Sweden.

Between 1600 and 1650 Sweden's foreign trade situation went through a dramatic change. It increased tenfold and its major markets shifted from the old Hansa towns to the Dutch Republic. This shift in the markets for Swedish goods meant that Sweden became integrated into the world trade system. This integration into the world trade system could be seen as a first step in Sweden's move from the periphery to the semi-periphery.[19] If we look at the general features of this integration into the world trade system, we can see that it followed the pattern typical for colonies in the Americas, Africa and Asia. Sweden's exports mainly consisted of two commodities: iron and copper. Sweden had a very limited ability to affect the conditions of sale in Amsterdam and other markets. At the same time, there was an influx of high-value processed commodities into Sweden, especially from the Dutch Republic. Commodities, both imports and exports, were carried on Dutch ships and were financed and insured by the Dutch. Furthermore, a major part of the services involved in shipping and commerce was organised by the Dutch. As was mentioned above, there was also a significant influx of merchants and skilled labour. To conclude, the integration of the Swedish market sector within the world system was carried out in accordance with Dutch interests and Dutch priorities. Sweden could play its role as a great power in militarily and diplomatic endeavours, but in commercial dealings, the country was closer in nature to a colony rather than a powerful nation.

---

svensk järnhantering från ca 580 till 1700 (Uppsala: Uppsala University Library, 2001), pp. 104–96.

[18] Leos Müller, *The Merchant Houses of Stockholm, c. 1640–1800. A Comparative Study of early-Modern Entrepreneurial Behaviour* (Uppsala: Uppsala University Library, 1998), p. 55.

[19] Sandström, *Mellan Torneå och Amsterdam*, op. cit., p. 387.

Swedish colonial endeavours in America and Africa

At the same time that Swedish foreign trade was growing, Sweden also strove to establish its own colonial empire overseas. Two spectacular attempts should be mentioned here. Between 1638 and1655 Sweden was in possession of a colony known as New Sweden in the Delaware Valley in America. The colony was established as a fur-trading outpost and the Swedes were successful in cooperating with the indigenous people. However, the population of the colony was limited to about 400 people and it could never compete with its much stronger neighbours in the North and South. In 1655, the Dutch from nearby New Netherland conquered New Sweden.[20]

Another spectacular colonial endeavour was the Swedish Africa Company.[21] It was established in 1649 to promote Sweden's trade in Africa. In order to get a foothold in Africa the Swedes built a fortress at Cabo Corso on the Guinea Coast. This outpost traded in gold, ivory and sugar imported from Africa to Europe. The Swedish Africa Company also took part in the slave trade between Guinea and São Tomé. Nevertheless, the volume of trade never became particularly voluminous, and the Company never presented a serious danger to the Dutch and English. At its peak, the Company's imports from Guinea reached 77,000–90,000 guilders.[22] The Company's activities in Africa ended in 1658 when the Danes conquered the Swedish possessions.

Both the American and African colonial endeavours were organised by Dutch merchants linked to the Swedish crown. In the case of New Sweden's, Peter Minuit played an especially important role. He had previously served as a Governor of New Netherland. The Africa Company was basically a creation of the fore-mentioned Louis de Geer. In fact, Dutch entrepreneurs used these Swedish institutions as a front against the Dutch chartered monopolies. Therefore these companies had practically no impact on Sweden's commerce or economy.

---

[20] Stellan Dahlgren and Hans Norman, eds., *The Rise and Fall of New Sweden. The Governor Johan Risingh's Journal 1654–1655 in its Historical Context* (Uppsala: Uppsala University Library, 1988).

[21] György Nováky, *Handelskompanier och kompanihandel. Svenska Afrikakompaniet 1649–1663. En studie i feodal handel* (Uppsala: Uppsala University Library, 1990).

[22] Nováky, *Handelskompanier och kompanihandel*, op. cit., p. 242.

Mercantilist policy in Sweden

The Dutch role in the Swedish colonial enterprises is just one more bit of evidence demonstrating Dutch dominance over Swedish commercial life. The leading politicians in Sweden were well aware of this Dutch dominance and disliked it intensely. They were not unconscious of the discrepancy between Swedish and Dutch economic interests. But until the mid-1640s, cooperation between these two Protestant states seemed to be advantageous for both parties. This cooperation ended in 1645 when Sweden, after its victory over Denmark, became the undisputed leading power in the Baltic—a situation that did not fit in well with the Dutch policy of balanced power in the region. In the 1650s, the relationship between Sweden and the Netherlands became even tenser.[23] Charles X's aggressive policy against Poland and Denmark directly violated Dutch commercial interests. In the years between 1658 and 1660, the Dutch navy, supporting the Danes, turned against its former ally.

From a commercial point of view, the most obvious indication of the changed relationship between the two states was Sweden's emerging mercantilist policy. In the 1650s, Sweden introduced an ambitious mercantilist programme, aimed at diminishing Dutch dominance over Swedish economic life. This mercantilist policy followed the same pattern as French and English mercantilism. A number of privileged trading companies were founded, yet without much success. In 1651, the Board of Commerce was established to encourage Sweden's foreign trade and shipping. A series of new regulations for customs duties was introduced. These new regulations drew distinctions between export and import duties, and between the duties charged for domestically built versus foreign ships. The aim was to promote domestic products and shipping. This policy has to be seen as at least partly successful, due to the increasing share of Swedish shipping.[24] The above-mentioned colonial endeavours can also be seen as part of Swedish mercantilist policy.

[23] Israel, *Dutch Primacy in World Trade, 1585–1740*, op. cit., pp. 216–21.

[24] On the development of Swedish shipping, see Birger Fahlborg, "Ett blad ur det svenska handelsflottans historia (1660–1675)," *Historisk tidskrift*, 1923, and Oscar Bjurling, "Stockholms förbindelser med utlandet under 1670-talets växlingar," in *Forum Navale*, 1951.

It is very difficult to judge the total impact of mercantilism in the second half of the 17th century. On the one hand, the colonial adventures failed. Some chartered companies survived for a longer period, but, despite their survival, they cannot be seen as successes. On the other hand, there are some more indirect data on Sweden's diminishing dependency on the Dutch, and the concomitant rise in the complexity of Swedish commerce and shipping patterns. Some historians also believe that the Swedish economy, especially after 1680, became as closed as it had been previously.

Characteristics of Sweden's foreign trade, 1650–1700

Perhaps the best evidence of the loosening links with the Dutch Republic is the declining Dutch share of Sweden's foreign trade. In 1650, the Dutch market accounted for about 50% of Stockholm's exports. For the most important commodity—iron—the Dutch share was about 48%.[25] And, for some commodities, the Dutch dominance was even greater. For example, about three-quarters of copper was destined for the Dutch Republic.[26] In the following two decades, the Dutch share of the Stockholm exports declined substantially. In 1669, it was just about 30% of Stockholm's exports, whereas England's share rose to 25%. The main reason for the decline is the shift in the Stockholm iron trade. The Dutch share of Stockholm's iron exports declined from 48% in 1650 to 27.5% in 1669, while England's share rose from a tiny 6% between 1646–1650 to 41% in 1669.[27]

In the course of the War from 1675 to 1679, when the Dutch discontinued trading with the Swedes, and Swedish ships disappeared from the Baltic Sea, English merchants took over a major part of the iron trade and shipping. Their share in the iron trade rose to 50%. Stockholm's iron exports reached their maximum in 1686 and 1687, when, on average, 166,200 ship-pounds—or roughly 22,000 tons—were exported from the Swedish capital. In 1687, over 100,000 ship-pounds, or 55% of the total volume, went to England.[28] The new pattern of Anglo-Swedish trade established in the period between

[25] Åström, *From cloth to iron*, op. cit., p. 35.
[26] Sandström, *Mellan Torneå och Amsterdam*, op. cit., p. 343.
[27] Müller, *The Merchant Houses of Stockholm*, op. cit., p. 89.
[28] K. G. Hildebrand, *Fagerstabrukens historia. Sexton- och sjuttonhundratalen* (Uppsala: Uppsala University Library, 1957), pp. 36 and 49.

1650–1680 was based on a triangular exchange.[29] The Swedish iron exports to England were not balanced by English commodities as there was limited demand for them in Sweden. They were paid for by imports from third markets—most often from the Dutch Republic—or else by letters of exchange. These commodity flows were then balanced by sales of English colonial goods in the Dutch Republic.

The newly established connection with the English market became the most significant feature of Sweden's foreign trade for the next 100 years. Iron continued to predominate as Sweden's main export product for the whole 18th century, and England continued to be the major market for it. Nevertheless, the English market for iron did not result in English dominance over Sweden's economy. Relatively few English (more precisely Britons of Scottish and Irish origin) settled in Sweden. There is no evidence of any significant investment flow from England to Sweden. In comparison with the Dutch entrepreneurs of the 1620s–1640s, the English seemed to have a very limited interest in developing the Swedish iron industry. There was also a significant difference between the Dutch and the English impact on Sweden's economic life.

Neither did the political situation strengthen the relationship between England and Sweden. On the one hand, England and Sweden had common interests in weakening Dutch influence in the world. On the other hand, Sweden's traditional ally—France—became England's major rival as the Dutch Republic declined. The solution for this divergence between economic interdependency and politically opposed allies was for the two countries to maintain a strictly businesslike relationship.

More evidence of the growing independence of the Swedish commercial system was the growth in Swedish shipping. The Sound Toll statistics show an increase in Swedish passages, especially in the 1680s and 1690s. The highest point was reached in 1693 when 884 Swedish passages were registered. The average for the 1690s was 675 passages. This can be compared with the average of 350 passages in another peaceful decade—the 1660s.[30]

[29] On establishing of the new pattern of Sweden's foreign trade in 1650–80, see Leos Müller, "Britain and Sweden: the changing pattern of commodity exchange, 1650–1680," in Patrick Salmon and Tony Barrow, eds., *Britain and the Baltic. Studies in commercial, political and cultural relations, 1500–2000* (Sunderland: University of Sunderland Press, 2003).

[30] Nina Bang and Knud Ellinger-Korst, *Tabeller over skibsfart och varetransport gennem Øresund 1661–1783* (Köpenhamn: Norsk Forlag, 1930).

At the same time, there was a decline in the Dutch and English share of Swedish commodity shipping. The Dutch decline was especially dramatic. In the mid-17th century, the Dutch carried between two-thirds and one-half of Sweden's exports and imports.[31] By the 1690s, the Dutch had practically stopped shipping Swedish commodities. In the 1680s the Swedish share of shipping between the Dutch Republic and Stockholm increased from 43.3% in 1682 to 96.6% in 1691. The low figure in 1682 should be seen as a consequence of the war in 1675–79, in which Swedish ships disappeared from the Baltic. Swedish shipmasters also began to compete with the Dutch in the Eastern parts of the Baltic, which had traditionally been completely dominated by Dutch shipping. For example, they began to compete in the trade between Riga and France. The development of the Swedish share of shipping between Stockholm and England was not so precipitous. Nevertheless, the Swedish share rose substantially. In 1691, Swedish ships carried 78.5% of Stockholm's exports to England.[32]

Sweden's shipping tonnage rose in the same degree as Sweden's total shipping activity. In Stockholm, the number of ships increased twofold between 1682 and 1691—and the tonnage increased even more. The shipping boom of the late decades of the 17th century helped the Swedish shipbuilding industry, but quite a large share of that tonnage was purchased from abroad. In fact, many Dutch ships just changed their flag to the Swedish colours.[33] Recent research indicates that during this time period a number of Dutch shipmasters settled in Stockholm and other Swedish ports. Thus, Dutch decline and Swedish growth might partly be explained by the Dutch involvement in the war against France (1688–1697).[34] It is worthwhile mentioning that Danish shipping also expanded greatly in the 1690s. Perhaps in the 1690s, we can already see evidence of the beginnings of the neutrality strategy that became so typical for the Scandinavian merchant fleets in the next century.

---

[31] Fahlborg, "Ett blad," p. 207, Leos Müller, "Sjömakten och den civila sjöfarten i Sverige 1650–1809," in Hans Norman, ed., *Skärgårdsflottan. Uppbyggnad, militär användning och förankring i det svenska samhället 1700–1824* (Lund: Historiska media, 2000), pp. 343–44.

[32] Oscar Bjurling, "Stockholms och Sveriges sjöfart åren 1680–1692," *Forum Navale*, 1972/27, p. 46.

[33] Ibid., p. 47.

[34] Tonko Ufke, "Nederländska skeppare på stockholmska handelskepp 1685–1700," *Forum Navale*, 2000.

Figure 2. Passages of Swedish ships through the Sound, 1661–1701

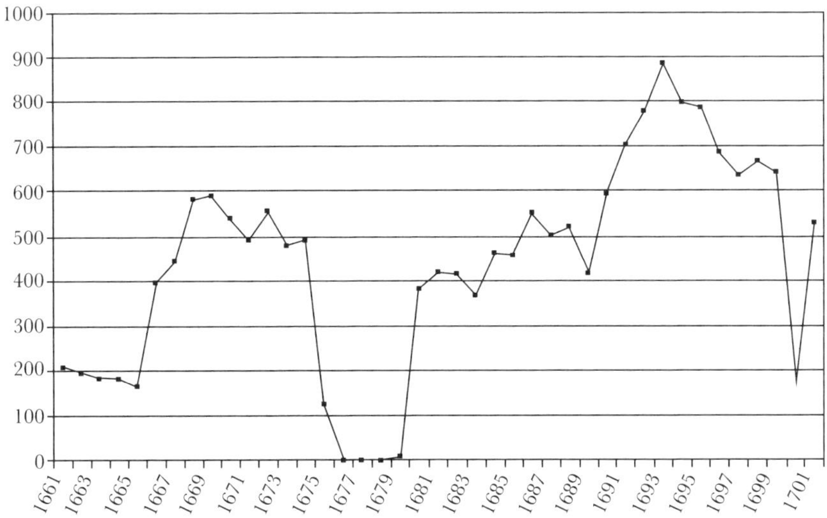

Source: Nina Bang and Knud Ellinger-Korst, *Tabeller over skibsfart och varetransport gennem Øresund 1661–1783*, op. cit.

To conclude, Sweden during the 17th century developed from a poor but ambitious military state on the periphery of Europe to an established great power with strong political and commercial links to Western Europe. The phase of territorial expansion was completed by 1660. After this year the leading objective of the Swedish administration was to maintain the status quo. Sweden's insufficient resources were one of the most serious problems for sustaining its great power status. The resource problem was managed in a variety of ways, demonstrating the capacity of Sweden's leaders to adjust and improvise.

From the point of view of the correlation between commerce and economic growth, the most interesting measure would be Sweden's conscious policy of commercial expansion. The Crown promoted industries supplying the world market with iron, copper, brass, tar and pitch. With these commodities Sweden could employ its natural comparative advantages and make use of the steadily rising demand in England, the Dutch Republic and France. The Swedish kings invited in foreign entrepreneurs and gave them privileges. These men brought to Sweden much-needed capital, technological and business know-how, and the necessary social networks. During the course of the 17th century, Sweden's market sector had been integrated into the orbit of the Dutch and, later on, the British markets. Sweden's mercantilist policy did play an important role in this process, and even if it failed in many arenas such as companies and colonial endeavours, this policy should, in the end, be seen as quite successful.

Yet, the Swedish market sector made up a very small part of the whole economy. Even if foreign commerce increased rapidly, it added little to the total. Commercial growth is not the same thing as economic development. Sweden's economy in 1700 was, just as in 1600, completely dominated by agriculture. The most important factors of economic development were, therefore, demography and agriculture.

But we should not underestimate the role marginal factors played, if these factors were dynamic. I will return again to the role of the iron trade and iron industries. Above, I illustrated how important iron was for Sweden's foreign trade. But iron also had to be produced, and production was extremely labour intensive. Due to the nature of the production process, Swedish iron production was scattered around in about 400 iron-works, with peasant populations nearby involved in charcoal burning, transportation and other production-related work. Thus, a significant proportion of the population was at least partly dependent on the iron industry.[35] Therefore, even peasants in Sweden's agrarian inland became linked to the world market economy, and were at least partly dependent on what happened in London or Amsterdam.

Reshaping Sweden's commercial system after 1718

The dramatic death of Charles XII marked not only the end of Sweden as a great power, but also marked the end of the military state fiscally. From that moment onwards, priorities in Swedish policy shifted from military expansion, following the logic of a feudal state, to economic development, population growth and welfare.

[35] In the mid-18th century perhaps as much as 10% of Sweden's population was living of iron industries, see P. A. Karlsson, *Järnbruken och ståndssamhället. Institutionell och attitydmässig konflikt under Sveriges tidiga industrialisering 1700–1770* (Stockholm: Almquist & Wiksell, 1990), p. 16. For an introduction to the problematic of Swedish iron production see Karl-Gustaf Hildebrand, *Swedish Iron in the Seventeenth and Eighteenth Centuries. Export Industry before the Industrialisation* (Stockholm: Jernkontorets Bergshistoriska Skriftserie, 1992).

These changed priorities were a sign of the new political situation, in which the parliament (*riksdag*) instead of an absolute monarch controlled political power.

The Age of Liberty (1718–1772), as the period after Charles XII's death is called, was a period of limited experiments with democracy. Perhaps a more exact term to describe this system would be parliamentary oligarchy. But the parliament became a forum in which different aims and priorities were discussed and argued. These discussions were relatively free. And it was in this environment that the first political "proto-parties" were born.

From our perspective, the most interesting aspect of this new parliamentary rule is its economic policy. The parliament became a place where different groups struggled for the power to shape economic policy. The victorious group monopolised the right to define what the national interest and welfare were. So private interests could thus be presented as national interests. At a very early moment during the Age of Liberty, the fighting groups coalesced into two political proto-parties—the Caps and the Hats. The Hats succeeded in keeping power for a longer period (1739–1766) than the Caps and, therefore, became the authors of the economic policy of the period. The Hats carried out policies of protectionism in commerce and manufacture and by providing easy credit. They were proponents of a classical mercantilist policy. The second group, the Caps, in a later period advocated free trade, less protection and a tighter credit policy.[36]

Perhaps the most typical feature of the Hat economic policy was institutional modernisation. Many institutions, with multiple, ever-shifting purposes, had been founded. One of the most important political questions of the time centred on these institutions. Did the institutions promote the general welfare of Sweden, or did they only serve the interests of powerful insiders?

Generally, the aim of these institutions—called usually *kontoret*—was to make Sweden more independent in trade and industry. Some of them were established as credit institutions, others were aimed at diminishing Sweden's dependency on imports. The Association of

[36] For an introduction of Sweden's political history in the Age of Liberty see Michael Roberts, *The Age of Liberty, Sweden 1719–1772* (Cambridge: Cambridge University Press, 1986). However, to describe the Hats as protectionists and the Caps as free-traders is too simple, see Gunnar Sundberg, *Merkantilism, partipolitik och ståndscirkulation*. Ministudier 6 (Stockholm: Almquist & Wiksell, 1987).

Iron Masters (*Jernkontoret*) was founded to co-ordinate Sweden's iron production and iron exports and provide credit to iron masters. The Office of Manufactures (*Manufakturkontoret*) provided the Swedish manufacturers, especially textile manufacturers, with credit. It was financed by special import duties. The Salt Office's aim (*Saltkontoret*) was to organise sufficient salt supplies and to keep salt prices low. One of the strangest institutions was the Exchange Office (*Växelkontoret*). Its purpose was to keep Sweden's exchange rate stable. The parliament farmed this task out to a group of financiers. Naturally, the question of whether these men manipulated the exchange rate for their own profit was soon posed.[37]

The parliament issued charters for monopoly companies: the East India Company, the Levant Company and the Canary Company. During Gustavus III's reign (1772–1792) the West India Company was also established. Further on, I will pay some more attention to the Companies' trade due to their importance in the development of Sweden's foreign trade and shipping.

One of the first and most successful mercantilist measures after the end of the Great Nordic War was the Navigation Act of 1724 (*produktplakatet*). It was shaped according to the English prototype and its primary target was Dutch shipping. During the Great Nordic War, foreigners conducted Sweden's trade. The Dutch made an especially strong comeback. Therefore, one of the first actions of Sweden's mercantilist policy after 1721 was directed against them. The Swedish Navigation Act prohibited foreign ships from carrying commodities produced in countries other than their homelands.

The 18th century economic policy was crafted for the conscious promotion of Swedish interests. There has been extensive debate about the consequences of this protectionist policy. This debate can be traced back to the political discussions in the parliament, newspapers and pamphlets of 18th century Sweden. Both parties—the

[37] On the specific institutions: Office of Manufactures, see Per Nyström, *Stadsindustrins arbetare före 1800-talet* (Stockholm: Almquist, 1983); Salt Office, see Stefan Carlén, "An Institutional Analysis of the Swedish Salt Market, 1720–1862," *Scandinavian Economic History Review* 1994; Association of Iron Masters, see Bertil Boëthius and Åke Kromnow, *Jernkontorets historia. Grundläggningstiden*, vol. 1 (Stockholm: Almquist, 1947); Exchange Office, see Leos Müller, "Economic policy in eighteenth-century Sweden and Early Modern entrepreneurial behaviour. A case of the Exchange Office," in Ferry de Goey and Jan Willem Veluwenkamp, eds., *Entrepreneurs and institutions in Europe and Asia, 1500–2000* (Amsterdam: Aksant, 2002).

protectionist Hats and free trader Caps—solidified their arguments in the course of these debates. But the same debate is going on amongst Swedish economic historians today. Did the 18th-century mercantilist policy promote economic development in Sweden or not?

Eli F. Heckscher, the founder of Swedish economic history, was the foremost critic of mercantilist policy.[38] However, his arguments against it seem to be motivated more by ideology than by evidence.[39] His conclusions concerning 18th-century economic development have been modified and corrected by later historians. For example, Heckscher's interpretation of the development of the iron industry was one of stagnation and failure in comparison to the Russian iron industry. A more nuanced picture of development, in which the Swedish policy is seen as economically rational and, in fact, quite successful, has replaced this view. Similar re-interpretations have been made with regard to the interaction between institutional change and the rapid development of agriculture from the mid-18th century.[40] Modern historians believe that, even if mercantilist policy failed in many ways, it contributed substantially to institutional modernisation. The institutional framework created in the course of the 18th century was a necessary precondition for 19th-century economic development.

With the exception of iron exports, very little attention has been paid to the impact of mercantilist policy measures on the development of foreign trade in the 18th century. However, foreign trade was one of the few dynamic factors in economy, just as it had been during the 17th century. Due to competition in the world markets, commerce and shipping were also the most developed sectors of the economy. In the concluding part of this essay, I will present some evidence on the commercial development in this period, and I will then link this data to the Swedish economy as a whole.

---

[38] See especially his major work on Sweden's economic history E. F. Heckscher, *Sveriges ekonomiska historia efter Gustaf Vasa*, 3 vols. (Stockholm: Bronnier, 1935–49).

[39] Lars Magnusson, *Eli Heckscher and mercantilism. An Introduction.* Uppsala Papers in Economic History, nr. 35, Uppsala, 1994.

[40] Göran Rydén and Maria Ågren, eds., *Ironmaking in Sweden and Russia. A survey of the social organisation of iron production before 1900* (Uppsala: Berghahn, 1993); on the relationship between legal changes and agriculture, see Christer Winberg, "Another route to modern society. The advancement of the Swedish peasantry," M. Lundahl and T. Svensson, eds., *Agrarian society in history. Essays in honour of Magnus Mörner*, (London: Routledge, 1990). Maria Ågren, *Jord och gäld. Social skiktning och rättslig konflikt i södra Dalarna ca. 1650–1850* (Uppsala: Universitetet, 1992).

The development of Sweden's foreign trade and shipping in the 18th century

One of the signs of the dynamism of Sweden's foreign trade after 1718 was the remarkable renewal in shipping. As was mentioned above, this increase in shipping has to be related to the introduction of the Swedish Navigation Act in 1724. The number of registered Swedish ships rose from 228 in 1723 to 480 in 1726. In the late 1740s, there were 515 ships registered in Sweden.[41] In fact, the increase in the Swedish merchant fleet in the 1720s was so rapid that it cannot be explained in other way than through the purchase of foreign ships. The Sound Toll statistics testify to a steady rise in Swedish shipping as well. But this increase was not without periods when shipping numbers fell off. Swedish success is more obvious regarding the increase in the Swedish share of shipping. This share rose from 50% in 1734 to about 80% in 1776.

The shipping boom left a mark on the Swedish shipbuilding industry. The number of shipyards and the number of ships they produced rose even more impressively than the shipping activities. Stockholm was the major home to shipbuilding, and had a number of leading shipyards where the "Swedish Chinamen" were built.[42] For example, in one of the leading shipyards in Stockholm, Terra Nova, more than 24 ships of over 100 lasts were built in the period between 1725–1771. Nine of them with larger average tonnages were built for the Swedish East India Company.[43] After 1765, the shipbuilding industries dispersed to the Northern parts of Sweden, especially to the small port-towns of Ostrobothnia.

[41] Eli F. Heckscher, "Produktplakatet: Den gamla svenska sjöfartspolitikens grundlag," *Ekonomi och historia* (Stockholm: Almquist, 1922), pp. 253–55.

[42] Gustaf A. Zethelius, "Stockholms-varven under 1700-talet," *Sjöhistorisk Årsbok* (Stockholm: Almquist, 1955–56).

[43] L. Müller, *The Merchant Houses of Stockholm*, op. cit., pp. 198–99. Here it is worthwhile to note that the Swedish Chinamen had in average much bigger capacity then their Dutch and English rivals. Christian Koninckx, *The First and Second Charters of the Swedish East India Company (1731–1766)* (Kortrijk: van Ghemmert, 1980), p. 449.

Geographic expansion of the Swedish shipping in the 18th century

Another feature of the successful development of shipping was the geographical expansion of shipping activities. Until 1700, Swedish ships rarely left the waters of the Baltic and North Seas. After 1724 this changed. Swedish ships replaced the Dutch carriers on the route from Sweden to Portugal and the Mediterranean, from whence salt was imported. It has been argued that salt imports were the main reason for the Navigation Act of 1724. But there were rising numbers of Swedish captains who were sailing within the Mediterranean looking for cargoes. These activities increased, particularly in the second half of the 18th-century, when Sweden had better opportunities to utilise its neutrality during periods of great conflicts (1756–1763, 1779–1783, 1793–1800). At the end of the 18th century, the Swedish shipping business became one of the more important businesses in the Mediterranean. Arrivals of Swedish ships in Barcelona and Livorno between 1795–1802 show Sweden as the fifth and sixth shipping nation in the Mediterranean, respectively. Annually, between 20 and 30 Swedish ship-arrivals there were registered at these two ports.[44]

Another testimony to the increase in shipping to and within the Mediterranean was the Swedish consular network in the area. In the 1720s and 1730s consulates were established in Livorno, Algiers, Marseilles, Smyrna, Tunis, Alicante, Malaga, Venice, and Tripoli. Sweden signed peace and trade treaties with Ottoman Empire and the so-called Barbary states of Algiers, Tripoli, Tunis, and Morocco. The peace treaties with these states were a precondition for shipping activities in the area.

Swedish commerce and shipping within the Mediterranean were open to any interested entrepreneur, with one exception. In the beginning, trade with the Levant coast was organised through the chartered Levant Company. It was founded in 1738 and obtained monopoly rights for Sweden's trade in the Eastern part of the Mediterranean. However, the Levant Company shared the destiny of its 17th-century forerunners. It was not a success. Only 14 voyages

[44] Dan H. Andersen and Hans-Joachim Voth, "The Grapes of War: Neutrality and Mediterranean Shipping under Danish Flag, 1747–1807," *Scandinavian Economic History Review*, vol. XLVIII, no. 1, 2000, p. 5.

were organised between 1738 and 1756. In 1756, the company was abolished and all Swedish trade in the Mediterranean was set free.[45]

There is no quantitative analysis of Swedish shipping activities within the area. However, the Sound Toll statistics once again can provide a fairly illustrative picture of this trade. In the 1720s, there were no registered Swedish ships returning from the Mediterranean, despite the fact that the traffic from Portugal was already vigorous—about 20 ships annually. In the second half of the century, this traffic increased rapidly.

The Swedish-China trade

Other than the competition in the Mediterranean, Sweden also competed with the maritime powers in the more "typical" colonial trade. The most successful enterprise of this part of the long-distance trade was the Swedish-China trade, carried out by the Swedish East India Company. Eli F. Heckscher called it Sweden's most successful trading enterprise.[46] The Swedish East India Company was established in 1731 as a joint venture between the Swedish state, Swedish merchants, investors from the Austrian Netherlands and Scottish adventurers with experience in China and the East India trade. There is a strong link between the dissolution of the Ostend East India Company (1727–31) and the foundation of the Swedish company. A lot of Flemish capital was transferred to Sweden and invested in the first Swedish voyages to China. There were also employees of the Ostend Company who moved to Sweden. Despite this heavy foreign involvement, over the course of time, the Swedish character of the company increased.

Despite its name, the Swedish East India Company was a quite different company from the Dutch, English or even the French East India Companies. Sweden had never seriously aspired to acquire colonies in Asia. This means that the company was focused only on dealing with countries where trade could be carried out without conquest and/or without maintaining trading posts. It also meant that the Company's operating costs were relatively low. Staff was limited

[45] Eskil Olán, *Sjörövarna på Medelhavet och Levantiska compagniet. Historien om Sveriges gamla handel med Orienten* (Stockholm: Almquist, 1921), pp. 62–63.

[46] E. F. Heckscher, "Sveriges Framgångsrikaste handelsföretag. Ostindiska Kompaniet," *Historieuppfattning, materialistisk och annan* (Stockholm: Almquist, 1944).

Table 2. Swedish-registered ships passing the Sound from the Mediterranean, Portugal, Spain and France, 1723–1783

Year	France	Portugal	Spain	Italy	Remaining Mediterranean
1723	9	14	1	0	
1730	17	27	0	0	
1735	44	32	7	5	
1740	26	15	4	7	
1745	28	16	5	1	
1750	31	30	15	24	1
1755	32	31	9	18	1
1760	33	34	0	9	0
1765	38	40	8	14	0
1770	37	26	6	27	1
1775	49	15	21	47	0
1780	32	41	12	24	1
1781	27	81	15	17	
1782	32	61	16	15	
1783	40	111	21	38	

Source: Nina Bang and Knud Ellinger-Korst, *Tabeller over skibsfart och varetransport gennem Øresund 1661–1783*, op. cit.

and the number vessels was low. The company usually sent one or two vessels to China annually.

In the beginning, the Swedes hoped to follow the English model of Asian trade. They aimed to sell Swedish commodities such as iron in India and then exchange Indian textiles in China for tea and other desired China goods. It did not work. The English East India Company disrupted the Company's activities on the Malabar Coast, and the Swedes were unable to fight off the English. Naturally, both the English and the Dutch did everything possible to impede their annoying Swedish rivals. After a few such incidents, the Swedish Company focused all its attention on Canton and the tea trade. Over the course of the 18th century, the Company sent 132 vessels to Asia, of which as many as 124 were destined for Canton only. Under Chinese legislation, the Swedish Company traded under the same conditions as did the English and Dutch giants. In fact, the limited size of the Swedish company could have even been an advantage for them.

The Swedish Company concentrated more or less on tea—the most profitable Asian commodity. An average of 80–90% of its cargoes consisted of tea.[47] This was a smart strategy as long as the European consumers, especially Britons, were thirsting after this fashionable drink. And it worked excellently until the 1780s, when the English and Dutch exerted their power and implemented measures to diminish their tea imports.[48] After 1800, the operations of the Swedish Company were stopped. The Company was formally abolished in 1813.

The Swedish company was a serious player in the world tea market. It imported huge volumes, and the prices of Swedish imports were competitive. In the period between 1739–1767, the Swedish Company carried 590 tons of tea to Europe annually, on average. It is important to mention, however, that the annual supply of tea fluctuated greatly.[49] European demand for tea in the mid-century was estimated at over 5,000 tons. Together with the Danish East India Company, which employed a strategy similar to that of the Swedes, the Scandinavian Companies could supply as much as one-third of all tea consumed in Europe.[50] Practically all tea was re-exported from Gothenburg and Copenhagen, the staple ports of the Companies, to the Dutch Republic, Austrian Netherlands, France and other markets. Much of the Swedish re-exports ended up as smuggled goods in Britain.

The importance of the Swedish-China trade for Sweden's economy appears to be underestimated. Of course, judging by the tonnage and by manpower, the Company had a quite limited impact. Only one or two Chinamen annually arrived from Canton to Gothenburg. But the relative values of China cargoes were very high and the profitability of trade for most of the period was very good. Contemporaries saw the China re-exports as a very important item in Sweden's balance of trade. In fact, the importance of the China trade was so great that the sale of one cargo could affect the exchange rate.[51] A comparison with Sweden's total exports, including the staple iron exports, shows that the re-exports of Chinese commodities

---

[47] Koninckx, *The First and Second Charters*, p. 271.

[48] H. S. K. Kent, *War and Trade in Northern Seas. Anglo-Scandinavian economic relations in the mid-eighteenth century* (Cambridge: Cambridge University Press, 1973), pp. 113, 125.

[49] Koninckx, *The First and Second Charters*, op. cit., pp. 211, 451–52.

[50] Kent, *War and Trade*, op. cit., p. 117.

[51] Ibid., p. 123.

(they were not included in the official trade statistics) were valued at between 20 and 30% of total Swedish exports.

Because of the volatility of the Chinese imports, the proportion of the China trade could be much higher. In the years after 1776, when England, France and the Dutch Republic were involved in the war in America, the re-exports reached its highest point. In the period between 1777–1783, Sweden re-exported Chinese commodities valued at 2.2 millions rixdollars (13.3 million of dollars-silver-money) annually. The peak year was 1782 when Sweden's China re-exports were valued at four million rixdollars (24 million dollars-silver-money).[52] The situation between 1777–1783 must be seen as quite exceptional and the conditions for the Swedish-China trade deteriorated quickly thereafter. In 1784 Britain had already reduced duties on tea (Pitt's Commutation Act) and the English East India Company increased its imports. The market for smuggled tea dwindled and so did the profitability of the Swedish tea trade.[53]

The successful operations of the Swedish East India Company demonstrate the capacity of the Swedish business elite to find and employ profitable opportunities—despite their lack of capital and despite their peripheral location. But does this mean that Sweden's engagement in colonial trade had any significance for domestic economic development? As was mentioned above, practically all tea was re-exported. And the Company activities were based on foreign

Table 3. Sweden's total exports and re-exports of China commodities, 1738–1740 (dollars-silver-money)

Year	Total exports	Company's re-exports	Percent
1738	7,172,000	1,402,972	19.56
1739	7,006,000	2,109,495	30.11
1740	6,521,000	1,330,499	20.40

Source: Christian Koninckx, *The First and Second Charters of the Swedish East India Company*, op. cit.

[52] Calculations based on Joh. Fr. Nyström, *De svenska ostindiska kompanierna. Historisk-statistisk framställning* (Göteborg: D. F. Bonniers, 1883) statistical appendix. In 1776 the monetary system of Sweden was changed and single unit was introduced: rixdollar (valued at six dollars-silver-money).

[53] Hoh-cheung Mui and Lorna H. Mui, *The Management of Monopoly. A Study of the East India Company's Conduct of its Tea Trade, 1784–1833* (Vancouver: The University of British Columbia Press, 1984), p. 13.

expertise and money. This means that a share of the profits from the Company's trade returned to the Austrian Netherlands, the Dutch Republic and Britain. Moreover, the tonnage and the labour involved in Company operations were insignificant overall.

Nevertheless, the China trade also had a number of important and dynamic side effects. First of all, as an increasing share of Company capital originated in Sweden, the profits made in this trade stayed in the country. The analysis of the investment strategies of the Company's shareholders and employees shows that most of them invested in estates and iron-works. A typical career of such a shareholder consisted of a few voyages to China, followed by the purchase of big iron-works and then living near the iron-works for rest of his life.[54] It should be pointed out here that Swedish iron-works were not only seen as production units. They also usually included large woods and farmland and they were regarded as suitable objects for investment. Other favourite investments were real estate in towns, shares in ships, shares in the East India Company or other chartered companies, and canal projects. Thus, tea profits were invested in dynamic sectors of the economy: agriculture, the iron industry, commerce, shipping, and manufacture.

The China trade was also a catalyst for the technological development of Swedish shipbuilding. As was mentioned above, practically all Swedish Chinamen were built in Sweden. Also, the know-how for long-distance sailing became a useful asset in the late 18th and early 19th century, when Swedish shipping extended its activities as far afield as the Americas. It is difficult to imagine this step without the experience acquired in the China trade.

Transatlantic links—St. Barthélemy colony

Sweden's commercial links across the Atlantic appeared much later than its links with Southern Europe and China. And they remained, until the end of the Napoleonic Wars, less important economically.

[54] Martin Åberg, *Svensk handelskapitalism—Ett dynamiskt element i frihetstidens samhälle? En fallstudie av delägarna i Ostindiska kompaniets 3:e oktroj 1766–1786* (thesis, Department of History, Gothenburg University 1988), pp. 73–87, Leos Müller, "Mellan Kanton och Göteborg. Jean Abraham Grill, en superkargörs karriär," in Janne Backlund et al., eds., *Historiska etyder. En vänbok till Stellan Dahlgren* (Uppsala: Uppsala University, 1997), pp. 159–60.

Sweden's appearance on the other side of the Atlantic was a direct consequence of the American Revolution. The independence of the American colonies opened up a niche for the Swedes in which they could make use of their neutrality.

At the same time as the American colonies struggled for independence, Sweden established its own colony in the Caribbean. Sweden had aspired to have a colony in the Caribbean for most of the 18th century. Different alternatives were discussed without any serious attempt to take the next step. In 1731, the Swedish frigate *Fortuna* was sent to the River Orinoco's estuary to investigate the area as a potential colony.[55] From time to time, Tobago was discussed as a possible area for colonisation. Yet, until the end of the 1770s, all ideas for colonisation stayed just that—ideas with no reality. After France's entrance into the American War of Independence, the situation was ripe for a more serious attempt at colonisation. Sweden expressed, through its ambassador in Paris, a wish to take over a French colony in the Caribbean. The colony was meant to be a reward for Sweden's mediating role in the French-English conflict, but the French did not take the request very seriously. However, the discussions continued and, after the war, in 1784, the French decided to accede to the Swedish request. They turned over to Sweden the tiny rocky island of St. Barthélemy, in exchange for trading rights in Gothenburg.[56]

St. Barthélemy was an insignificant colony from a commercial point of view. The island had practically no agriculture and a small population. But during the dangerous years between 1792 and 1814, St. Barthélemy began to play a role similar to that of the Danish St. Thomas, or the Dutch St. Eustatius and Curaçao—as a safe heaven for merchants of warring countries. Shipping between the Caribbean Islands and St. Barthélemy, and between the United States and St. Barthélemy, increased rapidly, but there was no significant trade with Sweden. The high expectations for the sugar and slave trades failed to become a reality. The Swedish ships participating in the transatlantic trade sailed as carriers between the Mediterranean, the USA and the West European ports, but they seldom had a

[55] Ingegerd Hildebrand, *Den svenska kolonin S.t Barthélemy och Västindiska kompaniet fram till 1796* (Lund: Lindstedt, 1951), p. 1.

[56] Ibid., pp. 2–39.

reason to visit the Swedish colony in the Caribbean. Also, the direct trade with the United States was a disappointment. This dismal situation changed, however, in the 1820s. Even then, though, the trade did not centre on colonial commodities, as the Swedes had hoped in the 1780s, but on the traditional Swedish staple commodity—iron. The slave trade was a part of the commercial activities in St. Barthélemy, but the trade never reached a significant level. At the Congress of Vienna, Sweden signed a treaty on the abolition of the slave trade which officially ended this trade. The remaining 500 Swedish slaves in St. Barthélemy were liberated by the state in 1846–47.[57]

In the course of the 18th century Sweden became engaged in three areas of long-distance commerce and shipping: the Mediterranean, the China trade, and the transatlantic trade. The expansion of commercial and shipping activities testifies to the transformation of the Swedish overseas trade. By 1800, Sweden was a small but competitive and niche-focused actor. It played a role in international commerce and shipping that was similar to that of the other small maritime states: Denmark, the USA and the Dutch Republic. This successful development has to be seen, on the one hand, as a result of an effective mercantilist policy, and, on the other hand, as a consequence of Sweden's new role in the changed conditions of international trade in the 18th century.

Iron trade

Long-distance trade was a dynamic factor in Sweden's commercial development over the course of the 18th century. Yet this does not mean that the traditional sectors of foreign trade, established in the mid-17th century, played a less important role. Of the total amount of foreign trade, iron exports and, especially, iron exports to Britain, continued to play a leading role. With regard to other staple commodities, there was an increasing share of trade going to timber exports, mainly to the new markets in the Mediterranean. For imports, grain, imported from the other side of the Baltic, continued to be the major article. Between 1734–1737, grain imports made up 30.8%

[57] Per Tingbrand, "A Swedish Interlude in the Caribbean," *Forum Navale*, 2002, p. 75.

of import value. Salt took up a large share of the shipping capacity, but the values of salt imports were low. The remaining imports were made up of many items arriving from widely different markets.

I will focus again on iron exports, as they remained of such importance to Sweden's foreign trade. In the years between 1734–1737, iron exports made up 72.2% of exports, and this share did not decline very much until the end of the century.[58] The export figures for iron indicate a quite stable level of trade. After the Great Nordic War, exports rose from about 200,000 to 300,000 ship-pounds—or roughly 27,000 to 40,000 tons—a quite remarkable increase, but less impressive if we compare it with the growth between 1610–1650. From the 1730s onwards, export volume varied from around 300,000 ship-pounds—or roughly 40,000 tons—with a strong development at the 1780s and 1790s. About one-half of the iron exports were destined for the British market. This was a very stable share. The decline at the end of the century us linked to a technological change in Britain—the introduction of the puddling process. Of the other markets, the only significant change is the rising share of the Latin markets (France, Portugal, Spain, and the Mediterranean) from 14% between 1738–1740 to 34% in 1786–1789.[59] This development confirms the rising importance of the Mediterranean trade as was discussed above in connection with Swedish shipping activities.

Swedish iron exports were not important only to Sweden. They were, in fact, a very important factor for British iron production. Britain's iron consumption increased during the course of the 18th century from 35,000 tons around 1720 to at least 90,000 tons at the end of the century, and domestic production could not meet this increasing demand. Over the course of the century, British iron imports more than doubled, from c. 20,000 tons to 40,000–50,000 tons in the second half of the century. Swedish bar-iron made up about 15,000–19,000 tons (112,000–142,000 ship-pounds) of this volume.[60] The volumes of Swedish bar-iron imported into Britain were fairly stable. This means that, in relative terms, Sweden's share

[58] Boëthius and Heckscher, *Svensk handelsstatistik*, pp. 620–21.

[59] Staffan Högberg, *Utrikeshandel och sjöfart på 1700-talet. Stapelvaror i svensk export och import 1738–1808* (Stockholm: Almquist, 1969), p. 75.

[60] Åsa Eklund, *Iron production, iron trade and iron markets. Swedish iron on the British market in the first half of the 18th century* (thesis, Dep. of Economic History, Uppsala University), Uppsala, 2001, pp. 80–81.

Figure 3. Sweden's iron exports 1706–1799 (annual averages in 000 ship-pounds)

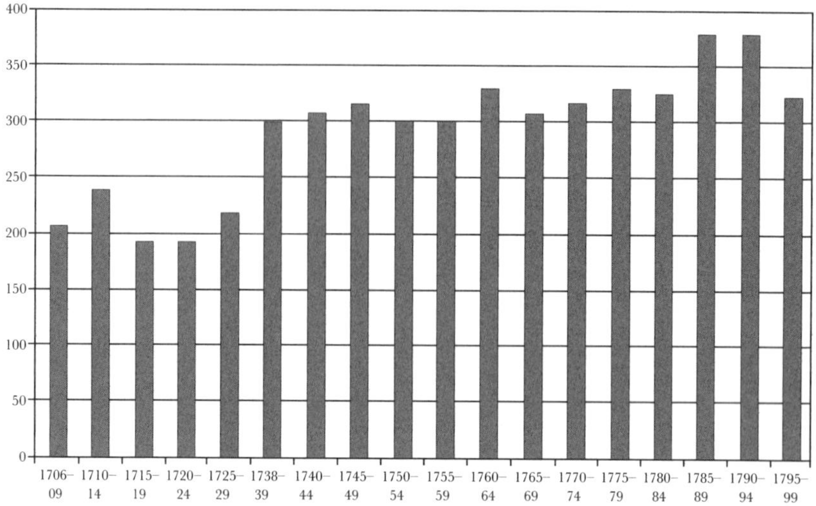

Source: K. G. Hildebrand, *Fagerstabrukens historia. Sexton- och sjuttonhundratalen*, op. cit., pp. 91, 96.

declined. But, at the same time, Sweden increased its iron exports to other areas such as the Mediterranean, Spain and Portugal.

What happened to the Swedish bar-iron in Britain? Obviously, a major part of it was consumed in Britain, in factories in the Midlands area, in Sheffield and in other industrial centres. It is estimated that in the mid-18th century, of the total of 60,000 tons of iron imported to Britain, only a tiny share of 15–2 tons was re-exported.[61] Nevertheless, some Swedish iron was surely used in international trade. There was already evidence of the use of Swedish iron in the Africa trade in the 17th century.[62] An analysis of the commercial links between Bristol, one of the leading centres of the British colonial trade, and Stockholm shows that the Bristol purchasers of Swedish iron were involved in sugar, tobacco and the slave trade. The firm of Prankard, the leading importer of Swedish iron, was heavily involved in the tobacco trade. There is also direct evidence of iron re-exports to the

[61] Ibid., p. 88.

[62] K. G. Hildebrand, *Fagerstabrukens historia. Sexton- och sjuttonhundratalen* (Uppsala: University of Uppsala, 1957), p. 122.

Caribbean and to the American colonies.[63] In London, another purchaser of Swedish bar-iron was the English East India Company. The Company also exported significant volumes of iron to India.[64] In addition, it should be mentioned that Swedish iron bars were considered a perfect ballast cargo for long voyages.

Evidence of iron re-exports to the colonies demonstrates the long commodity chain from Sweden's inland to the Caribbean and the American colonies. Yet, re-exports made up but a tiny share of the exported iron. The rapidly expanding British market mainly consumed this iron. To conclude, Swedish iron was a precondition for the growth of the British iron industries in the 18th century, and, therefore, an important factor for British economic development. This situation changed dramatically with the introduction of puddling technology, but, until the late 18th century, iron imports were indispensable for Britain.

In Sweden, the iron industry and iron exports played a key role in the development of the market economy. It was not the most dynamic market sector, but it had the largest effect on Sweden's total economy. It employed, either directly or indirectly, a large proportion of the population, though mainly as part-time workers. It provided a stable basis for Sweden's market sector. Due to this stability, iron-works were a preferred investment object for money made in more insecure enterprises.

Swedish iron had to compete on the world market with other iron producing nations. Therefore, Swedish iron masters and iron exporters had to adjust to changing market conditions. They kept up-to-date with new technologies, some of which they introduced, if the introduction was profitable. They looked continuously for new markets, and searched for information about competitors. The Association of

---

[63] For example, the firm of Lyonel Lyde & Co., a leading tobacco firm in Bristol, was second bigger purchaser of Swedish iron in Bristol in the late 1730s. At the same time this firm imported pig iron from Virginia. Eklund, *Iron production, iron trade and iron markets*, pp. 86–87.

[64] The house Andrew and Charles Lindegren, based in London, of Swedish origin, was one of the leading importers of Swedish iron, and at the same iron supplier of the English East India Company. Müller, *The Merchant Houses of Stockholm*, pp. 127–28. Huw V. Bowen, "Sinews of trade and empire: the supply of commodity exports to the East India Company during the late eighteenth century," *Economic History Review*, 2002/3.

Iron Masters sent its own industrial "spies" to Britain and other iron-producing countries to study the technology used by the competition, products, quality, prices, markets and so on.[65] There was a steady exchange of people. Travellers and immigrants came with new ideas, new knowledge and a new capitalist culture. Simply put, the iron sector was not only a very important sector; it was also a competitive sector.

The iron industry and trade were highly regulated. The Association of Iron Masters regulated prices, volumes, and the quality of produced iron. But these regulations did not seem to have had a negative effect on the profitability of this business. Some historians such as Eli F. Heckscher thought that these regulations were a cause of the stagnation of Sweden's iron production and also as a cause of Sweden's "failure" in competition with Russia for the British iron market. Today, this regulatory policy is interpreted as a rational response to changing conditions in the market. In the second half of the 18th century it became more profitable to invest in other sectors of Sweden's economy or to specialise in the most profitable iron brands. Agriculture has been identified as a dynamic sector with rising numbers of people involved in it and increasing output.[66] But it should be stressed that the diversification of Sweden's economy also affected the maritime sector, and that this sector was also highly dynamic.

Preconditions of 19th-century economic growth in Sweden

By 1800, Sweden was still an agriculturally based economy on the European periphery, with a very small urban sector. Peasants made about 90% of the population. In relative terms, Sweden was a poor country. The standard of living was lower than in Western Europe and economic growth per capita was almost insignificant.[67] Yet, from the mid-18th century, there was stable population growth. In the second half of the century, Sweden's population increased by 30%. The Malthusian circle of population increase and decline was bro-

---

[65] Anders Florén and Göran Rydén, "A Journey into the Market Society. A Swedish Pre-industrial Spy in the Middle of the 18th Century," in Ragnar Björk and Karl Molin, eds., *Societies made up of history* (Stockholm: Akademitryck AB, 1990).

[66] Schön, *En modern svensk ekonomisk historia*, pp. 53–57.

[67] Ibid., p. 50.

ken. This figure also very roughly indicates growth in agricultural output, and the potential of the domestic market. The growth in agriculture was not rapid, but it was stable and it definitely changed the countryside.

If capitalist agriculture with stable property rights, social differentiation, and production for the market are the preconditions of a capitalist economy then such preconditions existed in the Sweden of 1800. Yet, there was also a dynamic industrial and commercial sector, whose importance should not be undervalued. Sweden's preconditions for modern economic growth were based on the interaction between the domestic agriculturally based economic sector and the export and maritime-focused economic sector.

In spite of its relative backwardness and peripheral status, Sweden in 1800 was well-integrated economically within the Atlantic or even the world at large. Swedish iron producers and shipowners were competing in the world markets. In the case of iron, Swedish producers focused on the most profitable products and shifted to new markets. It was obviously a rational choice. In the dynamic maritime sector, Sweden succeeded in employing the advantages that it possessed, such as being a small neutral actor in the global market. Similar to Denmark, Sweden expanded its shipping, especially during the 1780s, 1790s and the first decade of the 19th century. Swedish ships could be found in the Mediterranean and in transatlantic shipping. Another good example of this niche strategy on the global level was the Swedish East India Company. It focused its activities almost exclusively on tea. Profits from shipping made up as much as about one-half of Sweden's export income in the first decade after 1800.[68] In the first half of the 19th century, Sweden, in union with Norway, has to be seen as an important maritime economy. The two countries combined had the third largest merchant fleet in the world. But it must be stressed, however, that Norway's share made up three-fourths of this fleet.[69]

Another key factor of 19th century economic development was innovation in the institutional structure. Institutionalisation of ownership

[68] Ibid., p. 60. Transparency of Sweden's shipping is a problem. Sweden, as well as many other countries, regulated shipping activities by Navigation Acts, which makes it difficult to calculate the competitiveness of specific countries.

[69] Yrjö Kaukiainen, *History of Finnish Shipping* (London and New York: Routledge, 1993), p. 89.

in agriculture was a necessary precondition of capitalist agriculture. But institutional innovation in the commercial sector was important as well. Institutional innovation mainly followed the ideas of the mercantilist system. However, not all new institutions were growth-promoting institutions. Some mercantilist institutions worked well and survived, while others were abolished after few years. It should also be pointed out that new institutions were either modelled on or designed with the foreign institutions in mind. A consequence of this policy was that by 1800 Sweden had a well-developed institutional structure; in many ways comparable with much more affluent countries. Also, the educational level in Sweden was comparatively high, which did not correspond to the low standard of living. Due to its institutional framework and the high level of education within the country, Swedish economic historian Sandberg has called Sweden an "impoverished sophisticate".[70] This is a quite accurate term to describe the weakness of Sweden's domestic market and the sophistication of the institutional infrastructure and the maritime economy. Without these institutions and outer commercial networks, the rapid economic growth of Sweden in the second half of the 19th century would not have been possible.

Conclusions

In the beginning, the question was put forward as to the significance of foreign trade in the development of Sweden. What is the answer now, at the end of the essay? Apparently, the impact of foreign trade was marginal in quantitative terms, but trade did play a significant role in qualitative terms. In fact, the process of change usually starts in the margins of the economy and only affects the whole economy over time. So, the sustained economic growth of the modern capitalist economy has to be seen as a result of a number of marginal qualitative changes. Here foreign trade is a factor that should be counted.

The importance of foreign trade for modern economic growth has been discussed mainly in the context of the history of the Dutch Republic, as the first modern economy, and of the British economic

[70] L. G. Sandberg, "The Case of the Impoverished Sophisticate. Human Capital and Swedish Economic Growth before World War I," *Journal of Economic History*, 1979.

development in the 18th century and during the Industrial Revolution. The quantitative evidence proves that foreign trade cannot explain modern economic growth, but at the same time, it cannot be ignored either.[71] In the Swedish case, the importance of foreign trade was pointed out in the classical export model for economic growth in the late 19th century. Yet, this model did not pay any significant attention to Sweden's commercial expansion in the Early Modern period. The modern economic growth after 1850 has been presented as a very dramatic shift of a quite primitive and backward economy—a shift based on outer factors such as foreign demand and investment, as well as new technologies. This model has been modified recently. The domestic market model pointed out, instead, the importance of population growth, and also the role of agriculture. The domestic market model characterises Sweden's economic development as a slow and long-running process, and stresses the role of institutional changes. Neither of these models gives much credit to Sweden's foreign trade in the 17th and 18th centuries.[72]

Yet, Sweden's foreign trade in the Early Modern period is important for both models. In the 17th century Sweden had already become an integrated part of the world commercial system. Then the Dutch Republic and Britain, the two most developed economies in the world, became key markets for Swedish staple commodities. Consequently, when the export boom started after 1850, Sweden could utilise its well-established commercial channels with the Atlantic economy—channels which had been built up over the course of two centuries. In regard to the domestic market model, the institutional change in Sweden was carried out in accordance with mercantilist policy, and this policy was shaped according to the priorities of commercial development. There existed in Sweden a strong awareness of the conditions of trade, and of agricultural and industrial development in Western Europe. In addition, there was a strong link between iron exports and agricultural development in iron-producing areas. In Sweden, the iron sector played a similar role as proto-industries in other countries.

---

[71] For example, see Roderick Floud and D. McCloskey, *The Economic History of Britain since 1700*, volume 1:1700–1860 (Cambridge: Cambridge University Press, 1994); De Vries and van der Woude, *The First Modern Economy*, op. cit.

[72] Schön, *En modern svensk ekonomisk historia*, pp. 34–37, 50–119.

INDEX

THE ATLANTIC WORLD

ISSN 1570–0542

1. Postma, J. & V. Enthoven (eds.). *Riches from Atlantic Commerce.* Dutch Transatlantic Trade and Shipping, 1585-1817. 2003. ISBN 90 04 12562 0
2. Curto, J.C. *Enslaving Spirits.* The Portuguese-Brazilian Alcohol Trade at Luanda and its Hinterland, c. 1550-1830. 2004. ISBN 90 04 13175 2
3. Jacobs, J. *New Netherland.* A Dutch Colony in Seventeenth-Century America. 2004. ISBN 90 04 12906 5
4. Goodfriend, J.D. (ed.). *Revisiting New Netherland.* Perspectives on Early Dutch America. 2005. ISBN 90 04 14507 9
5. Macinnes, A.I. & A.H. Williamson (eds.). *Shaping the Stuart World, 1603-1714.* The Atlantic Connection. 2006. ISBN 90 04 14711 X
6. Haggerty, S. *The British-Atlantic Trading Community, 1760-1810.* Men, Women, and the Distribution of Goods. 2006. ISBN 90 04 15018 8
7. Kleijwegt, M. *The Faces of Freedom.* The Manumission and Emancipation of Slaves in Old World and New World. 2006. ISBN 90 04 15082 X
8. Emmer, P.C., O. Pétré-Grenouilleau & J. Roitman. *A Deus ex Machina Revisited.* Atlantic Colonial Trade and European Economic Development. 2006. ISBN 90 04 15102 8